The Prophet of Islam in History

The Prophet of Islam in History

Shahid Ahmad

PARTRIDGE

ISBN: Hardcover   978-1-4828-7001-5
               Softcover   978-1-4828-7000-8
               eBook   978-1-4828-6999-6

To order additional copies of this book, contact
Partridge India
000 800 10062 62
orders.india@partridgepublishing.com

www.partridgepublishing.com/india

PREFACE

The life of *Muhammad*, the founder of Islam, is a widely written-about subject; we have a plethora of biographical and historical books on him in different languages written by believing as well as unbelieving scholars. Yet, ironically enough, it is still difficult to understand his true historical personality. He never claimed to possess any superhuman qualities and categorically stated that he had no power to perform miracles, which were the domain of God alone. The *Qurān* also reiterated that he was only a human being but pointed out his exceptional role as a messenger and special personality as a man. A 'mercy for the worlds' (Q 21/107), a 'beautiful model' (Q 33/21), and 'a person on whom God and His angles utter blessings' (Q 33/56) were the epithets used to describe his extraordinary status as the 'first Muslim'. Verse 3/31 remarked, 'Say, if you love God, follow me, then God will love you and forgive your sins.' It is on the basis of these Qurānic remarks that, in course of time, a mass of colourful legends and traditions developed around different events of his life. These traditional stories, which the Muslims regard as true to this day, were reverently incorporated in his first biographies compiled by the Muslim scholars during the classical period of Islam, becoming source books for later historians to sketch his life. In course of centuries, the Islamic historians of the prophet developed elaborate theories regarding his unique religious status which almost amounted to his deification, and in this way, his historical personality tended to disappear behind the colourful veil of legends.

From the eighteenth century, however, when the West started recovering from the hangover of the medieval Christian polemics about the founder of Islam, and the Western historians started studying and sketching his historical biographies from the original Arabic sources, the pendulum swung to the other extreme. Instead of making an analytical use of the Islamic traditions, which had substantial historical value, they, in the name of scientific and critical historiography, tended to totally disregard them or subject them to their own interpretations in order to find fault with his character. In complete disregard of his religious personality, they viewed his life in pure mundane terms, depicting him as a purely worldly character devoid of any genuine religious attributes.

That he was merely a product of the socio-economic conditions of *Makkah* in the beginning of the seventh century, was an extraordinarily intelligent person having great leadership qualities and political insight, was amenable to the vices of the time, expressed his political personality in religious terms, was even willing to compromise religious principles in order to manipulate situations, was a crafty statesman who used religion for political purposes, resorted to violence and other political means to strengthen his political position in the name of religion, mixed religion with politics, had a weakness for the fair sex, contracted multiple marriages for pleasure and even kept concubines, and by a masterly display of diplomacy and military power, managed to carve out the first powerful empire in Central Arabia based on a unifying ideology which changed the course of history—these are the highlights of their critical historiography about the Prophet of Islam. There is hardly any attempt to view his wars, conquests, and other activities as responses to the total historical situation under which he found himself; nor is there inclination to see the simplicity and austerity with which he spent his life. Do the genuine *ahādīth* (Islamic traditions) with confirmed veracity not throw ample light on his greatness as a religious figure? What were the ideals for which he was struggling throughout his life? What impact did gaining of political power had on his personal life? In what way did he make personal use of his rise to political as well as religious power? How many times did he avoid violence despite military ascendancy? Did he not evolve humane ethics about protection of the civilians during wars and treatment of war prisoners which were far in advance of his age? Was he not fighting for his and his community's life throughout his career? Were not his expeditions defensive in nature under the situation he found himself? Why did he remain a strict monogamist during his twenty-five years of married life with *Khadījah* and enter into many marriages during the last decade of his life only? These and many other such questions which focus on his true character have not been responded to by the Orientalists of the eighteenth and nineteenth centuries. Realization started dawning on a few of the Western historians only in the twentieth century, but still there has been an inhibition in accepting his genuine religious status. The trend is to suggest that he was sincere in his convictions and genuinely believed himself to be a messenger of God under some delusion. Implicit in this contention is the suggestion that neither the revelations were genuine nor was he an apostolic figure.

The true historical sketch of the life of the Prophet of Islam, therefore, gets blurred in biographical works of both categories— hagiographical accounts of the Muslim writers and motivated critical historiography of the Orientalists, and the great mass of literature on the subject falls in either of the two categories to the disappointment of a student today. It was only in the last century that a few Muslim historians, using the same scientific method of historical criticism as adopted by the Orientalists, were able to compile unbiased works. But, more often than not, they are either apologetic or concerned more about refuting the allegations of the Western writers rather than presenting a total history of their subject in a systematic and chronologically acceptable manner with different events of his life integrated in their true historical contexts so as to form an organic whole displaying gradual evolution of his religious as well as political personality. This book is an attempt in this very direction. An effort has been made to present a complete picture of the life of the Prophet with different significant events arranged in a sequence without missing links so as to form an integrated whole.

The book is based on the premise that traditional stories clustering around the personality of a religious leader cannot be totally separated from his history because they are necessary to recognize his charisma as well as historical image. This is also because they represent how he was seen by his contemporaries and what he was believed to have been by his followers of the succeeding generations. Any attempt to segregate the traditions from history in such cases may, therefore, amount to producing half the history only even though a few of them do not stand to reason today. An attempt has been made in this book to sketch the life of *Muhammad* without divesting it of his legendary image; the traditional stories associated with different events of his life have been described alongside plain historical facts. It may look like a combination of critical history writing and legendary stories, but it does present the things in full relief.

The book has been designed to cater to the need of the common readers, millions of whom have a quest to know what the founder of Islam actually preached and what Islam actually stands for. Since the life of *Muhammad* is the key to understanding of true Islam vis-à-vis current aberrations as well as misrepresentations in this regard, the subject assumes great importance. It is in order to make the subject easily comprehensible that a simple and lucid style of presenting plain historical facts with brevity has been adopted; and for sparing the readers of going through volumes of lengthy critical discourses on controversial issues, the traditional versions as well as critical theories and arguments in respect of important events have been briefly referred to so as to drive home a generally acceptable position. For a better understanding of the manner in which the history of the Prophet has been written by different groups having their own motives, a full chapter on the sources of his history has been added with detailed discussions on them, evaluating their relative historical importance. An attempt has also been made to trace the evolution of history writing about the Prophet since the beginning to the present times. Further, with a view to present his life and teachings in proper historical perspective, a detailed description of the legendary background of his family including traditional history of the *Kābah* and *Makkah,* of the social and economic conditions prevalent during his time, of the regional history of the peninsula in its geographical background, and of the religious beliefs and practices which he encountered, have been included in the second chapter titled 'The Setting', which describes the total conditions obtained in Arabia on the eve of the rise of Islam. The remaining nine chapters are devoted to the actual history of his life, tracing stages in the development of his personality, evolution of his religious status, as well as political power coming by default and shifts in his extraneous policies from time to time—all tending to display that his outwardly actions too were either divinely inspired or based on some noble considerations rather than imperialistic designs.

AN OVERVIEW OF MAIN TRENDS AND IMPORTANT EVENTS OF THE PROPHET'S LIFE IN CHRONOLOGICAL ORDER

1.	Birth of the Prophet in Makkah in the 'Year of the Elephant' a few weeks after the attack on Makkah by the Christian Abyssinian governor of Yaman—570 AD	- 570 AD
2.	Suckling and upbringing with Sād B. Bakr under the care of Halīmah for about four/five years. • Picks up purest form of Arabic. • The miracle of splitting of his chest takes place during the last part of his stay with Halīmah.	- 570–575 AD
3.	Spends about two years with his mother Āminah. • Visits Yathrib along with his mother.	- 575–576 AD
4.	Death of his mother Āminah.	- 576 AD
5.	Remains for about two years under the guardianship of his grandfather Abd al Muttalib.	- 576–578 AD
6.	Death of Abd al Muttalib.	- 578 AD
7.	Remains under the guardianship of his uncle, Abū Tālib, for about seventeen years. • Spends hard life in poverty. • Initially works as a shepherd. • Accompanies his uncle on a trade journey to al Shām at the age of 12 (about 582 AD)—meeting with the Christian monk, Bahīrah, who recognizes him as a prophet. • Plays a minor role in Harb-al Fijār (the sacrilegious war) in his mid teens (about 585 AD) and also participates in conclusion of the peace pact known as Hilf al Fudūl. • Grows into a man of high character, free from every vice of his time—comes to be known as al Amīn (trustworthy). • Engages in trade with Syria as an agent or manager and earns name—attracts the attention of the wealthy widowed merchant, Khadījah, who appoints him as her trade manager.	- 578–595 AD

8.	Marries Khadījah—shifts to her house—his economic condition radically improves. • Khadījah gifts to her husband a 15-year-old slave boy named Zayd Bin Harīthah who is subsequently adopted by the Prophet as his son and plays an important role in the history of Islām. • Four daughters (Zaynab, Ruqayyah, Umm Kulthūm, and Fātimah) and two sons born out of his marriage with Khadījah, but both the sons die in infancy.	- 595 AD
9.	Takes charge of his cousin (Abū Talib's son) Alī who enters his household.	- 605 AD
10.	Takes part in the repairs/renovation of the Kābah and solves a dispute regarding refixing of the Black Stone in its wall.	- 606 AD
11.	Spends about five years in spiritual preparation without knowing that he was going to be assigned prophethood. • Generally keeps himself aloof and spends time on meditation and search of truth. • Starts annual spiritual retreats during Ramadān to Ghār Hirā (in 610 AD, he was having his fifth annual retreat when the first revelation came).	- 606–610 AD
12.	Receives the first revelation of the Qurān (assignment of prophethood) on one of the last nights of Ramadān (said to be twenty-seventh) during his spiritual retreat in Ghār Hirā. • The first revealed are the first five verses of Surah 96 (Al Alaq). • Some other revelations follow. • After some initial puzzlement and doubts, he believes the words revealed as those of God and also believes himself to have been appointed by God as his messenger.	- 610 AD
13.	al Fatrah or temporary suspension of revelations for a short period ranging from six months to two and a half years, depending on the sources—causing great disappointment to him.	- 611–612 AD

14.	Resumption of revelations (with the coming of Surah 93—Ad Duhā) and private preaching. • Gabriel teaches him the manner of ablution and prayers (Salāt). • Islām believed and practised in camera.	- 612–613 AD
15.	After receiving God's command, carries out public preaching of Islām in Makkah. Since Islām challenges their ancestral religion and culture as also their economic system, the Quraysh gang up to oppose and exterminate it and carry out well-organized persecution of the Muslims. • Islām, however, survives due to support of Hāshim clan headed by his uncle Abū Tālib. • The powerful uncle of the Prophet, Hamzah, embraces Islām, giving it great vigor.	- 613–615 AD
16.	Emigration of many of the Muslims to the Christian kingdom of Abyssinia (ruled by the Negus) due to increasing persecution and harassment. • The Prophet, however, stays back in Makkah and continues preaching. • After about three months of emigration, one of the most vehement opponents of Islām, Umar, enters Islām giving it new strength.	- 615 AD (in Rajab, the seventh month of Islamic calendar)
17.	The alleged incident of the 'Satanic Verses'.	- 616 AD
18.	Boycott of the Muslims/Banū Hāshim by Quraysh for about three years causing great misery and hardship.	- 617–619 AD
19.	Death of Khadījah and Abū Tālib soon after lifting of the boycott. • After death of Abū Tālib, his brother, Abū Lahab, takes over as chief of Hāshim (he was absolutely hostile to the Prophet and Islām). • The Quraysh redouble persecution of the Muslims.	- 619 AD (the year of sorrow)

20.	Abū Lahab withdraws clan protection from the Prophet. • The Prophet visits Tāif to seek protection but is humiliated and driven out—returns to Makkah after obtaining protection of Nawfal clan (of Mutīm). • The Quraysh leaders remain impregnable to Islām, forcing the Prophet to preach the faith to outsiders visiting Makkah for pilgrimage • Starts searching for dependable and powerful supporters outside Makkah in order to emigrate and continue preaching and practising Islām. • Starts receiving encouraging signals from Yathrib.	- 620 AD
21.	The great spiritual experience of Al Isrā and Mirāj (the command for five daily prayers is received).	- 621 AD (twenty-seventh Rajab, about a year before Hijrah)
22.	The first Pledge of al Aqabah with twelve Yathribites.	- June, 621 AD
23.	Pledge of the Second al Aqabah with seventy-five Yathribites. • The Yathribites invite the Prophet to emigrate and pledge to work for spread of Islam and also provide protection to the Muslims.	- June, 622 AD
24.	The Hijarah—The Prophet's Emigration to Yathrib (Madinah) following emigration of most of the Muslims (immediately preceding his Hijrah, the Quraysh leaders conspired to kill him, but he managed to depart evading their vigilance. They even chased him during his Hijrah journey but could not lay hands on him)	- September, 622 AD (Rabi al Awwal)

25.	During the first two years, the Prophet consolidates his position in Madinah. • Becomes the religious as well as political head of the Muslim community, now known as Ummah. • For strong integration, introduces the system of brothering or fraternization between Muhajirūn (Emigrants) and Ansar (the converted Muslim supporters of Madinah)—pairs of each Muhajir with one of the Ansar is formed. • Concludes an agreement known as Constitution of Madinah (623 AD) with Jewish and Muslim tribes/clans of Madinah for its protection from Quraysh who plan to attack the Ummah. • Construction of a mosque in Madinah (subsequently known as Masjid al Nabwi) which is completed seven months after Hijrah. • Revelations continue and become more frequent and prolific dilating on socio-economic as well as legal reforms—Zakāt and fast of Ramadān made compulsory. • Due to impending attack of Quraysh, the Prophet adopts a policy of fighting in defense after receiving Quranic command—several expeditions are sent against Makkan caravans.	- 622–623 AD
26.	Expedition to Nakhlah leads to killing of a Makkan and provokes Quraysh.	- January, 624 AD
27.	The Battle of Badr against the Makkan invading army under the command of Abū Jahal—the Muslims achieve a miraculous victory despite numerical inferiority. • Islām emerges as a regional political power. • The Quraysh take vow to avenge the defeat.	- March, 624 AD
28.	Expedition against Banī Qaynuqah (a Jewish tribe of Madinah)—leads to their expulsion.	- 624 AD
29.	The Battle of Uhud fought against the invading Makkan army near Madinah—the Muslims defeated—Hamzah and a large number of Muslims killed. • Prestige of the Ummah receives a beating.	- March, 625 AD

30.	Expedition against the Jewish tribe of Banī Nadīr—their expulsion from the oasis of Madinah.	- August, 625 AD
31.	The Second Badr—the Prophet reaches with his army to fight Abū Sufyān as per promise given at Uhud, but Abū Sufyān fails to turn up—the incident largely retrieves prestige of the Ummah.	- April, 626 AD
32.	Expedition against the pro-Quraysh tribe of Banī Mustaliq—the Muslims successful.	- January, 627 AD
33.	The incident of Ifk or false accusation against the Prophet's wife Āishah after return to Madinah.	- January/February 627 AD
34.	The Battle of the Trench (also known as Battle of the Confederates—al Ahzāb)—the final attack by Quraysh along with allied tribes on Madinah with an army having a strength of 10,000—due to Muslims' strategy of digging a trench, the attack ends in a siege which continues for twenty-five days with intermittent fights—the Makkans forced to retreat. • The Ummah emerges as one of the strongest military powers of the Peninsula.	- April, 627 AD
35.	Punitive expedition against the Jewish tribe of Banī Qurayzah due to their treachery—Qurayzah defeated and about 600 of their males executed. • With strengthening of the Ummah's military power, threat to its existence decreases. • The Prophet adopts a policy of peace and conciliation towards Quraysh.	- April/May, 627 AD
36.	The Treaty of Hudaybiyah with Quraysh—a pact of peace and nonaggression. • But serious threat emerges from Khaybar where the Jews gang up against Islām. • The great Quraysh generals, Khālid ibn al Walīd and Amr ibn al Ās, enter Islām.	- March, 628 AD
37.	The Battle of Khaybar—the Jews defeated and enter into protective agreement with the Prophet.	- April, 628 AD

38.	The Prophet plans preaching Islām outside Arabia—sends envoys with diplomatic letters to eight foreign potentates including the Byzantine and Iranian emperors, inviting them to Islām—many of them react adversely. • The King of Egypt, though not accepting Islām, sends gifts to the Prophet including two beautiful slave girls, one of them Mariyah, who becomes one of the Prophet's wives.	- 628 AD
39.	The Prophet performs Umrah or the Lesser Pilgrimage of the Kābah in accordance with terms of the Treaty of Hudaybiyah.	- March, 629 AD
40.	The Battle of Mūtah (in modern Jordan) fought against the Syrian Governor of the Byzantine Empire and different north Arabian tribes—the expedition was sent due to impending danger of attack on Madinah from them. The Muslims defeated. • The famous Muslim leaders Zayd B. Harithah, Abdullāh B. Rawāha, and Jāfar killed in the battle. • Encouraged by the Ummah's defeat, the Quraysh abrogate terms of the Treaty of Hudaybiyah and engineer killing of men of a pro-Ummah tribe in the sacred area of the Sanctuary.	- September, 629 AD
41.	The Prophet attacks Makkah commanding an army of 10,000 and conquers it virtually without bloodshed. • The Kābah is taken control of and is purified by breaking all idols. • A general amnesty of the Makkans is announced. • Large-scale voluntary conversion to Islām takes place. • Apprehending danger to their temple of goddess al Lāt, the Hawazīn tribes assemble a big force to attack the Ummah.	- February, 630 AD
42.	The Battle of Hunayn against Hawaizīn—after initial reverse, the Muslims defeat Hawaizīn inflicting heavy causalities—their commander, Mālik, retreats along with men of Thāqif to the latter's fort at Tāif.	- February, 630 AD

43.	Siege of Tāif by the Prophet—continues for twenty days—the Muslims fail to break into and withdraw.	- February/March 630 AD
44.	Expedition to Tabūk (on Syrian border) against the Byzantine Empire—strength of the Muslim army 30,000, largest ever mobilized in Arabia—the Prophet camps at Tabūk for about twenty days, but no fight takes places as information regarding mobilization of the Byzantine army turns out to be wrong—the Prophet returns after entering into peace treaty with some of the frontier tribes.	- October, 630 AD
45.	The 'Year of Deputations' (al Wufūd). • Due to the emergence of the Ummah as undisputed military power in Arabia, a large number of nomadic tribes from different corners of the peninsula send delegations to the Prophet and enter into protective alliances with or without conversion—Arabia brought under the Pax Islamica. • Effort of the Prophet to spread Islām leads to religious as well as political unification of almost the whole of Arabia. • The first-ever state or empire is established in Arabia. • Almost the whole of Arabia is Islāmised.	- 631 AD
46.	The First Pilgrimage or Haj by the Muslims—due to preoccupation, the Prophet sends Abū Bakr with 300 Muslims for the purpose to Makkah. • After their departure, the first twelve verses of Surah 9 are revealed putting restrictions on entry of idolators to the Sanctuary—Alī sent to Makkah to announce it. • Qurānic command (Q 3/97) is received, making Haj compulsory for every Muslim having means to do it.	- March, 631 AD

47.	The Prophet's first Islamic Haj (the Farewell Pilgrimage) • Correct Islamic rites and rituals of Haj ceremony established. • During Haj, the last verse of the Qurān (5/3) is revealed, which confirms completion of evolution of Islām as the final religion for mankind.	- March, 632 AD
48.	The mission of the Prophet having been completed, he has intuition of approaching death—expires after a sickness of twelve days.	- 8 June 632 AD (Corresponding to 12 Rabi al Awwal, year 11 of the Hijrah).

CONTENTS

Maps and Appendices

1. Map of Arabian Peninsula on the eve of the rise of Islam
2. **Appendix I**: A chronological list of the Prophet's wives (basic facts about them)
3. **Appendix II**: Descendancy chart of the Prophet's line of *Quraysh* Tribe (*Quraysh* of the Hollow)
4. **Appendix III**: Family tree of the Prophet

CHAPTER I

WRITING OF
THE PROPHET'S HISTORY

It has been remarked[1] that unlike other prophetic figures, *Muhammad*, the Prophet of *Islām*, was born within the full focus of history. The remark is prompted by the fact that there is abundance of historical literature throwing light on even the minutest details of his life. During the classical period of the history of *Islām* itself, numerous Arab scholars, who developed a flair for writing historical literature, compiled hundreds of books on the life and work of the Prophet and his associates. But it is an irony that in spite of copious sources, writing of the history of the Prophet has created a series of controversies with the Muslim and the Western scholars sharply differing on a good number of points. The differences of opinion are mainly due to the nature of the sources and difficulties involved in their critical evaluation

---

1 *Earnest Renan.*

1

though historical prejudice of the Western writers and a general hagiographical approach of the Muslim scholars are also strong factors working behind their attitudes.

There are two primary sources for constructing the history of the Prophet: the *Qurān* and the Islamic traditions. The latter have come down to us in the form of six canonical collections of *ahādīth* (*Sihah Sittah*), the collections of the jurists (*Imāms*), but most importantly, in the historical works of the Arab writers of the first few centuries of the Islamic era. The last mentioned historical compilations are mainly based on the religious traditions of *Islām* and are in the form of *Sirah* (biographies) and *Tārīkh* (chronicles narrating events in order of time). They are the most popular sources of information on the subject and have served as the main source books for subsequent historians down the modern age.

The *Qurān* is accepted as a source of unquestionable authenticity for constructing the history of the Prophet. Believed by the Muslims as a book of divine origin, it was revealed to the Prophet in short and long passages over a period of twenty-three years through the angel named Gabriel.[1] It contains a whole lot of information about different aspects of life and activities of the Prophet. Apart from describing details of his religious teachings in their historical background, it refers to almost all major events and developments of his life, both public and private. Social and religious conditions in which he found himself, the manners in

---

1   *In its final form, as arranged by the Prophet himself under divine inspiration, the Qurān as a book is divided into 114 chapters (Surah), further divided into sections (Rukū) and finally into verses (Ayah). There are 6,353 verses in the Qurān including 113 Bismillāh verses. Further, for facilitating recitation, the book is divided into 30 equal parts called Juz or Saparā which is again subdivided into 4 equal parts (Ar Rub-1/4; An Nisf-1/2; At Thalāthah-3/4). Thus, recitation of Qurān can be ideally completed in 30 days by a Muslim covering 1 Saparā or Parā per day. However, in order to complete recitation in 7 days only, the holy book is also divided into 7 equal parts called Manzils. Of the 114 chapters, 92 are said to have been revealed in Makkah while the remaining 22 are believed to have been revealed during the Madinan period of the Prophet's life.*

which he received the revelations, his specific role as a preacher and warner, the way the unbelievers opposed his message and raised objections, the demands of the unbelievers and replies which he gave to their objections and demands, the manner in which the *Quraysh* persecuted the Muslims, the conspiracy they hatched against him and the way they attempted to kill him, the precarious situation under which he decided to migrate from *Makkah* along with his followers, the wars he had to fight against the unbelievers, the divine help he received during his battles and struggle, the treaty he made with the Makkans and their ultimate surrender to *Islām*, the manner in which he completed his mission step by step—all these historical facts are referred to in the *Qurān*. There are references also to his personal life prior to assignment of prophethood, his life as an orphan, his earlier poverty and subsequent affluence, his relationship with his wives, the false accusation spread against his wife, *Āishah*, and even undue demands of his wives making him annoyed. In short, there is hardly an aspect of the Prophet's life and mission which has not been referred to, directly or indirectly, in the *Qurān*. In fact, almost each passage or its part in the *Qurān* relates to some occasion or incident of his life; the verses were revealed either to expound theological doctrines of *Islām* or to guide him in respect of manifold problems encountered during his lifetime. In order to further illustrate the prophet's mission so as to provide him detailed guidance, the *Qurān* also alludes to past peoples and civilizations, the previous Prophets and their struggle, hostile response of the unbelieving peoples and punishment inflicted on them by God. The event of Abrahah's invasion of *Makkah* for destroying the *Kābah* has also been referred to. Even contemporary events like war between the Roman and Persian empires as also beliefs, customs, and superstitions of the *Jāhiliyah* period have been mentioned which provide background information on the Prophet's life and mission.

The high degree of historical authenticity of the *Qurān* is based on two main factors. First, it stands historically established that its contents have not undergone any change whatsoever

ever since their revelation.[1] In fact, the Prophet took special care to ensure that the revelations were preserved intact in memory as well as in writing. Immediately after coming down of the revelations, the Prophet as well as many of his close Companions used to memorize them for reciting in the prayers. The Prophet had been spiritually empowered to retain in his memory whatever was revealed to him whereas the Companions, like the Arabs in general, had been specially gifted with the skill of memorization. Therefore, in course of time, the Prophet as also many of his Companions had the entire *Qurān* committed to memory. However, to be doubly sure, the Prophet, at regular intervals, but especially during the month *Ramadān,* used to revise recitation of the whole *Qurān* so far revealed under the guidance of Gabriel. It was during such sessions of revision that he used to arrange the passages into chapters and sections as per divine guidance received through Gabriel. In addition to memorization, the Prophet also took care to get the revelations written down on available materials. This was in accordance with the advice given by God in the very first revelation (Q 96/4 and 5), which emphasized preservation of knowledge by means of the pen. The process of writing down the text started from the very beginning, the Prophet employing a number of his literate followers as copyists. In due course, four of the *Ansār* were specially engaged as scribes, the most competent of them being *Zayd b. Thābit.* Written records of the revealed text were kept with the Prophet as well as many of his Companions.

However, the work of written compilation of the text of the *Qurān* was done much later. Immediately after the death of the Prophet, when a number of Arab tribes revolted and attempted to renounce *Islām,* the war of *Riddah* was fought against them in which a large number of *Huffāz* (those who had memorized the *Qurān*) were killed. Alarmed by this, the *Khalīfah Abū Bakr,* acting on the suggestion of *Umar,* deputed *Zayd Bin Thābit* to arrange the written record of the *Qurān* into a final written

---

1   *The Qurān itself declares its absolute immunity from external interference and interpolations (Q-41/41 and 42).*

text in order of chapters and sections as taught by the Prophet and as learnt by the *Huffāz*. The master copy of the *Qurān*, thus prepared, was kept with *Abū Bakr* during his lifetime, and then with *Umar*, the next *Khalīfah*; after Umar's death, it was in the custody of his daughter and the Prophet's wife *Hafsah*. Subsequently, during the Khilafat of *Uthmān* (24–35 H), a tendency towards variant readings of the *Qurān* was noticed in the far-flung provinces. On Uthmān's direction, copies of the *Qurān* from the master copy in Hafsah's keeping were prepared and sent to different provinces, simultaneously withdrawing the variant versions therefrom. Since then, the same original version of the *Qurān* has been in circulation in writing and has also been preserved in memory, transmitted from generation to generation through memorization. Thus, the *Qurān* has been preserved in its original form in memory as well as in writing.

The second factor which confirms the highest degree of reliability of the *Qurān* as a source of history is that its revealed verses were not withheld from public view for any length of time; immediately on being revealed, they were made public and communicated to the people. The *Qurān* itself mentions that in his early prophetic career, the Prophet used to hurriedly repeat the revealed verses so that he did not forget them (Q 75/16–18). He had to be advised by God not to utter the words in haste without understanding and he was also assured that God would enable him to retain whatever was revealed. The fact of immediate communication of the revealed messages disproves the suggestion made by some of the Orientalists that he modified or altered the text of the *Qurān* with the progress of his mission. For, had he done so, his enemies and even his followers would have found fault with him. Further, the facts mentioned in the revelations were known to his contemporaries to have been correct; anything running counter to the known facts of the time would have damaged his mission. The absolute contemporaneity of the revealed Qurānic verses make them invested with a peculiar authenticity.

However, though highly authentic, as a source of history, the *Qurān* has its own limitations. It is a religious scripture and not a history book; it only refers to the incidents but it does not narrate the historical details. It simply alludes to but does not elaborate or give details of the Prophet's life and activities. Moreover, as complained by the Western scholars, its form of presentation is very often allegorical and metaphorical; nor does it have any chronological arrangement. Its contents are, therefore, not easily comprehensible without additional information regarding circumstances under which each revelation was delivered, and such additional information can be had from Islamic traditions only which, more often than not, are themselves matters of dispute. Nevertheless, as a highly authentic contemporaneous commentary on the life of the Prophet, it can generally be very well used to corroborate or contradict facts disclosed by the traditions.

The *Qurān* not providing complete historical details, the historians of the Prophet, therefore, had to heavily fall back on the other source, that is, religious traditions of *Islām*. In Islamic literature, the traditions are known as *ahādīth* (plural of *hadīth*), which are reports of the sayings, deeds, and even tacit approvals of the Prophet as narrated by his Companions and transmitted orally or in writing through generations.[1] In several verses,[2] the *Qurān* admonishes the Muslims to obey the Messenger, making it clear that obedience to the Prophet is equal to obedience to God. The Companions believed that whatever the Prophet said or did was on behalf of God and by his command and so his actions and sayings were divinely inspired. They also believed that the Prophet could not err.[3] Therefore, the highest degree of love and reverence of the Prophet, obedience to his commands and imitation of his actions became essential components of the faith-commitment of the Muslims. As a result, the Companions numbering several thousands, minutely watched the Prophet's actions, listened

---

1 *The sayings of the Companions not attributed to the Prophet are also generally placed in the category of ahādīth.*

2 *Quran 4.59, 4.65, 4.80, and 59.7.*

3 *Qurān 53.2–4.*

to his utterances, and preserved the same in their minds or in writing for transmission to others. Thus, a great mass of religious traditions connected with the Prophet came into currency. *Abu-Hurayrah*, an enthusiastic propagator of the Prophet's *Sunnah*, is credited by historians to have alone transmitted as many as 5,374 traditions. Similarly, *Anas ibn Mālik, Āishah*, and *Umar ibn al Khattāb* are said to have transmitted 2,286, 2,210, and 1,630 *ahādīth* respectively.

Although there are stray traditions indicating that a few of the Companions[1] had written down the sayings of the Prophet after obtaining his permission, such instances appear to be exceptions rather than the rule. It is generally accepted by the scholars that the large mass of *hadīth* traditions were written down only about a century or so after the death of the Prophet. There are traditions recorded by *Muslim* which indicate that the Prophet forbade the writing down of his statements and ordered to erase them if anyone had already done it. Such traditions are attributed to *Abu Hurayrah, Zayd ibn Thābit*, and *Abu Saīd al Khudri*. The discouragement by the Prophet of recording of *ahādīth* was, perhaps, due to apprehension of the same getting mixed up with the Quranic revelations.

The nonrecording of *hadīth* traditions for about a century led to developments which seriously impaired their very credibility. Lapse of considerable time in their recording left scope for fading of memory as well as lexicographical changes due to verbal transmission through individuals. Worse than this, the period following the death of the Prophet was one of intense internal conflict between families, political factions, and religious or theological sects within the Islamic world. In order to obtain public support in respect of their point of view regarding any issue, each one of the groups freely distorted and even invented

---

1 *Abd-Allāh-ibn-Amr-ibn-al-Ās, Abu-Rāfi, and Anas ibn Mālik— According to a tradition recorded by Abu Dawūd, when Abdullah asked the Prophet whether he could write his utterances even when he was angry, the Prophet replied pointing to his lips: 'Do write, for nothing but truth can escape from them.'*

ahādīth to justify its own cause. Similarly, the Muslim conquest of territories outside Arabia brought in a new set of social, political, legal, and religious concepts and practices; the unrecorded mass of *hadīth* traditions provided ample opportunities to protagonists of such foreign customs to obtain sanction for them by fabrication of *ahādīth*. Such motivated fabrication of stories and *ahādīth* by different groups soon reached alarming proportions and during the reign of the Abbasid caliph, *Mamūn* (813–33), when the *hadīth* literature was being finally compiled, 'the true *hadīth* was as discernible from the false as a white hair is in the fur of a black bull'.[1] Some of the religious teachers are also said to have made the most of the situation for making a fast buck by inventing *ahādīth*. *Tabari* has recorded the story of *al Āwja* who, at the time of his execution in 772, confessed to having circulated 4,000 traditions of his own invention. We can only imagine of the travails of the *hadīth* compilers when indentifying true *ahādīth* from the false ones. It is reported that *al Bukhāri,* while compiling his *Sahīh,* came across some six lakh *ahādīth* then current, out of which he could confirm only 7,397 as genuine. Taking into account a good number of repetitions, the actual number of sound traditions recorded by him came down further. Thus, according to a rough calculation,[2] out of every 150 traditions circulating in the market, not more than one or two were found genuine by him. The suspect *ahādīth*, thus, numbered in lakhs and contained a great deal of contradictions and unreasonableness. The stories of the Satanic Verses, of *Zaynab*'s marriage with the Prophet, and of the various miracles performed by the Prophet are but a few examples of such distorted or manufactured traditions.

It was during the reign of the *Umayyad* caliph, *Umar ibn Abd al Azīz* (717–20), who is often described as the fifth rightly guided caliph due to his piety, that we get first information regarding recording and compilation of *ahādīth* on official direction. Guided by the religious need to disseminate sayings of the Prophet to the conquered territories and, perhaps, also in order to put a stop to

---

1 *Dāraqutni.*

2 *Haykal.*

the practice of inventing *ahādīth*, he promulgated orders all over the Empire for compilation of the sayings of the Prophet in the form of books. *Sād ibn Ibrahīm* accordingly wrote into books a large number of traditions which were sent to different parts of the Empire.[1]

The *hadīth* traditions contained a storehouse of information regarding life and preaching of the Prophet as well as the circumstances leading to revelation of different verses. Meanings of many verses were also hidden in the statements of the Prophet. A detailed but accurate knowledge of the *ahādīth* was, therefore, essentially required by Islamic scholars of different disciplines for their intellectual pursuits. As a result, during the second and third *Hijrāh* centuries, there was a sort of movement in the Islamic world for collection and compilation of *ahādīth* by different groups of scholars. *Sirah* writers and historians, writers of interpretation (*tafsīr*) of the *Qurān*, the jurists or *Shariah* writers like *Malīk ibn Anas* (d. 795), *as Shāfi* (d. 820), and *Hanbal* (d.855), and most importantly, the pure hadith compilers known as the traditionalists (*Muhaddathīn*) competed with one another for collection of traditions. In order to collect material for their works as well as to earn religious merit, they undertook great pains, travelled from place to place, went from door to door, met persons who had anything to narrate, and collected *ahādīth* which were in circulation. But they were aware of a large number of spurious *ahādīth* in currency which were required to be excluded. The traditionalists, therefore, developed an elaborate science of *hadīth* criticism. According to its methodology, each *hadīth* was to be thoroughly investigated in order to establish authenticity and completeness of its chain of narrators (*isnād*) leading directly to the Prophet through an eyewitness Companion. This necessitated detailed enquiries into life and character of each transmitter. The veracity of the *hadīth* was to be suspected or rejected if there was interruption in the chain or any of the narrators was found untrustworthy due to prejudiced mind, educational deficiency, temperamental weakness, immature age, or bad reputation due

---

1   *Ibn-Abd-al-Barr*— *'Jami Bayan al Ilm'*.

to any other reason. These enquiries into the characters of a large number of transmitters gave birth to a unique branch of knowledge known as *Asma ar Rijāl* (biographies of the narrators of the Prophet's sayings) of which the *Tabaqāt* of *Ibn Sād* is an example. According to the famous German Orientalist A. G. Sprenger, the Muslim scholars compiled such biographies of about five lakh narrators. Thus, as far as *isnād* was concerned, the traditionalists developed a thorough and effective method of ascertaining the authenticity of each *hadīth*. In accordance with degree of trustworthiness of the chain of corroborators, the traditionalists classified the *ahādīth* into categories like sound or genuine (*sahīh*), good or fair (*hasan*), and weak or untrustworthy (*daīf*). However, a *hadīth* that had three or more complete and authentic chains of transmission was considered of the highest degree of trustworthiness and accepted as a *mutawātir* one. There was yet another method of classifying *ahadīth* into *sālih* (healthy) and *sāqim* (infirm).

By the middle of the third Islamic century, after a long process of investigative and editorial treatment, the voluminous mass of the Prophet's traditions were finally compiled into six standard collections to which no new element could be added and from which fabrications had been purged. These six collections of *ahādīth*, known as *Sihāh Sittah*, were accorded canonical status and became integral part of the science of jurisprudence intended as sources to be used by later jurists. All of the six traditionalists who compiled these collections were interestingly from Central Asia or Persia. The most authoritative and revered of them was a*l Bukhāri* (d. 870), whose *Kitāb al Jāmi al Sahih*, popularly known as *Bukhāri Sharīf,* has acquired a quasi-sacred character, next only to the *Qurān*; an oath taken on it is religiously valid. According to a tradition, he was inspired to the task of compilation of genuine *ahādīth* by a dream in which he saw the Prophet being disturbed by flies while asleep and he himself was fanning them away from the Prophet's face. As per interpretation, the flies represented the mass of spurious traditions damaging the true image of the Prophet, and the person who was removing them was *al Bukhāri* himself. And so he devoted his life to the job and after sixteen years of travel to different Islamic kingdoms involving considerable editorial pains, he finally collected 7,397 genuine *ahādīth* which he classified according to subject matter. Of comparable stature was *Sahih* of *Muslim ibn al Hijjāj* (d. 875) of Nishapur. Although the book of *Muslim* is sometimes considered better organized and methodologically superior to that of *Bukhāri*, the latter is accorded the first place in awe and esteem. Both *Bukhārī* and *Muslim* were contemporaries but they did not know each other. Yet, interestingly enough, the contents of both the collections are almost identical suggesting existence of unity of methodology and materials.

The other four of the canonical collections were *Sunan* of *Abu Dāwūd* (d. 888), the *Jāmi* of *al Tirmidih* (d. 892), the *Sunan* of *Ibn Mājah* (d. 886) and the *Sunan* of *al Nasāi* (d. 915). The technique of scrutiny and system of organization of all the six traditionalists were similar. Their collections were organized as legal manuals, dealing first with laws governing the rituals of worship and next with the laws regulating the social, political, and economic life of the community. The six collections were considered perfect by the Muslims and subsequent *hadīth* compilers followed their principles.

A *hadīth* consists of two parts, the chain of transmission (*isnād*) and the main statement or text (*matn*). The scope of *hadīth* criticism in the classical period, however, remained largely confined to investigation of the *isnād* only. The traditionalists did set some rules for *matn* criticism as well, which was known as *dirāya*. Unfortunately, however, these rules were not applied rigorously, perhaps, due to overreliance on truthfulness of the narrators or fear of stiff political opposition or else due to apprehension of the same introducing too great a danger of independent judgment opening up a Pandora's box. As a result, a few *ahādīth* of questionable contents crept into some of the collections giving rise to serious historical controversies. This method of *hadīth* criticism sans critical examination of the subject matter of the *hadīth*, especially in respect of those which had historical connotations, failed to satisfy the subsequent Muslim scholars. They felt that a *hadīth* was liable to rejection if its content contradicted the *Qurān* or the Prophet's known teachings or did not fit into the character of the Prophet or otherwise ran contrary to reason. To them, even if the *isnād* of a *hadīth* was trustworthy, its veracity was to be suspected if its subject matter did not conform to logic on historical and psychological analysis.

Apart from the fact that the classical traditionalists failed to subject the text of the *hadīth* to critical examination in the light of relevant historical and psychological facts as well as reason, the Western historians have challenged the authenticity of the canonized traditions from yet other angles. According to them, scrutiny of the chain of narrators in order to find out veracity of a *hadīth* had its own limitations. If the content of *hadīth* could be fabricated, then it was also possible to forge a chain of narrators. Further, rejection of the narrators on the basis of alleged political affiliation or sectarian conviction merely indicated victory of one opinion over the other.

One of the first to collect the orally transmitted Islamic traditions and make use of them was the group of the Prophet's biographers and historians. They included documents and poems also in their works, but their main source of information was the large mass of memorized traditions which they painstakingly collected after undertaking journeys to different places and interacting with the people having knowledge of the same. Their initial compilations were biographical and included three types: *Sirah* or biography of the Prophet, *Maghāzī* or account of wars and conquests of the Prophet, and the biographical dictionary which contained details of the lives of the Prophet, his Companions, and their successors (*tabiūn*). Immediately following these, books of formal history were also written. Thus, starting from the second Muslim century, hundreds of historical books of the four descriptions were penned down. Four of them—*Sirat Rasūl Allāh* of *Muhammad ibn Ishāq* (d. 767) of *Madinah*, the *Maghāzī* by *al Wāqidī* (d. 822) of *Madinah*, *Tabaqāt al Kubrā* (biographical dictionary) by *Ibn Sād* (d.845) of Baghdad, and *Tarīkh al Rusūl wal Mulūk* by *Jāfar Muhammad ibn Jarīr* al *Tabarī* (d. 923) of Persia—are, however, the best representatives of each of the four classes of historical compilations and are of seminal importance. All subsequent biographers and historians down the ages extensively borrowed materials from these works using them as the main source books.

The *Sirāh* of *Ibn Ishāq* was the first in point of time and, therefore, became the fundamental source book for the historians who succeeded him. But it has not come down to us in its original form; what is available now is its abridged and edited version as left by *Ibn Hishām* (d. 834), which is regarded as true. The most popular of the four masterpieces, however, was the *Tarīkh* of *Tabarī*. This monumental work on world history served as a source for later historians like *Miskawayh*, *Ibn al Athīr*, *Abu al Fidā*, *al Masūdi* (d. 957), and finally, the famous critical historiographer, *Ibn Khaldūn* (d. 1406). There are traditions which speak about *Tabarī*'s passion for writing history; he wandered from place to place in search of materials, writing forty sheets per day for forty years and had to once sell the sleeves of his shirt to buy bread for sustenance. The fame of *Tabarī*, however, equally rests on his commentary of the *Qurān* which turned out to be a standard work upon which other commentators drew.

However, the four foundational compilations have been subjected to severe criticism. The classical traditionalists and jurists doubted the authenticity of their accounts and charged their authors of including unattested information in their compilations. Even their intellectual integrity was suspected and it was suggested that they were susceptible to external influences including the opinions of the ruling authorities. *al-Wāqidī* was specially criticized for his baseless reports and it was alleged that in his enthusiasm for collecting colourful stories for his work, he even coined and fabricated traditions. In the opinion of *Imām as Shāfi*, his book was full of lies. Although opinions about reliability of *Ibn Ishāq* differed, *Imām Bukhāri* is said to have not included any of his traditions in his *Sahih* and criticized him for borrowing from the Jews. *al-Wāqidī*'s secretary, *Ibn Sād*, however, passed off with a rather positive reputation. But on matters regarding the life of the Prophet, he had extensively borrowed from *Wāqidī*; hence this part of his work was no better. Although *Tabarī* was held in high esteem for his profound learning, he was also accused of Shiaite inclinations. It is held by modern scholars that although these Arab historians mentioned *isnād* and conducted some enquiries into the sources, they generally ignored the rigorous principles of scrutiny and criticism of traditions as set by the traditionalists and cared little for their authenticity. Perhaps, keen to collect as many facts as in currency, they included all sorts of reports, spurious as well as genuine, in their writings. Thus, the controversial account about the verses relating to the three goddesses and the irresponsible story regarding the Prophet's alleged infatuation for *Zaynab* came to form part of the Islamic history; such unwarranted stories were made use of by the Western scholars to criticize the Prophet. Similarly, on the basis of unattested traditions, they included numerous miraculous stories about the birth and childhood of the Prophet which smacked of hagiography.

If we look at these historical compilations from the angle of modern historiography, we will definitely be left disappointed. There are shortcomings in these works. Their form of presentation is the stereotype used by the *hadīth* writers, that of recording statements with reference to the sources. They are almost devoid of historical criticism; not exercising any significant power of analysis, comparison, or drawing inferences; their authors have simply narrated stories without even commenting on contradictions. For example, *Tabarī* narrates two separate stories about the Satanic Verses and *Ibn Ishāq* puts two mutually exclusive versions of the conversion of *Umar* without even commenting on the apparent contradiction. They generally leave the judgment part on the readers themselves. There are also lacunae in their accounts. Whereas, they have incorporated abundant information in respect of the Madinan period of the Prophet's life, we get very little material about his early prophetic career in *Makkāh*. In respect of his early life till he began receiving revelations, there is hardly any concrete information. What have been recorded are only religious legends regarding the Prophet's birth, childhood, and youth, which have little historical value.

It will, however, be unfair to judge the historical compilations of these first writers according to the parameters of modern historiography. They were men of their own age and were constructing the history of a great man out of a scattered mass of stories and traditions. The man whose life they were attempting to portray was the subject of their greatest reverence. Nevertheless, they honestly and truthfully collected whatever information was available and wrote no uncritical hagiography. Despite their reverence for the Prophet, they did not hide stories which showed their hero in an undesirable light. Thus, *Tabarī* mentioned the controversial affair of the Satanic Verses which showed the Prophet committing a mistake. Similarly, the unappealing stories about impertinence of the Prophet's wives and his alleged affair with *Zaynab* were scrupulously recorded. They described every account they came across giving equal weight to each of them with utmost impartiality, caring little for their bearing on history. In each case, they even listed the sources though the chain of authorities would not meet modern requirements. With whatever defects, they created vital sources for reconstructing the history of the Prophet for all ages to come.

Unfortunately, there is hardly any contemporary chronicle or historical account about the Prophet from the neighbouring countries like Egypt, Abyssinia, the Byzantine Empire, and the Persian Empire although the last two used to have their official chroniclers. Perhaps, it was too early for them to attach importance to the land of the nomads, which was a cultural backwater. In the absence of any significant historical information coming forth from non-Islamic sources, the Islamic traditions, either in the form of *hadīth* collections or early historical compilations, remain the main sources of the Prophet's history. But due to large-scale pious or impious frauds suspectedly involved therein, the Western scholars treat them of little historical value and harp on paucity of authentic material for writing the history of the Prophet. Some of them like the Italian, Leone Caetani (d. 1935), and the Belgian Jesuit, Henri Lammens (d. 1935) even go to the extreme of rejecting the entire historical validity of the tradition literature. While there is some element of truth in

15

the criticism of the modern Western historians, their attitude appears to be too extreme; for after elimination and sifting on the basis of scientific historical criticism, there still remains enough traditional material to enable a historian to form a much clearer sketch of the Prophet's life than that of any other founder of a universal religion.

It is surprising that while all these literary activities regarding compilation of history of the Prophet was going on in the Muslim world, the Christendom was absolutely unaware of these facts; and this continued for about a thousand years after the birth of *Islām*. During that period, Europe remained in the make-believe world of its own imagination about *Islām* and its Prophet which was, perhaps, a calculated move. The widespread popularity and expansion of *Islām* as a religion within a short period seemed to engulf Christianity, causing serious consternation. At the same time, the rapid expansion of the military power of the Muslims on the three continents including the conquest of Spain (711) threatening the European heartland, caused great fear in the Christendom. The initial reaction was, therefore, one of abhorrence of *Islām* and its founder. Before organizing themselves to face the challenge militarily, however, the Christians initially started a campaign of vilification and calumny against the emerging religion; this was in order to inculcate hatred against *Islām*. The false propaganda resulted in elaboration of what has been called a 'deformed image' of *Islām* and its founder. The anti-Islamic propaganda originated in Muslim Spain (*al Andalus*). In 850, a Christian monk called Perfectus started publicly hurling the ugliest abuses on the Prophet and was executed at Cordova, the capital of Muslim Spain. This incident started an anti-Islamic movement of Christian fanatics in Spain, the members of which used to publicly deliver venomous statements about the character of the Prophet and court martyrdom. With the execution of the leaders like Ishaq, Eulogio, and Alvaro, this aggressive cult of martyrdom fizzled out after some time. The members of this anti-Islamic cult had in their possession a brief biography of the Prophet which had been prepared in one of the Christian monasteries. This composition contained a series of unimaginable lies about the Prophet intended to assassinate his character and the same used to be used by the Cordovan martyrs for abusing him.

According to this fantasy, which was a product of hate and fear, the Prophet was an impostor and a charlatan who impersonated as a prophet to deceive the world. He was a sexual pervert who promoted licentiousness which attracted his followers. He forced the people to convert to *Islam* at the point of sword, glorified war and slaughter, and his religion was one of violence. *Islam* was depicted as a transient Christian heresy[1] rather than an independent religion and the *Qurān* was described as a pirated but mutilated version of the Jewish and Christian scriptures. This fictional portrait of the Prophet and *Islam* passed on to other countries in Europe, influenced the minds of the masses, resulted in concoction of more and more such legends, and finally prepared the way for transformation of the war of ideology into long-drawn military campaigns against the Muslim enemies. The Christians of northern Spain began the Wars of Reconquest against the Muslims of Spain and conquered Toledo (1085). The Normans started attacking the Muslims in southern Italy and Sicily, conquering the area in 1091. And finally, in 1095, on the summon of the Pope, Urban II, to liberate the tomb of Christ in Jerusalem, the knights of Europe started a long-drawn religious war against the Muslim kingdoms which was known as the Crusades (1095–1291); the Christians managed to conquer Jerusalem in 1099 and established colonies in the Near East. During the war period, hatred against the Muslims further heightened and the fictional image of the Prophet and *Islam* got finally crystallised. Many more calumnies were levelled against the Prophet. The legends described him as a magician who concocted false miracles to mislead the Arabs; the physical states undergone by him while receiving revelations were claimed to have been epileptic attacks. The Prophet was depicted as the Antichrist of the New Testament, the great pretender. It was also said that while receiving one of the revelations, he was torn

---

1 *Islam was first so depicted by the Syrian John of Damascus during the Umayyad period.*

apart by the pigs, a fitting end for a heretic. During the wars of Crusades, a number of songs were composed which also directed bitterest diatribes against the Prophet. The Song of Roland which was composed during the First Crusade depicted the Muslims as idol-worshippers, bowing down before a trinity of Gods— 'Apollo, Tervagant, and Mahomet'. Thus, this distorted image depicting Muslims as the biggest enemy to be exterminated at all cost and describing the Prophet as the incarnation of all that was evil, was firmly established in the Western imagination; and it was, perhaps, this myth about the Prophet which made it difficult for the Christians to see him as a historical character even in the modern age.

Beginning from the twelfth century, however, a few Christian intellectuals started trying to obtain a more accurate view of *Islām* and the Prophet. William of Malmesbury was the first European to distinguish *Islām* from paganism in 1120. A more important attempt to know the reality about *Islām* was made by Peter the Venerable, the influential abbot of Cluny in France, by studying the *Qurān* and some other Islamic literature. He commissioned a team of Christian and Muslim scholars under an Englishman, Robert of Ketton, to translate some Islamic texts; the project was completed in 1143 and they produced the first Latin translation of the *Qurān*, a collection of Muslim legends, a Muslim history of the world, and a copy of the polemical literature circulating in Spain. The Christian intelligentsia had, perhaps, now started realizing that the Muslims were too powerful to be physically subjugated; the realization was soon confirmed by the major military defeats suffered by the Christians in the Crusades. It was now being felt that *Islām* could be successfully confronted with the power of words and reason only for which an accurate knowledge of their scriptures and literature was necessary. It was probably with this realization that during the Fifth Crusade (1218–19), Francis of Assisi attempted to teach the message of Christianity in the Muslim land. Subsequently, the Dominican scholar, Monte Croce, travelled in Muslim countries and was impressed by the quality of piety of the Muslims. In the fourteenth century, Raymond of Lull organized training of Christian missionaries in Arabic language and Islamic doctrines. The tradition of Peter the Venerable was carried forward in the fifteenth century by scholars like John of Segovia (d. 1458) and Nicholas of Cusa who made a beginning of systematic examination of Islamic history and theology.

The distorted image of *Islām*, however, still exercised a powerful hold in the Western imagination and the scholars who attempted to take a more objective view of *Islam* did not dare speak openly in its favour for fear of public reaction. The Christian Reformers like Luther and Zwingli still spoke of *Islām* as a Christian heresy, equating the Prophet with the Pope as the enemy of religion. Dante in his *The Divine Comedy* put the Prophet in the Eighth Circle of the Hell with the schismatics.

From the sixteenth century onwards, however, there were some major developments in Europe which paved the way for a more realistic and daring study of *Islām*. The conquest of the Christian Empire of Byzantium by the Ottoman Turks in 1453 and subsequent expansion of the Muslim Empire in European territories made the Christians realize that in order to counter the challenge, it was important to know the secrets of their strength. For this purpose, an accurate information about *Islām* and its history was desirable. The growth of international trade and commerce followed by colonialism of European countries was another factor which necessitated awareness of the language and cultural traditions of the Muslim-inhabited lands in the East. Similarly, a sound knowledge of Arabic and Islamic scriptures and history was a *sine qua non* for promotion of Christian missionary activities in the newly-explored Muslim lands. The Reformation of the sixteenth century also contributed in its own way to the study of *Islām*; a knowledge of Arabic philology was important for understanding the cognate Semitic roots of the Hebrew Bible. And most importantly, the Renaissance and the following 'Age of Enlightenment' widened the mental horizon of the European scholars and encouraged a thirst for more and more knowledge of Arabic and *Islām*; Arabic was seen to be the key to the writings of Muslim philosophers and scientists hitherto known only in imperfect medieval Latin translations.

Thus, with whatever motives, from the seventeenth century onwards, there emerged a group of scholars all over Europe who started a movement of modern study of *Islām* and its history. These scholars undertook intensive linguistic training in Arabic and other Islamic languages, explored the sources of Islamic history, and translated and published them in Arabic as well as European languages. In order to quench their intellectual thirst, some of them even visited different places in the Middle East for collecting first-hand historical information; a few of them[1] even became Muslims through their study of *Islām*. They made a thorough study of the *Qurān*, Islamic chronicles, and other books and, subjecting the sources of Islamic history to the principles of critical historical enquiry, attempted to write books on different subjects of Islamic history with considerable objectivity challenging the deformed image of *Islam*. Such Western scholars of Islamic studies were, by the end of eighteenth century, known as the 'Orientalists'—a term first used in England in 1779 in an easy about Edward Pocock.

In the seventeenth century, the lead was taken by the Dutch scholars Thomas Erpenius (d. 1624) and Jacobus Golius (d. 1667), who took initiatives in publication of Islamic literature and collection of manuscripts; Leiden soon became the *Makkah* of Arabic studies. The English Orientalist, Edward Pocock (d. 1691), who was incumbent of the first Arabic Chair at Oxford, wrote *Specimen Historiae Arabum* which prepared the way for a more accurate and dispassionate view of *Islām* than the deformed image. But the crowning achievement of this century was the *Bibliotheque Orientale* of Bartholemy d' Herbalot. Based on Arabic, Turkish, and Persian sources, this work was published in 1697 and is regarded as the encyclopaedia of *Islām* serving as the most authoritative source of reference in Islamic studies

---

1 *Rene Guenon and V. M. Nonteil of France, Frithi of Schuon and T. Bockhardt of Switzerland, Abdul Karim Germanus of Hungary, Martin Lings of Britain and Thomas Irving of America.*

in Europe. Though Herbalot made a bold step to break out of the medieval Christian approach, he still regarded the Islamic Prophet as a false one.

Another Orientalist, Henery Stubbe, attempted a fair and courageous account of the Prophet in his book[1] which, however, could be published only in the twentieth century due to fear of the Church's reaction. In the same century, however, there were Orientalists like Humphry Perideaux, J. H. Hottinger, and Abbe Maracci whose minds still shuddered at the mention of the Islamic Prophet and whose books were works more of controversy rather than scholarship. In his book *Mahomet: The True Nature of Imposture*, the English Orientalist, Perideaux described *Islām* as a mere imitation of Christianity and repeated the old irrational obsessions of the past. According to him, the Prophet's two predominant passions were ambition and lust. Nevertheless, the early Orientalists laid the foundation of an objective study of *Islām* on the basis of original sources and started the process of correcting the distorted reporting of the Middle Ages. Arabic language was exposed to Europe and the *Qurān* was translated and published. The study of Arabic was established in European universities.

In the eighteenth century, which witnessed the blooming of the 'Age of Enlightenment', the new approach to the study of *Islām* was further extended and systematized and some of the Orientalists wrote in modern languages conveying the information to the common readers of Europe. In 1708, Simon Ockley published his *History of the Saracens* which rather upset the readers because he did not present *Islām* as the religion of the sword and tried to see the Prophet's wars from the Islamic point of view. In 1734, George Sale published a remarkable English translation of the *Qurān* which is still regarded as accurate. His preliminary discourse to this translation was a milestone; with a fair estimation of the Prophet and his work, it put the study

---

1 *'Account of the Rise and Progress of Mahometanism, with the Life of Mahomet and a Vindication of Him and His Religion from Calumnies of the Christian.'*

of the *Qurān* on a new basis. The Dutch scholar H. Reland spoke in terms of doing historical justice to *Islām* which had long been denied. In 1730, Comte de Boulainvilliers wrote favourably about the Prophet in his *Vie De Mahomed*, describing him as the forerunner of the age of reason. Though holding that the Prophet used religion for political purposes, he compared him with great military heroes like Julius Caesar and Alexander the Great. His book was, however, severely criticized by his contemporaries as 'an anticlerical romance', and Jean Gagnier, the then professor at Oxford, even wrote another book of the same title in refutation, calling the Prophet 'the greatest villain of mankind and the most mortal enemy of God'. Francois Voltaire published a book in 1751[1] in which he praised the Prophet as a profound political thinker and founder of a rational religion. Another Dutch Orientalist, Johann Jakob Reiske (d. 1774), created a philosophical basis for Islamic studies and wrote wide-ranging works on Islamic history, Arabic poetry, numismatics, and so on. He brought out in five volumes a Latin translation of the work of *Abu al Fidā* along with marginal notes. His interpretation of Islamic history as a paradigm of universal history was ahead of his age. He was the first Orientalist who tried to notice divine qualities in the life of the Prophet; but for this, he was strongly criticized by his colleagues.

It was during this century that schools were started for oriental studies, oriental libraries were established, and Asiatic Societies were founded, which gave an impetus to the modern study of *Islām*. The school of De Sacy (d. 1838) in Paris influenced a whole generation of European scholars. The Dutch were the first to establish an Asiatic Society in the occupied East Indies. Following their example, Sir William Jones founded the Asiatic Society of Calcutta in 1784. As a result of remarkable research and studies by the Orientalists, a somewhat corrected picture of the Prophet's history now started becoming familiar to educated Europeans. History of *Islām* was now firmly established as an accepted field of study. This was manifested in the *Decline*

---

1 *'Les Moeurs et l'esprit des nations'.*

and Fall of the Roman Empire of Edward Gibbon, which was published in 1788. In this book, out of seventy-two chapters, nine were devoted to the history of *Islām*. Gibbon praised the lofty monotheism of *Islām* and showed that its history deserved a place in the history of world civilization. The exposure of a truer image of the Prophet and his religion was attempted to be made political use of by some European statesmen. In 1798, Napoleon led an expedition to Egypt accompanied by a good number of French Orientalists hoping to subjugate the Islamic world and challenge the British hegemony in India. In his address to the Egyptian ulema, he praised the Prophet and his sympathetic presentation of *Islām* impressed the Egyptians. The expedition, however, failed as he was defeated by the British and Turkish armies.

The Orientalists of this period used the original Islamic sources instead of hearsay and gossips of the past. They could not, however, totally cast aside the medieval legends; still remaining captives of the old prejudices, they continued to use the old material now and then to make their narration spicy. In spite of their positive writings, therefore, they did not recognize the Islamic Prophet as a religious figure and the *Qurān* as a revealed book. Thus, Simon Ockley described the Prophet as a crafty man who posed as a prophet while his basic motives were ambition and lust. Even in the opinion of George Sale, *Islām* was merely a human invention and it spread by sword. Voltaire also repeated the theory of the Prophet being an impostor who had led the people to accept *Islām* by means of trickery and lies. The final analysis of Gibbon, too, was no different; he argued that the Arabs had been motivated to join his religion due to temptation of loot and sex.

During the nineteenth century, oriental research and studies were further perfected. The idea of unity of research and studies was encouraged, and with this view, a good number of academic institutions[1] were founded. The work of opening up of various sources for the study of *Islām* was almost completed;

---

1   *Societe Asiatique in Paris, Royal Asiatique Society of Great Britain, the American Oriental Society, etc.*

most of the source books of the classical period were edited, published, and even translated into European languages and made available to the common readers. The *Sirah* of *Ibn Ishāq* by Ferdinand Wustenfeld (1860), the *Maghāzī* of *al-Wāqidī* by A. Von Kremer (1856) and again by J. Wellhousen (1882), the great history of *al Masūdi* by De Meynard (1877), the great annals of *Ibn al Athīr* by Toruberg, the *Tārīkh* of *al Tabarī* by De Goeje, *Mislat al Masabih* by A. N. Mathews, and the *Tabaqāt* of *Ibn Sād* by Edward Sachau are examples of the work done by the Orientalists in this field. And this work was done by the Orientalists to the highest standards of scholarship; most of these nineteenth century editions of original chronicles have neither been replaced nor superseded and are being pirated today even by Muslim scholars. Apart from opening up of historical sources, the auxiliary disciplines of historical research like archaeology, epigraphy, palaeography, and numismatics were also developed and treated scientifically.

The most important contribution of the Orientalists in this century was, however, application of the modern methods of historical criticism to Islamic historiography. Finding the traditional sources as of doubtful origin, the Orientalists resorted to sifting the material by eliminating the improbable and choosing between contradictory data by means of critical comparison and analysis. Thus, critical biographies of the Prophet and early history of *Islām* were compiled on the basis of traditional Islamic sources by German scholars, Gustav Weil and A. Sprenger and the British Orientalist, William Muir. Although the historical diagnosis of Sprenger was disputable, he for the first time made use of Islamic traditions in extenso. More important, however, was *Geschichte des Quorans* of Theodor Noldeke (1860), which is still considered a standard work. Julius Wellhausen fully used the critical method of writing history in his books. A highly significant work in this regard was *Muhammedanische studies* of the Hungarian Orientalist, Ignaz Goldzihar (d. 1921); he viewed the life of the Prophet as a phenomenon of cultural history inspired by religious ideas. A significant development of the nineteenth century was that a few moderate Orientalists started showing a tendency to view the Islamic Prophet as genuine and sincere in his conviction. The first to do this was Thomas Carlyle, who, while delivering lectures on 'Hero and Hero-worship' in 1840, stressed the sincerity of the Prophet, maintaining that he sincerely believed himself to be a messenger and the recipient of God's revelations; but he doubted the genuineness of the Qurān. Taking cue from Thomas Carlyle, some of the Orientalists following him tended to present his prophethood as a psychological phenomenon wherein he sincerely believed himself to be a prophet under some genuine delusion. The evolution of this type of interpretation can be traced in the works of the succeeding generations of the Orientalists represented by Sir William Muir (d. 1905), D. S. Margoliouth (d. 1940), and W. Montgomery Watt. The famous books of the last mentioned author *Muhammad at Mecca* and *Muhammad in Medina* were published in 1953 and 1956, respectively.

However, excelling in a field which was foreign to their cultural orientation, the Orientalists, over a period of a few centuries, evolved the scientific method of critical historiography about *Islām*, largely correcting the medieval distorted image. But whereas the medieval myths were exploded one by one, by the end of the nineteenth century, some of them developed new stereotypes which manifested their ingrained contempt for *Islām*. Under the influence of the success of European colonialism and imperialism, with Muslim countries succumbing one by one, such writers developed a false sense of racial superiority. They started talking in terms of carrying the 'whiteman's burden' of civilizing the savage peoples of Asia and Africa. They also spoke of *Islām* as the enemy of decent civilization and the Muslims as incapable of reforming their condition. Such were the views expressed by the French scholar Chateaubriand, who even thought of revival and extension of the Crusades.

Such unscientific expressions by a few Western writers were, however, exceptions rather than the rule. A majority of the Orientalists continued to present an objective image of *Islām* on the basis of critical historicism. From the beginning of the twentieth century, it was not only the political history of *Islām* but also the study of the religion of *Islām* which became established as a special discipline of learning in Europe and America. At the same time, materials were collected and study started of contemporary Islamic regions in their historical context. A crowning achievement of the Orientalists at the beginning of the twentieth century was consolidation of their knowledge about *Islām* and its history in the *Encyclopedia of Islām: A Geographical, Ethnographical and Biographical Dictionary of the Mohammadan Peoples*. It was compiled by Goldzihar, De Goeje, and Karabacek by the collaboration of about a hundred scholars and appeared in Leiden (1908) in German, French, and English.

With due regard to the Orientalists' great contributions to modern Islamic historiography, however, it may be concluded that in its final analysis, history writing about the Prophet by them smacks of motivated reporting though differing in degrees from writer to writer. In fact, the Orientalists were a heterogeneous group; while some were serving the purposes of the colonialist governments, others were supporting the viewpoints of the Christian missionaries; and yet there were others who showed ethnocentric inclinations. It was only a small group of them which had a thirst for true knowledge; but they also appear to have failed in totally freeing themselves from medieval prejudices. Therefore, more often than not, their interpretation of data fails to meet the standards of unbiased research. Perhaps, they have a psychological limitation which inhibits them from seeing the true religious character of the Prophet. In their subconscious mind, they have a preconceived image of an ideal religious figure; but when they find the Islamic Prophet leading an apparently worldly life, his character would not measure up to their expectations. Hence, they would hesitate in recognizing the Prophet as a spiritual leader and would tend to overplay his role as a statesman. Without regard to the total situation in which the Prophet found himself and his religiously inspired reactions, all the time showing a policy of peace and conciliation, his Western historians would view his wars and conquests only as examples of violence and political aggrandizement. Similarly, they would not be able to visualize the real intentions of the Prophet behind each of his multiple marriages and would tend to describe him as a person having weakness for the fair sex. Another feature of the Orientalists' approach is an extreme skepticism about the traditional sources of the Prophet's history. But when the same suits their inner feelings, they would freely use them in order to drive home their viewpoint.

It was under the influence of the Orientalist movement that from the end of the nineteenth century, side by side with Orientalist research, in Islamic countries, also a group of Muslim scholars started research work on *Islām* and the Prophet using the same scientific methodology. The works of Taha Husayn in Egypt, Md. Kurd Ali in Syria, and Syed Amir Ali in India were not motivated by theology alone but were scholarly in the Western sense. One of the most popular twentieth century Arabic biographies of the Prophet was the *Life of Muhammad* by Muhammad Husayn Haykal. The eighth edition of this book published in1935 was translated by Ismāīl Rājī al Fārūqī. Written in response to Emile Dermenghem's biography of the Prophet (1928), the book of this Egyptian writer is a beautiful example of modern critical history writing. He blamed the misrepresentation of the Prophet on the fertile imagination and uncritical scholarship of early Muslim writers who had failed to distinguish between historically sound and mischievously planted traditions. Warning against the irresponsible use of Muslim sources, he was responsible for re-evaluation of the Prophet on the basis of reason and scientific research. A similar biography of the Prophet with refutation of the Orientalists' misrepresentation was the *Sirat un Nabi* by Shiblī Numānī. There followed many other Muslim writers who attempted to present the correct picture of the life and character of the Prophet by critical examination and reinterpretation of the original sources. Attention was also paid to presenting the Prophet as a model of social and political ideologies.

CHAPTER II

THE SETTING

The sudden emergence of Islam as a world religion and one of the most powerful empires of the world in the second quarter of the seventh century was a highly unexpected phenomenon of history. It arose from the north-western part of the Arabian Peninsula, an area of barren mountains, deserts, and steppes known as *al Hijāz*. The area was geographically one of the least favoured, politically without any tradition of state-building and culturally too underdeveloped to give rise to such a great revolution. No wonder, the faithful historians would consider it a part of divine dispensation only. Some modern historians have, however, suggested that the Islamic revolution did not irrupt out of the blue. According to them, in Arabia preceding the rise of *Islām*, there were undercurrents of developments which favoured such a change. The relative strength of the two theories may be better appreciated after seeing through the total situation that prevailed in the peninsula on the eve of the rise of *Islām*.

Arabia is the largest peninsula on the map and spreads over an area which is almost as big as that of India. Some Muslim writers would suggest that the choice of area of the origin of *Islām* was, perhaps, due to its strategic location at the meeting point of three continents and roughly the centre of the then known world. The peninsula is bounded on the north by territories known as the 'Fertile Crescent' which includes areas of Iraq, Syria, and Palestine and which, according to orthodox geographers, is not part of the peninsula. On the east, south and west, the peninsula is bounded by the Persian Gulf, the Indian Ocean, and the Red Sea, respectively. Barring a small area in the south-west[1] which is well watered, the whole of the peninsula is one of the hottest and driest regions of the world, highly inhospitable and almost totally barren. With no river, lake, or other source of water and hardly any rainfall, the physical features of the country those days mainly consisted of sun-scorching deserts, waterless steppes, and rugged mountains. This landscape was broken only by a few oases generally falling in the peripheral area. To this general physical feature of the peninsula, the only contrast was presented by the south-western portion which is known as *Yaman*. This area had the benefit of monsoon rains which permitted large-scale agriculture and development of advanced sedentary civilization from the ancient times. But the remaining vast area of the peninsula did not leave scope for rise of agriculture and settled life except in a few oases, and permitted only the nomadic way of living.

The classical Greco-Roman writers divided the area of the peninsula into three parts—Arabia Petraea, Arabia Felix, and Arabia Deserta. The first corresponded to the northern area including *al Hijāz*, the second referred to the rich area of *Yaman*, while the third included the whole area of central Arabia consisting of deserts and steppes. This categorization, however, did not bring into full relief the total geographical configuration of the peninsula. The Arab geographers are more precise and divide the peninsula into distinct geographical divisions. The

---

1 *Covering about 10 per cent of the total area of the peninsula.*

northern area consists of desert marches adjoining Syria and Iraq and is known as *Hamad*. The south-western corner of the peninsula encompasses the cultivated area of *Yaman* and *Hadramawt* as we have already seen. The rest of the peninsula, from west to east, has three distinct divisions. The sandy coastal area adjoining the Red Sea with generally sharp slopes towards the sea is known as *Tihāma*. To the east of *Tihāma* lies a range of mountains descending from Palestine and running almost parallel to the Red Sea and the Indian Ocean. The range is called *Shammār* with height ranging from 9000 to 14,000 feet above sea level. The Arab geographers have named the mountain area as *al Hijāz*, meaning barrier, which roughly includes the *Tihāma* as well. At places the mountains run close to the Red Sea and at times they draw far away from the sea coast, thus, leaving the *Tihāma* or the coastal area varying in width from place to place. As the region which became the cradle of *Islām*, *al Hijāz* is the main area of interest of the Muslim historians. The cities of *Yathri*b, later known as *Madināh*, *Makkāh*, the seat of the *Kābah* and the birth place of the Prophet; and the beautiful hill station, *Tāif*, are all situated in *al Hijāz*. The area to the east of the mountains gently sloping towards the Persian Gulf forms a huge plateau which is known as *Najd*. This is the large central area of the peninsula which mainly consists of deserts surrounded by steppes. The northern desert is called *al Nufūd* whereas the southern one is known as *Rub ul Khāli* (empty quarters); both are joined by a strip of red desert called *al Dahna*, about 600 miles long. To the east of *Najd* are the areas of al Bahrain (*al Asha*) and Kuwait on the Persian Gulf. In the south-eastern corner of the peninsula lies the country of Oman.

In the absence of any navigable river, communication between different zones of the peninsula was very difficult. The only means of access was provided by the dried-up river beds known as *Wādis*. These *Wādis* were responsible for giving rise to some well-defined land routes within the peninsula connecting the Indian Ocean with the Mediterranean countries in the north, thus leading the peninsula emerge as a transit region for trade with 'Further East' from the very early times. The first of these trade routes was the *Hijāz* route, running from the ancient towns of Palestine and Jordan along the Red Sea coast to *Yaman*. A second route ran through *Wādi al Dawasīr*, running from north-eastern *Yaman* to central Arabia where it linked up with another route along *Wādi al Rumma* to southern Iraq. There was yet a third route provided by *Wādi al Sirhān* which connected central Arabia with southeastern Syria.

The Arabians of history belong to the Semitic race. But whether the peninsula was the original home of the Semites or it was peopled by different races during different prehistoric times remains obscure. The most plausible theory in this regard is, however, the one advocated by Winckler and Caetani. According to this theory, in very early times, Arabia was a land of great fertility and was the original home of the Semitic people. Subsequently, through millennia, it underwent a climatic and physical change through a process of desiccation which resulted in desertification of almost the entire peninsula. The declining productivity coupled with overpopulation led to a recurring cycle of invasions of the neighbouring countries by the Semitic people of Arabia. It was this process which carried the Semites to Syria, Iraq, and Palestine. Although there is no geological survey report of the peninsula to support this theory, the deep dried-up river beds provide evidence of the same. We also have some philological evidence in support of the theory. The Arabic language has been found to be the oldest of the Semitic languages in terms of grammatical structure.

Based on local traditions, the Arab historians have divided the population of the peninsula into three broad ethnic groups. The first was named *Arab ul Baīdah* which included tribes like *Ād, Amālika, Thamūd, Jadīs,* and so on, all extinct by the time the Prophet emerged. The second group was called *Arab ul Ariba* (or *Mutāriba*). The people of this group are said to have been the descendants of *Qahtān* (Joktan), one of whose sons, *Yāreb,* gave his name to the country. This group originated in *Yaman* and, in course of time, was subdivided into three main divisions of *Qudāa, Kahlān,* and *Azd,* each having a good number of tribal subdivisions. The third group was the *Arab ul Mustāriba* or naturalized Arabs who were the progeny of *Ismaīl*. The group was also known after the name of *Adnān*, one of its important chiefs and included two major branches known as *Khindif* and *Qais*, each having a large number of tribes. *Quraysh*, the tribe of the Prophet, was related to *Khindif* branch of the *Adnān* group.

The Muslim traditions supported by the Book of Genesis and the *Qurān* have vividly described the story of *Ismaīl*'s emigration from Palestine to *Makkāh* and origin as well as spread of the Abrahamic group of population in the peninsula which came to be known as *Arab ul Mustāriba*. According to the story, the great Quranic prophet, *Ibrahīm*, was born in Iraq where he started preaching the rejection of paganism and worship of one God. The people reacted violently and tried to burn him alive, which forced him to run away along with his wife, *Sārah*, first to Palestine and then to Egypt. The king of Egypt gifted him a maid servant or slave girl named *Hāgar*.[1] Subsequently, *Ibrahīm* went back to Palestine along with *Sārah* and *Hāgar*. *Sārah* was then 76 years old and *Ibrahīm* 85; but to their great disappointment, they had no issue. God, however, promised *Ibrahīm* that his progeny would be countless like the stars. With the permission of *Sārah*, he took *Hāgar* as his wife. She soon gave birth to *Ibrahīm*'s son named *Ismaīl*. After a few years, *Sārah* also bore a son who was called *Ishāq*. But bitterness of feeling soon arose between the two ladies and as per advice of God, *Ibrahīm*, travelling in a caravan, dropped *Ismaīl* and *Hāgar* in the uninhabited valley of *Makkāh* and went back. When the stock of water was exhausted, *Hāgar* feared that the child might die of thirst. She, therefore, started searching water and food in the valley and ran to and fro seven times between the hills of *Safā* and *Marwāh*, but returned unsuccessful in despair only to find that the child had miraculously discovered a great spring with abundance of excellent water. This spring

---

1   *According to Bukhari (60:11), the Pharoah had given Hāgar as a servant to Sārah. As per interpretation of the famous commentator of the Bible, Rabbi Saloman, Hāgar was the daughter of the Pharoah. When the latter had seen the miracles, he thought that it was better for her daughter to be a servant of Abraham and Sārah than mistress with someone else.*

came to be known as *Zamzam*. Thenceforth, the place became a stopover for the trade caravans and *Hāgar* and *Ismaīl* were sufficiently provided for. In due course, due to availability of abundant water from the *Zamzam*, a number of tribes found it convenient to settle around the valley and a township developed there. *Jurhum* was the first such tribe to settle in *Makkāh* though some versions maintain that *Jurhum* was already settled there.

It is said that after *Ismaīl* reached his holy destination, *Ibrahīm* still lived for seventy-five years and at times visited his son and *Hāgar*. The *Quran* tells us that during one of the visits, *Allāh* commanded him to construct a sanctuary for His worship and guided him about the exact place near the well of *Zamzam* where it was to be built, and the shape in which it was to be erected. Thus, the house of *Allāh* was built by *Ibrahīm* and *Ismaīl* together. The building was called *Kābah* by virtue of its cube-like shape with its four corners pointing to the four directions of the compass. The Muslim traditions maintain that the *Kābah* had originally been constructed by *Adam*, according to a celestial prototype but was destroyed in the great deluge. The building as constructed by *Ibrahīm* and *Ismaīl*, however, had no roof or door, which were much later constructed by the *Quraysh*. The most holy object in the *Kābah* was a celestial stone, the famous black stone, which is said to have been handed over to *Ibrahīm* by the archangel, Gabriel, and which was fixed into the eastern corner of the *Kābah*. According to a *hadīth* mentioned by *Tirmidhi*, this sacred stone was whiter than milk when it descended from the Heavens but the sins of the sons of *Adam* made it black. After the construction of the *Kābah* was complete, *Ibrahīm* was commanded by God to institute the practice of pilgrimage to the sanctuary which was to include circumambulations on foot, and bows and prostrations in prayers.[1] *Ibrahīm* then prayed to God to take care of his son in the barren valley, provide him supporters, establish regular prayer at the new House of God, and make the same a place of peace and prosperity. The prayer was answered

---

1   *Quran 22: 26–7.*

and the *Kābah* soon became a place of regular pilgrimage for the people of the entire peninsula which, in its turn, brought wealth and prosperity. Thus, because of the sacred house, *Makkāh* emerged as a pre-eminent town of the peninsula and even the descendants of *Ishāq* started paying visit to the sanctuary.

Separation with *Ismaīl* and *Hāgar* was a great trial for *Ibrahīm*. But soon, God was to put him through a much greater test of faith and sacrifice. During one of the visits to *Makkāh*, he was commanded by God in dreams to sacrifice his son to Him. We are told by the Muslim traditions that despite dissuasion by *Shaitān* not to obey God's command, *Ibrahīm, Ismaīl*, and *Hāgar,* all accepted the will of God with alacrity and went ahead to act on the same. But as *Ibrahīm* prepared for the sacrifice, bound down the 15-year-old *Ismaīl* and laid him down to cut his throat with a knife, he was called by God to stop. He had given evidence of his obedience to God's command, and accepting his sacrifice, God had ransomed his son with a sheep which he found close by and sacrificed in lieu of *Ismaīl*. In verses 102–7 of *Surah 37*, the *Quran* itself refers to the story without mentioning the name of *Ismaīl*. The Jewish legends maintain that the sacrificial son was *Ishāq* and the sacrifice took place in Palestine. But according to Islamic traditions, the episode of sacrifice definitely related to *Ismaīl* and the venue was the hill of *Minā* near *Makkāh*. As a supreme example of sacrifice for and obedience as well as devotion to God, the event, however, was established in *Islām* as a part of *haj* and an annual festival throughout the Muslim world.

As per story of the Genesis, God had promised that he would make *Ismaīl* a great nation. The same came true in the succeeding centuries. *Ismaīl* settled down in *Makkāh* and married the daughter of one of the leaders of the *Jurhum* tribe. Out of this marriage, *Ismaīl* had twelve sons who became ancestors of the twelve tribal groups of naturalised Arabs or *Arab ul Mustāriba*. In the long run, these groups proliferated into a large number of tribes and clans and spread over the whole of the peninsula. We are told by traditions that *Adnān*, one of the descendants of *Ismaīl*, flourished in the first century BC. He, like *Ismaīl*, married the daughter of a Jurhumite chief and established himself in

Makkāh. It was his son *Maād* who became a prominent leader and the real progenitor of the Ismailites inhabiting *Hijāz* and *Najd*. Subsequently, one of his descendants called *Fihr* flourished in the third century and became the founder of the famous tribe of *Quraysh* to which the Prophet belonged. *Fihr* was a successful merchant and was, therefore, popularly known as *Quraysh*, which means a merchant.

The guardianship of the *Kābah*, however, did not remain with the Ismailites for long and passed into the hands of the Jurhumites. As the centuries passed under the Jurhumites, the purity of worship of the one God came to be polluted. The descendants of *Ismaīl* who settled away from *Makkāh* started carrying stones from the holy precinct for performing rites in their honour. Later, under the influence of the neighbouring pagan tribes, idols came to be added to the stones which led to the practice of the pilgrims bringing idols to *Makkāh*. The idolators thought that their idols had the power to act as mediators between God and men. The Jurhumites, too, spoilt by the incoming wealth, forgot their religious duty and neglected the maintenance of the *Zamzam*, which is reported to have dried up. The Jurhumites continued in control of *Makkah* and the *Kābah* until the third century when their power was threatened by a Qahtanite tribe called *Banī Khuzāh*. Realizing the danger ahead, the Jurhumites dug a deep hole within the well of the *Zamzam*, buried the accumulated wealth of the holy house along with two golden gazelles, and covered them all under sand. They hoped that they would return some day to power and reclaim the treasure as well as the *Zamzam*. Thus did the Jurhumites commit the great sin of concealing the *Zamzam*. The control of *Makkāh* and custody of the *Kābah* soon passed on to the *Khuzāh* who remained in power until the middle of the fifth century but shared the guilt of the *Jurhum* by not making any attempt to rediscover the *Zamzam*. They are also charged of bringing idols to the *Kābah*. One of their chiefs named *Amr ibn Luhayy* is said to have brought the idol of *Hūbal* from Syria which he set up within the holy building as the chief idol of *Makkāh*.

After many centuries of Jurhumite and Khuzaite control, guardianship of the *Kābah* was restored to the Ismailites by a *Quraysh* leader named *Qussay* (398–480) in the middle of the fifth century. *Qussay* was an outstanding leader of his time and was the fifth grandfather of the Prophet. He married the daughter of *Hulayl* who was then the chief of the *Khuzāh* tribe. On the death of *Hulayl*, he, enlisting the support of different *Quraysh* clans scattered over *al Hijāz*, claimed the guardianship of the *Kābah* and after a fierce battle which resulted in arbitration became the ruler of *Makkāh* and the guardian of the *Kābah*. Thenceforth, the control of *Kābah* remained with the *Quraysh*.

Qussay took a series of measures in order to strengthen his tribe's political power over *Makkah*. He brought about a unification of the hitherto scattered *Quraysh* clans and made them settle down in and around *Makkah*. Those who were his nearest of kin[1] were settled in the valley around the sanctuary; the group was subsequently known as '*Quraysh* of the Hollow'. Those *Quraysh* families which were remotely connected to *Qussay* were allowed to settle down in the outer areas of the town; and they came to be known as '*Quraysh* of the Outskirts'. Further, until Qussay's time, perhaps, due to extreme sanctity of the *Kābah*, no building had been constructed near it. In order to make the sanctuary well protected, *Qussay* induced the *Quraysh* families to construct well-fortified houses made of stone around the sanctuary leaving sufficient space for its circumambulation (*tawāf*). He also built near *Kābah* a palace called the *Dār un Nadwā* (House of Assembly) where all public affairs used to be transacted. It was *Qussay* who introduced the practice of providing free food to the poor pilgrims. For raising funds for this purpose, he succeeded in inducing the *Quraysh* to make an annual payment of poor tax called *Rifādah*. Apart from this, *Qussay* was able to organize the administration of the city as well as the sanctuary on a sound footing, establishing six departments for handling of different affairs and concentrating control of each of them in his own hands. These departments, *inter alia*,

---

1   *Zuhrah, Taym, Makhzum etc.*

included *Hijābah* (maintenance of the house and custody of its keys), *Siqāyah* (provision of water to the pilgrims), and *Rifādah* (provision of food to pilgrims).[1]

Apart from ethnic division of the inhabitants of the peninsula as described above, Arab historians have further divided the Arabs into two main branches, the southern belonging to *Yaman* and *Hadramawt* and the northern belonging to the rest of the peninsula. This division was based on factors like ecological order, linguistic traits, and cultural development of the two regions. Although both belonged to the Semitic race, the Arabic language of the south is different from the language of the *Qurān* which was the language of the north Arabians. The alphabet of the southern language is also different and is related to Ethiopic. Further, unlike their northern cousins, the south Arabians were a sedentary people. The mental gulf between the two Arabian stocks continued, to some extent, even after the advent of *Islām*.

As far as the peninsula's historical role in ancient times is concerned, it was south Arabia which was the region of dominance. Favourable geographical conditions and strategic location on the sea-route to India helped this region to develop an economy based on agriculture and commerce, evolve a highly developed civilization, and establish kingdoms as far back as the eighth century BC. The region, therefore, played an important role in international affairs of the pre-Islamic millennium. Our knowledge of its history is based on legendary traditions preserved in Arabic literature, Semitic and Greco-Roman writings of the classical period, and above all, on the local epigraphic sources discovered by Halevy and Glaser. There are about 4000 such inscriptions on different subjects.

Of the kingdoms that rose to prominence in south Arabia, four, lying from north to south west, were important. They were *Māin* (capital-*Qarnaw*), *Sabā* (capital-*Mārib*), *Qataban* (capital-*Tamna*), and *Hadramawt* (capital-*Shabwa*). While the

---

1 *The other departments were Nadwāh (chairmanship of the House of Assembly), Qiyādah (leadership of the army at war) and Liwā (possession of the flag at the time of war, that, is a secondary command).*

first two of the kingdoms existed in the eight century BC, the remaining two were of a later origin. The Sabāean kingdom[1] was the most prominent of them and tended to form a larger political aggregation by absorbing the remaining three kingdoms; and this was finally accomplished in the beginning of the Christian Era. Magnificent temples, forts, and citadels constructed by these kingdoms are indicative of the level of civilization achieved by the south Arabians in ancient times. The Sabāean kings constructed the great dam of *Mārib*, the older portions of which appear to have been constructed as far back as the seventh century BC. This dam regulated agriculture and irrigation in the region.

Towards the close of the second century BC, another south Arabian tribe called *Himyār* captured the throne of *Sabā* and shifted the capital to a place called *Zafar*. They spoke the same language and were close kinsmen of the Sabāeans. Under them, south Arabia reached its zenith of political consolidation and development of trade and commerce. Around 300 AD, their rule is said to have been terminated[2] following which there was a short Abyssinian rule. One of the most important incidents of the first Himyarite period was the invasion of south Arabia by the Roman army under Aelius Gallus[3] in 24 BC with the object of capturing and controlling the trade routes to 'Further East' which had been monopolized by the Arabians. The Roman army entered Arabia through the Red Sea, captured *Najrān*, and penetrated further south. The expedition, however, was a complete failure. Another noteworthy development of the period was the south Arabian colonization of *Abyssinia*.[4] In order to protect their kingdom from the raids of the central Arabian nomads, the Himyarites constructed a number of citadels, the most famous of which was the one known as *Ghumdan* in *Sanā*. This castle was twenty-storied and has been called the first skyscraper in recorded history.

---

1   *Identified as Biblical Sheba whose queen entered into relations with King Solomon.*

2   *This is known as end of the first Himyarite period.*

3   *During the time of the Roman emperor, Augustus Caesar.*

4   *Modern Ethiopia.*

The second Himyarite period from the fourth century onwards was a period of decline inviting interference from external powers. The two superpowers of the age, that is, the Eastern Roman Empire of Byzantium[1] and the Sassanian Empire of Persia,[2] tended to drag their struggle for supremacy to south Arabia due to a combination of political and economic motives. Internally also, a new dimension was added to the local politics of south Arabia by introduction of Christianity and Judaism to the region. Christianity spread to the area and a few churches were built. *Najran* emerged as an important centre of monophysite Christianity.[3] Judaism also spread and the last Himyarite king *Dhu Nuwas* was a Jew. He was responsible for the massacre of the Christians of *Najrān* in 523 which invited the wrath of the then Christian powers. At the instance of the then Byzantine emperor, the Christian king of *Abyssinia*, known by the title of *Negus*, in order to avenge persecution of the Christians, invaded and defeated the Himyarites. The Himyarite king was killed and Abyssinian colonial rule was established in south Arabia in 525.

The Abyssinians ruled south Arabia from their capital at *Sanā* where they constructed a magnificent cathedral called *al Qālis*. An interesting episode of the Abyssinian period was the bursting of the *Mārib* dam, which is placed by some scholars in 570. Some sources, however, indicate that the process of breaking of the dam had started much earlier and symbolized the economic decline and political disintegration of the south Arabian empire. It was during this period of decline that two of the important tribes of south Arabia, *Banū Ghassān* and *Banū Lakhm*, migrated to Syria and Iraq border, respectively. In due course, they founded their own small kingdoms.

The Abyssinian governor of *Yaman* named *Abrahah* was a zealous Christian; he publicly expressed his intention of making the cathedral at *Sanā* supersede the *Kābah* as the great place

---

1   *Established by Constantine in 327* AD.

2   *Established in 226* AD *as a result of a national revolt led by Ardeshir against the Greek–Parthian rule.*

3   *This Christian sect held that the Christ had only one divine nature.*

of pilgrimage for entire Arabia. The prospect of getting the great wealth which the *Kābah* attracted, diverted to his own city might have further motivated him. The desecration of the *Sanā* church by a man of the *Kinānah* tribe provided him the desired opportunity. He vowed that in revenge he would raze the *Kābah* to the ground and raising a large army, which included an elephant, set out for *Makkah*. The entire story of this incident has been graphically described by *Ibn Ishāq*. Some of the Arab tribes on way attempted to stop *Abrahah*, but they were put to flight and their leader, *Nufayl*, was captured and forced to act as a guide. *Abrahāh* camped at the outskirts of *Makkah*, captured some booty which included 200 camels of *Abd al Muttalib*[1] and informing that he had gone there not to fight but only to destroy the *Kābah*, invited the chief of *Makkah* to negotiate. As the de facto leader of the city, *Abd al Muttalib*, cleverly negotiated with *Abrahah*, took back his camels and warned him that God of the *Kābah* himself would protect His house. After returning to *Makkah*, he advised the *Quraysh* to withdraw to the hills and with others took hold of the *Kābah*'s door and prayed to God to protect the holy building.

The next morning when Abrahah's army started its march to *Makkah* with the richly caparisoned elephant in the front, the animal stopped and knelt down. The keeper of the elephant, *Unays*, tried all tricks to make him stand and move, but he would not budge. Despite this clear portent, however, *Abrahah* decided to march in order to destroy the great rival of his newly constructed church. As per the traditional story recorded by *Ibn Ishāq*, God intervened at this stage to save the *Kābah* from destruction. Suddenly, the entire sky was full of small birds, turning it black and creating a strange sound. Each bird had three small pebbles, two in the feet and one in the beak. They swooped to and fro over the ranks and pelted the stones with such a velocity that they even pierced through the armours of men. Whosoever was hit by the pebble died instantaneously and the dead body started rotting. Terror stricken, the main part of

---

1   *The Prophet's grandfather.*

the army ran back in disorder. Many of the soldiers died on way while a good number of them, including *Abrahah*, died soon after their return to *Sanā*. *Unays* and the elephant were, however, left unhurt.

The miraculous incident which greatly enhanced the prestige of the *Kābah* is reported to have taken place in 570, a year which came to be known in the history of *Islām* as the 'Year of the Elephant'. The story finds mention in the *Qurān* also in the short but popular *Surāh* numbering 105. In order to explain the miracle of the birds in mundane terms, some writers,[1] taking cue from a reference by *Ibn Hishām*, have suggested that Abrahah's army was routed by the outbreak of some epidemic like small pox. Dr Krenkow opines that the flying creatures may well have been swarms of insects carrying infection. The 'Year of the Elephant' was, however, soon to witness an event of much greater importance and that was the birth of the Prophet himself some fifty days after the incident.

After the death of *Abrahāh*, a freedom struggle was started against the unpopular Abyssinian regime in south Arabia which was led by a scion of the *Himyār* royal family known as *Sayf*. He was successful in obtaining military help from the Sassanian emperor, defeated the Abyssinians, and freed the country in 575. But independence proved to be a mirage as soon *Yaman* was converted into a Persian province.

The south Arabian kingdoms of the pre-Islamic millennium were the earliest states of the peninsula. Their real significance in international politics of the time, however, lay not in their military exploits but in their remarkable management of a commercial empire based on international trade of the 'Near East'. The south Arabians were expert navigators and controlled the maritime trade with India and the countries of south-east Asia including China. From these countries, they imported fabrics, silk, slaves, and a number of other luxury items which were in high demand in the Mediterranean countries. From the Persian Gulf, they brought pearl. They also maintained commercial link

---

1   *Caussin de Percevel.*

with the African coastline and imported items like ivory, gold, and ostrich feathers from Ethiopia. Apart from these imports, they locally produced spices and a number of aromatics, the most important being frankincense, which was highly sought after in Egypt for temple use and mummification. All these highly priced items were exported to the Mediterranean countries through the Red Sea. But due to inherent difficulties involved in navigating the Red Sea, the Sabaeans and the Minaeans developed land routes between *Yaman* and Syria as well as Iraq, passing through *Makkah*. For this purpose, they are said to have established trading stations along the routes, thus introducing sedentary life in the deserts of the peninsula. In this manner, under the south Arabian kingdoms, *Yaman* emerged as the transit point of ancient international trade between the Mediterranean countries and East Asia as well as Red Sea coast countries of Africa. And the monopoly of this international trade remained in the hands of the Sabaeans and the Himyarites. This international trade was highly profitable and in classical literature south Arabia had a legendary reputation as a land of wealth and prosperity, named as 'Arabia Felix'. The real strength of the south Arabian kingdoms, therefore, lay in their control of the international trade of the 'Near East', both through land and sea.

In the early centuries before Christ, the Ptolemys of Egypt gave a stiff competition to the south Arabians in the Red Sea trade. Subsequently, the Roman Empire adversely affected their commercial interest by entering the Indian Ocean and controlling the trading centres of Petra and Palmyra. Their caravan trade through land routes was also frequently subjected to raids and plunders by the Bedouins of the peninsular deserts. In the early centuries of the Christian era, therefore, the foreign trade of south Arabia was rather slipping out of their hands. In the fourth century, the trade routes seemed to have been diverted from Arabian Peninsula to other channels.

To this record of impressive material development and historical role of south Arabia, history of central and northern Arabia presents a contrasting picture. Due to hostile ecological environment, the Arabs of this area could not develop an agriculture-based economy; nor could they develop a higher civilization or political states. In the deserts and steppes of *Hijāz* and *Najd*, even subsistence agriculture was not possible. It was only in a few oases having source of water that limited agriculture was possible giving rise to some sedentary life. The vast majority of the people of inner Arabia, therefore, lived in a state of perpetual poverty and hunger. Consequently, the area could not play any significant role in the history of the pre-Islamic period and remained in a state of cultural isolation, the neighbouring political powers not making any serious attempt to penetrate it. Rather, the untamable and war-like Arabs of this area always remained a source of nuisance to them. It is indeed an irony of history that *Islām* and its powerful empire arose from this cultural backwater.

Barring a small group of people leading a semi-sedentary life in a few oases, the vast majority of the inhabitants of the barren deserts had to take to the life of camel-based nomadism, dwelling in tents and wandering from place to place in search of food and pasture. Known as *badawah*,[1] their life displayed the best adaptation to the extremely difficult geographical conditions. Hard desert life made them physically sturdy and fostered a mental state marked by fearlessness, arrogance, roughness of temperament, love for freedom and equality, disregard of authority and discipline, weakness for sensuous pleasures, and above all, an urge for fighting. A Bedouin was a compulsive fighter, ready to kill or get killed at the slightest provocation. Cattle rearing and hunting were their main occupation which, however, failed to satisfy their economic needs, leaving them always on the brink of starvation. They, therefore, adopted raiding and plundering (*ghazwa*) as an essential institution of their economy. They would regularly invade the territories of the neighbouring tribes, the nearby settled areas, and the trade caravans in order to carry off their cattle, slaves, and other properties. In our time, *ghazwa* will amount to the serious crime of dacoity; but in Bedouin society, this type of razzia was not considered reprehensible and

---

1   *In English, Bedouins.*

was socially sanctioned as an occupation, a kind of national sport. The Bedouins conducted such raids with remarkable skill according to clearly defined rules, avoiding killing anyone since this could lead to a vendetta. The *ghazwa* was thus a Bedouin way of redistributing wealth in a region where there was an acute scarcity of necessities of life.

Life in the extremely hostile environment of the deserts was always in peril. There was cut-throat competition for economic resources and the nomadic groups were constantly at war. Under such a situation, an individual alone hardly had any prospect of survival. The Bedouins, therefore, were compelled to evolve a highly specialized way of closely-knit group life which may be called tribalism. The groups were small as well as large bound by a common ancestry. Although the Bedouins used to call both the groups as *qaum*, the smaller one (clan) was a group of families only while the larger one (tribe) represented a group of clans. The tribe was the ultimate social and political entity beyond which the Bedouin's mental horizon could not reach. The unit of society was the group, not the individual; rights and duties of the individuals emanated only from his membership of the group. The tribe or the clan thus represented the strongest social bond held together externally by the need for self-defense against the dangers of desert life and internally by the tie of blood and kinship. Every individual was required to subordinate his interest to the general welfare of the group. An individual Bedouin must belong to a tribal group as without it his life had no identity. It was possible for an outsider to join a tribe by becoming a client (*māwla*). There are also instances of a weaker tribe or clan joining a bigger and stronger one for better protection.

Since the entire existence of the Bedouins depended on the strength of their group, an inviolable group unity and the highest degree of communal spirit as well as emotional attachment with the group were essentially required to be cultivated. In order to achieve this objective, the Bedouins, over a period of time, evolved an elaborate ideology known as *murūwah*. The word literally meant 'manliness' but actually had a much wider and complex connotation, encompassing all essential virtues required to make the group strong. It, above all, implied an absolute and unconditional loyalty to the tribe, a feeling of strong tribal solidarity and patriotism of the chauvinistic type. This was called *asābiyāh* and expressed in terms of love and concern for the fellow tribesmen. Additionally, *murūwah* meant courage in battle, patience, and endurance in suffering, a dedication to chivalrous duties of avenging a wrong done to the tribe, protecting its weaker members, and defying the strong. Glorification of one's own tribe, a regard for autonomy of the group, keeping one's covenant and generosity as well as hospitality for the friends were also important qualities of *murūwah*. Each tribe had its own special brand of *murūwah* which, the Bedouins thought, was inherited from the founding fathers of the tribe and passed on like genetic features from one generation to the other. Therefore, a high concern for purity of blood and noble ancestry as also a high regard for the *sunnah* or practices of the ancestors also became important elements of the concept.

Thus, on the basis of the virtues included in the concept of *murūwāh*, the Bedouins developed a whole code of conduct which was based on 'tribal humanism'.[1] It was the duty of each member of the tribe to cultivate the qualities of *murūwah* in order to ensure that the tribe survived. Due to emotional propaganda of the Arab poets, by the sixth century, the way of life propagated by *murūwah* had become normative. But the concept of *murūwāh* had a few negative aspects as well. As a sign of purity of blood and nobility, some negative qualities like arrogance, superiority complex, and a haughty self-reliance (*istighnā*) also came to be regarded as ideal values. The ideology no doubt encouraged unflinching fidelity for and emotional attachment to the tribe, but such a strong group loyalty made it almost impossible for the tribes to unite in order to form a larger political aggregation. Further, courage, bravery, selflessness, and concern for the others were within the context of the tribe only. There was no concern for the outsiders and no respect for their lives. The concept of *murūwah* taught the Bedouin to back his tribesmen and obey

---

1   *W. M. Watt.*

the chief without consideration for right or wrong. As the maxim ran, 'help your brother whether he is being wronged or wronging others.'

One of the major tribal values covered under *murūwah* was the principle of blood vengeance or vendetta. Each member of a tribe was duty-bound to avenge each and every injury caused to any member by an outsider. For example, if a member of a group was killed by an outsider, a vendetta was established imposing on his kin and even the whole tribe the duty of exacting vengeance from the murderer or one of his fellow tribesmen unless the negotiated blood money was paid. According to this principle of *lex talionis*, the entire tribe was responsible for the misconduct of a member when perpetrated on a member of another tribe. In the absence of a central authority or a common law, the Bedouin adopted the principle of vendetta as a means of social security and personal protection. But the custom let loose a vicious cycle of intertribal warfare. The century preceding the birth of the Prophet, therefore, witnessed a series of long-drawn intertribal wars known as *Ayyām al Arab*.[1] Arising out of petty disputes, these tribal hostilities were stoked by poetical exaggerations through which vendetta became a recognized institution in Bedouin life. In these clashes, there was a great deal of raiding and plundering but less of bloodshed as this would lead to new vendettas. One of the early such wars was *Harb al Basūs* fought from the end of the fifth century for about forty years between *Banū Bakr* and *Banū Taghlib* in north-eastern Arabia. The cause of this war was a petty one, that is, wounding of a she-camel. Silimar were the battles of *Dāhis* and *al Ghabra* fought between *Abs* and its sister tribe, *Dhubyān*, in central Arabia over the issue of unfair conduct of a horse race. The Day of *al Fijār* fought between *Quraysh* and *Hawazīn* and the Day of *Buath* fought between the two tribes of *Yathrib*, *Aws* and *Khazraj*[2] are other examples. It was due to intensive training received in the endless intertribal wars and the frequent plundering raids coupled with the committed mental

---

1   *The Days of Arabia.*
2   *Fought during the Prophet's time.*

outlook bred by *murūwāh* that the Bedouin had a latent power which was subsequently channeled by *Islām* in order to organize its wars of conquests. *Umar* was indeed right when he remarked that the Bedouin were the 'raw material' of Islam.

The pre-Islamic religion of the Bedouins as well as their sedentary brothers was of a low form with no well-developed ritual and belief systems. They had, of course, been aware of the monotheistic religions of Judaism and Christianity a long time before the arrival of *Islām*. In the millennium before the Prophet, following the Babylonian and Roman attacks on Palestine, the Jews had taken shelter in Arabia. There were Jewish settlements at *Yathrib*, *Khaybar*, and *Fadak*, all located north of *Makkah*. Subsequently, the faith spread to *Yaman* as well, and as we have seen, the last Himyarite king had embraced it. Similarly, a few centuries before *Islām*, Christianity with its deviant forms,[1] had spread to a few pockets in the peninsula. *Banī Hārith* of *Najrān*, *Bani Hanifā* of *Yamāmah*, *Banī Tay* of *Taymā*, the Ghassanides on Syrian border, the Lakhmids on Iraq border, and a few more of the Arabs professed the faith. But torn by violent mutual hostility and serious internal strife and schism, the sprinkling of the two monotheistic religions failed to attract the Arab masses who were, perhaps, expecting the arrival of their own Prophet. Moreover, the political background of the two religions made the Arabs suspicious of them. They, therefore, stuck to their heathenism which in its final pre-Islamic form[2] was represented by motley modes of worship and a multiplicity of primitive beliefs and practices ranging from nature worship and even atheism to totemism, fetishism, and idolatry.

---

1 *Monophysite and Nestorian—the first believing that Christ had only one divine nature and the second holding that he had two natures, human and divine.*

2 *Available sources on the subject do not throw sufficient light to trace the evolution of different religious practices of the Arabs and present a complete and vivid picture of the same.*

As referred to in the *Qurān* (45.24),[1] a section of the Arabs denied the existence of God and believed that Time or Fate or the Laws of Nature were the whole reality. Everything in the universe, they thought, was predestined and came under the sway of *dahr* (Time or Fate) which inflicted all types of suffering on humanity and would spare no one. There was, therefore, no meaning in this life of ceaseless struggle and so a person should make the most of his life and enjoy its pleasures and good things, specially wine, women, and poetry. Such sentiments have been expressed in the pre-Islamic odes. The belief, thus, combined pessimism about life and indulgence in hedonistic pleasures.

The vast majority of the Arabs, however, were polytheists worshiping a variety of deities in various forms. It appears, initially, overawed by the mystery of nature, they worshiped a host of natural objects like animals, trees, fire, stones, and a good number of celestial bodies. The tribe of *Himyār* that lived in *Yaman* worshiped the sun whereas the Kananites worshiped the moon. Likewise, different planets and stars[2] were objects of worship of different tribes of the peninsula. Side by side with worship of objects of nature, the Arabs also developed the cult of shrines. Various places were felt to be sacred and became the sites of shrines which had their own rituals centring around a particular deity. The most important and, perhaps, the oldest of these shrines was the *Kābah*, the legend about the construction of which has already been mentioned. As per tradition, after constructing the shrine, *Ibrahīm* had dedicated it to the worship of one God and had also instituted the practice of annual pilgrimage (*haj*) during an appointed month. In course of time, it became a centre of pilgrimage for the entire region. The rites of *haj* included the *tahlīl* (slogan),[3] *tawāf* (seven clockwise circumambulations of the shrine), *wuqūf* (vigil on the mount of *Arafāh*), *Muzdālifah*

---

1   *'And they say, there is nothing beyond our life in this world; we live and die and nothing destroys us but Time.'*

2   *Mercury (Utarid), Venus (Zuhra), Jupiter (Mushtri), Saturn (Zuhal), Canopus (Suhail), Sirius (Shira), and so on.*

3   *'Labbaik! Allhumma Labbaik.'*

48

(session of prayer), seven rounds between *Safā* and *Marwāh*, hurling pebbles at the three sacred pillars of *Minā* and finally the animal sacrifice. Subsequently, however, during the Makkan domination of *Khuzah* tribe, idolatrous practices were introduced and the people forgot the real meaning of different rites of *haj*. It was after this degeneration of the worship at the *Kābah* that men and women started the practice of circumambulation in a state of nudity arguing that it was not justified to perform the holy ceremony in those very clothes in which they had committed sins.

Apart from the *Kābah*, there were some other shrines in the peninsula which were centres of pilgrimage and in which similar circumambulation and other practices were followed. The most important of these were the shrines dedicated to the three goddesses—*al Lāt, al Uzzah,* and *Manāt*—who were called daughters of God (*banāt Allāh*). Their shrines were located in the vicinity of *Makkah* at *Tāif, Nakhlah,* and *Qudayd,* respectively. They were deities of great antiquity and were very popular throughout *Hijāz,* their shrines being next only to the *Kābah* in importance. In the sources, we do not come across any mythology to explain the symbolic importance of these divine beings. Some scholars think that they were moon goddesses representing bright moon, dark moon, and the union of the two, respectively. Others, however, opine that whereas *Manāt* represented the ancient goddess of love (Venus) and *al Uzzah* was the goddess of fate, *al Lāt* simply meant the goddess. They were worshiped in their shrines not as personalized statues but as large standing stones. The worshippers believed that through these three daughters of God, they could get close to Him. The *Qurān* refers to the three goddesses in *Surāh Najam* (53)[1] but repudiates them as absolutely powerless calling them mere names.

Apart from worshipping the gods and goddesses in the shrines at periodic gatherings, the Arabs subsequently developed the practice of worshiping personal gods of families and tribes in the form of shapeless stones (a*snāb*) and idols (*asnām*). They used to carry stone pieces from different shrines, believing them

---

1 *Verses 19 to 23.*

to be sacred and representing the gods. Traditions, however, suggest that idol worship was a relatively new religious passion which had been imported from Syria and other Mediterranean countries. On the eve of the rise of *Islām*, idol or totem worship was the most popular practice. Each tribe had its own god in the form of stone or statue, was guarded by the house of the *Sheikh*, and accompanied the tribal group to the battlefield serving to reinforce tribal identity and unity. However, at places having more complex settlement, widely shared deities also emerged which transcended tribal boundaries. Thus, the *Kābah* came to have as many as 360 idols or totems placed by different tribes for worship during pilgrimage. In addition, almost every house in *Makkah* had a personal image of some god.

Important of the idols worshiped were *Wudd*,[1] *Suwa*,[2] *Yagūth*,[3] *Yauq*,[4] *Usaf*,[5] *Nailah*,[6] and *Nasr*.[7] But the greatest of all was *Hūbal* which had been imported from Syria by a chief of *Khuzah* tribe. Placed inside the *Kābah*, it was the chief deity of the shrine and specially worshiped by the *Quraysh* at times of war. Beside this idol stood the ritual arrows used for divination. Since *Hūbal* means vapour, it might have been associated with rains also. This idol was carved out of red granite in the form of a man. One of its arms subsequently broke off and was replaced by one made of solid gold by the *Quraysh*. The idols of the gods were of different shapes. *Nailah* and *Suwa* were shaped as women. *Yagūth* carried the shape of a lion whereas *Yauq* was like a horse. The image of *Nasr*, the deity of *Yaman*, was having the shape of a vulture. Apart from idol worship, an important element of the peoples' faith was belief in spirits, jinns, and a host of superstitions and omens. The poets were also included in the

---

1 *Deity of Banū Kalb.*

2 *Worshiped by Banī Hudhayl.*

3 *Worshiped by the tribe of Madhhij.*

4 *God of Hamdan.*

5 *Placed near Kabah.*

6 *Placed near Kabah.*

7 *Worshiped in Yaman.*

category of mysterious beings who were thought to be endowed with powers. Some believed that the ghost of a slain man would hover over the grave in the form of a bird crying for revenge until the murder was avenged.

With all this idolatry and belief in a multiplicity of gods, however, the Arabs still had faith in a supreme God whom they called *Allāh*. This high God, they thought, was the creator and sustainer of the universe, the master of life and death; the whole mechanism of nature was operated in accordance with His command. There are several verses in the *Qurān* which confirm that the pre-Islamic Arabs very well believed in the existence of *Allāh* as the supreme power[1] and prayed to Him in emergencies, but once the danger had passed, they forgot about him. In fact, the Arabs felt that although *Allāh* was omnipotent, He had delegated powers to many subordinate gods, animate as well as inanimate, who served as the media through which the worshiper could earn His pleasure. *Allāh* was, thus, the most important god and was revered as the lord of the *Kābah,* but He was a distant figure without having much influence on the peoples' daily lives. Therefore, He had no cult and was never worshiped in the form of idol.

With no complex theology and no hope of an after-life, the Arab religion of pagan pluralism failed to evoke much interest in the life of the people. In fact, in the Bedouin society, the tribe, not the deity, was the supreme value; social ideals and customs transcended the religious doctrines. As a result, though they worshipped different gods and goddesses following the time-honoured customs of their forefathers, it was without any particular feeling of devotion and moral commitment. Such a lifeless religion naturally failed to satisfy the spiritual quest of a few thoughtful persons who were in search of *Dīn Hanīfī*, the pure religion of *Ibrahīm*. They found it meaningless to run around and worship stones and idols which could neither see, nor hear, nor harm, nor help. They, therefore, withdrew from the pagan religion of the *Kābah* and denounced idol worship.

---

1 *31. 10.22–24, 24.61 & 63, 29.61 & 65, 39.38, 43.87, 106.1–3.*

They were known as *Hanīf*,[1] a word occurring in the *Qurān* also. We are told by *Ibn Ishāq* that *Waraqah ibn Naufal* (cousin of the Prophet's wife, *Khadījah*), *Abd Allāh ibn Jahsh* (a nephew of the Prophet's uncle, *Hamzah*), *Uthmān ibn Huwairith* (a son of *Abd al Uzzah*), and *Zayd ibn Amr ibn Naufail* (an uncle of *Umar*) represented the *Hanīfiyyah* revolt against idol worship in *Makkah* shortly before the Prophet began his mission. All the four belonged to the tribe of *Quraysh* and were associated with the life of the Prophet in some way or the other. The *Hanīfs* believed in the pure monotheism of *Ibrahīm* but were confused regarding the form and mode of worship of their faith. *Zayd* is said to have once remarked while standing beside the *Kābah*: '*Oh Allāh! If I knew how you wished to be worshiped, I would have so worshiped you; but I do not know.*' Sometimes, the *Hanīfs* expected that an Arab prophet would come with a divine mission to revive the pure religion of *Ibrahīm*. Three of them,[2] however, converted to Christianity as an interim measure. The fourth one, *Zayd ibn Amr*, as a reaction to his outspoken criticism and disrespect for the gods and goddesses, was driven out of the city. He travelled in the civilized countries of Syria and Iraq, met the Jews and Christian monks, but none of them could satisfy him. Eventually, he met a monk who told him that a prophet was about to emerge in *Makkah* who would preach the religion he was looking for. So, *Zayd* left for home but was killed on the way.

Of those who rejected idol worship and propagated the *Hanīfiyyah* ideology, *Ibn Hishām* has named only four as mentioned above. We learn of a few other individuals[3] who rejected idol worship immediately before the rise of *Islām*. The *Hanīfiyyah* sect was, however, microscopic and had a negligible impact on the contemporary religious system of *Makkah*. It has

---

1   *The word means to turn away from or to revolt.*

2   *Waraqah, Abd Allāh, and Uthmān.*

3   * *Umayyah ibn Abisalt, a chieftain of Tāif and a famous poet.*
    * *Quss ibn Saida al Lyadi, the famous orator of Arabia.*
    * *Qais ibn Nushba.*

been remarked[1] that the *Hanīfs* were chiefly concerned with their own personal salvation rather than reformation of the religious and moral life of Arabia. The theology of the sect was negative; they had a clear idea of what they did not want than a positive conception of what they wanted to establish. Nevertheless, the movement represented a kind of spiritual awakening in *Makkah* immediately before the emergence of *Islām*.

The superficial religion, which the Bedouin Arabia had, failed to ameliorate the conditions of its society, which remained steeped in vices, superstitions, and barbaric practices. With no concern for social justice and human rights, the society was based on exploitation of the weak. There was hardly any regard for moral values and little respect for sanctity of matrimonial relations. Adultery and fornication were common and polygamy was practiced to an unlimited extent. Polyandry is also referred to by Strabo. The famous pre-Islamic poet, *Imrū al Qais*, in his *qasīdah*, took delight in narrating his illicit sexual intercourse with his own cousin. The people were passionately addicted to drinking, gambling, and music. A class of women known as *Kiyān* were specially known for dancing and singing. Their immorality was proverbial, but they were held in high esteem and had access to even the greatest chiefs. We also hear of human sacrifice as a religious ritual. The position of women in the society was deplorable. Like slaves, they had no human or legal rights but were considered mere chattels and were cruelly treated. The birth of a daughter was regarded as a great misfortune and the people used to bury the female infants alive for fear of getting impoverished by providing for them. That the atrocious practice of female infanticide was quite common is confirmed by its condemnation in a few verses of the *Qurān*.[2] The women had no right of inheritance in the property of husbands, parents and other relatives. A widow was considered an integral part of the deceased husband's patrimony, and if she was a stepmother, the son inherited and used her. Real sister could be co-wife to

---

1   *Karen Armstrong.*

2   *6:141, 6:152, 16:57 to 59, 17:33.*

the same husband. The slaves used to be treated inhumanely, their masters possessing authority of life and death over them. Marriage among the slaves themselves was not legal. The slave girls were often used as concubines of the masters.

The political system of the Bedouin tribes was rudimentary. The chief of the tribe, known as *Sheikh*, was elected by the elders on the basis of merit-cum-seniority. But he had no absolute authority, being first among equals only. His main work was arbitration rather than command. His decisions were based on public opinion which was the law of the tribe and was in accordance with the *Sunnah* or practices of the ancestors. In order to aid and advice the *Sheikh*, every tribe had a council of elders known as *Majlis* which consisted of the heads of the families and representatives of the clans within the tribe. Beyond this intra-tribal elementary arrangement, Bedouin Arabia did not have any larger political entity. Due to strong tribal loyalties, *Hijāz* and *Najd* could not develop any empire or state. The only attempt at establishment of a supra-tribal kingdom in pre-Islamic Arabia was that of emergence of the petty kingdom of *Kindah* in central Arabia. This confederacy of several central Arabian tribes was their first joint venture in the last part of the fifth century. The kingdom was founded by *Hujr*, a scion of the Himyarite royal family. *Al Hārith* was the most powerful king of the dynasty who is said to have subjugated the Lakhmids but was subsequently defeated and killed by them in 529. The kingdom proved ephemeral and soon collapsed due to succession disputes and lack of inner cohesion. One important contribution of the *Kindah* kings was patronage of the Arabic poets of the 'heroic age'. The great Arabian poet, *Imrū al Qais*, was a descendant of the royal *kindah* line and attempted restoration of the kingdom both through power of pen and sword, but in vain.

Barring this attempt at empire building, inner Arabia, throughout the pre-Islamic period, remained a region politically divided on lines of tribes. The inhospitable region, therefore, could not play any significant role in international affairs of the contemporary 'Middle East'; nor were the superpowers[1] of the age ever interested in penetrating the barren land. But though inner Arabia[2] remained immune to political developments of the age, in the bordering areas of Syria and Iraq, the Arabs did develop petty states which during their heydays included portions of northern Arabia. These border kingdoms were of Arab origin, used Arabic language in speech but wrote in Aramaic and had a culture largely under Hellenic and Aramaic (Syrian) influence. Drawing their main strength from exploitation of the Arabian trade routes, they were basically commercial rather than military kingdoms and were used by the two superpowers as buffer states. Nevertheless, they represented the Arabs in international relations of the time.

The earliest but the most important of them was the kingdom of Nabataeans, which had its capital at *Petra* in Jordan and prospered from the fourth century BC to the beginning of the second century AD. The kingdom maintained friendly relations with the Roman Empire, but actually the latter used it as a buffer for protection of its territories from the untamable Bedouin. The Roman Emperor, Pompey, is said to have visited *Petra* in 65 BC, and later the Nabataean kingdom served as a base for the Roman expedition of south Arabia by Gallus. Subsequently, due to deterioration in the Roman-Nabataean relations, the Roman Emperor, Trajan, converted this kingdom into a Roman province in 105 AD. After the fall of the Nabataeans in the second century AD, another petty Arab kingdom of *Palmyra*[3] rose into prominence in the Syro-Arabian desert. This kingdom was located at the starting point of the western trade route and its importance was due to the gradual diversion of the east to west caravan route to a more northerly region centring on *Palmyra*. The present ruins of the city of *Palmyra* are reminiscent of its magnificence and grandeur. According to Arab storytellers, the city had been built by the jinns for king Solomon. This kingdom was also a buffer state between the Roman East and the Parthian

---

1   *The Byzantine Empire and the Persian Empire.*
2   *Hijāz and Najd.*
3   *Based on the oasis of Tadmur.*

Iran, and therefore, its security depended on its neutrality. In the third century, however, its king, *Odaynath*, sided with the Romans in their war against the Persians for which he was granted recognition as a king by the Roman Emperor. But subsequently, after the assassination of *Odaynath* and his son, suspectedly at the instigation of the Romans, the former's wife, Zenobia, defied the Roman Empire and conquered Egypt and a part of Asia Minor whereupon the Romans defeated and crushed *Palmyra* in 272 AD. The Palmyrene civilization was an interesting blend of Greek, Syrian, and Iranian elements.

After the fall of *Palmyra* in the third century, two other petty kingdoms of Arab origin emerged on the Arabian frontiers of Syria and Iraq. They were the kingdoms of *Ghassān*[1] in the Syrian Desert and *Lakhm*[2] on Iraq-Arab border. According to Arab traditions, the two kingdoms were founded respectively by the people of *Hawrān* and *Tanukh* tribes of south Arabia after they migrated in the wake of breaking of the *Mārib* dam. The rise of the two kingdoms was encouraged by the Byzantine and Sassanian empires in order to use them as buffers or client states as also to get Arab auxiliaries for their wars. The kingdom of *Ghassān* and *Hirā* both were Christians, the former Monophysite and the later Nestorian; both drew their culture from the Hellenic civilisation of Syria. The two kingdoms fought against each, patronized Arabic poetry of the 'heroic age', and played an important role in political affairs of the region during the sixth century. The kingdom of *Ghassān* attained its greatest importance under *al Hārith II* who was the contemporary of the formidable Lakhmid king, *al Mundhīr III*. After ups and down in battles, the latter was killed by his Ghassanide rival in 554. Whereas the Lakhmid kingdom was converted into a Persian province in the beginning of the seventh century, that of *Ghassān* was terminated by the Muslim invasion only. The petty border States were but transitory affairs which could neither affect the political life of inner Arabia nor bring about cultural transformation of

---

1   *Capital at al Jabīyah.*

2   *Capital at al Hirā.*

the Bedouin. The kingdom of *Ghassān* and *Lakhm*, however, did provide arms and military expertise to the Arabs. It was from *al Hirā* that the *Quraysh* are said to have learnt the art of writing.

The conditions prevailing in inner Arabia during the pre Islamic century is referred to by the Muslim historians as *Jāhiliyah*[1] which literally means the age of ignorance. But the actual meaning of the term was much wider as it covered the whole gamut of civilization and included all values which were not in consonance with the principles of *Islām*. In common historical parlance, however, the term signified a period of low cultural values when the Arabs led a barbaric way of life in which there was political anarchy, socio-economic injustice, and above all, prevalence of a low form of religion marked by absence of dispensation, inspired prophet and a revealed book. But everything in the age of *Jāhiliyah* was not negative. The period witnessed a few intellectual developments to which the term would be difficult to apply. The first was the development of a common poetic Arabic language which was independent of tribal dialects and which reached its maturity during the sixth century. This was a highly forceful language exercising an irresistible influence over the Bedouin' minds. No wonder, it was described as a 'lawful magic' (*Sihr halāl*). The language provided the Arabs extraordinary eloquence and united the tribes in a single oral tradition. It was the same language in which the Quranic revelations subsequently came.

Side by side with evolution of this Arabic *lingua franca*, there was efflorescence of the great Arabic poetry, there being a symbiotic relationship between the two. Evolving over a long period of time and passing through stages of the rhymed prose of the soothsayers (*kuhhān*) and the song of the camel drivers (*hudā*), the powerful poetical tradition reached its classical perfection

---

1 *A term used in the Qurīn several times.*

in the form of ode (*qasīdah*) in the sixth century.[1] This was a highly finished type of poetical composition, extremely forceful and passionate, and reflected a technique of excellence in terms of meter, rhyme, and diction. As models of excellence, the odes of the *Jahiliyah* period remained unsurpassed even to this day. Since the art of writing was not common, these early poems were committed to memory, sung in social gatherings, and transmitted orally through generations. They were finally reduced to writing during the Umayyad period only. The main theme of the *Jahiliyah* poetry was glorification of the tribes by describing their wars, giving accounts of courage, chivalry, and other *murūwah* qualities of the tribal heroes and exposing turpitude of their enemies. But the poets also sang of wine, love, and hunting as well as the landscapes of mountains and deserts. Strangely enough, however, religious themes are conspicuous by their absence in the poems. There is no mention of stories of gods or devotion to them. Viewed from the angle of literary criticism, the horizon of the pre-Islamic Arabic poetry was thematically limited; it lacked in thought-provoking imagery and had only local appeal. Nevertheless, it was a true and passionate expression of the life of the Bedouin. Among the earliest odes of the 'heroic age', the collection known as '*Seven Muallaqāt*' holds the first place. In addition to this, there is another collection called '*al Mufaddaliyāt*' containing 120 odes composed by lesser known poets. We also find a number of *diwāns* (anthologies), the most popular being *Hamāsah*, edited by *Abu Tammām*.

Poetical congregations were the main events of the Bedouin' cultural life. According to traditions, every year at the fair of *Ukāz*, the Bedouin used to organize a sort of literary congress where the poets used to compete for annual prizes. The poems awarded prizes used to be inscribed in golden letters and hung on the walls of the *Kābah*. The earliest odes are ascribed to *Muhalhil*,

---

1 *The period is known in the history of Arabic literature as the 'heroic age'. During this period though there was absence of literature in prose, extremely popular poems (odes) were composed in praise of the heroes of the tribal wars.*

the *Taghlīb* hero of the *Basūs* war. But a more renowned poet was *Imrū al Qais* of the *Kindah* royal family whose ode was said to have been the first to receive prize at *Ukāz*.[1] A typical poet-hero was *Shanāfara* of *Azd* who completed his oath of killing hundred men of *Banu Salamān*. His splendid ode, *Lamiyyātul Arab*, describes his own heroic character. The poets were held in high esteem and were the heroes of their age personifying all qualities of *murūwah*. The Arabs considered poetry as super-human and thought of the poets being possessed by jinns and, therefore, having magical qualities. The poet was the spokesman of his community, its historian, and its propaganda minister. He performed an important political role, provided the main inspiration for intertribal wars, and stirred the Bedouin to action. Negatively, however, he glorified intertribal wars and violence to a dangerous extent. Covering almost all aspects of the Bedouin' life, the pre-Islamic poetry provides significant source material for study of the history of the period.

The most consequential development of the *Jahiliyah* period, however, was the rise of *Makkah* as the regional centre of trade and commerce. This development, which cristallized the Makkan situation before the rise of *Islām*, was the result of several factors. Though not centred on an oasis to support agriculture-based economy, *Makkah* still had enough well-water to provide for a large number of camels. Situated at the junction of the major north-south and east-west trade routes, the city had a highly favourable location for serving as a centre of trade and commerce. The international situation of the sixth century was also in favour of *Makkah*. In the fourth century, international trade route had been diverted from western Arabia to other channels—through Egypt and the Red Sea and through Euphrates Valley and Persian Gulf. Due to this, the peninsular trade route had fallen into significance. But in the sixth century, due to continuous wars between the Byzantine and Persian Empires, trade through the Iraq-Persian Gulf route became difficult. Egypt was also in a

---

1   *Other popular poets were Amr ibn Kulthūm, Antarāh al Absi, Hārith bin Hilliza and Tarafa bin al Abd.*

state of disorder and no longer offered an alternative trade route through the Red Sea. Consequently, international trade between the Mediterranean countries and 'Further East' again resumed through the Arabian trade route via *Yaman*. However, since *Yaman* itself was under political disorganization and foreign rule, the opportunity was seized by the city of *Makkah* to establish monopoly of this trade. And this became possible mainly due to political stability which the rule of the *Quraysh* tribe provided to the city and the wiser economic policies adopted by its leaders.

Qussay, who had established the supremacy of *Quraysh* over *Makkah* and systematized the administration of the city as well as management of the *Kābah*, died in 480. As nominated during his lifetime, his eldest son, *Abd ud Dār*,[1] succeeded him and ruled. But after his death, serious disputes broke out between *Abd ud Dār*'s grandchildren and sons of his brother, *Abd Manāf*, for control of the *Kābah* and the city of *Makkāh*. Different *Quraysh* clans and their supporters ranged themselves on either side.[2] The situation was on the verge of a civil war but was ultimately saved by a compromise under which the real powers, represented by *Siqāyah* and *Rifādah*, were entrusted to *Adb Manāf*'s son, *Abd Shams*, while the secondary matters like *Hijābah*, *Nadwah*, and *Liwā* remained in the hands of the children of *Abd ud Dār*. *Abd Shams*, however, transferred his powers to his highly competent and wealthy brother, *Hāshim*. *Hāshim* proved a great leader; in addition to discharging his assigned duties excellently, he was able to control the mercantile activity within Arabia. The system of organizing a series of annual markets in different parts of Arabia, with *Makkah* as the centre, was developed. The first market (*sūq*)

---

1   *He is said to have been the least competent of his sons. The most competent was his brother Abd Manāf.*

2   *The group of Abdu ud Dār's children was supported by Makhzum, Sahm, Jumah, and Adi and was known as Ahlāf (the confedrates). The group of the children of Abd Manāf was supported by Asad, Zuhrā, Tāym, and Hārith ibn Fihr and was known as Mutayyābūn (The Scented Ones) because they had dipped their hands in a bowl of perfume at the Kābah and taken oath of unity.*

of the year was held in Bahrain followed successively in *Oman*, *Hadramawt*, and *Yaman*. The cycle of markets concluded with five consecutive fairs in and around *Makkah*, the last being held in *Ukāz* immediately before the month of *haj*. Thus, caravans laden with merchandise started coming to *Makkah* from all directions for exchange and sale of commodities. The *Quraysh* monopolized the trade. *Hāshim* regulated and standardized the system of sending two main caravan trips of the Makkan traders every year, the winter trip to *Yaman*, and the summer trip to al *Shām* (Syria). In addition, smaller caravans were sent at other times. Every *Quraysh* family associated itself in commerce, as bankers, financiers, and merchants; and soon they acquired a capital surplus that made a settled life possible without depending on agriculture. In order to ensure obstruction-free movement to the trade caravans, the *Quraysh* under *Hāshim*'s leadership entered into agreements of peace and friendship with the rulers of the neighbouring countries[1] and obtained from them exemption from payment of taxes. Further, in order to obtain security on the roads, *Hāshim* concluded treaties with various Bedouin tribes of the peninsula guaranteeing safety to the trade caravans of *Quraysh*. Thus, as a result of the diplomatic policies of *Hāshim*, *Makkah* prospered and its power and position rose tremendously making it the cynosure of the peninsula.

Hāshim died in 510 leaving his only son, *Shaybāh*, by a Yathribite lady named *Salmā* of the Khazraj tribe. After his death, he was succeeded by his younger brother *Muttalib* who was known for his generosity and goodness. *Muttalib* brought his white-haired nephew, *Shaybāh*, from *Yathrib* to *Makkāh*. On arrival at *Makkāh*, the *Muttalib*, a name by which he was thenceforth popularly known. After the death of *Muttalib* in 520, the young *Abd al Muttalib* succeeded him and held position as the *de facto* head of the Makkan administration for fifty-nine years. Meanwhile, the children of *Abd ud Dār* were growing rich and jealous of the Hashimites and trying to compete with the

---

1   *Which included the Byzantine Emperor, the Negus of Abyssinia and the kings of Ghassān and Yaman.*

latter for leadership. They were joined and led by *Omayyah*, the ambitious grandson of *Abd Shams*. But due to his high character and contributions, *Abd al Muttalib* was held in such a high veneration by *Quraysh* that he was always regarded as the virtual chief of the city and *Omayyah* had to spend ten years in exile in *al Shām*. The period of *Abd al Muttalib* was quite eventful. His greatest achievement was the rediscovery of the sacred well of *Zamzam* and the wealth hidden by *Jurhum* for which he had received guidance in his dreams. *Abd al Muttalib* had twelve sons and six daughters. As per the custom of the time, he had vowed to sacrifice one of his sons to God, should all his sons grow to maturity. His wish came true, and when the priest decided by drawing lot that the most handsome and favourite of his sons, *Abd Allāh*,[1] should be sacrificed, a hue and cry were raised by the *Quraysh*. As told by the classical historians, on the advice of the priests, it was decided to ransom *Abd Allāh*'s life by sacrifice of 100 camels. A great event of *Abd al Muttalib*'s time was the invasion of *Makkah* by the Abyssian governor of *Yaman* in 570 and the miraculous failure of the attack. As regards administrative structure during the days of *Abd al Muttalib*, the city state of *Makkah* has been described as 'a merchant republic governed by a syndicate of wealthy businessmen'.[2] On the nomadic model, each clan had its own *Majlis*. From the *Majlises* were drawn members of a bigger council known as *Mala* which was actually an oligarchy of the ruling families. But the *Mala* had no coercive authority; its role was only persuasive and moral. The real basis of authority remained the class solidarity of the merchants. Formal administration was, however, carried out by a governing

---

1 *He was to become father of the Prophet.*

2 *Lammens*

body consisting of ten senators (*Sharifs*) holding the charge of 10 separate departments.[1]

Side by side with economic development, under the *Quraysh, Makkah* emerged as the greatest centre of Bedouin religion. With political stability in its surrounding area, the spring of *Zamzam* rediscovered, its administration streamlined and the attack on it by *Abrahah* miraculously repulsed, the prestige of the *Kābah* radically enhanced, and the people from different parts of the peninsula flocked there for pilgrimage.[2] Annual pilgrimage (*haj*)[3] to the sanctuary, which had effigies of almost all Bedouin tribes placed in its precincts, developed as the most important religious custom of the Bedouin. The *Quraysh* were able to exploit the increasing importance of the *Kābah* to serve the interest of the Makkan trade and commerce. Apart from organizing different

---

1 *During the Prophet's time, charge of these ten departments was held by the leading men of the house of Qussay as under:*
   (1) *Hijābah (guardianship of the keys of the Kābah)—held by Uthmān of the house of Abd ud Dār;*
   (2) *Siqāyah (provision of water to the pilgrims)—held by Abbās of the house of Hāshim.*
   (3) *Diyat (civil and criminal magistracy)—held by Abdullāh ibn Kuhāfa of the house of Tāym.*
   (4) *Sifārah (settling disputes arising between the Quraysh and other tribes)—held by Umar.*
   (5) *Liwā (possession of the flag at the time of war)—held by Abu Sufyān of the house of Omayyah.*
   (6) *Rifādah (provision of food to pilgrims and administration of the taxes)—held by Hārith of the house of Naufal.*
   (7) *Nadwah (chairmanship of the house of Assembly)—held by Aswad of the house of Abd al Uzzā.*
   (8) *Khaimmeh (guardianship of the council chamber)—held by Khālid ibn Walīd of the house of Makhzūm.*
   (9) *Khāzina (administration of public finances)—held by Hārith ibn Qais of the house of Kāb.*
   (10) *Azlām (guardianship of the divining arrows)—held by Safwān of the house of Omayyah.*
2 *Both haj and umrāh.*
3 *Performed in Dhu al Hijjāh, the twelfth month of the Muslim calendar.*

fairs in the vicinity of *Makkah* during months preceding and following the pilgrimage, they allowed utilization of the campus of the sanctuary as a market for sale and exchange of commodities at all times. But the endemic tribal violence was a serious threat to Makkan commerce. The *Quraysh*, therefore, persuaded the Bedouin to establish a zone of peace in and around the *Kabāh* which came to be known as the *harām*. This was a zone of a twenty-mile radius with the *Kābah* as its centre. This was regarded as a sacred area where all violence was forbidden. The measure, apart from providing peace in *Makkah* for business activities, put an end to violent tribal conflicts around the sanctuary for gaining control of the prestigious site. In addition to establishing the *harām*, the *Quraysh* were instrumental in getting the four months of business transaction and religious festivities declared as the months of 'holy truce' during which all intertribal hostilities were to be kept under suspension and all violence was to be abjured. These holy months included the eleventh, twelfth, and first month of each year of the Muslim calendar together with the seventh month in the middle.[1] Thus were the *Quraysh* able to incorporate the *Kābah* into the Makkan economic system establishing a 'market-shrine complex' which provided an uninterrupted flow of revenue and great prosperity to the city.

Some modern Western historians have overemphasized the social aspect of the rise of mercantile economy in *Makkah* as a factor which helped the rise of *Islām*. The rise of the Makkan commercial system within a Bedouin milieu, they would argue, created a set of social problems. Even after more than a century of sedentation, the *Quraysh* had not severed links with the nomadic culture and still idealized the Bedouin way of life. But the rise of capitalism resulting in accumulation of wealth in a few hands had radically transformed their social values;

---

1 *The names of the four months of the 'holy truce' are*
   (i)   *Dhu al Qadah—eleventh month,*
   (ii) *Dhu al Hijjāh—twelfth month,*
   (iii) *Muharram—first month,*
   (iv) *Rajab—seventh month.*

by the time the Prophet emerged on the scene, the Makkan society was unlike that of the Bedouin. Whereas stratification was minimal in Bedouin society, a hierarchy based on wealth appeared among the *Quraysh*.[1] Further, unlike other Bedouin tribes which freely indulged in intertribal warfare and raiding, the *Quraysh*, due to their vested economic interest, became men of peace and neutrality and were successful in avoiding conflicts periodically during pilgrimage and fairs. And, most importantly, their commercial ethos made them accept materialistic values and an individualistic spirit, taking them away from many of the traditional values of *murūwah*. The clans and individuals were engaged in an aggressive competition and were keen to have economic dealings with members of the other clans neglecting the interest of their own needy people. Instead of sharing their wealth equally as the old ethic demanded, individuals were now building up their own fortunes. In the greed for acquiring wealth, they were even exploiting the rights of orphans and widows and were neglecting the traditional duty of looking after the poorer and weaker members of their own clans. All this was in violation of the Bedouin code of conduct and tended to break up the tribal solidarity which had been a prominent feature of the Bedouin society. Under the changing social dynamics, the individuals who gained economically dominated the scene to the deprivation of others. The clans and individuals who lagged behind and lost power and importance stood dissatisfied, ready to join a movement which challenged the authority of the established order and spoke in terms of social justice. The consequence was social tension, a crisis in society. *Islām*, it has been suggested, represented a reaction to this socio-economic situation. This view, however, exaggerates one particular aspect of Islām's teachings to the detriment of the rest.

---

1   *On the eve of the rise of Islam, Makkāh had a divided society consisting of*
    (i)   a higher class of merchant aristocrats (Quraysh of the Inside),
    (ii)   a middle class of the small traders of humbler status (Quraysh of the Outside), and
    (iii)   a 'proleteriat' of outsiders (bedouins from outside and slaves etc).

ARABIAN PENINSULA

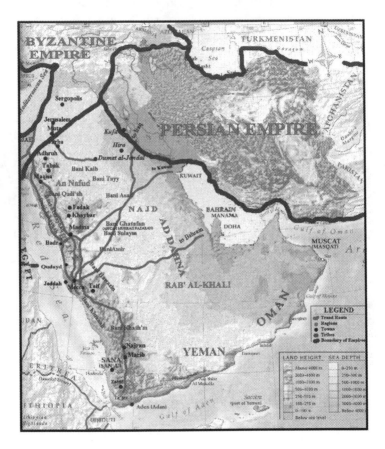

ON THE EVE OF THE RISE OF ISLAM

CHAPTER III

EARLY LIFE
(Preapostolic period)

As compared to the post-apostolic period, our historical information regarding the early life of the Prophet remains scanty. It is the *Qurān* which provides us the most authentic and basic information about the same. The following three verses of *Surāh* 93[1] give vital clues to his experience during early life:

Did He not find thee an orphan, and give thee shelter?
And He found thee wandering, and gave thee guidance.
And He found thee in need, and made thee independent.

The above lines of the *Qurān* confirm beyond doubt that the Prophet's premarital life was one of financial difficulties and, till the revelation came, he was struggling in search of truth

---

1   *Verses 6 to 8.*

having no inkling about his future status. Apart from such bare facts, the *Qurān*, however, does not mention other details of his early life. Greater details are provided by the mass of Islamic tradition as recorded by the Prophet's biographers of the classical period. Though not as copious as in respect of the later period, the tradition is our main source of information on the subject. But based on legendary details, it, *inter alia*, incorporates a series of miraculous stories regarding his birth, infancy, and childhood, which are treated by the Western historians as apocryphal and, therefore, ignored. Nevertheless, for a better appreciation of the Prophet's history, it may be prudent to refer to such stories as well, for many of them are believed by the Muslims to be true.

The Islamic tradition indicates that before the birth of the Prophet, there was an expectancy in some sections that an Arabian messenger would be born who would bring the true message. The Arabian poets and soothsayers were referring to such a forecast. *Zayd ibn Amr*, the *hanīf*, who had been in search of the true religion of *Ibrahīm*, had been informed by a Christian monk about the imminent arrival of an Arabian prophet. We are told that the Jews of Arabia including those of the agricultural settlement of *Yathrib* also believed that a prophet would emerge in the peninsula. A pious rabbi had emigrated to *Yathrib* from Syria, and when asked the reason for his emigration, he explained that the time of coming of the prophet in *Hijāz* had come and that he wanted to be there during the occasion. The religious scriptures of the time also supported the traditional theory of the prophet's expected arrival. According to the version of the Gospels then prevalent in Syria, Jesus had said that after his death, a 'Comforter' would be sent by God who would remind the people of everything he had taught them and help them understand the same. There was a similar expectation of a prophet in Palestine, too. The *Qurān*[1] also refers to the belief that Jesus had foretold that another prophet named 'Ahmad' would come after him and confirm his message.

---

1   *Q 61.6.*

The Prophet was the son of *Abd Allāh* of the then dominant Hāshimite family of *Quraysh*. The family was considered one of the noblest, and as we have seen, the Prophet's grandfather, *Abd al Muttalib*, was the virtual chief of *Makkāh*. But the financial status of the family was in the wane. *Abd Allāh* was proverbially handsome and when he was 24 years old, his father arranged his marriage with one of the most excellent women of *Quraysh* named *Aminah*, daughter of *Wahab*, chief of *Zuhra* clan who had died a few years ago. Hence, *Āminah* was under the guardianship of her uncle, *Wuhayb*, who also had a daughter of marriageable age named *Hāla*. Though *Abd al Muttalib* was over 70 years old at the time, he fixed his marriage, too, with *Hāla* and the double wedding took place at the same time. It was *Hamzah*, of the same age as he. Interestingly, *Hamzah* was also his cousin from his mother's side. We are told by *Ibn Ishāq* that when the father and the son were proceeding for the wedding, they passed through the dwellings of *Bani Asad*. *Qutaylāh*, the sister of *Waraqah*,[1] impressed by the beauty of *Abd Allāh* and, noticing a radiance which lit his face, invited him to sleep with her; but the offer was refused. The same night, Abd Allāh's marriage was consummated and *Āminah* is said to have conceived the Prophet. The next day, when *Abd Allāh* again happened to pass through the house of *Qutaylah*, he expected the same offer but she was not interested because the extraordinary light was no more there on his face signifying that another woman had conceived the Messenger of God.

Though there is divergence of opinion regarding the Prophet's date of birth, it is broadly accepted that he was born on a Monday, on the twelfth of *Rabi al Awwal*[2] in the 'Year of the Elephant' corresponding to 570 AD.[3] It is a tragedy of the Prophet's life

---

1 *The cousin of the Prophet's first wife, Khadījah. He was a hanīf converted to Christianity and was aware of Christian scriptures and also knew that an Arabian prophet was likely to come with the same message.*

2 *The third month of the Islamic calendar.*

3 *According to Gregorian calendar, the Prophet was born on twenty-ninth of August.*

that his father had died shortly before his birth.[1] The fact that on his death, *Abd Allāh* was able to leave for his widow only five camels, a small herd of sheep and a young slave girl named *Barakah* (subsequently known as *Umm Ayman*) shows that the family was under a difficult financial situation. According to Muslim traditions, the gestation and birth of the Prophet were attended with many signs and portents. *Āminah* experienced no discomfort while carrying the child; instead, she was conscious of carrying an extraordinary child. As per a story, while pregnant, she heard a voice which told her that she was carrying the lord of the Arabs and she also saw a light emanating from her belly in which she could notice the castle of *Basrā*.[2] The delivery of the child took place at the house of Āminah's uncle and was extraordinarily easy. The child was born circumcised and carried on his back, between the shoulders, an oval mark which was later identified by the Muslims as the 'seal of prophethood'. *Abd al Muttalib* was overjoyed at the birth of his grandson, took the newly born baby in his hands, went to the *Kābah*, and gave him the unfamiliar name of '*Muhammad*', which means 'the praised one' by the Muslims as the 'seal of prophethood'. *Ibn Ishāq*, however, says that this unusual name came to his mother in the vision as mentioned above. Since the newborn was the only issue of his favourite deceased son, *Abd al Muttalib* felt great affection for him which was further heightened when he personally had vision indicating great future of the child.

It was a customary practice of the sedentary noble families of *Makkah* to hand over their newly born male babies to wet nurses of the nearby Bedouin tribes for suckling and upbringing for a few years[3] in the desert. Though sedentised, they still idealized the Bedouin way of life and thought that the child's initial upbringing in the pure atmosphere of the desert would be more congenial for his health and help him pick up the purest form

---

1   *He is reported to have died of sickness at Yathrib while returning from a trade journey.*

2   *In Syria.*

3   *For as many as eight years according to one author.*

of Arabic language. Further, such a step would also spare the child from the vices and addictions of town life and lead him to imbibe the ideal values of the Bedouin life. *Āminah*, therefore, decided to hand over the infant to some wet nurse. Some of the tribes had a high reputation for nursing and rearing children and *Bani Sād ibn Bakr*[1] was one of them, and their wet nurses were expected to visit *Makkah* shortly for taking over nurselings. For a few days before the arrival of the wet nurses, however, the holy infant was suckled and looked after, in addition to his mother, by *Thuwaybāh*, the female slave of the Prophet's uncle *Abū Lahab*. This lady is said to have subsequently suckled the Prophet's uncle, *Hamzah*, making the two foster brothers also. When the wet nurses of *Bani Sād* arrived at *Makkah*, *Āminah* offered her son to them, one by one, but they all refused because they did not expect adequate return from the poor mother of an orphan. The group included *Halīmah*, daughter of *Abū Dhuayb*, who was accompanied by her husband, *Hārith*, and a recently born son. She was the poorest of the visiting wet nurses and had a shabby look. It was a year of drought and her family had no provisions. The she-ass and the she-camel which she had brought as the family's mount were emaciated and did not have any milk in their udders. The lady herself did not have enough in her breasts to feed her own infant. *Halīmah* also, however, was initially unwilling to take Āminah's infant for nursing. But due to her poverty, she could not get an infant from other families who preferred the wet nurses having better look and resources. At last, in order to save herself from humiliation of not receiving a nurseling, she accepted the child of *Āminah*.

Halīmah left an account of what happened to her and her family after she took over charge of the holy baby and the same was recorded by *Ibn Ishāq*. According to the story, different types of strange favours of God started coming to her. As soon as she put the baby in her bosom, her breasts overflowed with milk which he and his foster-brother drank to fill. The she-camel also gave abundant milk which more than satisfied *Halīmah* and her

---

1 *An outlying branch of Hawāzin tribe.*

husband's hunger, and during the return journey, the weak donkey that was not able to keep pace with others surprised everyone by her swift speed and overtook others in the convoy. After the family reached home, there was abundance and prosperity for them; their flock started yielding a lot of milk while the animals of others went dry. Assisted by her daughter, *Shaymā*, *Halīmah* nursed and reared the child who grew well. On completion of two years, he was weaned and taken back to *Āminah*. But due to the disguised blessings which *Halīmah*'s family was receiving by the presence of the holy baby, she begged to *Āminah* to leave the child under her care for sometime more which was agreed to. Historians disagree whether *Halīmah*'s extended charge of the child was due to her own or Āminah's wishes. It appears, *Āminah* agreed to the same due to an epidemic which had afflicted *Makkah* at the time. The Prophet is said to have remained under the care of *Halīmah* for four or five years.[1] To the Muslim writers, the early years of childhood with *Bani Sād* in the difficult environment of the desert fashioned his outlook and prepared him for the future role of the Messenger. The environment was surrounded by pure nature reflecting everywhere signs of the Creator which the child could observe. Moreover, he was able to learn the purest form of Arabic for which the *Bani Sād* were renowned and which accounted for his powerful eloquence in later life. It has been reported by *Ibn Ishāq* that the Prophet was always proud of his *Bani Sād* connection and used to tell his Companions that '*I am the most Arab of you all. I am of Quraysh and I was suckled among the Bani Sād.*' All through his life, *Halīmah* and her people remained the object of the Prophet's great love and admiration, and during her occasional visits, he was always extremely generous and regardful to her. When following his marriage with *Khadījah*, a severe draught occurred and she visited them, she was gifted with fourty heads of cattle and a camel loaded with water. Whenever she visited, the Prophet used to stretch out his mantle for her to sit

---

1 *There is difference of opinion among scholars regarding the number of years the baby Prophet stayed with Halīmah. It ranges from three to five years.*

as a sign of respect. The affection he showed to his foster-sister, *Shaymā*, on a much later date when she was brought as captive after the Battle of *Hunayn*, will be referred to in due course.

It was during the last part of his stay with *Halīmah* that the great miracle of the splitting of his chest is reported to have taken place. As per the version recorded by *Ibn Ishāq*, one day when the holy child along with his foster brother was with the lambs behind the tents, the latter suddenly came running to his parents in fright and reported that '*two men clothed in white have seized that Qurayshi brother of mine and thrown him down and opened up his belly, and are stirring it up*'. *Halīmah* and her husband ran to the spot in nervousness and found the child shaken and pale. When asked, he confirmed the story of his foster brother adding that after opening up the belly they searched something in it which he did not know. There was no sign of any person at the place, nor was there any blood on the spot or trace of any bodily injury or mark on the child to confirm the reported story. In spite of repeated questioning, however, the two little boys would not change their version. According to traditions recorded by the biographers, in later life, the Prophet was able to describe the event with more details: '*There came unto me two men, clothed in white, with a gold basin full of snow. Then they laid hold upon me, and splitting open my breast they brought forth my heart. This likewise they split open and took from it a black clot which they cast away. Then they washed my heart and my breast with the snow.*'[1] Other stories add that after completing the miraculous surgery, they lifted the child's body on a pair of scales and declared that he was heavier than all the Arabs put together. In other traditions, the Prophet even explained the spiritual meaning of the event during discussion with some Companions. '*There is no one among you but is accompanied by a jinn or an angel specially assigned to him*', he said. They asked, '*Even you Messenger?*' The reply was, '*Even me, but God has helped me and he (the jinn or the evil spirit) has submitted, so he only enjoins me to do what is good.*'[2]

---

1 *Ibn Sād.*
2 *Hadīth reported by Muslim.*

The western writers do not trust the story and find the evidence therefore spurious. But as interpreted by most of the Muslim scholars, the *Qurān* makes a mention of the incident in *Surah* 94[1] as under:

Had we not opened your chest for you
And dissipated your burden
Which was galling your back.

The Muslim writers find in these verses testimony of the truthfulness of the incident. To them, this was a purification of the heart of the Prophet by *Allah* and was necessary for his preparation for receipt of the divine message by making him immune to evil feelings and vices. Some Muslim writers, however, place the incident immediately before the Night Journey while others maintain that the miracle of the surgical purification was performed a second time on the later occasion when he was about 50 years old.

The incident badly shook *Halīmah* and her husband who felt that the child had been possessed by some evil spirit. They, therefore, immediately took the child to his mother for being handed over back before the harm was apparent. When told the story, *Āminah*, however, brushed aside the apprehension recounting the experiences she had had during pregnancy and confirming that her child was an extraordinary one having a great future ahead. But this time, *Āminah* decided to keep her son. According to a story recorded by *Ibn Ishāq*, however, another reason which induced *Āminah* to keep the child was disclosure by *Halīmah* that some Abyssinian Christians wanted to kidnap him. The child stayed happily with his mother for two years or so[2] winning the affection of his grandfather and other relatives. He grew specially attached to *Hamzah* and *Safiyyah*, the children of *Abd al Muttalib*'s last marriage. While *Hamzah* was almost his

---

1   *Verses 1 to 3.*

2   *Scholars differ regarding the exact number of years the Prophet spent with his mother.*

own age, *Safiyyah* was a little younger. When he was about 6 years old, his mother, accompanied by her slave girl, *Barakah*, took him to *Yathrib*[1] to meet her relatives and, more importantly, to visit her husband's grave. But while on her way back to *Makkāh*, she fell ill and died and was buried at a place called *Abwā*. In later life, the Prophet had sweet reminiscences of the days spent in *Yathrib* with his mother. He used to recount how he learned to swim in a pool belonging to his Khazrajite kinsmen, how he stayed in the house of a relative of *Abd al Muttalib* belonging to *Banū an Najjār*, and how the boys taught him to fly a kite. He particularly remembered a girl named *Unaisah*, with whom he used to play and have fun making a bird fly away from the top of the tower of the building upon which it wanted to perch. But he always remembered his mother with grief, and each time he passed through *Abwā* during his expeditions, he used to stop at her tomb and shed tears.

After the death of his mother, the child, who was doubly an orphan, was brought to *Makkāh* by *Barakah*. The complete charge of the child was now taken over by his old grandfather, *Abd al Muttalib*, who treated the child with great affection and care, his special love for *Abd Allāh* now transferred to the latter's son. It was Abd Al Muttallib's wont to spend most of the time in the shade of the *Kābah* for which a couch used to be spread there every day. None of his children, not even *Hamzah*, were allowed to sit on it. But there was no restriction for his little grandson who used to freely sit and play on the couch beside his grandfather. *Abd al Muttallib* even used to take him along to attend the meetings of the Assembly where the forty chiefs of the city used to meet to discuss various matters. Sometimes he even took the opinion of the 8-year-old boy which used to be objected to. *Suhaili* mentions that he loved his grandson so much that during a drought, he prayed to God to send rains in the name of his grandson, and he was not disappointed. The child was so intelligent that each time when his grandfather or other relatives lost something, they asked

---

1   *Later known as Madinah.*

him to go and search it, and he always found out the same.[1] But when he had hardly completed two years under the guardianship of his grandfather, attaining the age of 8, the latter died; at the deathbed, however, *Abd al Muttallib* entrusted the charge of his grandson to *Abū Tālib*, who was full brother to the boy's father. The death of such a loving grandfather shocked the child who was continuously crying at the funeral. The memory of his grandfather was always present in his mind despite the love and care of his next guardian, *Abū Tālib*.

The next phase of the Prophet's life under the guardianship of his uncle, *Abū Tālib*, was a long one. He shifted to the house of *Abū Tālib* at the age of 8 and continued to stay there till his marriage at the age of 25. Apart from being a gifted poet, *Abū Tālib* was the nicest and the most respectable of the Hāshims and succeeded his father as the chief of the clan. But the death of *Abd al Muttalib* gave a hard blow to the Hāshims who began fast losing their commanding position in *Makkah* to the rival branch of *Omayyah*. Only *Siqāyah* remained in the hands of *Abd al Muttalib*'s son, *Abbās*, and *Rifādah* passed out of their hands. Since the fortunes of *Abd al Muttalib* had waned during the last part of his life, he could not leave any substantial property for his children. Though some of them, like *Abū Lahab*,[2] had acquired wealth of their own, *Abū Tālib* remained poor. The impact of his uncle's financial strains was felt by the Prophet also who was obliged to pasture cattle of the Makkāns for remuneration in order to contribute to maintenance of the house. The Prophet working as a herdsman for several years at a young age was, however, important for preparation for the spiritual role he was to play subsequently. As a shepherd, his long hours of loneliness in the lap of nature enabled him to observe the signs of God and learn patience, contemplation, and concentration. '*There was no prophet who was not a shepherd,*' the Prophet is reported to have remarked in later life, according to a *hadīth* reported by *Bukhāri*. The financial difficulties he faced at his uncle's house

---

1 *Balādhuri.*

2 *Original name—Abd al Uzzah.*

was, however, more than compensated by the great affection *Abū Tālib* and his wife *Fātimah* had for their nephew. They treated him as their own son. In later life, the Prophet used to recall their affection and kindness and remark that they would have let their own children go hungry rather than him. In Abū Tālib's house, he had a happy life in the company of his sons *Tālib* and *Aqīl* and daughter *Fakhita*.[1] Later on, when the Prophet was about 16, *Jāfar* was born with whom the Prophet developed great attachment, and the youngest son of *Abū Tālib*, *Alī*, who was born a few years after the Prophet's departure from the household, was to be subsequently brought up by the Prophet himself.

According to a story based on traditions, when the Prophet was 12 years old,[2] *Abū Tālib* took him along to Syria on a trade caravan. On the way, they stopped at *Basrā* near the dwelling of a Christian monk named *Bahīrah*. *Bahīrah* had in his possession some old Christian manuscripts which contained prediction of the coming of a prophet to the Arabs and also had details of his signs and features. Like a few other Christians and Jews, he also believed that the arrival of the Arabian prophet was imminent. When the caravan was approaching *Basrā*, the monk was amazed to notice that a small cloud was moving above the caravan so as to provide it protection from the hot sunrays. A more amazing fact was that when the party halted, the cloud ceased to move and remained stationary over the tree beneath which they took shelter, while the tree itself lowered its branches so as to keep them doubly in the shade. The portent made him expect some spiritual presence in the caravan and he immediately thought of the expected prophet. In order to ascertain the truth, he invited the entire party to a meal. But while all members of the party went to Bahīra's cell, the Prophet, being the youngest, was left behind to guard the camels and the baggage. Not noticing the things he was looking for in any of the individuals, the monk enquired about anyone's absence and, learning about the small boy left behind, called him also for the meal. One glance at the

---

1   *Later known as Umm Hāni.*

2   *According to some scholars, his age was then only 9.*

boy's face explained to the monk the miracle of the cloud. He was able to notice many features of both face and body which corresponded to what was in his book. After the meal, the monk further satisfied himself by asking the boy many questions about his way of life, about his sleep and dreams, and about his affairs in general. When asked to swear by *Al Lāt* and *Al Uzzah*, the boy refused and swore by *Allāh* only and replied to the questions. And finally, the monk persuaded the boy to show his back. *Bahīrah* already felt certain about his finding and when he noticed the expected mark, 'the seal of prophethood', he firmly recognized him as the expected prophet. He is said to have then told *Abū Tālib*: '*Take thy brother's son back to his country, and guard him against the Jews, for by God, if they see him and know of him that which I know, they will contrive evil against him. Great things are in store for this brother's son of thine.*' This story has been related in detail by *Ibn Hishām* and some other biographers of the Prophet, but some scholars have doubted the correctness of the report, both on account of weak chain of narrators as well as circumstantial evidence cited in its support. Many Orientalists have, however, claimed that it was from *Bahīrah* that the Prophet learned about monotheism and developed hatred of idol worship.

The Prophet's uncles saw to it that he, as also *Abbās* and *Hamzah*, received some military training. The Prophet, being of average height and strength, was no match for *Hamzah*, who had a huge body and proverbial physical strength and was to be outstanding on the battlefield. But still he had his training well, became a competent swordsman and wrestler, and showed a marked aptitude for archery. A strong point about his bowmanship was his extraordinarily powerful eyesight; he was able to count the stars of the constellation with naked eyes. But the Prophet did not receive any formal education and was not able to read and write. In the *Qurān*, he is referred as the *Ummi* Prophet which means that he was unlettered. However, since his illiteracy goes to prove the miraculous nature of the revelation, some Christian writers do not accept this interpretation of the meaning of the word *Ummi*, which to them, means a Prophet for the unlettered people who had not received a scripture from

God. They would claim that during his frequent journeys to the civilized cities as a merchant, he might have learnt the art of writing to some extent. But, it should be noted that in the early sources, there is no mention of the Prophet's ability to read and write. Instead, we come across a number of instances showing that when the Prophet wanted to write any document or letter, he used to give dictation to some literate person like *Alī*. It would not have been possible for him to conceal his literacy from his own family members and followers with whom he used to live so closely.

It was when the Prophet was in his mid-teens that he had an opportunity to witness the viciousness of intertribal warfare. A bad character of *Kinānah* treacherously killed a man of *Āmir*, one of the *Hawazīn* tribes of *Najd*, and took refuge at *Khaybar*. In order to take revenge in accordance with the tribal principle, the *Āmir* tribe attacked the tribe of the murderer, and before long, numerous allied and confederate tribes of the two also joined the war. The *Quraysh* were also involved in the conflict as allies of *Kinānah* and fought against *Qays*. This was a spasmodic conflict which came to be known as *Harb al Fijār* or the sacrilegious war, so named because it had started in one of the sacred months. The conflict dragged on for three or four years in which there was only five days of actual fighting. The Prophet's uncles *Zubayr* and *Abū Tālib* took their nephew also with them to one of the first battles, but he, being too young, was not allowed to fight. He was assigned the only duty of collecting enemy arrows which had missed their mark and handing them to his men for being shot back. But as reported by *Ibn Sād*, in one of the subsequent battles when the *Quraysh* were having a bad time, he was allowed to show his skill as a bowman and his performance impressed everyone. The war finally ended in a peace treaty, the *Quraysh* paying blood-wit of twenty men to *Hawazīn*.

Shortly after the sacrilegious war, the *Quraysh* took a great measure for the noble cause of maintenance of peace in *Makkah* in which the Prophet is said to have enthusiastically participated.[1] Under the prevailing Bedouin institution of vendetta, even a petty dispute between individuals had the potential of leading to high-magnitude tribal conflagration. The *Harb al Fijār* had made the *Quraysh* realize that unlike the civilized cities of Syria and Iran, they had no machinery for redressal of grievances and adjudication of disputes. There was a general consensus among the *Quraysh* to take initiative in this direction; and their consideration for justice was soon put to test by a scandalous incident that took place in *Makkah*. An important individual of the clan of *Sahm* bought some valuable goods from a Yamani merchant but refused to pay the promised price. The merchant, being a stranger to *Makkah*, had no supporter in the city and appealed to the *Quraysh* as a whole for help. The clans which had no traditional alliance with *Sahm* responded immediately. The *Quraysh* wanted to take action unitedly but the rift between the 'Scented Ones' and the 'Confederates' still continued and *Sahm* were from the group of the 'Confederates'. The lead was, however, taken by the chief of *Tāym*, *Abd Allāh ibn Judān*, who offered his house as venue of the meeting. Most of the clans of the group of the 'Scented Ones'[2] were well represented in the meeting and they were joined by *Adī* from the other group. After thorough deliberations, they formed an order or committee for the furtherance of justice and protection of the weak. They went in a body to the *Kābah* and took a vow that thenceforth, in respect of every act of oppression, they would unitedly support the oppressed against the oppressor without consideration for tribal alliances or other interests until justice was done. Thereupon, the Sahmite fellow was compelled to pay his debt. This pact was known as *Hilf al Fudūl*[3] which

---

1 *According to some scholars, the Prophet played a major role in this peace initiative.*

2 *Hashim, Muttalib, Zuhrah, Asad and Taym.*

3 *This name was in the memory of an ancient society instituted with a similar objective by the Jurhum tribe. This society of the ancient days had been composed of four persons named Fadl, Fadāl, Mufaddal, and Fudayl—collectively called Fudūl.*

has been translated as the 'League of the Virtuous'. Though short-lived, the League represented a laudable movement for maintenance of peace, for suppression of violence and injustice, and for vindication of the rights of the weak. Together with his uncles, the Prophet is said to have taken an active part in its formation and became one of its principal members having taken part in the oath. Another youth present in the meeting was *Abū Bakr ibn Abū Quhāfah* of *Tāym*, who was younger to the Prophet by a year or so and was destined to become his close friend. In later life, the Prophet was proud of having been a part of this historic peace meeting and remarked, '*I was present in the house of Abd Allāh ibn Judān at so excellent a pact that I would not exchange my part in it for a herd of red camels; and if now, in Islām, I were summoned unto it, I would gladly respond.*' It is sometimes argued[1] that the *Hilf* had a commercial objective, too. The clans which united in this League were in a weaker position than the Confederate clans and this might have been their instrument for fighting against the monopolists.

During his childhood, the Prophet used to accompany his relatives to the great fairs at *Ukāz, Majannah,* and *Dhū al Majāz* and listen to recitations of the hero poets as well as speeches of Christian and Jewish scholars who criticized paganism. These fairs were great cultural events and had significant educative value. Apart from these fairs, however, there used to be many other festivals, feasts, and social gatherings in which drunkenness and lack of restraint prevailed. But as reported by traditions, God persistently protected the Prophet from idol worship and such social gatherings where pagan practices used to prevail. There are numerous stories which, again and again, assert that the life of the Prophet remained free from all impurities of *Jahiliyah* since his very childhood. One evening, he heard that a wedding was to be celebrated and wanted to attend the same; but on the way, he suddenly felt tired and slept and was not able to attend the function. According to *Halābi*, once he was forced by his aunts to attend the festival of *Buwānah* in which one had to shave

---

1   *Karen Armstrong: 'Muhammad'.*

head and sacrifice animals. The Prophet went to the function but withdrew in the midst. He later informed that he had seen strange figures asking him not to take part in the festival. As per a *hadīth* reported by *Bukhāri*, once when the Prophet was served with food from an offering made to the gods, he refused to eat it. *Sūyūti* narrates a story attributed to *Alī* that the Prophet was once asked if he had ever worshipped an idol. He replied, *'Never.'* He was again questioned, *'Have you ever tasted wine?'* He emphatically said, *'No,'* and added, *'I always looked down upon these acts as shameful acts of kufr, even during that period of my life when the Holy Book had not been revealed to me and I had no idea of faith.'*

It was after the Prophet entered his twenties that his personality crystallized. Although of average built, he grew into a handsome and smart man with a luminous and highly attractive face. Most of the sources have mentioned that in addition to his natural beauty, there was a glaze or light on his face, the same which was there on his father's face, but in the son, it was more powerful. In manners and habits, he was far removed from other young men of the society and kept himself aloof from all the vices of the age. Sweet and gentle of disposition, he was highly sensitive to human suffering and had a special love for the company of the children. In his conduct, he was so perfect that he became the beloved of all with whom he came in contact. With a keen intellect, he had a great power of observation and possessed a powerful memory. It was his habit not to look over his shoulders. When he shook hands, he was never the one to withdraw his own first. After attaining adulthood, he started participating in trade journeys as agent of other merchants. He was highly successful in the job and built a reputation of great honesty and efficiency. It was due to his numerous qualities of character, his reputed truthfulness, and his absolutely fair dealing that he became an object of praise all over *Makkah*; the people started calling him *al Amīn*, which meant the reliable, the trustworthy, and the honest. In due course, after marriage with *Khadījah*, his popularity had risen to such an extent that the chiefs of *Quraysh* considered him as one of the most capable men of the generation who would not only restore the glory of *Hāshim* but also maintain the honour and power of the whole tribe throughout Arabia. And it was due to his great popularity that subsequently *Abū Lahab* proposed marriage of his two sons[1] with his daughters, *Ruqayyah* and *Umm Kulthūm*.

After joining the occupation of a trader and achieving success in that capacity, the Prophet was in a position to earn a better livelihood and might have thought that he would be able to afford marriage. We are told by some sources that he had developed a liking for *Fakitah*, daughter of *Abū Tālib*, and wanted to marry her. But those days marriage used to be considered more an instrument for cementing alliances with families and clans, and *Abū Tālib* preferred to marry his daughter to his cousin, *Hubayrah*,[2] of the clan of *Makhzūm*, whose power in *Makkah* was greatly on the increase. *Hubayrah* himself was rich and was a gifted poet. Attributing this humiliation to his lowly financial status, the Prophet might have had his confidence shaken as far as the question of marriage was concerned. Little did he, however, know that there was in store for him a far better and advantageous match. One of the wealthiest merchants of *Makkāh* was a twice-widowed woman named *Khadījah*, daughter of *Khuwaylid*, of the clan of *Asad*. A distant relative of the Prophet, she was a cousin of *Waraqah*, the Christian *hanīf*, and had a number of children. Though rather elderly, she was a 'determined, noble, and intelligent' lady of impeccable character, known in Makkan circles as *tahirah*.[3] She was still quite beautiful, and in view of her dignity, reputation, and wealth, many wanted her hand, but she refused. Since the death of her second husband, she had been personally managing her trading business for which she used to hire employees to carry merchandise to and fro on her behalf. She had heard much about the high character and fair performance of *al Amīn* as a trading agent. She, therefore, sent word to him, asking him to take some of her goods to Syria at double the fee she used to pay to others. She also offered him for the journey

---

1 *Utbah and Utaybah.*

2 *The son of his mother's brother.*

3 *Of a pure character.*

the services of her servant named *Maysarah*. The Prophet accepted
the proposed offer and set off with her goods.[1] The biographers
have narrated a few miraculous stories about this journey of the
Prophet as well. When he along with *Maysarah* reached *Basrā*,
he sheltered under the shadow of a tree near the cell of a monk
named *Nestor* which was perhaps the same tree under which he
had taken shelter some fifteen years ago, and *Nestor* was probably
the incumbent of the same cell in which *Bahīrah* used to live.
During conversation with *Maysarah*, the monk informed that
the man accompanying him was none other than a prophet.
Soon, *Maysarah* himself had a brief but clear vision of two angels
shading his companion from the sun's rays and he could know
why throughout the journey, the heat had been so unoppressive.

After returning to *Makkah*, they straightaway went to
Khadījah and explained the details of their business transaction.
The trip proved highly profitable and sale of the commodities gave
double of what had been paid for them. When the Prophet was
explaining the things to *Khadījah*, she was carefully observing
the appearance and behaviour of the young man. Subsequently,
Maysarah also informed her about the two angels and the
statement of the monk. He was full of praise for the extremely
good conduct and sincerity of the Prophet. On hearing the story,
Khadījah consulted her cousin *Waraqah*, who informed her that
if the story was true, then *Muhammad* was none other than
the Arabian prophet he had been expecting. The description
of *Maysarah* coupled with her personal observation of the
personality and conduct of the young man left *Khadījah* highly
impressed, and the high impression soon transformed into love.
The attraction was so intense that, against the usual practice, she
sent a woman friend of hers named *Nufaysah* to the Prophet to
find out whether he could be persuaded to marry her. *Nufaysah*
went to the Prophet and had talks with him. When asked why
he had not yet married, the Prophet truthfully replied that he
had no means to do so. She then suggested whether he would

---

1 *Ibn Sād reports that it was Abu Talib who went to Khadījah and
   arranged for Prophet's engagement as her trade manager.*

agree to marry a rich and respectable woman like *Khadījah*. The Prophet apologized saying that *Khadījah* was too highly placed for him. The woman undertook to sort out the problem of disparity of status whereupon the Prophet gave his consent. On receiving the tidings from *Nufaysah, Khadījah* called the Prophet and straightaway proposed marriage to which he agreed. '*Son of mine uncle,*' she is reported to have told him, '*I love thee for thy kinship with me, and for that thou art ever in the centre, not being a partisan amongst the people for this or for that; and I love thee for thy trustworthiness and for the beauty of thy character and the truth of thy speech.*'[1] Both agreed to speak to their uncles who were their guardians. Since Khadījah's father had died, she was under the guardianship of her uncle, *Amr*. The wedding was arranged and solemnized[2] by the two families in the presence of the two guardians.[3] Most of the traditions report that *Khadījah* offered her hand to the Prophet immediately after return from the trade mission; but a few reports suggest that this was nearly after three months of the same. The age of the Prophet at the time of marriage was 25 whereas it is reported by most of the traditions that *Khadījah* was then about 40. A few of the writers,[4] however, have mentioned that she was only 28 at the time of marriage. Considering the fact that she gave birth to as many as six children during the next ten years, the second report seems more likely.

After marriage the Prophet shifted to the house of *Khadījah*. The marriage proved a turning point in his life; overnight he became prosperous and entered the class of the Makkan nobility though he was generous enough to distribute among the poor whatever he received from her. Now relieved from financial

---

1 *Ibn Ishāq.*

2 *For a mahr of twenty camels or five hundred dirhams according to two different reports.*

3 *Some sources report that due to low financial status of the Prophet, Khadījah had not dared ask for the prior consent of her uncle, Amr. He was made to get drunk and sleep during the wedding ceremony and came to know of it only after the marriage was solemnized.*

4 *Ibn Habīb, Balādhuri and Abd Allāh ibn Masūd.*

hardships, he was in a position to spare maximum time on his natural inclination i.e. spiritual meditation and contemplation. Some of the Orientalists felt that the decision of the Prophet to wed *Khadījah* was one of convenience rather than of love and that marriage with such an elderly lady might have been emotionally frustrating for him. But on the contrary, the post-marital developments as recorded by the biographers prove that the marriage turned out to be 'wondrously blessed and fraught with great happiness, though not without sorrows of bereavement'.[1] One after another, *Khadījah* bore him six children, two sons, and four daughters. The eldest was a son named *Qāsim*[2] who died before completing two years of age. The next four consecutive issues were daughters who, in order of age, were *Zaynab*, *Ruqayyah*, *Umm Kulthūm*, and *Fātimah*, and the last was another son, *Abd Allāh* who died in infancy. Apart from being mother to his children, *Khadījah* turned out to be an indispensable companion to her husband, remarkably sharing all his feelings and inclinations and becoming his adviser in all matters. Subsequent history shows that during the early years of the Prophet's mission, it would have been very difficult for him to manage without her support and counsel. As a lady and wife without any failing, she is considered an exemplar among the womanhood of *Islām*. It needs to be noted by those who criticize the Prophet for his multiple marriages and alleged weakness for the fair sex that throughout the twenty-five years of his married life with *Khadījah*,[3] he remained totally devoted to her and did not think of marrying any other wife. And even after her death when he was in power and had a number of wives, he always missed her and continuously praised her. On one occasion, his face turned white with grief when he thought he had heard her voice. Such a high regard and affection for his deceased wife were

---

1 *Martin Lings.*

2 *It was after his birth that according to the Arabian practice, the Prophet came to be known as Abu al Qāsim meaning the father of Qāsim.*

3 *The marriage of the Prophet with Khadījah took place in 595. Khadijah died in the year 619.*

a source of irritation to *Āishah*, his favourite wife in later life, who is reported to have said, '*Never was I more jealous of any of the Prophet's wives than I was of Khadījah, although I never saw her; for the Prophet remembered her much. Once I hurt his feelings on this issue and he replied gravely, "God has blessed me with her love."*'

It is said that on the happy occasion of his marriage, the Prophet freed his female slave, *Barakah*, who was after sometime married to a Tadmibite.[1] The same day, *Khadījah* gifted to him a slave boy named *Zayd bin Hārithah* who was about 15 years old. Though he belonged to a respectable family,[2] he had been captured by some bandits and sold in *Makkah* as a slave. Before long, however, he was able to notice a few persons of his tribe who had visited *Kābah* for pilgrimage and through them managed to inform his father of his whereabouts by means of some verses he had himself composed. Receiving clues, Zayd's father and uncle came to *Makkah*, traced him out in the house of the Prophet, and requested for his liberty, offering to pay as much ransom as the Prophet should demand. The Prophet replied that from his side, *Zayd* was free and could go with them if he so wished even without any ransom. But *Zayd* had grown so attached with the Prophet that despite great insistence of his father, he refused to leave the Prophet and preferred to stay as a slave with him rather than live with his family as a free man. The biographers report that at the repeated persuasion of his father and uncle, *Zayd* told them that he had seen such great qualities in his master that he could never choose any other man above him. Thereupon the Prophet announced Zayd's freedom and also declared: '*All yee who are present, bear witness that Zayd is my son; I am his heir and he is mine.*'[3] From that day, *Zayd* became his adopted son and came to be known as *Zayd ibn Muhammad*. Seeing their son freed and established in honour, Zayd's father and uncle went back without

---

1 *After this marriage, she bore a son and, according to the Arabian custom of adopting Kunya, came to be known as Umm Ayman.*

2 *His father was of the famous northern tribe of Kalb and his mother belonged to the illustrious tribe of Tayy.*

3 *Ibn Ishāq.*

any bitter feeling. The story of Zayd's choice of slavery above freedom, speaks volumes about the magnetic personality of the Prophet even before revelation.

After ten years of marriage with *Khadījah*, when the Prophet was about 35 years old, his five-year-old cousin, *Alī*, the youngest son of his uncle, *Abū Tālib*, was adopted by him and entered his household.

The financial condition of *Abū Tālib* had become worse and he seemed not in a position to support his big family. The Prophet had consultations with another of his uncles, *Abbās*, who was a successful merchant; as advised by him, *Abbās* took charge of *Jāfar*[1] and the Prophet brought *Alī* to his house for upbringing. The Prophet's youngest son *Abd Allāh* had died about this time and in a sense *Alī* replaced him. Now their four daughters together with *Zayd* and *Alī* formed the immediate family of the Prophet and *Khadījah*. It was at this time that *Umm Ayman*, now divorced by her husband, came back to the household. She was now quite elderly, but due to the Prophet's great affection and regard for her,[2] *Zayd* subsequently married her. She bore a son to *Zayd* named *Usāmah* who was very dear to the Prophet and was brought up as his grandson.

It was when the Prophet was in his thirty-fifth year that he showed remarkable sagacity of a prophetic nature in sorting out a serious dispute in connection with reconstruction of the *Kābah*, which otherwise would have plunged the *Quraysh* in bloodshed. The building of the Sanctuary had short walls of the height of a man only and so, even when the door was locked, it was easily possible to get access to the same. And recently, there had been a case of theft of the property kept inside. Besides the fact that the building did not have a roof, the foundation of the building had been shaken due to floods, cracking its walls, and loosening the stones. The Quaysh, therefore, decided to demolish the walls and reconstruct the building raising the height of the walls and

---

1 *Now about 15 years old.*

2 *The Prophet is said to have remarked that anyone who wanted to marry a woman of paradise should wed Umm Ayman (Ibn Sād).*

providing it a roof. The required wood for constructing the roof became available from a wrecked ship at Jeddah and service of a Roman carpenter was also arranged. But such was the awe of the Sanctuary that the people were scared in laying their hands on the building lest it should cause divine wrath. The appearance of a large snake in the building further added to their fear and hesitation.

But the snake was soon caught and taken away by an eagle which served as an omen for starting the work. The work of demolition was hesitatingly started by the Makhzumite, *Walīd*, son of *Mughirah*. When no divine reaction was noticed, the work was started on a full swing and as a communal effort, responsibility of different sections was given to different clans.[1] *Bukhārī* mentions that the Prophet personally took part in the construction like an ordinary labourer, carried heavy stones on his shoulders getting the same bruised. However, when the reconstruction work was started and it reached the height at which the Black Stone was to be fixed, a serious dispute arose among the clans; each clan wanted the honour of lifting and fixing it to its place. The impasse continued for a few days and tension mounted to the extent of formation of alliances and preparations for fight. A few clan chiefs, in the customary style, dipped their hands in blood and pledged themselves to fight unto death for the cause. Large-scale bloodshed seemed imminent and the situation was on the verge of a civil war. In order to avert violence, the oldest

---

1   *The story of reconstruction of the Sanctuary has been described in detail by Ibn Ishāq and other biographers. It has been mentioned that from inside the corner of the Black Stone, a piece of writing was found which read as under:*

> *'I am God, the Lord of Becca. I created her the day I created the heavens and the earth, the day I formed the sun and the moon, and I placed round about her seven inviolable angels. She shall stand so long as her two hills stand, blessed for her people with milk and water.'*

Again, a manuscript was found beneath the Station of Ibrahīm in which was written: 'Mecca is the holy house of God. Her sustenance cometh unto her from three directions. Let not her people be the first to profane her.'

man present there suggested that whosoever was the first to enter the gate of the mosque the next morning should be allowed to arbitrate the dispute. The proposal was agreed to by all the clan chiefs. And the first man to enter the Mosque the next morning was none other than the Prophet himself. The very sight of *al Amīn* pleased and satisfied all who were convinced that he was the right person sent by God for the task. The Prophet at once understood the crux of the problem. He asked them to bring a piece of cloth. Placing the Black Stone on it, he asked each clan chief to take hold of different ends of the cloth and lift it to the required height. When the people lifted the stone placed on the cloth to the desired height, he took the same and placed it in the corner with his own hands, and this was accepted by everyone. The incident shows that even before prophethood, he wielded a type of public authority, had wide acceptability as a leader and arbitrator, and was able to inspire confidence in all.

What has been told above is all we know of the Prophet's public life during the first fifteen years[1] after his marriage. The period, specially the five years preceding the revelation, appears to be a silent phase of preparation during which there was an awakening of spiritual consciousness in his heart. Therefore, during this period, he generally kept himself aloof from public affairs and spent most of the time in introspection, meditation, and search of truth. Solitude now became dear to him. We are told by the biographers that adopting the age-old Abrahamic practice of meditation and prayer in solitude, he started going on long spiritual retreats. This practice was known as *Tahannūth* and was followed by the *Hunafa* and Christian hermits as well. For this purpose, he discovered a cave called *al Hirā*[2] on mount *an Nūr* which was ideally located for the job. Though hardly a mile or so away from the Prophet's house, it was in complete isolation and provided perfect silence and solitude for spiritual contemplation, and most importantly, the *Kābah* was clearly visible from there. The cave itself was so small that it would have been difficult to

---

1   *From 595 to 610.*

2   *Located to the north-east of Makkah.*

accommodate more than one person there. The Prophet started spending the whole month of *Ramadān* every year in this cave for meditation. He used to carry his provisions along and sometimes share his food with strange travellers there. Occasionally, he used to go home himself to fetch provisions in case of shortage, but sometimes, his wife used to carry the same to the cave. After completion of the period of retreat, it was his wont to proceed to the *Kābah* and perform the seven ritual circumambulations before going back home. Some sources have mentioned that he used to make his pious retreat along with his wife, but this sounds strange. Perhaps the narrator means that she used to visit the cave from time to time to replenish food and drinks. In the sources, we do not find any details about the thematic evolution of the Prophet's thinking during the retreats. Perhaps, he meditated on the meaning of life and death, mysteries of nature, and the Creator of the universe though social and moral evils of *Jāhiliyah* also might have been a subject of his thought. *Bukhārī* records a hadith attributed to *Āishah* that during the years preceding the revelation, the Prophet started seeing powerful dreams which used to come 'like the breaking of the dawn'. Such dreams have been called true visions (*al ruyah al Sādiqah*) because they used to be meaningful and turned out to be true. A story recorded by *Ibn Ishāq* informs that slightly before revelation, while approaching the cave, the Prophet would distinctly hear the words *'Peace be on you, O Messenger of God'*.[1] But looking here and there, he would not find anyone except trees and rocks and would be left amazed and frightened. Thus, during the last few years preceding the revelation, he was unobtrusively being prepared for the great spiritual task that lay ahead. But, as confirmed by the *Qurān*,[2] he was absolutely unaware that he was going to be commissioned by God as the last of the prophets.

---

1 *As salāmu alayka, ya rasūl Allāh.*
2 *Surah 28, Verse 86.*

CHAPTER IV

THE CALL
AND PRIVATE PREACHING
(610–13)

I t was during his annual retreat[1] at *ghār Hirā* in 610, after attaining the age of 40, that the Prophet had the extraordinary experience of receiving the first revelation. During one of the odd nights falling towards the end of *Ramadan*,[2] when he was alone in the cave and was either sleeping or in a trance, an angel (later identified as Gabriel) appeared before him in the form of a man. The angel asked him: *'Recite'*[3] and he replied, *'I am not a reciter.'*[4] Thereupon, the angel took hold of him and pressed him

---

1 *This is said to be the fifth annual retreat of his life.*

2 *Though there is disagreement regarding the exact date of the first revelation, many scholars regard it as twenty-seventh of Ramadan.*

3 *'Iqra' in Arabic. The word is sometimes translated as 'read'.*

4 *'Ma aqrau' in Arabic. Also translated as 'I cannot recite or read'.*

so tightly that he reached the limit of endurance. Thereafter, he released the Prophet and again asked, '*Recite*,' to which he gave the same reply. The angel repeated the direction for the third time also receiving the same answer and again squeezing the Prophet's body, but this time, he continued to hold him tightly and completed his command as under:

Recite in the name of your Lord who created,
Created man from a blood clot.
Recite, for your Lord is most magnanimous,
Who taught by the pen;
Taught man that which he knew not.[1]

Under the impact of the divine embrace, the Prophet recited the words after the angel whereupon the latter released him and vanished, and as the Prophet himself informed later on, he found the recited words permanently inscribed on his heart. Thus was he spiritually initiated into the process of receiving God's revelations. Different canonised *ahadīth* as well as traditions recorded by the biographers have reported the incident and its aftermath, though with minor differences in narration of facts as well as sequence of events. The *Qurān* in a subsequently revealed chapter[2] referred to the night of the first revelation as the'Night of Power'[3] on which God's decree's for the year are brought down to the earthly plain by angels and spirits.

---

1   *The first five verses of Surāh 'al Alaq' (ninety-sixth Surah) of the Qurān.*

2   *Surah 97, al Qadr. It runs as under :*
    'Verily we have sent it down on the night of destiny.
    And what has shown you what night of destiny is?
    The night of destiny is better than a thousand months.
    In it the angels and the spirits descend by their Lord's permission with every matter.
    It is peace until the rise of dawn.'

3   *The Muslims call it 'Laylat al Qadr' and consider it specially sacred for prayers.*

It is, however, confirmed by all sources that the Prophet's initial reaction to the vision was one of utter bewilderment and fear; he thought that he had been possessed by some evil spirit or had become a jinn-inspired *Kāhin*. Highly frightened, he fled from the cave and started descending down the mountain. When halfway down the slope, he heard the same awe-inspiring voice above his head, saying, '*O Muhammad! Thou art the apostle of God and I am Gabriel.*' Then the Prophet raised his eyes and saw the angel in the form of a man in the sky above the horizon, repeating the same announcement. The Prophet stood still, turning away his face from the brightness of the vision, but whichever direction he turned his face, the angel was always there.[1] The Prophet remained there for a while till the angel vanished. Even after the second vision, the Prophet remained utterly confused, not in a position to establish whether the vision he had had was a friendly one or associated with some demonic spirit. In great distress of mind, he rushed to his house, trembling with fear, and asked *Khadījah* to cover him with a cloth which she did. After getting calmed down, he explained to her what had happened and also expressed his fear of having been possessed. *Khadījah* did her best to reassure him and remove his misgivings, saying that his conduct had been so noble that God would not let a harmful spirit come to him. '*You have,*' she is reported to have said, '*nothing to fear. Have a rest and calm down. God will not let you suffer any humiliation, because you are kind to your kinsfolk, you speak the truth, you help those in need, you are generous to your guests and you support every just cause.*'[2] She is also said to have expressed her hope that he was to become prophet of his people. The reassuring and sympathetic talks of *Khadījah* allayed his fears to some extent. In order to

---

1   *Tabri says that the idea of having been possessed or forcibly made a poet was so loathsome to the Prophet that immediately after the vision of the cave, he began running towards the top of the mountain in order to commit suicide by jumping down; and he was prevented from taking this step by the reappearance of Gabriel who addressed him as the apostle of God.*

2   *Bukhāri and Muslim.*

obtain advise regarding her husband's experience, she then went to her blind cousin *Waraqah* who was well-versed in Christian and Jewish scriptures and had been expecting the emergence of an Arab prophet.[1] On hearing the story, the old and experienced *Waraqah* instantaneously recognized her husband as the expected messenger and remarked, '*Holy! Holy! by He who holds Waraqah's soul, it is the sublime Nāmūs*[2] *who has come to Muhammad; the same who had come to Moses. Indeed Muhammad is the Prophet of this people.*'[3] *Khadījah* immediately went back home and narrated Waraqah's remarks to the Prophet who returned in a comparative peace of mind to the cave in order to complete the duration of his retreat. This completed, he, in accordance with his practice, went to the *Kābah* for circumambulations. *Waraqah* happened to meet him there and no sooner had he seen him than he remarked, '*Surely, by Him in whose hand is Waraqah's soul, thou art the prophet of this people. There hath come unto thee the greatest Nāmūs, who came unto Moses. Thou wilt be called a liar, and they will use thee despitefully and cast thee out and fight against thee. Verily, if I live to see that day, I will help God in such wise as He knoweth.*'[4] After saying these words, *Waraqah* kissed his forehead.

The Prophet's initial diffidence and extreme distress of mind were, perhaps, due to the fact that he, like the *hunafa*, hated the idea of union or association with spirits which the sorcerers and soothsayers used to have. Moreover, he was a man of reclusive disposition, a lover of quiet and solitude. The very thought of being chosen as the messenger of God to face the entire mankind alone, a task involving tremendous responsibility, appalled him at first. But the reassurances of *Khadījah* and *Waraqah* helped restore his confidence and lightened his anxiety. This was followed

---

1   *According to some traditions, she went to Waraqāh alone leaving the Prophet sleeping, while a hadīth attributed to Āishah reports that the Prophet also accompanied her to Waraqah's house.*

2   *Identified as the angel who used to bring God's revelations to previous prophets i.e. Gabriel.*

3   *Ibn Ishāq.*

4   *Ibn Ishāq.*

by a reassurance from God in the form of a second revelation, though the manner in which it came is not known. This time, the revelation consisted of the first six verses of Surah *al Qalam*, numbering 68, which ran as under:

> *Nūn. By the pen and by that which they write.*
> *You are not, by the grace of your Lord, possessed*
> *Verily, yours is an unfailing reward*
> *And surely you have sublime morals.*
> *You will soon see, and they will see, which of you*
> *is afflicted with madness.*

Following this, some other revelations came which together with the reported trial of the angel by *Khadījah*,[1] further strengthened the Prophet's conviction about his new role. With the available data, we do not know as to how many revelations were there during the initial days; nor is it possible to identify the verses revealed.[2] But we do know that in course of a few days, as a result of intermittent revelations, the gloom which had gripped

---

1   *Ibn Ishaq reports that during the initial days Gabriel had been coming and transmitting revelations again and again. In order to totally remove doubts from the mind of the Prophet about the angel's genuineness, Khadījah once tried him with the help of the Prophet when the angel was present. After ascertaining from the Prophet that the angel was there, she sat beside the Prophet and removed her veil whereupon, as told by the Prophet, the angel immediately vanished.*

2   *Some scholars, however, opine that it was during the initial days only that once the Prophet, when again visited by Gabriel, came running to the house shivering and perspiring and covered himself with a cloak; and then were revealed the first seven verses of Surah al Mudaththir (74):*
   'O you who lie wrapped in your mantle.
   Arise and warn.
   Glorify your Lord.
   Purify yourself.
   Shun uncleanliness.
   Give not in order to have more in return.
   For the sake of your Lord endure patiently.'

the Prophet's mind finally dispersed and he genuinely believed that the messages coming through the angel were words of *Allāh* and that he had been chosen by Him as a messenger, and so he accepted the great task imposed on him. It should, however, be noted that the conduct of the Prophet following the first revelation, which has been vouched for by all sources, is a strong evidence of his genuineness and sincerity as a prophet.

After receipt of the first few messages during the days immediately following the incident of mount *Hirā*, the coming of revelations stopped for quite sometime.[1] This period of silence has been called *al Fatrah* by Muslim scholars. We are told by the biographers that this temporary discontinuation of revelations caused serious despair and desolation in the mind of the Prophet who feared that he had either incurred the displeasure of God or had been found unworthy of receiving revelations. Though *Khadījah* continually reassured him, he started having the ambivalence he had experienced during the days immediately following the first revelation. We learn from a *hadīth* reported by *Bukhāri* that during these days, in utter grief and agitation of mind, he used to feel like ending his life by throwing himself from the top of a steep mountain. But each time he reached the top of the mountain to do so, Gabriel would appear and convince him that he was truly the messenger of God. The words of the angel used to momentarily bring peace to his mind and he used to try to concentrate on his prayers and meditations. Muslim scholars have explained this period of silence as a trial by God for preparation of the messenger for receiving the voluminous message; it was necessary for him to develop need and love for his Master by a period of eager wait.[2] At last, however, the silence was broken by

---

1   *Traditions sharply differ as to the duration of suspension of revelation, the same ranging from six months to two and a half years depending on the tradition cited.*

2   *The unexpected period of silence is another testimony of the sincerity of the Prophet; it proves that revelation of God's messages was totally beyond his control.*

the revelation of *Surah* 93—the *Surah* of Morning[1]—which gave a further reassurance and the first command to start his mission:

> *By the morning brightness*
> *And by the night when it is still*
> *Thy Lord hath not forsaken thee nor doth He*
> *hate thee*
> *And last shall be better for thee than the first*
> *And thy Lord shall give unto thee and thou shalt*
> *be satisfied.*
> *Hath He not found thee an orphan and sheltered thee*
> *And found thee astray and guided thee*
> *And found thee needy and enriched thee?*
> *So for the orphan, oppress him not*
> *And for the beggar, repel him not*
> *And for the bountiful grace of thy Lord, proclaim it.*

The concluding part of this revelation contained a command to proclaim the message of God, and in accordance with it, the Prophet now started his mission; though the contours of the message were not yet clear enough, he began to privately preach his closest relatives and friends about the revelations and his prophethood. Before long, however, the ritual prayer (*salāt*) was prescribed. We are told by *Ibn Ishāq* that one day Gabriel appeared before the Prophet on the high land of *Makkah*, dug a hole on the ground with his heel from which a spring gushed out and taught him how to perform ritual purification (*wadū*) by giving a demonstration. After teaching the manner of purification which was essential for the worship, the angel, again by giving a demonstration, made him learn the method of worship. He showed him the postures and movements of the prayer—the standing, the inclining (*rukū*), the prostrating (*sajdā*), and the sitting positions—the Prophet repeating the actions of the angel. He also taught him the repeated magnification, i.e., the words

---

1 *Quranic name—Ad Duhā.*

Allāhu Akbar[1] and the final greeting, i.e., *as–Salāmu Alaykum.*[2] This was the main ritual prayer of the Muslims and was based on recitation of the *Qurān* in cyclical units of gestures, each single unit known as *rakah.*[3] After returning to his house, the Prophet taught his wife all that he had learnt and both started praying together.[4]

Reinforced by the newly prescribed ritual purification and prayer, preaching of the new faith met with considerable success in the coming months. The Prophet's better half had already embraced it from day one. She was followed by *Alī* and *Zayd*, both belonging to the Prophet's household. *Alī*, who is generally considered to have been the first male to enter the faith, was about 10 years old at the time.[5] *Zayd*, the adopted son of the Prophet, had hardly any influence in *Makkāh*. Before long, however, *Islām* was to receive an influential convert from outside the family and he was *Atīq ibn Uthmān* of *Tāym*, better known by his *kunya*, *Abū Bakr*. A wealthy merchant,[6] a widely knowledgeable person of gentle temperament and sociable nature, skilled in interpretation of dreams, possessing a wise judgment and having a good knowledge about the genealogy of *Quraysh*, *Abū Bakr* was a man of substance; he was liked and respected by all and the people used to frequently visit him for advice on different matters.

---

1 *God is most great'.*

2 *'Peace be on You'.*

3 *The physical movements of the salāt symbolized total surrender of one's being to God.*

4 *During early years, the ritual prayer was performed only twice a day, in the morning and in the evening. The five daily prayers were made obligatory after the mirāj which happened before the hijrah.*

5 *According to a story, one evening Ali noticed the Prophet and his wife offering salāt. Becoming curious, he enquired about the same and was invited to accept Islām. But due to the fear of his father's reaction, he initially dithered. The next morning, however, he joined the faith, deciding to conceal the same from his father.*

6 *According to Ibn Sād, he had 40,000 dirhams in his possession at the time of joining Islām.*

As a close friend of the Prophet, he reposed a high degree of trust in him and is reported to have accepted the faith without any hesitation, becoming a zealous Muslim. According to a tradition referred to by *Ibn Ishāq*, the Prophet later remarked about him: '*I have never invited anyone to accept Islām but he has shown signs of reluctance, suspicion, and hesitation, except Abū Bakr. When I told him of it, he did not hold back or hesitate.*' Since he had wide social contacts, his conversion to *Islām* gave a fillip to the mission; using his entire energy and resources, he was successful in inducting a number of trustworthy individuals to its fold, some of them from powerful families. *Ibn Ishāq*, in his *Sirah*, has listed out the first eight male Muslims. They, apart from *Alī*, *Zayd*, and *Abū Bakr*, included *Abd ar Rahmān bin Auf*[1] of *Zuhrā*, *Uthmān bin Affān* of *Umayyah*, *Zubair bin al Awwām* of *Asad*, *Sād bin Abū Waqqās* of *Zuhrā*, and *Talha bin Ubaydullāh* of *Taym*—all the five entering the fold of *Islām* through *Abū Bakr* and becoming enthusiastic Muslims. Of the many converts who embraced *Islām* slightly afterwards on the invitation of *Abū Bakr*, the names of *Abu Ubaydā bin al Jarrah* of *al Hārith*, *Abd Allāh ibn Masūd* of *Zuhrā*, and *Khālid ibn Saīd of Abdū Shams* stand out prominently.

During the first phase of preaching, which lasted for about three years, *Islām* was believed and practised in camera, the Muslims concealing their religion from the Makkans and dissimulating as belonging to the traditional faith. In order to avoid being seen, they used to perform prayers in some glens in the suburbs of *Makkah*. Towards the close of the period of concealment, they shifted their base to the house of *al Arqām*,[2] a wealthy Makhzumite. His large house was near the foot of mount *Safā* where the Muslims were able to preach and pray unobtrusively. But why did the Prophet decide to initially conceal the faith? In fact, he had been fore-warned by *Waraqah* that he would face violent criticism, rejection, and even banishment as

---

1 *His Original name was Abdū Amr which was subsequently changed by the Prophet in order to give it a pure Islamic colour.*

2 *He entered the faith through Abū Salāmah, the son of the Prophet's aunt, Barrah.*

a messenger. Being an ordinary human being grown like others and without any supernatural power to work miracles, he was sure, his claim to prophethood would be rejected and ridiculed. Moreover, the religion he was preaching violated the *Sunnah* and traditional gods of the Makkan traders; deeply attached to their customs, they were likely to treat the new faith as a sacrilege. The form of *salāt* with a Muslim grovelling on the ground in total submission to God was in contravention of the lofty tribal independence, pride, and arrogance and was sure to be rejected by the aristocratic Makkan leaders.

Despite secrecy, however, during the initial phase, an ever-increasing number of persons of both sexes, related to the Prophet or otherwise, pronounced the *Shahādah*[1] and entered the fold of *Islām*. The Prophet's four daughters and most of his cousins as well as aunts with some of their relatives joined the new faith. The group included *Jāfar ibn Abū Tālib*, *Abdullāh*, and *Ubaydallāh* sons of *Jahsh*, their sister, *Zaynab*, *Abū Salāmah*, son of the Prophet's aunt, *Barrah*, and *Umayr*, son of *Abū Waqqās*. From the female side *Umm al Fadl*[2] is said to be the first woman to enter *Islām* after *Khadījah*. Others who joined were the Prophet's aunt *Safiyyah*, Hamzah's wife, *Salāmah,* Jafar's wife, *Asmā*, and Umm al Fadl's sister *Maymunah*. Another to respond very early was *Umm Ayman*. By the end of the period of concealed mission, which is placed somewhere in 613, the Prophet was thus surrounded by a substantial group of Muslims. We, however, do not know their exact population; nor do we have definite information regarding sequence and chronology of these early conversions. According to W. M. Watt, when the faithful adopted the house of *al Arqām*, the total number of Muslims was 39. Pertaining to the same period, *Ibn Ishāq* gives a bigger list which, in addition to *Khadījah* and the first eight Muslims, includes 46 other names. From other sources, however, we get some more names and considering the fact that many Muslims used to strictly hide their faith, the total number might have been even larger.

---

1   *Lā ilahā illallāh, Muhammad ar Rasulullāh.*
2   *Wife of the Prophet's uncle Abbas.*

While most of the conversions took place after a good deal of persuasion, as per stories referred to by *Ibn Sād*, in a few of the cases, there was hardly any human effort. *Khālid Ibn Saīd* of the influential Shamsite family dreamed that he was being pushed into a big pit of raging fire by his own father and *Al Amīn* saved him by physically holding fast onto him. He hurriedly went to *Abū Bakr* for interpretation of the dream; on the latter's advice, he went straight to the Prophet, entered *Islām*, and kept it a secret. Similarly, another merchant of a powerful family of *Umayyah*, *Uthmān ibn Affān*, while returning from Syria, was one night awoken by a powerful voice: '*Sleepers, awake, for verily Ahmad hath come forth in Mecca.*' The words had a powerful influence on him but he did not know who *Ahmad* was. Before reaching *Makkah*, however, he was overtaken by *Talhā* of *Taym*.[1] During his journey, *Talhā* had passed through *Basrā* where a monk had asked him if *Ahmad* had yet appeared at *Makkah*. He narrated his story to *Uthmān* and both of them went to *Abū Bakr* for consultation. *Abū Bakr* seized on the opportunity and took them to the Prophet under the spell of whose personality, they professed *Islām*. Another story relates to *Abd Allāh ibn Masūd*,[2] who used to pasture flock. Once, the Prophet along with *Abū Bakr* passed by him; in order to satisfy his hunger, the Prophet extracted abundant milk from the udder of a tender eve which had never become pregnant. The mind-blowing miracle was enough to goad him to enter *Islām*.

Though a fair number of the Prophet's relatives joined the new faith, those who commanded significant status did not. His uncle and guardian, *Abū Tālib*, who was the chief of the Hashimite family, refused to give up the faith of his forefathers. Having seen his nephew offering *Salāt* together with his son, *Alī*, he had become aware of the new faith; but though he rejected the offer to profess *Islām*, he allowed them to continue with the new faith and decided to provide them full tribal protection. His other uncles, *Abbās* and *Hamzah*, also kept aloof from the new faith;

---

1 *A cousin of Abū Bakr.*
2 *A confederate of Zuhrah.*

and the fourth uncle, *Abū Lahab*, remained absolutely hostile to it. The Prophet's son-in-law, *Abū al Ās*,[1] refused to even consider the faith. From outside his family, the Prophet wished conversion of the top Makkan leaders, but none came forward. However, those who entered *Islām* remained committed and devoted to the Prophet and the faith to the highest degree. Developing great love and respect for him, they were keen to learn more and more about the revelations and imitate the Messenger in prayers and daily actions as also to brave all dangers involved in sticking to the new faith. They, especially those belonging to the family, lived in his closest association and watched all his daily activities. Had there been any failing or deception in the life of the Messenger, they would surely have detected the same. The unflinching faith and conviction of the Prophet's immediate followers is indeed a great testimony of his genuineness.

The class composition of the early Muslim community has been a subject of keen interest of modern historians. On the face of it, it was a disparate group of persons belonging to different backgrounds of society. While some were alienated younger sons, brothers, and cousins of the rich and powerful merchants, many were from the poor classes harbouring a feeling of deprivation. *Abd Allāh ibn Masūd* was a shepherd, *Khabbāb ibn al Arātt* had the profession of a blacksmith, and *Suhayb ibn Sinān* as well as *Ammār ibn Yasīr* were freedmen. There were many tribeless slaves and foreigners who had no tribal protection. The best known of the slaves was *Bilāl*, an Abyssinian negro who had a powerful and attractive voice, a quality which later made him the first *muezzin* of *Islām*. The community included a substantial number of females, too, both from the Prophet's family or otherwise, and included a few slave girls. But though from different walks of life, the vast majority of early converts belonged to two particular groups—the young and the weak. 'Weak' was a technical tribal term denoting inferior tribal status or no tribal protection rather than poverty. Coincidentally, however, most of the weaker members of the community also happened to be economically

---

1 *Husband of the Prophet's eldest daughter Zaynab.*

poor having lowly social status. From yet another viewpoint, the early Muslims had a unifying feature—they mainly belonged to the *Hilf al Fudūl* group representing the weaker clans[1] in the city. It has been remarked by some modern scholars that in the beginning, *Islām* was a movement of young and the poorer people, a peripheral group which felt deprived and did not matter much in the society. Many of the Makkan aristocrats who were not aware of the new faith, therefore, used to wonder why *al Amīn* was associating with such lowly elements.

What motivated these people to join the new faith despite apprehension of stiff opposition of the established order? This question has been debated at length by modern historians who attribute it to the social tension which the new Makkan society had generated due to concentration of wealth in a few hands. Rise of capitalism accounted for an attitudinal change of the leaders and represented a collapse of the tribal code of conduct. On the other hand, Quranic revelations negated the power and wealth of the merchant-leaders and talked in terms of socio-economic equality and justice. Therefore, the persons from such classes which had lost power and importance and stood dissatisfied had a significant motivation to flock to the new faith. This was what may be called a socialistic theory of the origin of *Islām* viewing it as the result of a class conflict between the infant Muslim community and the Makkan oligarchy. Such a view, however, exaggerates one particular aspect of the Islamic message to the detriment of others. Moreover, as abundantly reflected by the traditional sources, different conversions took place under different circumstances in which a variety of motivating factors were at work and, therefore, it would not be fair to generalize the same. While moral uprightness and egalitarianism of *Islām* were factors in some cases, no less important was the spiritual attraction of the new faith, and one cannot ignore the magnetic personality of the Prophet himself whose personal example was a great inspiration. A yet more important factor was the mesmerizing linguistic beauty and extraordinary eloquence of

---

1 *Hāshim, Al Muttalib, Zuhrah, Taym, Al Hārith and Adi.*

the *Qurān*, recitation of which had a spellbinding effect. Many a conversion took place due to the irresistible impact of the Qurān's recitation, the best example of which is the conversion of *Umar ibn al Khattāb* who is reported to have said, *'As I heard the Qurān, my heart was softened and I wept, and Islām entered into me.'*

While the secret mission was going on leading to many conversions, there was a continuous flow of revelations which had now become more copious. We do not have definite information regarding all revelations received during the period, but it is generally believed that many important verses of *Surah 73— al Muzammil, 74—al Mudaththir, 88—al Ghāshiyah, 80—al Abasa, 84—al Inshiqāq, 104—al Humazah, 69—al Haqqāl, 101—al Qāriyah, 81—al Takwīr,* and so on relate to this early period. The faithful used to keenly wait for new revelation, and immediately after it came down, the Apostle used to transmit it to those with him; then it used to pass on from mouth to mouth, memorized and recited. Apart from being taken by heart, the followers also used to write it down on whatever material was available. The work of writing was later carried out by the Apostle's secretaries, the most famous of whom was *Zayd bin Thābit.* However, the revelations were not being placed chronologically in the book[1] which was taking shape. The verses used to be arranged in an order that Gabriel advised each time. We are told that each year, the Prophet would recite to the angel all the verses that had been revealed so far in order to ascertain the correctness of the arrangement. As regards transmission of the revealed verses, the Prophet, in the early days, had the habit of repeating loudly whatever was revealed, even during the course of revelation. Subsequently, however, he was instructed by God[2] to listen carefully to each revelation and not to impose a meaning on a verse prematurely. After that, whenever any new message was revealed and recorded by the writers, the Prophet used to get the material read over immediately in order to verify its correctness.

---

1 *Now known as Qurān.*

2 *Qurān 20: 114 and 75: 16–18*

There was no uniform pattern of the manner in which revelations were received; they came in different ways at different times. Some of the ways have been mentioned in the *Qurān* itself: '*It was not for a human being that God should speak to him except by revelation, or from behind a veil, or that he should send a messenger to reveal what (God) willed by His permission.*'[1] Based on the statements of eyewitnesses as well as description by the Prophet himself, Muslim scholars have listed different manners of revelation which included a few others besides those mentioned in the verse; but their interpretation of the details is sometimes different. The most common manner of revelation was through the voice of Gabriel without vision, though sometimes the Prophet used to distinctly see as well as hear the angel,[2] and in this type of revelation, the message used to be clear enough. But, more often than not, the voice used to be obscure, though finally the words used to be totally comprehensible. According to a *hadīth* referred to by *Bukhāri*, the Prophet himself remarked, '*Sometimes it comes to me like the sound of a ringing bell and that is the hardest to bear; then it stops, whilst I remember everything that has been revealed, well impressed on my memory. On other occasions, the angel appears to me in the form of a man, and I retain well what he says.*' The sources, however, inform us that whatever was the manner of revelation, the process generally was a painful and difficult one, characterized by convulsions, nervousness, perspiration, and so on.[3] The Prophet is reported to have once remarked, '*Never once did I receive a revelation without thinking that my soul had been turned away from me.*'[4] Sometimes he would grow pale with the effort and cover himself with his cloak. The Companions have mentioned some other physical states—like

---

1 *Qurān 42: 51.*

2 *Sometimes in angelic persona and other times in the form of a human being.*

3 *It is on the basis of the disturbed physical state of the Prophet during revelations that some medieval polemicists coined the absurd theory that the Prophet was suffering from epilepsy.*

4 *Suyūti.*

motionlessness, reddening of the face, and a condition showing
as if he was intoxicated or hypnotized—which used to be visible
during different revelations. On a few occasions, when the
revelations came on mount, a sudden increase in weight used
to be noticeable which tended to disbalance the camel as if the
weight would break its legs.[1] *Zayd bin Thābit* relates[2]: '*One day
there was a great crowd and everyone was sitting on the ground with
folded legs; revelation began to arrive, his knee was on my thigh and
weighed so heavy that I feared that my femur will break.*'

By the end of the phase of in-camera preaching, the volume
of revelations in proportion to the total length of the *Qurān*
was still negligible. Nevertheless, the revelations so far received
were able to crystallize the fundamental elements of the Quranic
message:

1. The foremost was the oneness of God, His greatness,
    goodness, benevolence, omniscience, omnipresence, and
    unlimited power. The revelations sang of his glory as
    the Creator and Sustainer and associated his name with
    mercy (*ar Rahīm*), compasion (*ar Rahmān*), and peace
    (*as Salām*). By extension, they also referred to his signs,
    the marvels of nature, and to their harmonious working
    together which testified so eloquently to the oneness of
    the sole originator.

2. The verses mentioned of the ephemeral nature of all
    earthly things, of death and life after death. They
    warned of the impending destruction of the world and
    also spoke of the certainty of Resurrection and of the
    Last Judgment followed by Hell and Paradise.

3. They also instructed that in response to God's favours
    and benevolence, human beings should worship Him
    and thank Him by prayers—*salāt*, *zakāt*, night vigil,
    and recitation of the revealed messages.

4. Implied in the revelations was a belief in the special
    status of *Muhammad* not only as a warner (*Nadhīr*) but

---

1 *Hanbal.*

2 *Bukhāri.*

also as a Messenger of God (*Rasūl*),[1] to be respected and imitated to the highest degree.

5. Contained in the revelations was also the exalted status of the *Qurān* as the revealed words of *Allāh*, sacrosanct and infallible, to be accepted as a miracle and accorded the highest degree of reverence. One of the verses of the *Qurān* itself revealed its importance: '*Had we sent this Qurān on a mountain, you would have seen it humble itself and cleave asunder in awe of God.*'[2] It was later that the *Qurān* was to be regarded as the earthly reproduction of an uncreated and eternal heavenly original.[3]

6. Last but not the least, the message described the socio-economic and moral dimensions of the new faith, stressing on social justice and economic equality. It contained an admonition to care for the orphans, to feed the hungry, to help the poor and the destitute, and to redistribute wealth by alms giving. It enjoined the people to be generous with their wealth and not to amass riches.[4]

Thus focused, the new faith now came to be known as *Islām*, which meant surrender or submission (to the will of God). The believers now started greeting each other by the phrase given by Gabriel: '*Peace be on you*'; to this the answer used to be '*and on you be Peace*'. The sacrament of thanksgiving and that of consecration or dedication were also adopted from the revealed verses. The first read '*Praise be to God, the Lord of the Worlds*'[5] whereas the second

1 *This word was to be later distinguished from 'Nabi' which meant Prophet whereas.*
 'Rasul' implied a Nabi who brought a Book or message.

2 *Quran 59: 21.*

3 *Quran 75: 22*

4 *Quran 93:9-10, 104:1-3 and 69:33-35.*

5 *Al hamdu lillāhi Rabbil Ālameen.*

was '*In the name of God, the infinitely good, the all merciful*'.[1] The second one became the first verse of every *Surah* of the *Qurān* except *Surah* 9; the Prophet used it to inaugurate every Quranic recitation, and by extension, every act or initiative.

----

1 *Bismilla hir Rahmān ir Rahīm.*

CHAPTER V

PUBLIC PREACHING
AND ITS REACTION
(613–15)

I t was after about three years of the concealed mission that the Prophet received clear-cut command from God to openly preach and propagate the revealed religion. '*Proclaim what you have been ordered and turn aside from the polytheists*,' instructed one of the verses.[1] Another verse directed: '*Warn thy family, thy nearest relations, and lower thy wing to the followers who follow thee*.'[2] This was a great responsibility and knowing that such a move was likely to invite violent reaction from the Makkan leaders, the Prophet was mentally disturbed. We are told by *Balādhuri* that following the command, the Prophet remained confined to his house for about a month; thinking

---

1   *Qurān 15: 94*.
2   *Qurān 26: 214–15*.

that he was ill, his aunts even went to enquire about his health. Eventually, Gabriel came and advised him to execute the instruction immediately failing which God might punish him. The Prophet, therefore, made up his mind to start with his own clan and invited forty of the leading men of *Hāshim* and *Abd al Muttalib* to a modest meal. According to a *hadīth* attributed to *Alī*, he, as advised by the Prophet, had arranged only a leg of mutton and a cup of milk which only one person could have finished. But before serving the food, the same was treated by the Prophet and all the invited leaders were miraculously able to have their fill out of the meagre quantity. After the meal, the Prophet wanted to address the invitees in order to inform them of the message of *Allāh*. But, before he could speak, *Abū Lahab*, who was also present,[1] interrupted and alleged that the Prophet had bewitched his guests upon which the leaders went away. The task left unaccomplished, the Prophet again invited them to a feast the next evening. After the meal was over, he stood up and said, '*I know of no Arab who has come to his people with a nobler message than mine. I have brought you the best of this world and the next. God has ordered me to call you to Him.*'[2] He then asked if there was anyone to help him shoulder the great responsibility. Everyone remained silent except the 13-year-old *Alī* who stood up in support to address the audience. Though the Prophet had been able to convey the substance of his message, the men went away laughing and saying to *Abū Tālib*: '*He has ordered you to listen to your son and obey him.*'[3]

Undeterred by the setback, however, the Prophet now decided to direct his call to all Makkans as a whole. He climbed the top of mount *Safā* and gave a call to the people of the whole *Quraysh* tribe. Thinking that he had some important announcement to make, the clan leaders with their men assembled at the foot of the hill. As described by *Ibn Hishām*, he addressed them by taking names of the clans and asked, '*If I warn you that down*

---

1 *According to some sources, he attended the dinner uninvited.*

2 *Tabari.*

3 *Tabari.*

in this valley, armed horsemen are closing in to attack you, would you believe me?' They answered almost in one voice: *'Certainly. You are trustworthy and we have never heard you tell lies.'* The Prophet then continued: *'Well, I am here to forewarn you of violent torments! God has ordered me to admonish my nearest kinsmen. I have no power to protect you from anything in this life, nor to grant you blessings in the life to come, unless you believe in the oneness of God.'* But, once again, *Abū Lahab* intervened and remarked, *'Woe to you on this day! Did you assemble us for this?'* Thus instigated, the Makkan leaders became offended by the Prophet's warning and left in disdain.

The new religion had now become public, but though some tension was growing,[1] the *Quraysh* as a whole showed a tendency to tolerate it. In fact, they took *Islām* as only a minor religious development like that of the *hunafā* which would fizzle out in course of time. Their initial reaction was, therefore, simply one of ridiculing the Prophet and mocking at the principles of the new faith. But, before long, the real implications of the Islamic movement became clear to them and they conceived it as an extremely dangerous threat to their interest in more ways than one. The Prophet was now openly denouncing polytheism and idol worship, speaking against their traditional religious practices and insulting their revered gods and goddesses. Apart from asking the Makkans to adopt an entirely new religious attitude, he was impairing the religious status of the *Kābah* on which depended the name, fame, and prosperity of *Quraysh*. Further, *Islām* was attacking their social values—traditions, customs, principles,

---

1 *Tabari refers to a story that once when the Muslims were offering prayer in a glen outside Makkah, they were noticed by a number of idolators who rudely disturbed the Muslims and scoffed at them. Both came to blows and a Muslim, Sād ibn Abū Waqqās, a cousin of the Prophet, hit and wounded one of the disbelievers with the jawbone of a camel, thus shedding the first blood in the cause of Islām. This was, however, an exceptional incident and subsequently revelations were received (Qurān 3: 10 and 76: 17) commanding the Prophet to refrain from violence and take recourse to patience; and this was always scrupulously followed by the Muslims until, much later, command was received otherwise.*

and inveterate practices of their forefathers—to which they were so strongly attached. Their way of life was being declared foolish and their forefathers branded infidels. In addition to the Quranic attitude rejecting the values by which they lived, *Islām* was creating a fault-line in the society, separating a man from his father, brother, wife, and even the family in general and endangering clan and tribal loyalties; the new ideology was, therefore, viewed as splitting the tribe and endangering the society.

Added to these aspects of the new faith was the political and dynastic jealousy of the powerful clan chiefs and wealthy merchants. It was difficult for them to digest the idea of an unimportant individual acquiring the power and popularity of prophethood and becoming the ruler of *Makkah.* And if at all a Prophet was to come, they thought, he should have been one of the leading clan chiefs. It was, however, due to its economic configuration that the new faith became highly resentful to the Makkan merchant leaders. The power of the *Quraysh* in the peninsula largely depended on their trade and economic activities. Acquiring monopoly of the regional trade, they had built up a capitalistic society having a hierarchy based on economic status. The members of the commercial syndicate of the city who wielded all powers, therefore, had a strong vested interest in continuance of the existing socio-economic order. But now *Islām* was emerging as a critique of their economic policies and was attacking business practices which they considered essential to the successful conduct of commercial operations. The *Qurān* was advocating redistribution of wealth and socio-economic equality—a classless society. Wide acceptance of the new faith was, thus, sure to give a death-blow to the ascendancy of the merchant leaders.

Alarmed by disturbing dimensions of the Islamic movement, the *Quraysh* leaders, therefore, considered it not only sacrilegious but also a grave threat to their very existence. They decided to oppose it with all might and immediately arrest its spread at all cost; restraining the Prophet from spreading seditious and dangerous ideas was now the prime task. But use of force or physical violence against the Prophet was not possible as he had full protection of *Abū Tālib*, the chief of *Hāshim* clan; according to the Bedouin custom, any harm done to him could establish a vendetta and the power of a clan chief in this regard was sacrosanct. The *Quraysh* leaders, therefore, went in a delegation to *Abū Tālib* pressurising him to stop his nephew from spreading dangerous and undesirable ideas. Though the Prophet's uncle gave them a conciliatory reply, he did not do anything to prevent his nephew from spreading his religion. The *Quraysh* were consequently angry, took a second delegation, and threatened *Abū Tālib*: '*You have a high and lofty position among us, and we have asked you to put a stop to your nephew's activities, but you have not done so. By God, we cannot endure our customs mocked and our gods insulted. Until you rid us of him, we will fight the pair of you until one side perishes.*'[1] This time, *Abū Tālib* was mentally disturbed. He called his nephew and said, '*Spare me and yourself. Do not put on me a burden greater than I can bear.*'[2] Under the impression that his uncle was going to yield to the pressure exerted by *Quraysh* and withdraw his protection, the Prophet broke into tears and said, '*O my uncle, by God, if they put the sun in my right hand and the moon in my left on condition that I abandon this course until God has made it victorious, or I perish therein, I would not abandon it.*'[3] Making this remark, he got up to go but *Abū Tālib*, moved by the feelings and reaction of his nephew, stopped him and said, '*Go and say what you please, for by God, I will never give you up on any account.*' When the *Quraysh* perceived that *Abū Tālib* would not abandon his nephew, they again went to him and offered to hand him over the most handsome young man of *Quraysh*[4] to be adopted as son in lieu of his nephew who was to be handed over to *Quraysh*. But the offer was rejected outright by *Abū Tālib*. This was the parting of the ways between *Abū Tālib* and *Quraysh*. *Abū Tālib* then composed passionate verses indirectly attacking those

---

1 *Ibn Ishāq.*

2 *Ibn Ishāq.*

3 *Ibn Ishāq.*

4 *The name of the boy was Umāra.*

of the *Quraysh* who had abandoned him and strongly reaffirming his protection and support for his nephew. Those verses, however, won over the support of the clan of *Abd al Muttalib* for his cause.

In the meantime, the Prophet was preaching *Islām* unabated, its ranks getting swelled up by new converts every day. Failed in their attempt to persuade *Abū Tālib* and panicked by the increasing influence of the new faith, the *Quraysh* leaders now banded themselves more strongly to oppose and exterminate it. The biographers tell us of a dozen odd powerful individuals, mostly clan chiefs and wealthy merchants, who spearheaded the anti-Islamic movement. Foremost among them in status was *Walīd ibn al Mughīrah*, the chief of *Makhzūm*. As the chief of the most powerful clan, he was the unofficial leader of the whole *Quraysh*. But far more inveterate as an enemy of *Islām* was his nephew, *Abū al Hakām*, pejoratively called *Abū Jahal* (father of ignorance) by the Muslims out of hatred, and it was by this name that he became famous in the annals of *Islām*. An irascible character, he was known for his vindictiveness and ruthless behaviour. He was a successful merchant in his own right and had ambition to succeed his uncle as chief of *Makhzūm*. With his extreme hatred of *Islām*, he became the most vociferous critic of the Prophet and turned out to be the most relentless of the persecutors of Muslims. If a convert had substantial protection, he would merely insult him and indulge in character assassination. If he were a merchant, he would threaten to ruin his trade by boycott. And if a Muslim was weak and unprotected, he would have him tortured directly or through his influence with other clans. During the initial years, *Abū Jahal* was the virtual leader of opposition to *Islām*.

Less violent than *Abū Jahal* in hostility towards the Prophet was *Abū Sufyān*, chief of Ummayyad branch of *Abdū Shams* which was then the second most powerful clan of *Quraysh*. He had married *Hind*, the daughter of *Utbah*.[1] Though highly intelligent and successful both in politics and trade, he was an opportunist and was known for his calculative moves. Another leader known

---

1 *Chief of the other branch of Abdu Shams.*

for his wickedness and worst hostility to the Prophet was his own eldest uncle, *Abū Lahab*, who was actively supported in his anti-Muslim activities by his equally ill-famed wife, *Umm Jamīl*; she used to throw thorns on the Prophet's path for which she received the epithet 'bearer of the wood' in the *Qurān*. It was due to their harassment of the Prophet that the duo was made an object of sinfulness and divine displeasure in the *Qurān*.[1] Among other significant members of the opposition group were *Utbah ibn Rabīah* and his brother *Shaybah* of *Abdū Shams* and the elderly *Umayyah bin Khalāf*, chief of *Jumah*. While the first two were less violent and more conciliatory in the group, *Umayyah* was extremely hostile to *Islām*. Whenever he saw the Apostle, he slandered and reviled him for which he was condemned in *Surah* 104[2] of the *Qurān*. Another leader, *Ās ibn Waīl* of *Sehm*, was supposed to be the wealthiest person of the city and was also rich in children. *An Nadr bin al Hārith* of *Abdū Manāf* also figured in the group. A widely travelled person, he used to think of himself as highly knowledgeable, the ideologue of the opposition group; he used to frequently interrupt the Prophet in his speeches and claimed that he would be able to tell better stories than him, thereby getting indirect condemnation in the *Qurān*.[3] The group also included several other individuals—the notorious *Uqbah ibn Abū Muait* of *Umayyah*,[4] *Abul Bakhtarī* of *Asad*, *Aswad bin al Muttalib* of *Asad*, and also a few prominently able and successful young men of *Quraysh* like *Khālid ibn al Walīd*,[5] *Amr ibn al Ās*

---

1   *Surah 111 (Lahab):*
    'Abū Lahb and his hands, God blast
    His wealth and gains useless at last,
    He shall roast in flames held fast,
    With his wife, the bearer of wood, aghast,
    On her neck a rope of palm-fibre cast.'

2   *al Humazah.*

3   *Qurān 6: 104.*

4   *Who used to torture the Prophet during prayers by novel mischiefs.*

5   *The youngest son of the chief of Makhzūm — a great warrior.*

of *Sehm*,[1] *Safwān ibn Umayyah* and *Umar ibn al Khattāb* of *Adī*. *Umar*, who was the nephew of *Abū Jahal*, was to later become one of the strongest pillars of *Islām*. But then, as a young man of 26, he was fanatically devoted to the old religion. He was of a violent nature, always ready for more extreme methods. In the clash between *Islām* and *Quraysh*, he, therefore, became one of the fiercest opponents of *Islām*.

In order to combat the menace of *Islām*, various leaders of the opposition group chalked out their common policies by meticulous mutual consultations. Their strategy, however, was flexible and opposition to *Islām* took different forms at different times ranging from propaganda and inducement to violent persecution and boycott. First of all, a war of propaganda against *Islām* and its founder was launched. Serious calumnies were spread against the Prophet.[2] His prophethood was rejected and he was charged of being either a fraud or mentally sick. He was abused and reviled, accused of atheism and branded an enemy of gods. The people were warned to beware of him as he was propagating dangerous ideas and breaking families and society. Most of the *Quraysh* described him as a 'dangerous sorcerer' or a possessed poet or soothsayer who, by the power of his magical poetry and eloquence, was casting spell on the people. Some mischievously changed his name to *Mudhammam* which meant reprobate. Since the Arabs had a passion for poetry and considered the same as a very effective means of propaganda, *Quraysh* engaged their poets[3] to carry out a campaign of vilification against the Prophet through poetry. The principles of *Islām*, especially those of Day of Reckoning and Resurrection, were challenged on an ideological plain. How could dead bodies that had rotten away come to life again, they asked. How would it be possible for their ancestors to rise from their graves and stand before the Lord, they questioned.

---

1 *Warrior and diplomat.*

2 *We know of many of them from refutations in the Qurān.*

3 *Abū Sufyān ibn al Hārith, Amr ibn al Ās, Abdullāh ibn al Zibāri.*

The *Qurān* replied that if *Allāh* could create a human being out of a tiny drop of blood, he could easily resurrect the dead bodies.[1]

The propaganda campaign was initially limited to the inhabitants of *Makkah* alone, but soon, it became necessary to extend it to the outsiders visiting the city. The time for annual pilgrimage of the *Kābah* was approaching and it was feared that, failed in his attempt to induce *Quraysh*, the Prophet would now turn his attention to the visiting pilgrims. The pilgrims would hear their gods insulted by the Muslims and get invited to *Islām*. This, apart from casting an adverse effect on trade, would damage the image of *Quraysh* as guardians of the Sanctuary, and there was also apprehension of the irresistible magical effect of the *Qurān* leading to large-scale conversion of the outsiders. The *Quraysh* leaders, therefore, convened their Assembly and, after deliberations, decided to frustrate the designs of the Prophet by insulating him from the visitors. Following the advise of *Walīd ibn al Mughīrah,* they decided to warn the pilgrims before entry into the city of the 'dangerous sorcerer' who by the sheer power of his magic would destroy their religion and separate them from their families. When the pilgrims began to arrive, they posted their men on different approach routes and warned them accordingly, advising them not to meet or communicate with *Muhammad* lest they should fall under his spell.

The isolation strategy, however, proved counterproductive in the long run; little did the *Quraysh* leaders know that by opposing *Islām*, they were taking the first step towards its acceptance. When the pilgrims went back home, they carried the news of the strange preacher who, at the risk of his own life, was calling people from different corners of Arabia to give up religion of their forefathers. Moreover, although the Prophet could not have direct communication with the pilgrims, other Muslims did speak to them and well conveyed the unique message of the *Qurān*. Thus, *Islām* received a good deal of publicity and was talked about throughout Arabia. Its fame also reached *Yathrib* rousing tremendous curiosity as the Jews of that oasis had already

---

1   *Qurān 45: 23 and 26; 77: 83.*

been expecting arrival of a new prophet. Apart from leaving an unfavourable long-term impact, the policy of isolation could not prove impregnable and a few of the outsiders did manage to meet the Prophet, embracing *Islām* at the very first encounter.

One such person was *Abū Dharr* of *Banī Ghifār*. Though a highway robber, he had rejected idol worship and was a firm believer in the oneness of God. He had heard about the Prophet and his message and so, despite warning of the *Quraysh* on arrival, he managed to meet the Prophet and listen to the recitation of a *Surah*, and this immediately resulted in his profession of *Islām* whereupon the Prophet remarked, '*Verily, God guideth whom He will.*'[1] As advised by the Prophet, he returned to his native place, had many of his people enter *Islām*, and continued with the practice of looting the trade caravans, especially of *Quraysh*. But whenever he overpowered a caravan, he offered to give back the property if the men embraced *Islām*. In due course, he became a highly devoted and renowned Companion of the Prophet. Another famous conversion which took place despite insulation of the Prophet was that of *Tufayl* of *Banī Daws*, an outlying western tribe. On arrival at the city, he was warned against speaking or listening to *Muhammad*. Scared of being bewitched, he stuffed his ears with cotton before entering the Sanctuary. The Prophet was there reciting some verses, but though Tufayl's ears were stuffed, some sound of recitation did enter them, making him curious. He was himself a poet and a person of considerable standing in his tribe. The incident stirred his self-respect and he felt confident of distinguishing between good and evil if he heard the Prophet. He, therefore, went to the Prophet's house, listened to the latter's explanation of *Islām*, and entered the faith. Then he returned to his people and started preaching *Islām*. His father and his wife followed him into the faith immediately while others took sometime.

Derision and propaganda had so far failed to stop the Prophet from preaching *Islām* and conversions were also taking place. The *Quraysh*, therefore, decided to put down the new faith by

---

1 *Ibn Sād.*

force and embarked on a policy of well-organized persecution of the Muslims not refraining from resorting to violence whenever possible. Each family took upon itself the task of strangulating the new religion within its own circle; each household tortured its own members or clients or slaves who were believed to have attached themselves to *Islām*. Weaker Muslims of both sexes—slaves, servants, and those who had no support or protection—were subjected to physical violence in different ways. They were mercilessly beaten up, exposed to the burning heat and scorching sand of the desert, deprived of food and water and offered the alternative of recanting to the old faith or death. Muslims of noble descent were also victimized and subjected to brutal treatment by the family elders. Traditional stories throw light on how they were put into confinement, starved and beaten with sticks in order to bring them back to the old religion. *Uthmān ibn Affān* was cruelly treated, harassed, and even tied with rope by his uncle. The uncle of *Zubayr bin al Awwām* wrapped him in a skin-mat which was smoked from underneath causing torture by suffocation. According to a story referred to by *Suhayli*, *Saīd ibn al Ās* hit his own son, *Khālid*, who had turned a Muslim, breaking his head.

Since the Prophet himself was fully protected under *lex talionis*, he personally remained safe from severe physical violence, but the *Quraysh* did not spare him, too, from milder form of persecution, subjecting him to continuous harassment, mental torture, and occasionally, to mild physical assault. They scorned at him, derided him, abused him on his face, and insulted him on every occasion. The biographers have preserved many such stories. Thorns were put on his path, filth was thrown on him while praying, garbage used to be dumped at his door,[1] and street urchins used to be engaged to abuse and manhandle him. He was asked not to visit the *Kābah* for prayers, and when he did, he was subjected to torture. *Abū Lahab* compelled his two sons to repudiate the Prophet's daughters, *Ruqayyah* and *Umm Kulthūm*,

---

1 *Abū Lahb's wife, Umm Jamīl, was notorious for doing this.*

with whom they were married or betrothed.[1] We learn from *Ibn Ishāq* that once the Prophet became irritated by the slanderous remarks of the *Quraysh* leaders and reacted angrily. One day, when the *Quraysh* leaders were sitting together in the *hijr*, the Prophet appeared and started circumambulations of the *Kābah*. Each time he took a round and passed by them, they loudly made highly offensive and insulting remarks against him; when the same thing happened the third time, he burst out of anger and remarked, '*Will you listen to me O Quraysh? By him who holds my life in His hand, I bring you slaughter.*' The tone of his remark was so powerful that the leaders were left dumbfounded, not daring to utter a single word. But the next day, they decided to punish and manhandle to him at the Sanctuary. *Uqbah ibn Abū Muait* flung a sheet of cloth round his neck and dragged him so forcefully that he fell on his knees.[2] Seeing his plight, *Abū Bakr*, who was present, intervened and with tears in his eyes cried, '*Would you kill a man for saying Allāh is my Lord*?' Thereupon, they left him but fell upon *Abū Bakr* dragging him by his beard and hair. *Abū Bakr* was a very hairy man and that day he returned with some of his hair torn. *Bukhāri* narrates another hateful story of maltreatment of the Prophet. One day while he was praying at the Sanctuary, a group of *Quraysh* turned up for committing mischief. *Uqbah ibn Abū Muait* brought a foetus of a she-camel from somewhere and when the Apostle prostrated in prayer, he laid it on his back and shoulders. Under the weight of the dirty stuff, he could not get up while the disbelievers laughed at him until his daughter *Fātimah* came running and threw it off. According to yet another story referred to by *Ibn Hajār* in his *Isābah*,[3] once, the *Quraysh* started manhandling the Prophet in the *harām* when *Hārith ibn Abi*

---

1 *Ruquyyah was one of the most beautiful women of her generation. The breaking of the relationship with Abū Lahb's son proved a blessing in disguise for her because after divource she was taken in marriage by Uthmān ibn Affān, making a highly pleasing pair.*

2 *Bukhāri.*

3 *An article on Hārith ibn Abi Hala.*

Hala, believed to be the son of *Khadījah* from her first husband, intervened in defense of the Prophet but was himself put to death.

In their reaction to persecution unleashed by the *Quraysh*, the Prophet and his followers, however, showed remarkable patience and perseverance, facing violence with nonviolence and evil with good. To those who left no stone unturned to harass and harm him, the Prophet responded by praying to God for their guidance and liberation from the evil of paganism. Showing a rare example of passive resistance, the Muslims braved all atrocities and continued with practicing and preaching *Islām* unabated; in fact, the more they were persecuted, the more patience and resolution they displayed. Sometimes, even the enemies wondered why the Muslims were bearing all these tortures. But the blood of the martyrs was to become the seed of the Church and persecution only added to the strength of the new faith. The ill-treatment of the Prophet had started earning sympathies of a few of the *Quraysh*, and it was soon to attract to his fold his brave uncle, *Hamzah*, who was known as physically the strongest man of *Quraysh*. Once, when the Prophet was sitting outside the mosque near the *Safā* gate, *Abū Jahal* publicly reviled him with the ugliest abuses and also spoke spitefully of *Islām*. The insult caused was so offensive that even the non-Muslims considered it having transgressed the code of honour. But the Prophet did not utter a word and went away. Within a short while, *Hamzah* appeared at the *Kābah*; he was returning from hunting, with his bow hanging from his shoulder. A freed-woman belonging to the house of *Abd Allāh ibn Judān* having sympathy for the Prophet informed *Hamzah* of the outrageous treatment meted out to his uncle. Provoked by her taunts, *Hamzah* was full of rage, went straight to *Abū Jahal*, struck him a blow with his bow, and roared, '*Will you insult him when I follow his religion, and say what he says? Hit me back if you can!*'.[1] Seeing his anger, *Abū Jahal* preferred not to react. This was Hamzah's own way of professing *Islām* which he faithfully maintained for the rest of his life. His conversion provided tremendous strength to *Islām*;

---

1   *Ibn Ishāq.*

the Apostle found another powerful protector and the *Quraysh* were left scared.

The conversion of *Hamzah* indicated that the policy of persecution was a double-edged weapon which could prove counterproductive, too. In one of the meetings of their Assembly, the *Quraysh*, therefore, decided to change their strategy. They thought that the real motive of *al Amīn* behind his movement was to realize his personal ambitions. Therefore, on the advice of *Utbah ibn Rabīah*, a leading man of *Abdū Shams*, they agreed to make attempt to buy him off by making him offers of highly desirable worldly gains like power, prestige, wealth, and hands of the most beautiful women of *Makkāh*. Due to his conciliatory nature and close links with *Hāshim*, *Utbah* himself was chosen for the job. *Utbah* went to the Prophet, and after narrating the harmful effect of his preaching on *Quraysh*, asked him to stop preaching *Islām* in lieu of any or all of the offers he was to make. In the words of *Ibn Ishāq*, he told the Prophet:

> *If what you want is money, we will gather for you of our property so that you may be the richest of us; if you want honour, we will make you our chief so that no one can decide anything apart from you; if you want sovereignty, we will make you king; and if this ghost which comes to you, which you see, is such that you cannot get rid of him, we will find a physician for you, and exhaust our means in getting you cured; for often a familiar spirit gets possession of a man until he can be cured of it.*

The Prophet rejected all the offers outright and in reply recited the first thirty-seven verses of the newly revealed *Surāh* 41, *Hā Mīm Sajdah* (also known as *Fussilat*). The verses recited spoke of the *Qurān* itself, of creation of the earth and the firmament, of the prophets of the past and of the people who resisted them and were destroyed by God. They also spoke of the promise of *Allāh* for protection, happiness, and satisfaction in this world and the other for the believers. The Prophet ended his recitation with this verse and prostrated: *'And of His signs are the night and the day and the sun and the moon. Bow not down in adoration unto the sun nor unto the moon, but bow down in adoration unto God, their Creator, if Him indeed ye worship.'* It was not difficult for *Utbah* to see through the true character of the Prophet, a person who had no ambitions and no desire for power, wealth, and other worldly gains. But more importantly, the beauty and sublimity of the Quranic revelation he had heard left him mesmerized and speechless. He immediately went back to his companions with a noticeable change of expression on his face and said that he had heard words from *Muhammad* as he had never heard before, which were neither poetry nor magic. He further said, *'Take my advice and do as I do, leave this man entirely alone for, by God, the words which I have heard will be blazed abroad. If Arabs kill him, others will have rid you of him; if he gets the better of the Arabs, his sovereignty will be your sovereignty, his power your power, and you will be prosperous through him.'* But the *Quraysh* leaders mocked at him and said that he had been bewitched by *Muhammad* with his language. Not satisfied by the performance of *Utbah*, they decided to make a final attempt in order to convince the Prophet and win him over. They, therefore, called him, repeated the same offers as made by *Utbah*, and requested him to stop his dangerous activities. The Prophet replied that he did not seek either wealth or power; he was only performing his duty assigned by God to announce His message and warn the people. It was up to them to accept the same or not.

The attempt at obtaining submission of the Prophet by tempting offers having fallen flat, the *Quraysh* leaders next decided to argue with him, defeat him in debates, and prove him wrong in his convictions. They asked him to work miracles in order to prove his spiritual status as a prophet. If his Lord was all-powerful as claimed in revelations, they argued, then let him ask Him to remove the mountains which surrounded the valley of *Makkah*, cause rivers to flow there as in Syria and Iraq, and resurrect some of their forefathers including *Qusayy*. They demanded that he should make visible his God and angels in order to confirm his prophethood and the truth of the message he was preaching. They further demanded of him to get built gardens and palaces and produce treasures of gold and silver, if his Lord had power to bestow the same. Some would ask him to make the sky fall in pieces as claimed in the *Qurān*.[1] *Abd Allāh bin Abū Umayyah* mischievously said, '*I will never believe in you unless you get a ladder to the sky and mount up it until you come to it, while I am looking on, and until four angels shall come with you, testifying that you are speaking the truth.*' Misunderstanding the opening words of *Surah Rahmān,* some of them alleged that the message that *Muhammad* preached was tutored by a man of *Yamāmah* called *ar Rahmān* and, therefore, they would not believe it. To these numerous demands for miracles, the Prophet's only reply was that they could be performed only by God; his only mission was to guide them and warn those who had turned away from God's commandments. They could either accept God's message with advantage or reject it and await God's judgment. He also recited some verses of the *Qurān*[2] which said that signs were for God only and that he was but a plain warner. Such demands for miracles, however, were raised during subsequent days also causing embarrassment and irritation the Prophet.[3] In a series of verses[4] revealed in the following days, the *Qurān* addressed most of these demands of the disbelievers and informed that the universe was full of numerous signs or miracles of God which could be observed if one had eyes and wisdom of the believers. The *Qurān* itself was a great miracle according to one verse.[5]

---

1   *Qurān 34: 9.*

2   *Qurān 29: 50–51.*

3   *As per a story reported by Bukhāri, on one occasion, however, a miracle did actually take place. On one of the nights of full moon, the moon was visible above the hill of Hirā. Some disbelievers came and asked the Prophet to split the moon into two parts in order to prove that he was a messenger of God. Much to their amazement, the moon suddenly got divided into two distinct parts, each shining brightly on either side of mount Hirā for a moment. Some of the disbelievers entered Islām seeing this miracle while others said that it was merely an optic magic. According to some of the scholars, it is this incident which is referred to in the first two verses of Surah Qamar (numbering 54).*

4   *Qurān 1: 78, 2: 118–9, 6: 50, 6: 35–7, 7: 188, 13: 27–33, 17: 90–3, 19: 50–1, 25: 7–8, 25: 21, 25: 45–59, 44: 36.*

5   *Qurān 29: 51.*

While the *Quraysh* leaders had been making all possible efforts to win over the Prophet and convince him to stop his mission, persecution of the Muslims was still going on unabated. The Prophet was extremely concerned about the safety of his followers, none of whom was a towering leader of consequence so as to bring relief through his influence. He, therefore, longed to win over some of the local chiefs, especially *Walīd ibn al Mughīra*, who happened to be the unofficial leader of the entire city. One day, the Prophet had an opportunity to speak to *Walīd* alone in order to obtain his support. But while the conversation was going on, he was interrupted by an old and poor blind man. He had converted to *Islām* recently and was requesting the Prophet to recite some of the *Surahs* for him. The discussion being so important, the Prophet asked him to be patient and come at a freer moment, but he insisted, causing irritation to the Prophet who frowned and turned away. The interruption, however, did not cause any loss as *Walīd* did not respond favourably to his message. Immediately after the incident, a new *Surah* named *Abasa*[1] was revealed in which the Prophet was reproached for neglecting a poor and needy person in preference to an important individual. This criticism of the Prophet's own conduct in the *Qurān* is one of the testimonies of genuineness of the revelations.

The *Quraysh* leaders were at a loss to decide how to arrest the spread of *Islām*. The matter was being regularly discussed in their Assembly. Believing that the claim of *Muhammad* to prophethood was a false one, they thought that an effective way of turning his followers against him would be to expose the falsehood of his claim. They knew that the Jewish rabbis of *Yathrib* had a good knowledge of the old monotheistic scriptures and so they would be the best persons to confirm the truthfulness or otherwise of Muhammad's message. Two of their leaders, *An Nadr* and *Uqbah bin Abū Muait*, were, therefore, sent as envoys to *Yathrib* for consultations. The rabbis told them that in order to test Muhammad's genuineness, they should ask him three questions:

---

1   *Qurān 80.*

- What is the wonderful story about the young men who disappeared in ancient days?
- What is the story of the mighty traveller who reached the confines of the earth in both East and West?
- What is the Spirit?

The *Quraysh* leaders publicly asked the Prophet these three questions. The Prophet did not know the answers but, thinking that he would get the reply from Gabriel who had been bringing revelations almost daily, he replied: '*I will give you answer tomorrow*,' but he did not say, '*If God will*'.[1] Gabriel, however, did not turn up for fifteen days and the disbelievers kept on demanding the answers every day to which the Prophet had no reply. This caused considerable distress and embarrassment to him. Finally, after a long wait, Gabriel brought a revelation disclosing the answers to the three questions, but along with the answers also came the admonition for not remembering God when promising a thing: '*Never say of anything, "I shall do that tomorrow" except: "If God will"; and remember your Lord when you forget, and say: "I hope that my Lord will guide me ever closer than this to the right course."*'[2] The answers to the first two questions formed part of *Surah al Kahf* (The Cave), numbering 18. As per the revelation,[3] the first question related to the story of the Sleepers of Ephesus which took place in the middle of the third century AD. Some young men had remained faithful to the worship of one God while the people at large had become idolators. In order to evade persecution, the young men escaped and took shelter in a cave where they were miraculously made to sleep for over 300 years. In addition to what the Jews already knew from the *Torah*, the revelation provided some additional information as to how the sleepers looked and how a dog guarded them. As regards the second question, the revelation[4] narrated the entire story of the

---

1   *Inshā Allāh.*

2   *Surah 18: 23–4.*

3   *Qurān 18: 9–25.*

4   *Qurān 18: 93–9.*

great traveller whose name was *Dhū al Qarnayn* (he of the two horns). Giving even additional information, it told the story of his mysterious third journey to a place between two mountains where he, after receiving power from God, confined the evil spirits who would get released before the final doom bringing terrible destruction. As to the third question, the revelation[1] informed: '*They will ask you about the Spirit, say, the Spirit is a matter for my Lord, and you have only a little knowledge about it.*' After receiving the revelation, the Prophet answered the questions of the disbelievers beyond their expectations, and this caused some conversions, but the worst enemies failed to draw lessons from it. The delay in receiving the revelation, although painful to the Prophet, has significant historical value. It powerfully corroborates the fact that the revelations came from God and that the same was totally beyond his control. If the Prophet had invented the previous revelations, it is not understandable, why there was so much of a delay in concocting this revelation, especially when the stake was so high.

---

1   *Qurān 17: 37.*

CHAPTER VI

ISLĀM UNDER SIEGE IN MAKKAH
(615–22)

All efforts of the *Quraysh* to suppress the Islamic movement or strike a deal with the Prophet had, so far, failed, and the number of the Muslims was multiplying; and the more the number increased, the more panicky they grew. In their assessment, the effective alternative now left was nothing but suppression of *Islām* by deterrent force. As a result, they intensified persecution of the Muslims to the maximum. The weaker Muslims on whom they could lay their hands were subjected to unprecedented violence and torture, a few of them even losing their lives. The traditions have preserved a number of such stories of cruel and barbaric treatment meted out to the faithful. The hill of *Ramdhā* and a place called *Bathā* turned into scenes of cruel tortures.[1] The most famous of such stories is the one of the Abyssinian slave, *Bilāl*, who had entered *Islām*

---

1 *Athīr.*

through *Abū Bakr* and was a firm believer. His master, *Umayyah bin Khalāf*, chief of *Jumah*, used to conduct him to *Bathā* each day when the heat of the sun was the maximum. There he used to be forced to lie on the burning sand barebacked and a large block of stone kept on his chest with these words written: '*There shall you remain until you are dead or you abjure Islām.*' But, though tortured beyond limits of endurance, his faith gave him remarkable courage and strength and never failed him. Lying thus in extreme pain and thirst, he still used to keep on uttering: '*Ahadun, Ahadun*',[1] emphasizing the unity of God. Sometimes a rope used to be put around his neck and urchins were made to drag him through streets and even across the hillocks of *Makkah*. Once *Waraqah ibn Naufal* happened to pass by and, witnessing the scene of torture, remarked, '*I swear by God that if you kill him thus, I shall make his grave a shrine.*'. The torture of *Bilal*[2] in this manner continued for days reducing him to the verge of death when he was bought and freed by *Abū Bakr*. In the like manner, *Abū Bakr* is said to be responsible for purchasing and setting free six other slaves—*Āmir ibn Fuhayrah* and five female slaves which included *Umm Unays, Nahdiyah, Zinnirah*, and *Lubaynah*. Spending a large chunk of his wealth, he thus earned great religious merit by relieving these helpless Muslim slaves of severe tortures. His father used to wonder why he was

---

1   *One, one.*

2   *In due course, Bilal became one of the favourite followers of the Prophet. He had an extraordinarily powerful and attractive voice due to which he distinguished himself as the first Muezzin of Islam. According to a story, being an African, he was not able to pronounce 'Ash hadu' properly and used to miss 'h' part of the word. Due to defective pronunciation, the Arab Muslims used to be critical of him; but the Prophet had great regard for the sincerity with which he used to deliver Azān. One night, due to repeated criticism of the Arab Companions, the Prophet asked him not to say Azān the next morning. However, so long as he did not personally give the call of Azān, much to the surprise of everyone, the Fajr did not break. In subsequent years, the Prophet appointed him secretary of treasury of the Islamic Kingdom.*

lavishly spending his wealth on liberation of such insignificant individuals.

Another poignant story of cruel torture recorded in the traditions is that of the family of *Ammār* (which included his father, *Yāsir*, and mother, *Sumayyah*)—the first 'whole family' to embrace *Islām*. They were ex-slaves and were confederates of *Makhzūm*. *Ammār* and *Yāsir* used to be made to lie on burning sand and beaten so severely that, on occasions, they became senseless. When *Summayyah* intervened, she was speared to death by *Abū Jahal*. She is said to have become the first martyr in the cause of *Islām*. According to *Ibn Sād*, *Yāsir* also subsequently succumbed to his injuries. *Ammār* sacrificed his life much later in the battle of Siffin in 657—the trio earning the distinction of also being the first whole family of martyrs in *Islām*. The Prophet was extremely pained to see tortures being inflicted on *Ammār* and his family and gave the tidings that they would enter Heaven. The physical tortures inflicted on the poor Muslims in order to force them to abjure *Islām* were extremely severe, but most of them braved the same by dint of strength of the faith. A few including *Ammār* were, however, subjected to such unbearable violence that they found themselves forced to apparently recant, though at heart still remaining Muslims, and this type of secrecy of faith or dissimulation (*Taqiyah*) was approved by the Prophet. The traditions furnish a long list of Muslims who were subjected to cruel violence which includes *Abū Fukaiyah, Khabbāb ibn al Arāt, Suhaib bin Sinān, Lubaynah, Zinnirah, Nahdiyah, Umm Unays*, and others. *Khabbāb* used to be tortured by fire due to which he was having permanent white leprous spots on his back which in later days he used to show to the Companions with pride. *Zinnirah* and *Lubaynah* were slave girls belonging to the family of *Umar* who, along with *Abū Jahal*, used to torture them. According to a story, *Zinnirah* lost her eyesight due to torture which she subsequently recovered and the *Quraysh* attributed this to the sorcery of *Muhammad*. *Umar* used to mercilessly thrash *Lubaynah* for long hours; when exhausted by continuous beating, he used to stop for a while and resume beating after a brief rest.

Due to increased persecution, it had become difficult for the Muslims to practice their religion freely. Till then, no one was allowed to recite the *Qurān* aloud in the precincts of the *Kābah*. *Abd Allāh ibn Masūd*,[1] who dared to recite *Surah Rahmān* aloud at the *harām*, was severely beaten up by the polytheists, leaving his face bruised. *Abū Dharr*, who had the temerity to pronounce *Shahādah* aloud in the *harām*, was also badly assaulted. The reported incident of slaughter of *Ibn Halā* while protecting the Prophet in the *harām* also appears to have taken place at this stage. Apart from serious restrictions being faced in practicing *Islām*, the tribulations and physical pains being suffered by the believers had become unbearable and their very existence was in peril. Unable to do anything to stop violence against his followers, the Prophet was in great mental agony. In order to save his nascent community from extermination, he, therefore, advised his followers to emigrate to *Abyssinia*,[2] which was a Christian kingdom. Its ruler, known as the *Negus*,[3] was famous for his justice and benign rule. Religious affinity between Christianity and *Islām* and Abyssinia's past history of hostility with *Quraysh* of *Makkah* might have been the guiding factors in the Prophet's mind behind selection of this country as an ideal place of refuge. Some Western scholars suggest that the emigration was not only to avoid persecution but had wider political and economic motives. It might have been an attempt by the Muslims to forge a political alliance with the *Negus* in order to obtain military support against *Quraysh*. Development of independent trade with African coastland for raising finances for the Muslim community was also a possible motive. But these are mere conjectures.

The first batch of the Muslims clandestinely went to *Abbyssinia* in the fifth year of the Prophet's mission i.e.

---

1 *He is said to be the first Muslim (except the Prophet himself) to recite the Qurān at the Kābah aloud.*

2 *Modern Ethiopia.*

3 *Personal name—As Hama (Arabic name—Najashī).*

615[1]; the incident is known as the first *Hijrah* in *Islām* and is referred to in the *Qurān*.[2] Authorities differ as regards identity and exact number of individuals included in this small group. But, it is generally held that it had eleven males and four females and included *Uthmān ibn Affān* and his wife *Ruqayyah*,[3] *Abd ar Rahman ibn Auf*,[4] *Abū Salamah* and his wife *Umm Salamah*[5] of *Makhzum*, *Zubayr ibn al Awwām*, and *Uthmān ibn Mazun*, the last acting as the leader of the group. More of the nature of a reconnoitring group, it was received well by the *Negus* and the Muslims were allowed complete security and freedom of worship. After receiving green signals from them, a large number of other Muslims from *Makkah* also joined them under the leadership of *Jāfar ibn Abū Tālib*, the elder brother of *Alī*, who carried the Prophet's letter to the *Negus* recommending hospitality to the Muslims. From the sources, it is not clear how and at what point of time they effected their flight. But since their flight was planned secretly and carried out unobtrusively, it is highly probable that they went in several small batches. There is divergence of opinion among classical historians regarding the total number of migrants. While *Ibn al Athīr* mentions it to be 101 (83 men and 18 women), according to *Baladhurī*, excluding the infants who accompanied and the children born after emigration, the total number of Muslim refugees in Abbyssinia was 109, which included 75 Makkan males, 9 females, and 25 clients or confederates. The Prophet had appointed *Jāfar* as the spokesman of the refugees as he was an eloquent speaker and had a prepossessing appearance; his wife also accompanied and

---

1 *In the month of Rajab, the seventh month of the Islamic calendar.*

2 *Qurān 16: 14.*

3 *Though well protected, they were sent by the Prophet as a source of strength and moral support to the group.*

4 *One of the 10 declared entitle to Paradise according to a hadīth.*

5 *She was to later become one of the wives of the Prophet. It was she whose later statements became the main source of information about the Abbyssinian emigration.*

the two together made a highly pleasant couple. Others who accompanied were *Musāb* of *Abd ad Dār*,[1] the exceptionally handsome young Makhzumite called *Shammās*,[2] and the two cousins of the Prophet, *Abd Allāh ibn Jahsh* and *Ubayd Allāh* together with the latter's wife *Umm Habibah*.[3] As per lists of the emigrants left by the classical historians, a majority of them were protected individuals belonging to well-off families. It is on this basis that some of the modern Western historians opine that persecution was not the main factor behind emigration. But, in fact, even persons belonging to well-protected stronger families were being harassed by their disbelieving relatives, and moreover, what they actually wanted was freedom of practicing *Islām*. Strangely enough, however, the names of some of the weakest and worst victimized Muslims, like *Bilāl* and *Ammār*, were conspicuous by their absence in the lists. Perhaps, they were too poor to afford expenses of the journey or else they did not want to part company with their beloved Prophet.

The flight of the Muslims to *Abbyssinia* had been effected in total secrecy eluding the attention of *Quraysh*. When *Quraysh* came to know of the same, their reaction was one of severe anger and panic. They apprehended that large-scale conversions and fast proliferation of a dangerous community on a foreign land beyond their control might pose a serious threat to *Makkah* in the long run. Deciding not to leave the emigrants in peace, they chalked out a plan of action and sent two of their smart leaders, *Amr ibn al Ās* and *Abd Allāh ibn Abū Rabīah*, as envoys to the *Negus* along with highly sought-after gifts in order to bribe the *Negus* and his courtiers who mattered. After winning over the generals and officials, the two delegates informed the *Negus* that the Muslims in *Abbyssinia* were not refugees from persecution but were escapees from law and justice, the blasphemers of their

---

1 *A highly competent Companion who was subsequently sent to Yathrib for preaching Islam preceding the Hijrāh and was remarkably successful.*

2 *His mother was the sister of Utbah.*

3 *Who was later to become one of the wives of the Prophet.*

religion, deserving severe punishments; and so they requested
the king for their extradition. But, true to his sense of justice, the
Negus called the Muslims and gave them opportunity to speak
in defense. At this point, the eloquent *Jáfar*, as the leader of the
community of the exiles, gave a memorable speech which was a
beautiful description of the doctrines of *Islám* and situation under
which it arose:

> *O King, we were an uncivilized people,
> worshipping idols, eating corpses, committing
> abominations, breaking natural ties, treating
> guests badly, and our strong devoured our weak.
> Thus we were until God sent us an apostle whose
> lineage, truth, trustworthiness, and clemency we
> know. He summoned us to acknowledge God's
> unity and to worship him and to renounce the
> stones and images which we and our fathers
> formerly worshipped. He commanded us to speak
> the truth, be faithful to our engagements, mindful
> of the ties of kinship and kindly hospitality, and
> to refrain from crimes and bloodshed. He forbade
> us to commit abominations and to speak lies,
> and to devour the property of orphans, to vilify
> chaste women. He commanded us to worship God
> alone and not to associate anything with him,
> and he gave us orders about prayer, almsgiving,
> and fasting. We confessed his truth and believed
> in him, and we followed him in what he had
> brought from God, and we worshipped God alone
> without associating aught with Him. We treated
> as forbidden what he forbade, and as lawful
> what he declared lawful. Thereupon our people
> attacked us, treated us harshly and seduced us
> from our faith to try to make us go back to the
> worship of idols instead of the worship of God
> and to regard as lawful the evil deeds we once*

> *committed. So when they got the better of us,*
> *treated us unjustly, and circumscribed our lives,*
> *and came between us and our religion, we came to*
> *your country, having chosen you above all others.*
> *Here we have been happy in your protection, and*
> *we hope that we shall not be treated unjustly while*
> *we are with you, O king.*[1]

When the meaning of Jāfar's speech was explained by the interpreters, the *Negus* was impressed and desired to listen to some verses revealed to the Prophet. Thereupon, *Jāfar* recited a passage of *Surah Maryam*[2] which contained the Quranic account of the extraordinary virginal conception of Jesus in the womb of Mary. The sublimity of the verses left the *Negus* electrified and he as well as his bishops wept; and when the meaning was explained, they wept more, wetting their garments. Becoming convinced of the truthfulness of *Islām*, the *Negus* said that the source of the Quranic verses was the same as that of the message brought by Jesus and added that the Muslims were free to live in his kingdom as long as they wished. The next day, however, *Amr ibn al Ās* again appeared before the *Negus* and tried to instigate him against the Muslims. He alleged that the Muslims rejected the divine nature of Christ and claimed that he was a servant of God, a mortal like other men. When asked to clarify, *Jāfar* replied, '*We say of him what our Prophet brought unto us, that he is the slave of God and His messenger and His spirit and His word which He cast unto Mary, the blessed virgin.*' Though there was no mention of Christ as son of God, the *Negus* was satisfied and remarked that Jesus was what *Jāfar* stated him to be and nothing more than that. Despite protest by his generals and bishops, he gave judgment in favour of the Muslims, remarking, '*Go your ways, for you are safe in my land. Not for mountains of gold would I harm a single man of you.*' He refused to deport the Muslims, returned the presents

---

1 *Ibn Ishāq.*
2 *Surah 19 verses 16–21.*

sent by *Quraysh*, and directed the ambassadors to go back, and thus they left ignominiously.

According to contemporary historical account, the Negus' favourable treatment of *Islām*, however, caused disaffection among the Abyssinian Christians who accused him of having left Christianity and rose in revolt against him. They were probably joined by other political elements who wanted to overthrow his regime. Realizing precariousness of his position and apprehending threat to the small community of Muslim refugees who were under his protection, he even advised the Muslims to be in readiness to sail back for *Makkāh* if the situation deteriorated. But much to the relief of the Muslims, he was soon able to win over the revolting leaders by convincing them of his religious bonafides and the revolt was finally put down by the Negus' military victory. The Muslim refugees thereafter lived in *Abyssinia* in peace, prosperity, and security. There are traditions which mention that in his subsequent life, the *Negus* had privately embraced *Islām* and was in contact with the Prophet. In 628, after the *Treaty of Hudaybiyah*, he represented the Prophet in the latter's marriage with *Umm Habibah*,[1] a marriage which took place in *Abyssinia* in the absence of the Prophet. After a few years, when the Negus died, his funeral prayer was performed by the Prophet in absentia. We have a *hadīth* attributed to *Āisha* which says, '*When the Negus died it used to be said that a light was constantly seen over his grave.*'

We learn from some historians that after the Muslims stayed in *Abyssiania* for about a year, they heard a rumour that the unbelievers in *Makkāh* had accepted *Islām*. The Muslims had already been feeling homesick; excited by the news, many of them left back for *Makkah*. But on approaching the city, they learnt that the information was baseless.[2] Many of them, therefore, went back to *Abyssiania* joined by some new faces. Some, however,

---

1   *Daughter of Abū Sufyan.*

2   *Some of the writers opine that the rumour had been deliberately planned by Quraysh in order to make the refugees return for persecution and even extermination.*

made a secret entry into *Makkah*, a few of them only after obtaining protection[1] of some significant families. Persecution at this stage was so intensified that it is said that even *Abū Bakr* attempted to migrate to *Abyssinia* proceeding towards Yaman, but returned after securing protection of *Abū Dughunnah*, chief of *Qarā*. *Ibn Ishāq* mentions that the total number of companions who entered *Makkāh* on return from *Abyssinia* was thirty-three. With the available historical data, our knowledge regarding return of the emigrants to *Makkah* and their remigration remains rather vague. While many of the Western historians maintain that return of the emigrants took place within a few months after the alleged incident of the 'Satanic Verses', there are Muslim historians who hold that the same occurred after the withdrawal of the boycott against *Banu Hāshim*, that is, in 619. There are still others according to whom, it was only after the reported episode of the 'Satanic Verses', that the subsequent emigrating groups under *Jāfar* left for *Abyssinia* followed by the visit of *Quraysh*'s delegation. It, however, appears highly probable that *Umar* accepted *Islām* after about three months of the first emigration and failure of the delegation sent to *Abyssinia* by *Quraysh*. It also remains established that though *Uthman ibn Affān*, his wife *Ruqayyah* and a few other individuals, after return from *Abyssinia*, stayed back with the Prophet in *Makkah*, a majority of the returnees including their leader *Jāfar*, went back to rejoin the Prophet in *Madinah* in 628 only.

Shortly after emigration, the dramatic conversion of *Umar* took place which is regarded as a turning point in the history of *Islām*. The failure of the diplomatic mission sent by *Quraysh* in order to obtain deportation of the runaway Muslims had caused considerable consternation as well as anger among the *Quraysh* leaders. In reaction, they immediately intensified repression and persecution of the left-over Muslims. *Umar*, who was a head-strong young man of great determination and extreme violent nature, decided to put an end to the root cause of the problem by

---

1   *Uthmān bin Mazūn received the protection of Walīd ibn al Mughira. Abū Salamah went under the protection of Abū Tālib.*

slaying the Prophet. He took his sword and left in search of him. On way, *Nuaym ibn Abd Allāh*, one of his own clansmen, who had entered *Islām* but kept it a secret due to fear of *Umar*, met him. Sensing danger from Umar's expression, he enquired about his intentions and was informed by *Umar* that he was going to kill *Muhammad*. *Nuaym* tried to stop him by pointing out that he would be inviting danger to his own life by harming *Muhammad* since that would raise the whole *Hashim* clan in revenge. *Umar*, however, turned a deaf ear to his advice whereupon, in order to divert his mind, *Nuaym* informed him that his own sister, *Fātimah*, and her husband, *Saīd*[1] had also entered *Islām* and so he should first set his own house in order before taking the extreme step of killing *Muhammad*.

Infuriated at this revelation, *Umar* at once turned and went straight to *Fātimah*'s house. At that point of time, his sister and her husband were reciting the newly revealed *Surah Tā Hā*[2] with the help of *Khabbāb*, a confederate of *Zuhra*. When *Umar* approached the house and they heard his angry voice, *Khabbāb* at once hid in a corner of the house and *Fātimah* concealed the page in her gown. *Umar* asked them what they were reading and whether they had turned Muslim. Not satisfied by their reply, he started beating *Saīd* and when *Fātimah* interposed, she also received a blow on her face and started bleeding from the nose. Infuriated at the misconduct of *Umar*, both openly accepted having entered *Islām* and challenged him to do whatever he felt like. But when *Umar* saw his sister's blood, he felt sorry and asked for the script so that he could personally read what was there in the *Qurān*.[3] *Fātimah* initially hesitated to hand over the same to a disbeliever lest it should be disrespected. But when *Umar* gave assurances and washed and purified himself as advised, she handed over the manuscript. *Umar* read the *Surah* which described glory of God and the story of Moses' conversation with God. The miraculous language of the *Qurān* worked its

---

1 *Umar's own cousin.*

2 *Surah No. 20.*

3 *Umar Knew how to read and write.*

magical effect, stirred his mind, and immediately forced him to remark, '*How beautiful and how noble are these words!*' Excited by the words uttered by *Umar*, *Khabbāb* at once came out of hiding and disclosed that just the other day he had heard the Prophet praying God to strengthen *Islām* by conversion of either *Umar* or *Abū Jahal* and that the change of his heart was the result of that prayer. After ascertaining the whereabouts of the Prophet, *Umar* straightaway went to *dar al Arqām* where the Prophet along with other believers was present. Umar's arrival there with sword created tension and misgivings and *Hamzāh* readied himself to attack *Umar* if he showed any harmful intentions. But to their great amazement and joy, Umar announced his acceptance of *Islām* and the Prophet loudly uttered, *Allahū Akbar*, the same being heard by all the forty odd Muslims present in the house.[1]

The opposition to *Islām* was then so strong and the situation so frightening and charged with tension that every Muslim on conversion used to conceal his faith fearing reprisal by the pagans. But the iron man of *Makkah*, with his obstinacy and high sense of tribal pride, considered it disgraceful to hide his faith and decided to publicly proclaim his conversion. He, therefore, immediately called *Jamīl bin Māmar*, known as the best at spreading news, and informed him of his conversion; within no time, the news had spread like a wild fire causing great sensation. The next morning, in order to challenge *Quraysh*, he singled out *Abū Jahal*, who

---

1   *This is the most popular story of conversion of Umar as recorded by Ibn Ishāq and most of the classical biographers. This story comes from Madinan narrators. Ibn Ishāq, however, has also recorded a different story of Umar's conversion based on narration of Makkan reporters. According to this, one night when Umar reached the Kābah to take its round, the Prophet was already there, praying and reciting the Quranic verses. Umar stealthily listened to the recitation from behind the covering of the Kābah. When he heard the Qurān, his heart was softened and he wept and Islām entered into him. Under the irresistible impact of the Quranic verses he had heard, Umar immediately went to the Prophet and pronounced Shāhadah. The biographer did not make any attempt to reconcile the two different stories of Umar's conversion. There is, however, hardly any taker for this second story.*

was known to be the most inveterate enemy of *Islām*, went to his house, and informed him of his conversion, to his great chagrin. Further, his ego did not allow him to tolerate the humiliation of offering prayers in hiding. So he soon went to the *Kābah* along with other fellow Muslims and performed prayers in front of it. *Dārqutni* reports that the people were astonished to find a procession of Muslims going to offer prayers in the precincts of the *Kābah* fearlessly and they were more amazed to find that Umar served them as guard. *Abdullah ibn Masūd* used to say, *'We could not pray at the Kābah until Umar became a Muslim; and then he fought the Quraysh until he could pray there and we prayed with him.'*

The conversion of *Umar* was a great victory for *Islām* giving it considerable strength. *Ibn Ishāq* says that the Muslims now got the better of *Quraysh*. With the two strong men of *Makkah*, *Hamzah* and *Umar*, on their side and a majority of vulnerable Muslims staying in a safe sanctuary in *Abyssinia*, the Muslims were now emboldened to challenge the pagans and pray openly in the precincts of the *Kābah*. Realizing the gravity of the situation, the *Quraysh* leaders, therefore, made a last attempt at compromise. They went to the Prophet and proposed that they would worship *Allāh* provided the Muslims also respected and worshipped their gods. The Prophet, however, outrightly rejected the offer of sharing of religion and *Surah Kāfirūn*—109 was then revealed confirming the decision and signifying the final rupture:

> *Say, O disbelievers,*
> *I do not worship what you worship,*
> *And you do not worship what I worship;*
> *And I do not worship what you worship,*
> *And you do not worship what I worship;*
> *You have your religion and I have mine.*

With strengthening of the Muslims' position and failure of all negotiations, a stage was now set when hardening of attitude on both sides was to be expected. Strangely, however, at this point of the Prophet's history, the Christian historians of

Islām, on the basis of a flimsy tradition, come out with a highly incongruous and illogical postulation suggesting that in order to reconcile the *Quraysh*, the Prophet momentarily recognized the three goddesses of *Quraysh* as intercessors with *Allāh* and, thus, compromised on the fundamental Islamic principle of oneness of God. The story is known as that of 'Satanic Verses' and has become highly controversial gaining a good deal of notoriety by Salman Rushdie's novel of the same name. The story was reported by a few classical biographers like *Ibn Sād* (d. 845), *Wāqidī* (d. 822), and *Tabarī* (d. 923). We are told that *Ibn Ishāq* (d. 768), the first biographer of the Prophet, did make a mention of this tradition but treated the same as a mischief of the disbelievers. Therefore, *Ibn Hishām* (d. 834), who collected and collated the work of *Ibn Ishāq*, omitted the same, finding it unreliable. However, in the commentaries on the relevant verses, the story is told by a few *Qurān* commentators such as *Baydāwi*.

According to the story reported by *Tabarī*, once when the Prophet was sitting before the *Kābah* in the presence of many pagan leaders, he longed for some message from God which would reconcile the *Quraysh* to *Islām*. At this moment, revelation of *Surah* 53—*An Najm*—began, which the Prophet started reciting aloud. When he completed verses 19 and 20,[1] which referred to *banāt Allāh*, Satan interfered with his reception of the divine message and put on his lips his own words, and the Prophet uttered the next two verses as '*These are exalted birds, whose intercession is approved.*' On hearing the verses, the *Quraysh* polytheists were highly delighted thinking that the Prophet had praised their goddesses and accommodated them in his religion as intermediaries between the worshippers and God. In the meantime, the Prophet continued to recite the verses until he reached the sign of *sajdah* (the last verse of the *Surah*) when he prostrated; and out of excitement, all polytheists present also prostrated except *Walīd ibn al Mughīra* who could not do so because of old age. The news spread rapidly and reached the

---

1   *The verses read as 'Have you considered al Lāt and al Uzzā
    And Manāt, the third, the other!'*

Muslim refugees in *Abyssinia* who heard that *Quraysh* had accepted *Islām* and many of them started to return. However, Gabriel soon appeared and informed the Prophet that he had read out to the people something which God had not revealed. The Apostle was highly frightened and bitterly grieved for having committed the mistake. But God immediately comforted him by the following revelation: '*We have not sent a prophet or apostle before you but when he longed Satan cast suggestions into his longing But God will annul what Satan had suggested. Then God will establish His verses, God being knowing and wise. That He may make what Satan suggested a temptation to those whose hearts are deaceased and hardened.*'[1] Thereafter, God abrogated what had been suggested by Satan and then finally revealed verses remained as under:

> *Have you considered al Lāt and al Uzzā*
> *And Manāt, the third, the other?*
> *For you males and for Him females?*
> *That would be unfair sharing.*
> *They are but names you and your fathers named;*
> *God revealed no authority for them;*
> *They follow only opinion and soul's fancies,*
> *Though from their Lord there has come to them*
> *guidance.*[2]

This story of Satan's interference with Quranic revelation, however, did not carry much significance in Islamic writings of the pre-Orientalist era. Though some of the Muslim historians and exegetes did make a mention of this tradition without attributing any negative implication to it, most of them[3] rejected its authenticity and regarded it as a mischievous invention of the enemies of *Islām*. It was only when the Christian Orientalists started their study of *Islām* that the story rose into prominence.

---

1   *Surah 22—Al Haj—Verses 52 and 53.*

2   *Surah 53—An Najm—Verses 19–23.*

3   *Like Ibn Ishāq, al Baihāqi, Qādi Iyād, al Āini, al Nawāi etc.*

To such disbelieving writers, the story offered a convenient piece of material which they made the most of in order to malign the Prophet and the *Qurān*. Arguing that verses 52–53 of *Surah 22* clearly refer to interpolations by Satan and their annulment by God, they regarded the story as true. It was also said that verses 73–74 of *Surah 17—Banī Isrāil*—referred to the same incident: *'And their purpose was to tempt thee away from that which We had revealed unto thee to substitute in our name something quite different; (in that case) behold! They would certainly have made thee (their) friend. And had we not given thee strength, thou woudst nearly have inclined to them a little.'* The story of return of many of the emigrants from *Abyssinia* after hearing the news of reconciliation was also cited by them as a strong circumstantial evidence in support of truthfulness of the tradition. On the basis of their interpretation of the tradition, such writers thus attacked sincerity of the Prophet as well as sanctity and integrity of the *Qurān*. To them, the Prophet was ready to compromise even on the basic issue of monotheism in order to meet exigencies of the situation. A genuine Prophet would have been able to distinguish between divine and a satanic inspiration.

In reaction to such a prejudiced view, Muslim writers and commentators of modern times also made a deep study of the tradition and construed it very differently. They have pointed out a series of infirmities in the story and concluded that it was nothing more than a motivated fabrication which managed to creep into the works of a few classical historians who were eager to narrate all available stories without regard to their trustworthiness:

- Judged in the light of events preceding and following the alleged incident, the story is historically incongruous and does not stand to reason. The incident is reported to have taken place after the Prophet had already rejected a series of offers for compromise. Most of the vulnerable Muslims whose lives were under threat had already migrated to *Abyssinia* and were safely entrenched there with full support of the *Negus*. Moreover, the powerful *Umar* had joined *Islām*, considerably strengthening community of the faithful which is vouched for by *Ibn Ishāq*. With the Muslims now in a position to openly offer prayers in the *Kābah*, their position was much stronger. The Prophet at this stage entering into a compromise—that too in respect of the central message of *Islām*—stands highly improbable and illogical. Further, even if the Prophet had entered into a compromise to end strife with *Quraysh* and get rid of persecution, it is not at all understandable why he should surrender the great advantages obtained shortly after the incident and revert to the same predicament.

- The contextual flow of *Surah An Najm* does not allow interpolation as claimed. In case it is assumed that the alleged interpolation did take place, then it will be contradicted by the subsequent verses; relevant portion of the *Surah* along with the interpolated verses will run like this:

    *Have you considered al Lāt and al Uzzā
    And Manāt, the third, the other?
    They are exalted birds,
    Whose intercession is approved
    They are but names you and your fathers named;
    God revealed no authority for them;
    They follow only opinion and soul's fancies,
    Though from their Lord there has come to them guidance.'*

    Does the alleged interpolation make sense? Is it not utterly out of context?

- The Prophet accepting the alleged interpolation, which was in violation of the most essential principle of *Islām*, would have been a highly significant development and so we would have come across a large number of s*ahīh ahadīth* on the subject, but there is none. The great collections of traditions compiled in ninth century by *Bukhāri* and *Muslim* do not mention the same. Further, there is no clear reference to it in the *Qurān*. The Quranic verses of *Surah* 17 and 22 which are referred to by the Christian historians do not clearly refer to the alleged incident. Verses 73–74 of *Surah* 17 and 52–53 of *Surah* 22 were revealed after several years of the incident according to many commentators and pertained to different contexts.

- The return of emigrants from *Abyssinia*, which is treated as an evidence in support of the story, was actually not because of the rumour of reconciliation but due to revolt which had broken out against the *Negus* and the consequent fear of losing his protection.[1]

- The allegation regarding deception on part of the Prophet stands unacceptable as it does not fit into his character. All historical sources confirm truthfulness of the Prophet who used to be called *al Amīn* even by the polytheists. There are numerous references in the sources which prove that even the disbelievers never doubted his truthfulness. Moreover, the story as presented in some of the sources does not at all suggest any intention of the Prophet behind the interpolation. Rather than putting character of the Prophet in a bad light, it actually sheds additional lustre on the same. Despite full knowledge of likely reaction by the whole city, he had the moral courage and frankness to accept the mistake caused by Satan's tampering and retract openly.

- As part of their general strategy, the *Quraysh* mischief-mongers used to set up a noise and interpose their own sentences in order to create confusion whenever the Prophet publicly recited the Quranic revelations. That

---

1 *This is the view of Muhammad Husayn Haykal in his* The Life of Muhammad. *Some other Muslim scholars, however, place the return of the emigrants much later in 619 and treat it as consequence of a rumour of reconciliation which reached Abyssinia in the wake of withdrawal of the 3-year economic boycott when there was a momentary impression that hostilities between the Muslims and Quraysh had ceased (Martin Lings).*

they frequently created this type of disturbance during recitation is confirmed by the *Qurān*: '*The unbelievers say: Listen not to the Qurān, but talk at random in the midst of its (reading) that yee may gain the upper hand.*'[1]. And this was what most probably happened in the instant case.

- When the Prophet completed recitation of verses 19–20, which referred to the names of *banāt Allāh*, the polytheists expected the next verses in their denunciation; in order to avert the same, they raised a disturbing noise while some mischief-maker loudly cried out the alleged interpolated words in similar tone as the Prophet's, the voice of the Prophet getting subsided. In the noisy confusion, the disbelievers misunderstood the mischief-maker's words as the Prophet's utterance thinking that he had praised their goddesses and sanctioned power of intercession to them. They were, therefore, extremely excited and prostrated along with the Prophet. But soon they realized their mistake, and out of frustration, concocted the story.[2]

It was the seventh year of the Prophet's mission towards the close of 616. Despite three years of relentless resistance by *Quraysh*, *Islām* was progressing well, its number slowly multiplying and the community gaining strength day by day. The Muslims now had the audacity to offer prayer openly in the *harām*. To the added consternation of *Quraysh*, the religion had started spreading even outside *Makkah* to the outlying tribes. The situation again forced the *Quraysh* to ponder and figure out what went wrong with their strategy and what was the reason for Islām's success even though all possible obstructive as well as persuasive efforts had been made to get rid of it. After a thorough reassessment, they realized that the main factor on which *Islām* thrived was the monolithic support of *Banu Hāshim*; so long as their strong

---

1 *Qurān 41: 26.*

2 *Such views have been expressed by scholars like Abul ala Maududi (founder of Jamat-e-Islami) and M. H. Haykal.*

protection continued, it was not possible to eliminate or effectively restrain the Prophet. All attempts at persuading or pressurizing *Abū Tālib* so far made having failed, it was now necessary to take some more radical measure against his clan, they thought. After mutual consultations in the Assembly, they, therefore, decided to totally boycott or ostracise the whole clan of *Banu Hāshim* while the previous policy of persecution and torture of all Muslims belonging to other clans was to continue. This stratagem was likely to be multipronged in its consequences. On the one hand, sufferings and starvation arising out of excommunication would force *Banu Hāshim* to abandon the Prophet and place him at the mercy of *Quraysh*; on the other, a prolonged boycott would ruin the clan's economy and be a befitting punishment for its vicarious responsibility for the rise of Islamic ideology. This was to be an appropriate tribal way of dealing with a people who violated own tribal customs and religion. And, more important than choking the financial resources of the Muslims and their supporters, it would isolate and marginalize the Prophet, stop conversions, and force him to submission.

The proposed interdiction was to be imposed on *Banū Hāshim* only, but since *Banū Muttalib*, the clan of Hashim's brother, did not consent, the latter was also included in the ban. It was applicable to all members of the two clans irrespective of whether they were Muslims or polytheists. The Muslims belonging to other clans were, however, to be beyond its purview. Though a few individuals of other clans were also not in favour of this extreme step, they were bought off. A document[1] was written down[2] and signed by as many as forty *Quraysh* leaders binding down all clans in and around *Makkah* for the purpose. Among the Hashimites, *Abū Lahab* was the only one who defected, joined the opposite group, and shifted to the district of *Abdū Shams*. In order to give the document a colour of solemnity, it was hanged in the *Kābah*. Though primarily so, the ban was not to be only

---

1 *A covenant called Sahīfah or Deed of Ostracism.*
2 *It was drafted by Mansūr bin Ikrimah. The Prophet subsequently invoked God against him and some of his fingers withered.*

economic in nature but a total one covering all social and cultural aspects. According to provisions of the pact, no one was to do any selling or buying or any other business dealing with anyone belonging to the excommunicated clans. None was to have any marital tie with them or associate with them in any manner; even speaking to them was prohibited. Special care was to be taken not to allow any provision to go to the banned people. The boycott was to continue until such time *Muhammad* renounced his claims to prophethood or else was outlawed by *Hāshim* and handed over for execution. The decision to impose the boycott made the situation so charged with tension that the Hashimites in general and the Muslims in particular apprehended violent attacks from the disbelievers; for better security, they decided to abandon their houses scattered all over the city and form a ghetto. Therefore, all families of *Banū Hāshim* and *Banū Muttalib* shifted along with the Prophet and *Abū Tālib* to a cave-type narrow mountain defile on the eastern outskirts of *Makkah* known as *Shib Abū Tālib*. This mountain pass was the ancestral property of *Hāshim* and was cut off by rocks or walls from the city except for one narrow gateway. Thus were the Hashimites and the Muttalibs confined to a state of siege and were cut off from the rest of the world for three long years.

The boycott was rigorously enforced by the *Quraysh* leaders under the direction of *Abū Jahal*, but due to some inherent problems, it could not be foolproof. It was a move that violated the tribal code of conduct and was, therefore, construed as unjust and unnecessary by many a rightly thinking leader right from the beginning. Moreover, the Hāshims and the Muttalibs had many relatives in other clans who were by no means prepared to disown the relationship and let their brethren starve to death. Therefore, eluding the vigilance of *Quraysh*, many relatives and philanthropic persons from other clans, though disbelievers, joined the Muslims like *Abū Bakr* and *Umar* in clandestinely sending food, water, and other provisions to the *Shib* from time to time. Thus, *Hishām ibn Amr*, related to *Banū Hāshim* through mother, used to send food- and water-laden camels to the ravine stealthily during night; once when caught, the stuff was seized and he was threatened. We are told that another person, *Hakīm ibn Hizām*, a nephew of *Khadījah*, used to similarly send supplies to the ghetto. One night while carrying a bag of wheat with the help of his slave, he was intercepted by *Abū Jahal* who wanted to confiscate it. He was soon joined by a nonbeliever, *Abul Bakhtarī*, who happened to pass through. As a matter of principle, he supported *Hakīm* as the latter was sending Khadījah's own food to her and no one had the right to stop the same. The situation occasioned a brawl; he came to blows with *Abū Jahal* and hit him with a camel's jaw, leaving him wounded.

Notwithstanding the help received from time to time, however, the prolonged boycott inflicted untold hardships on inmates of the *Shib*. Apart from perpetual hunger and sickness resulting from a famine-like situation, it subjected them to unbearable social and psychological pressures. Traditions recount a series of poignant stories of misery and suffering encountered by them, details of which may be found in Suhaili's *Raud al Unūf*. According to a *hadīth*, once during starvation, *Sād ibn Abū Waqqās* had to roast and eat a piece of leather which he happened to find. *Ibn Sād* reports that the unbelievers used to be amused to hear the cries of hungry children. No wonder, the death of *Khadījah* and *Abū Tālib* shortly after lifting of the boycott in 619 is attributed to suffering and sickness faced by them during these difficult days. To add to physical agony, the Prophet and his family were in perpetual fear of violent attacks by the pagans. It is said that extremely concerned about the Prophet's personal security, *Abū Tālib* used to shift him from one bed to the other during nights. Further, the ban ruined the economy of the proscribed clans and left the Muslims totally impoverished. The vast wealth of *Khadījah* was totally exhausted in procuring food and water at exorbitant rates. *Abū Bakr* also was no longer a rich man. According to a source, his wealth of 40,000 dirhams at the time of joining *Islām* had dwindled to a mere 5,000 after lifting of the ban.

Despite unpopularity and criticism, the boycott which began in the seventh year of the mission continued for three years.

With passage of time, the issue started dividing the *Quraysh* and opposition to it gathered momentum. Apart from being a shameful violation of the tribal ethics and arousing a wave of sympathy for the beleaguered clans, the ban was telling upon the commercial interest of many polytheists as well who were in favour of its withdrawal. Ultimately, a group of five disbelievers, all related to the two banned clans, decided to publicly oppose the boycott and get it revoked. This is sometimes called the 'revolt of the five'. Initiative in this direction was taken by *Hishām ibn Amr* of *Makhzūm* who used to secretly send provisions to the ghetto. He roped in four other important individuals—*Zuhair* son of *Abū Umayyah* of *Makhzūm*, *Abul Bakhtarī* of *Asad*, *Mutīm ibn Adī* of *Nawfal*,[1] and *Zamā ibn al Aswad* of *Asad*. All the five are said to have initially objected to the document of boycott at the time of its ratification. The group held its secret meeting at *Hajūn* in order to decide strategy and resolved to mobilize public opinion against the great injustice being done to the proscribed clans. The next morning, they went together to the *Kābah*, denounced the ban as utterly unjustifiable, insisted on the leaders to rescind the same by emotional speeches[2] and expressed their intention of tearing the document into pieces. *Abū Jahal* strongly protested but, noticing the mood of others, did not resist at the moment. Before he could plan to react, *Mutīm* grabbed the document, and to the great amazement of all, it was seen that worms had already eaten up the document except the traditional formula mentioning the name of God— *'Bismika Allā humma'*.[3]

This strong omen had a favourable psychological effect in silencing the opponents taking advantage of which, *Mutīm* at once tore it into pieces.[4] The boycott now stood annulled; the group of five immediately left for the *Shib* and escorted the inmates back to join the mainstream. *Abū Tālib* composed verses

---

1 *He was the chief of Nawfal clan.*
2 *Ibn Ishāq refers to the powerful speech of Zuhair.*
3 *It is said that the Prophet had already informed about eating up of the document by worms except the name of God.*
4 *Ibn Sād.*

in praise of the five disbelieving heroes who were successful in putting an end to the boycott. According to some biographers,[1] subsequently the disbelievers who had helped revoke the pact of boycott, went to the Prophet and vehemently requested him to give their gods some recognition as a gesture of reconciliation. The Prophet was rather inclined in gratitude for the favours they had shown, but God guided him, and he finally rejected their request. It was in this connection that verses 73–74 of *Surah* 17 were revealed. It is sometimes pointed out that some influential Muslims like *Abū Bakr*, *Uthmān*, and *Umar*, who belonged to other clans unaffected by the interdiction, could have effectively worked for its revocation or, at least, joined and supported the movement launched by the five. The sources, however, do not make any mention of their role in this regard. Perhaps due to extreme hatred of the pagans, they had ceased to exercise any influence on their society.

In its ultimate outcome, the much-hyped boycott failed to achieve effect as desired by *Quraysh*. Neither the Prophet nor the Muslims at large showed any sign of surrender or submission; instead, as enjoined by contemporary revelations, they endured unspeakable sufferings with greater faith, resolution, and patience. During the ban, a series of revelations descended which talked about stories of previous prophets who were subjected to persecution by the people but were helped by God by awarding exemplary punishments to their opponents. The Muslims derived great strength and enthusiasm from such stories. The interdiction also failed to break the unity and support of members of the two proscribed clans for the Prophet. In one sense, the boycott even proved counterproductive for *Quraysh*. The Prophet drew much attention out of the issue, the new religion was talked about throughout Arabia, and sufferings inflicted left a wave of sympathy for it. Nor did the Prophet ever cease preaching while shut up within the cave. During the four sacred months when violence was considered a sacrilege, he used to go out and preach the pilgrims at venues of different fairs like *Minā*, *Majannah*, and

---

1   *Saīd ibn Jubayr and Qatādah.*

Ukāz apart from *Makkah*, but the squint-eyed *Abū Lahab*[1] always followed him and spoilt his chances by mischievous remarks.

For sometime following withdrawal of the boycott, hostilities seemed to have relaxed bringing about much relief to the nascent Muslim community. According to some scholars, it was on hearing exaggerated reports about this temporary phase that many emigrants from *Abbyssinia* returned to *Makkah* but went back noticing that persecution was still continuing. The seemingly improved situation, however, was to shortly[2] get transformed dramatically ushering in the most difficult phase of the Prophet's life. This was due to the death of the two most important individuals in the Prophet's life—*Khadījah* and *Abū Tālib*—which made his position precarious. They were the two strongest pillars of his psychological and physical support and without them he was left extremely desolate and despondent. There is difference of opinion as to who of the two died first, but the two deaths certainly took place at a very short interval, perhaps due to sickness caused by hunger and hardships during the period of excommunication. Because of the highest degree of grief caused to the Prophet and the believers, the year 619 is known in the history of *Islām* as 'the year of sorrow'. *Khadījah* died in the month of *Ramadan* at the age of 65 and was buried at a place called *Hajūn*. The Prophet is said to have himself laid her in grave.[3] Her married life with the Prophet was a record of the highest degree of devotion and sacrifice. A lady of great wealth and fortune, she cheerfully shared all difficulties with the Prophet sacrificing not only her wealth but also her life for his sake; one of the richest traders at the time of marriage, she was penniless at the time of death, the household not even having money to buy a shroud for her burial. No wonder the loss of the most loving and supporting companion and the most dependable counsellor in temporal as well as spiritual matters was to prove irreparable and filled the Prophet's heart with the highest degree

---

1   *Whose name meant 'father of the flame'.*

2   *The same year i.e. tenth year after the mission corresponding to 619.*

3   *Ibn Sād.*

of sorrow, leaving a permanent emptiness in it. After her death, the Prophet bestowed on her the honour of belonging to the rank of four perfect women along with mother of Jesus, sister of Moses, and his daughter *Fātimah*. She was also the first Muslim to have received confirmation from God in the very early years of the mission regarding her place[1] in the Paradise—a rare divine tribute conveyed through Gabriel which was befitting her status in *Islām*.

The Prophet's uncle, *Abū Tālib*, died an octogenarian. When he fell sick, news quickly spread around *Makkah* that he was going to die. Since he had himself not become a Muslim, and yet was trusted by the Prophet, *Quraysh* saw him as a potential mediator through whom reconciliation could be negotiated with *Muhammad*. *Abū Jahal*, therefore, visited his deathbed along with *Abū Sufyān*, *Utbah*, and *Umayyah bin Khalāf* and requested to persuade his nephew to follow his own religion but stop tampering with theirs. The Prophet was called for the purpose but rejected their offer, remaining adamant on preaching unity of God. After the *Quraysh* leaders had left, uttering bitter remarks, *Abū Tālib* spoke approvingly of his nephew's decision. Hopeful that his beloved uncle might join his faith before death, the Prophet earnestly begged him to profess *Islām* so that he could intercede for him with God. *Abū Tālib*, however, did not agree and replied, '*If I were to embrace your faith, our tribal leaders would become even more hostile to you and rest of my family than they already are. Moreover, they would say that I had embraced your faith, not from genuine conviction but from fear of death.*' This is the version of *Bukhāri* and *Muslim* showing that *Abū Tālib* died an infidel. This view is considered more trustworthy and it is said that verse 28: 56 of the *Qurān* confirms this. *Ibn Ishāq*, however, mentions that when *Abū Tālib* was breathing his last, he was murmuring something inaudible. Another uncle of the Prophet, *Abbās*, who was present, put his ear near Abū Tālib's lips and heard him say the *Shahādah*; but when he informed the Prophet about this, the latter replied, '*I did not hear it.*' However, though dying a disbeliever, Abū Tālib's services to *Islām* were no less

---

1 *A palace of pearls in Jannat.*

significant than those of even many of the leading believers. Right from inception, he was the bulwark of support to the Prophet and *Islām* and made all conceivable sacrifices for the sake of his nephew whom both he and his wife loved more than their own children. It may not be far to see that but for his strong protection and fearless support, *Islām* might have died in its very infancy. 'A second *Khadījah* might be found, but not a second *Abū Tālib*,' remarked the Orientalist William Muir. Though the statement belittles the status of *Khadījah*, for a second *Khadījah* also could never be found, the remark sums up the importance of *Abū Tālib* in the history of *Islām*.

The death of *Khadījah* was undoubtedly a great personal loss to the Prophet. But more serious in its consequences was the demise of *Abū Tālib* who was the chief of *Hashīm* clan. Despite preaching a menacingly radical faith, the Prophet had so far escaped serious violence only due to the strong and unfailing protection of *Abū Tālib* and his whole clan. Now after his death, his brother, *Abū Lahab*, who was an inveterate enemy of *Islām*, took over as chief of the clan. Due to obvious social compulsions, however, he continued with the clan's protection to *Muhammad*, but it was only a nominal protection and *Quraysh* could well see through it. The arrangement thus failed to deter the disbelievers from harassing and torturing the Prophet with impunity and incidents started occurring frequently. We are told by traditions that the disbelievers started misbehaving with him day in and day out.[1] *Uqbah* again started his nasty games with sheep's uterus, throwing it on him during prayers and even into his cooking pot.

Throwing dust and filth on him while praying or otherwise became the order of the day. On one such occasion when he returned home with soil thrown all over his head and body, his

---

1 *Persecution of other Muslims was also redoubled. It was during these days that Abū Bakr and Talhā were subjected to torture by Nawfal, Khadījah's half-brother; they were left lying on public highway with hands and feet bound and roped together. Abū Bakr was also frequently targeted by Umayyah, Bilāl's former master. Apprehending serious hazard, he even attempted to migrate but came back when provided protection by the chief of Qarā.*

daughter *Fātimah* burst into tears, and the Prophet complained of superficiality of Abū Lahab's protection. But the situation was soon to become even worse as *Abū Lahab* cleverly prompted the Prophet to declare that ancestors of his clan including *Abd al Muttalib* had been suffering punishment in the Hell for infidelity. He was then charged of showing disrespect to the ancestors, an offence amounting to blasphemy according to tribal code of conduct; and on this ground, *Abū Lahab* not only withdrew clan's protection from him but also outlawed him. According to some scholars, it was due to this reason that *Abū Lahab* was subjected to severe damnation in *Surāh* 111 of the *Qurān*.

Without any tribal protection whatsoever, the Prophet's life in *Makkah* now became highly insecure. The *Quraysh* had not only turned a completely deaf ear to his message but were violently hostile and determined to annihilate *Islām*. The Prophet, therefore, desperately needed an asylum with tribal protection and a people receptive to his message. His choice fell on *Tāif*, a prosperous neighbouring city, about forty miles east of *Makkah*, which was inhabited by *Thāqif* tribe. Earlier, a rival to *Makkah* as a trading city, it was a hill station known for its fruit gardens and agriculture. As the seat of goddess *al Lāt*, the town was an important centre of pilgrimage also. Since it was the summer resort of the peninsula, the rich Makkan merchants had built houses and estates there, the town remaining under their sphere of influence. We do not exactly know what motivated the Prophet to seek help from *Tāif* which was apparently under his enemy's control. Perhaps he expected the needed help from the ruling clan of *Banū Abd Yalīl* which is said to have been related to him through mother. In addition, he had spent his childhood with *Banū Sād* who were settled near *Tāif* and were expected to have some influence there. Another probable reason could have been the influence of his favourably disposed uncle *Abbās* in *Tāif*; he was a banker and had lent money to many in *Tāif*.

The Prophet, however, kept his destination a secret and went alone to *Tāif* on foot. According to some authorities, his adopted son *Zayd* accompanied him. With a view to win over the leaders before approaching the public at large, he straightaway went to the three sons[1] of *Amr ibn Umayyah*,[2] who were leaders of the ruling family. He invited them to accept *Islām* and sought their protection, but was insultingly rebuffed. One of them said, '*I am no more convinced that you are messenger from God, than I am willing to go to Makkah and tear down the Kābah.*' The second leader said, '*Surely a messenger of God would be a more impressive man than you.*' And the third replied, '*Do not let me ever speak with you again. If you are truly a messenger of God, as you say, then I am not worthy even to be in your presence. But if you are lying, then I am in danger of being corrupted by you.*' In fact, the disdainful rejection of the Prophet by the *Thāqif* leaders was due to the fear of antagonizing the powerful *Quraysh* by providing support to their enemy. Further, any accommodation of *Islām* in *Tāif* would amount to rejection of *al Lāt* which, in its turn, would deprive the city of its importance as a place of pilgrimage.

To the Prophet, however, more disturbing than the humiliating treatment of the *Thāqif* leaders was the fear of the news of his failed mission reaching *Makkah*; that would surely encourage the *Quraysh* leaders in their attacks on him. So he requested them not to reveal the purpose of his visit. But they paid no heed to his request and instead instigated the street boys and slaves to harass him and drive him out. The rabble chased him, manhandled him, and pelted him with stones, leaving his feet wounded. With great difficulty, he managed to escape and take shelter in a grape orchard. Extremely dejected and disappointed at the humiliating treatment and in severe pain, the Prophet addressed a highly touching prayer to God seeking protection in the light of His face; the prayer has become famous as a paradigm

---

1 *Abdu Yālayl, Masūd, and Habīb.*
2 *Whom Walid used to consider as his Thāqif counterpart.*

of the faithful's response while put under serious trial by God.[1]
The response of God to the prayer seemed to come immediately.[2]
The orchard belonged to *Utbah* and *Shaybah*[3] who were then
present there and were watching the Prophet's predicament. They
did not like a respectable fellow *Quraysh* being subjected to such
a humiliating treatment, took pity, and sent a bunch of grapes to
him through their Christian slave named *Addās*. The slave was
highly impressed by the conduct and utterances of the Prophet
and when the latter informed him about his prophethood, he at
once recognized him. Like the *Negus*, he could see the connection
between the two religions, immediately embraced *Islām*, and
showed great reverence for the Prophet, covering his body with
kisses. Later, after the Prophet's departure, his masters brought
him to book for falling a prey into the hands of *Muhammad*,
but he informed them that only a prophet could know what that
man knew.

On his journey back to *Makkah*, the Prophet halted midway
at a place called *Nakhlah* to spend the night. It is said that when
he was reciting the *Qurān* during night, a group of seven *jinns*
passed through; greatly attracted by the power and beauty of the
Quranic verses under recitation, they all embraced *Islām*. This
story regarding conversion of the *jinns* has been referred to in the

---

1   *'O, al Llah, to Thee I complain of my weakness, little resource, and
lowliness before men. O Most Merciful, Thou art the Lord of the weak
and Thou art my Lord. To whom wilt Thou confide me? To one afar
who will misuse me? Or to an enemy to whom Thou hast given power
over me? If Thou art not angry with me, I care not. Thy favour is more
wide for me. I take refuge in the light of Thy countenance by which the
darkness is illumined, and things of this world and the next are rightly
ordered, lest Thy anger descend upon me or Thy wrath light upon me. It
is for Thee to be satisfied until Thou art well pleased. There is no power
and no might save in Thee.'*

2   *According to one tradition, the Lord then sent the angel of mountain
who sought the Prophet's permission to destroy Tāif by joining together
the two hills between which the town was located. But the Prophet asked
him not to do that.*

3   *The two brothers were pagan leaders of Abdū Shams branch of Quraysh.*

Qurān as well.[1] Given the violently hostile mood of the *Quraysh* leaders, however, it was not at all safe for the Prophet to re-enter *Makkah* without strong protection of some clan. He, therefore, stopped a few miles short of *Makkah* and sent messengers to two of the clan chiefs—*Akhnās ibn Shāriq* of *Zuhrā* and *Suhayl ibn Amr* of *Āmir*—requesting them to provide protection to him in *Makkah*; but both of them refused on points of tribal principle. *Akhnās* replied that since he himself was a confederate, he could not provide the needed protection. *Suhayl* replied that *Banū Āmir* could not give protection against *Banū Kāb*. Finally, a third leader, *Mutīm ibn Adī*, the chief of *Nawfal*, who was broad-minded and had played a leading role in annulment of the boycott, accepted to take him under his protection. Some authors suggest that his protection was with an understanding that the Prophet would reduce his religious activities, while others say that it was unconditional. He along with his sons escorted the Prophet,[2] first to the *Kābah* and then to his house, publicly announcing his protection. It is sometimes pointed out that some of the members of the Muslim community in *Makkāh* were themselves men of influence and physical strength but they did not come forward to provide protection to the Prophet or to guard him at this stage. In fact, the sources are silent about their role. It appears that such believers themselves were under heavy persecution and had been outlawed by their clans; what the Prophet actually wanted was a strong clan protection which was beyond their capacity as individuals.

It was during this phase of utter disappointment and distress following the humiliating experience of *Tāif* that the Prophet had the greatest mystical experience of his life, i.e. his miraculous transportation one night from the *Kābah* to the site of *Masjid al Aqsa* at Jerusalem, elevation therefrom through the heavens to the highest horizon and direct appearance before and dialogue with *Allāh* at the closest possible proximity. To the faithful, it was a

---

1   *Qurān 46: 29–32.*

2   *According to some writers, the Prophet had then taken shelter in mount Hira from where Mutīm escorted him.*

multipurpose move of God. Apart from removing demoralization of the Prophet due to setbacks suffered, it was meant to show him the extraordinary signs and glory of the Almighty, so essential for development of his knowledge and personality as the last but the most important prophet. It was also for the sake of imparting some special commands and instructions to His messenger in His immediate presence which were most important and fundamental to the faith. The event, therefore, amounted to the gift of the highest spiritual status to the Prophet, an object of great pride and glory for the community. Though the whole nocturnal experience is commonly known as *Mirāj*,[1] many scholars separate the journey into two parts:

- *Isrā* or the night journey from *Makkah* to Jerusalem performed horizontally on earth;
- *Mirāj* or the ascension to the heavens performed vertically in the space.

It is said that the event took place on the night of twenty-seventh *Rajab*[2] about a year before the *Hijrah*, that is, in 621. This night is celebrated by the Muslims with prayers and recitations; in some areas like Turkey, mosques are also decorated with lamps during the night.

The *Mirāj* was a purely religious or spiritual experience and so it is not to be seen in the light of concrete historical evidence. That an event of this type actually took place is confirmed by the *Qurān* itself which may be regarded as the basic source of information on the subject. The first verse of *Surah* 17—*Bani Isrāil*—refers to *Isrā*: '*Glory be to Him who carried His servant from the Sacred Mosque to the Distant Mosque the precincts of which We have blessed in order that We might show him some of our*

---

1   *Though the term literally means ladder, it conveys the meaning of ascent or ascension. In Urdu, the word also conveys the sense of climax.*

2   *Seventh month of the Islamic Calendar.*

signs.[1] Further, a few verses of *Surah* 53—*An Najm*—refers to the ascension and describe the Prophet's experiences in the heavens:

> *While he was in the highest part of the horizon:*
> *Then He approached and came closer,*
> *And was at a distance of but two bow-length or nearer;*
> *So did (Allāh) convey the inspiration to his servant what he (meant) to convey.*
> *The (Prophet's) heart in no way falsified that which he saw.*
> *Will Ye then dispute with him concerning what he saw?*
> *For indeed he saw Him at a second descent,*
> *Near the Lote-Tree of the uttermost boundary.*
> *Near it is the Garden of Abode.*
> *Behold, the Lote-Tree was shrouded with what shrouds.*
> *(His) sight never swerved, not did it go wrong!*
> *For truly did he see, of the signs of his Lord. The Greatest.*[2]

The information contained in the *Qurān*, however, was too brief and given in mystical terms. Subsequently, an elaborate story was developed about the event by a large number of canonical *ahadīth* as well as commentaries of the *Qurān*.[3] A mass of more beautiful and gorgeous legends was also woven around the nucleus provided in the *Qurān* by a series of untestified traditions taken note of by many of the biographers. In addition, in course of time, the event became the favourite subject of *Sufīs* and poets of different Muslim languages and inspired a voluminous literature

---

1 *Some authorities like Sulaiman Nadwi claimed that almost the whole of Surah 17 is related to the ascension in some or the other way.*

2 *Qurān 53: 7–18.*

3 *According to Al Zurqani, there were not less than 45 Companions who gave account of different details of the night journey.*

in which the story was embellished with more and more charming and even fantastical details in order to glorify the Prophet. The subject even inspired many beautiful paintings in Iran and other countries under the influence of Islamic culture. Thus, we have an extraordinarily large number of sources on the subject. Even if the story is kept confined to the description given by reliable *ahadīth* only, given the large number of narrators, there are inevitably some differences in sequence of events as well as details thereof.

As told by the biographers, the Prophet was very fond of visiting the *Kābah* during night hours for praying. Once he was spending the night at the house of his cousin, *Umm Hāni,*[1] which was located close to the Sanctuary. After spending some time in her house, he went to the Mosque for prayers but felt sleepy and lay down in the *Hijr.*[2] There, while he was asleep, Gabriel came, waked him up, and took him to the *Zamzam*. As an initiatory measure of spiritual purification, the angel opened his chest, washed his heart with *Zamzam* water, and closed it back. He next led him to the gate of the Mosque where a celestial steed was waiting which has been named *Burāq* (lightning) in the sources. The animal looked something between a mule and an ass, was white in colour, and had a human head with wings on sides. It was a high-speed flying creature whose every stride was as far as his eyes could see. The Prophet and the angel both mounted *Burāq*. It is said that when the Prophet was mounting the unique steed, he shied and was chided by Gabriel, who had to remind him that none more honourable before God had ever mounted him. The animal felt ashamed, started sweating, and stood motionless allowing the Prophet to mount with ease. Thus mounted on the heavenly animal, the Prophet along with the angel flew to Jerusalem, on way flying over *Yathrib* and *Khaybar*. According to a tradition, they first had a brief halt on mount *Sināi* for prayer where God had spoken to Moses; they then stopped at

---

1   *Her original name was Hind. She was daughter of Abū Tālib and sister of Alī & Jāfar.*

2   *An enclosed area to the north-west of the Sanctuary which houses the tombs of Ismāil and Hāgar.*

Bethlehem where Jesus was born and finally landed at the Temple of Solomon, the site of *Masjid al Aqsa* at Jerusalem. At Jerusalem, the Prophet met a group of previous prophets which included Abraham, Moses, and Jesus. There, a group prayer of the prophets was held under the leadership of *Muhammad* which shows his superiority over all other prophets. Then two vessels, one filled with wine and the other with milk, were offered to him; he took the glass of milk and drank whereupon Gabriel remarked that he had been rightly guided and that wine was forbidden for him.[1]

After completion of business at Jerusalem, the Prophet, accompanied and guided by Gabriel, undertook the second part of the night journey which was ascension to the heavens.[2] While some authors say that the Prophet's ascension took place mounted on *Burāq* itself, others mention that it was through an endless ladder[3] which appeared on 'Jacob's Rock' located at the centre of *al Aqsa*. During this transcendental journey, the Prophet guided by the archangel, passed through different levels of heavens beholding hidden wonders of the other world. The traditions have charmingly described the same. While ascending, they first reached the gate of the heavens called the 'Gate of the Watchers'. This area was under the charge of one angel called *Ismaīl* who had 12,000 other angels under his command, there being again 1,200 angels under each. Therefrom, the Prophet ascended the first heaven[4] which

---

1   *According to another tradition, three vessels — one of water, the other of milk and the third one of wine — were offered to him and he accepted that of milk. This signified adoption by him of the 'middle path' between extreme austerity and hedonism.*

2   *There is divergence of opinion among scholars regarding order in which the two parts of the journey took place. While it is generally believed that visit to Al Aqsa took place first, some place it after completion of the ascension. Ibn Kathīr placed visit to Jerusalem on return journey giving his own reasons for that.*

3   *According to one tradition, the Prophet remarked that this ladder was one of the most beautiful objects he had ever seen.*

4   *As per one story, the first heaven was made of pure silvers and stars were suspended from its vaults by chains of gold; each was being guarded by an angel to prevent demons and spirits from getting access to the holy place.*

was under the charge of Adam who was seen reviewing the spirits of his offspring. While taking round of the first heaven, Gabriel introduced him to *Mālik*, Keeper of the Hell, who unlike all other angels, did not smile and welcome the Prophet. But on advice of Gabriel, he showed him the Hell. As soon as he opened the door, a highly frightening scene of raging fire became visible. While taking round of the Hell, the Prophet witnessed different types of sinners being put through highly painful punishments. There were men having lips like those of camel who were continuously swallowing fire-like stones which were coming out of their posteriors; they were persons who had sinfully devoured wealth of the orphans. There were usurers gasping with thirst and having abnormally large bellies. They were being trampled by large ferocious creatures looking like camels. The Prophet also saw men who were having good as well as rotten meat before them; they were eating the latter and leaving the former. He was informed that they were adulterers who abandoned their own wives and went after the wives of others. The fate of women who had fathered bastards on their husbands was also shown to the Prophet; they were hanging with their breasts.

The Prophet continued his ascent through the seven heavens meeting different important prophets at different levels and exchanging compliments with them. But unlike what they appeared at Jerusalem, they were now in their heavenly forms and the Prophet wondered at their transfiguration. According to traditions, *Muhammad* met the following eight prophets in different heavens during his journey to the top:

First Heaven	–	Adam
Second Heaven	–	Jesus, son of Mary, and John the Baptist (*Yahyā*) son of *Zakariah*.
Third Heaven	–	Joseph (*Yūsuf*) son of Jacob.
Fourth Heaven	–	Enoch (*Idrīs*)
Fifth Heaven	–	Aaron (*Harūn*) son of *Imrān*.
Sixth Heaven	–	Moses (*Musā*) son of *Imrān*
Seventh Heaven	–	Abraham (*Ibrahīm*

As opined by some scholars[1] his meeting with only these eight prophets signifies the fact that they alone were the important prophets of the Abrahamic line who had had their own *mirāj* in some or the other way. Abraham's location at the highest level of the heavens shows his very special position in Islamic tradition. In different *ahadīth*, the Prophet is later said to have described the physical appearance of some of the prophets he met. Jesus was a reddish man of medium height with freckles on his face as if he had just come out from a bath. Aaron was an extraordinarily handsome man with white hair and long beard and Moses was a dark man with hooked nose. But supreme was the beauty of Joseph who, in the language of the Prophet, had been '*endowed with no less than half of all existing beauty*'. His face had the splendour of moon at the full. Abraham whom the Prophet met in the seventh heaven was sitting on a throne at the gate of the celestial mosque, *Bayt al Mamūr*.[2] The Prophet remarked that there was great resemblance between Abraham and him except that the former was older. On the highest floor, Gabriel showed him the Paradise. There the Prophet saw an attractive damsel with dark red lips and was quite amused when she revealed that she was meant for *Zayd bin Harithā*. The inexplicable beauty and charm of the Paradise was later on described by the Prophet in a *hadīth* collected by *Bukhāri*: '*A piece of Paradise the size of a bow is better than all beneath the Sun, whereon it riseth and setteth; and if a woman of the people of Paradise appeared unto the people of earth, she would fill the space between heaven and here below with light and with fragrance.*'

The highest point Gabriel could take the Prophet was 'the Lote-Tree of the Uttermost End'—*Sidrat al Muntahā*—as it is named in the *Qurān*. Since the Prophet's experience at this point was purely mystical and metaphysical surpassing all human understanding, it left the commentators baffled, impeding a clear comprehension and explanation of the same. The earliest

---

1   *Muhammad Hamidullah.*
2   *As per a tradition, everyday 70,000 angels entered the Mamūr not to come back until the day of Resurrection.*

commentator, *Tabarī*, on the basis of sayings of the Prophet has said, '*The Lote-Tree is rooted in the Throne, and it marks the end of knowledge of every knower, be he arch-angel or prophet–messenger. All beyond it is hidden mystery, unknown to any save God alone.*' The Lote-Tree marked the line of demarcation between the realm of God and that of spirits and angels. It is said that the divine writs are first sent to the Lote-Tree from where the angels bring it to earth. According to some commentators, the Divine Light, that is, God, descended upon the Lote-Tree and the Prophet could see Him without turning aside his eyes, and he received the special commandments at this very location. Others, however, opine that after reaching the Lote-Tree, Gabriel informed that he could not cross that line as in that case he would be burnt to ashes by manifestation of the Divine Glory (*tajallī*). But he advised the Prophet to proceed further alone as he had been invited by God. The Prophet, therefore, proceeded and as he approached, he heard the sound of pens writing up divine decrees; he then reached the 'Enclosure of the Holiness'—*Hadirat al Qudūs*, which was perhaps the same as the invisible Divine Throne. It is said that from this place, heaven and earth appeared reduced to the size of a mustard seed in the middle of a field.[1] As mentioned in verses 7–10 of *Surah* 53, it is at this point that the Prophet had rendezvous with God and dialogue with Him, receiving the divine commandments.

If the different views and opinions of authorities about God's commands and gifts received by the Prophet during *Mirāj* are taken into account, they were as under:

1. A command to the Muslims to perform fifty ritual prayers (*salāt*) a day. According to a tradition, while the Prophet was returning, Moses advised him again and again to go and request *Allāh* to reduce the same as ritual prayer was a very heavy responsibility which would fail his *Ummah*; and so the Prophet repeatedly went back to God requesting for reduction, the number of prayers finally getting reduced to five per day only. But it was the

---

1   *M. H. Haykal.*

supreme mercy and generosity of *Allāh* that He declared
that one who performed only five prayers a day in good
faith and in trust of God's bounty would get heed of fifty
prayers, that is, ten times.[1] The issue of command for
Salāt directly by God was, in course of time, interpreted
by the commentators as having given a new significance
and meaning to this fundamental prayer of *Islām*—
an individual elevation towards God of *Mirāj* by every
Muslim[2] five times a day.

2. The gift of the last two verses of *Surah 2—al Baqarā*[3]
which described the fundamental elements of the faith
in categorical terms including need for continuous
prayer for the Lord's help and forgiveness. Thus, unlike
the remaining portion of the *Qurān*, these two verses
are regarded as revealed on the highest horizon directly
by *Allāh* and so their recitation is considered highly
effective for all purposes.

3. Grant of right to intercession (*Shafāat*), to *Muhammad*.
In Islamic tradition it is believed that *Muhammad* is the
only Prophet who will be allowed to intercede with *Allāh*
for his *Ummah* on the Day of Judgment.

---

1 *Hadith Qudsi of Bukhari—This is as per principle contained in verse
6:160 of the Qurān.*

2 *In support of this contention, the following statement was coined: 'As
salātu Mirāj ul Mumineen.'*

3 *The two verses read as under:*
*'285: The Apostle believeth in what hath been revealed to him from his
Lord, as do the men of faith. Each one believeth in Allah, His angels,
His books and His Apostles. And they say—"we hear and we obey (we
seek) Thy forgiveness. Our Lord, and to Thee is the end of all journeys."
286: No soul doth Allah place a burden greater than it can bear. It
gets every good that it earns, and it suffers every ill that it earns. (Pray)
Our Lord! Condemn me not, if we forget or fall into error. Our Lord!
Lay not on us a burden like that which thou didst lay on those before
us. Our Lord! Lay not on us a burden greater than we have strength
to bear. Blot out our sins, and grant us forgiveness. Have mercy on us.
Thou art our Protector; help us against those who stand against faith.'*

4. The gracious promise given to the Prophet that every Muslim who believes in one God will be finally saved in eternal life and shall find a place in the Paradise even after being purged by some punishment in the Hell.[1]

5. Issue of twelve commandments (as against ten given to Moses) to *Muhammad* as recounted in *Surah* 17.[2]

After completion of business in the heavens, Gabriel took the Prophet back through the same route as they had ascended and dropped him back at the *Kābah*. We learn from a *hadīth* of *Bukhāri* that on return, his bed was still warm and that the pitcher of water, which had tumbled over when he was carried away, had not yet leaked out completely. Obviously, the extraordinary journey of *Isrā* and *Mirāj* was beyond the domain of earthly physical laws of time and space. Thus, to the Sūfis, this experience of complete timelessness became a model of ecstatic state in which a man can spiritually live in a single moment through years.

After return, the Prophet went to the house of *Umm Hāni*, performed the morning prayer, and narrated his experience of *Isrā* to her. She immediately advised him not to disclose the story to the people lest they should disbelieve him, mock at him, and declare him insane. But the Prophet did not pay heed to her advice, went to the Mosque then and there, and informed the *Quraysh* leaders

---

1 *Muhammad Hamidullah.*

2 *Hamidullah enumerates the commandments as under:*

(i) *Worship none save Allah.*

(ii) *Kindness to parents.*

(iii) *Give the kinsman his due.*

(iv) *Be neither miserly nor squanderous.*

(v) *Slay not your children for fear of poverty.*

(vi) *Don't come near unto fornication and adultery.*

(vii) *Save with right, slay none.*

(viii) *Come not near the property of the orphans except for his good.*

(ix) *Keep the covenant.*

(x) *Fill the measure.*

(xi) *Follow not that of which you have no knowledge.*

(xii) *Walk not in the earth exultantly.*

of the same. Since the story was beyond the bounds of reason, they laughed at him in disbelief and pointed out absurdity of his claim. To them, it was impossible to reach Jerusalem and get back in a few hours for it took a caravan a month to reach there and another to return. In fact, they were quite amused by the Prophet's claim; at last they had a point to prove that he had gone mad. Even some of the Muslims who heard the story disbelieved the same and began to doubt if he was truly a God's messenger. *Ibn Ishāq* says that a few of them even apostatized.[1] They went to *Abū Bakr* in a group, informed him of the matter, and sought his opinion. *Abū Bakr* first thought they were lying but when they informed that the Prophet was openly telling the story in the Mosque, he replied, '*If he says so then it is true. And what is so surprising in that? He tells me that communications from God from heaven to earth come to him in an hour of the day or night and I believe him; and that is more extraordinary than that at which you boggle.*' He then went along with others to *Muhammad* and asked him to describe Jerusalem. The Prophet did so accurately to the full satisfaction of all who had seen the city. It was on this occasion that he gave *Abū Bakr* the honourific title of *as Siddīq*,[2] an epithet which was subsequently always added to his name.[3]

According to another story attributed to *Umm Hāni*, many infidels as well as Muslims asked the Prophet to furnish proof about his claim. In response, the Prophet described to them a caravan he had encountered on way to *Makkah* from Jerusalem. He also informed how he had guided one of its leaders to one of the camels which had gone astray and how he drank water from a jar kept on the back of a camel and replaced the cover. He further informed that he had passed a particular caravan at *Dajanān* (twenty-five kilometres from *Makkah*) with the leading camel

---

1 *It is said that verse 13: 62 of the Qurān concerns such people who had a change of heart on this occasion.*

2 *Meaning 'the great confirmer of truth'.*

3 *It is said that at this stage, the Prophet had disclosed the story of visit to Jerusalem only. Story of the other experience of Mirāj was disclosed by him to Abū Bakr and others later.*

having a load of two sacks, one black and the other multicolour; and judged by the distance at which he had noticed the caravan, he also predicted the expected time of its arrival at *Makkah*. To the surprise of everyone, all facts narrated by the Prophet were found correct on subsequent enquiry.

In course of time, the ascension of the Prophet became one of the most theologically speculated subjects of *Islām*. Muslim mystics, philosophers, and poets pondered on the nature, hidden meaning, and significance of the experience. In the *Sūfi* effort to achieve access to God, the *Mirāj* became a paradigm of their philosophy; they devised spiritual means for achieving this very goal and spoke in terms of annihilation (*fanā*) of individuality to be followed by its revival (*baqā*) as an enhanced self-realization. The example of *Mirāj* even entered the Western tradition and inspired Dante's account of his imaginary journey through hell and heaven in his *The Divine Comedy*. The theological debate about the nature of *Mirāj*, however, gave rise to a few conflicting opinions. The most important issue debated was whether the Prophet made his journey only in spirit or physically in body as well. *Ibn Ishāq* referred to a *hadīth* of *Āishah*, according to which *'the Apostle's body remained where it was but God removed his spirit by night'*. The traditions attributed to *Muāwiyā* and *Hasan al Basri* are also put forward to emphasize that ascension was only a vision or dream—a purely spiritual experience. The Mutazilite School, which applied a rationalistic approach to Islamic theology, considered it as a vision only which was supported by most of the modernists. *Shah Waliullāh* of Delhi attempted reconciliation and held that the ascension was physical but the body was then in possession of spiritual attributes.

This view, however, was strongly contradicted by orthodox scholars to whom *Mirāj* was physical as well as spiritual, and this continues to be the view of a majority. The great classical historian and commentator, *Tabarī*, opined that the journey took place in the physical body. The authorities who support this view point out that the relevant verses of *Surah* 53 strongly suggest that it was a bodily rather than a dream experience. After all, why should the *Qurān* make specific reference to close proximity, that is, two bow length or less, if it was purely spiritual, they would argue. According to *Maulana Shibli Numāni*, had it been merely a dream, its special mention in the *Qurān* as an extraordinary favour was not required and the limited span of time involved would have been meaningless. Further, why would the Prophet have needed a mount like *Burāq* for a purely spiritual journey? The traditional stories unanimously imply that the Prophet claimed to have undergone the experience in body. This was the reason why the polytheists as well as some of the Muslims reacted against him accusing him of telling lies. If it were the question of merely a dream, the pagans had no reason to criticize the Prophet and mock at him; nor could a dream have created disbelief and stirred the minds of some of the Muslims to the extent of apostasy. Another controversial question about the experience was whether the Prophet had really seen the Lord, and if so, whether he saw Him with his physical eyes or just experienced His presence only in heart. Verse 17 of *Surah* 53 clearly mentions that Muhammad's eyes did not rove even during the immediate vision of the Divine Essence. 'Not turning away his eyes' was seen in terms of his superiority over other prophets. The *Qurān* thus strongly suggests that it was a real vision with physical eyes. In some of the traditions when the Prophet was asked to explain what God looked like, he said that he saw Him in the most beautiful shape and that He was nothing but light (*Nūr*). This controversy, however, was beautifully summed up by *Qastallāni*: '*Some said he saw Gabriel at the highest horizon; others say he saw Allāh with his heart and his inner view; still others say he saw Him with his eyes; but all of them speak the truth for they only tell what they have heard.*' The mystics explained the matter in terms of a paradox in which the Prophet both saw and did not see the Divine Essence.

Though accounting for the highest exaltation of the Prophet through ascension, in outwardly terms, this period was one of the most difficult and disappointing in his life. In personal life, the death of *Khadījah* had left a vacuum in his heart and he was feeling absolutely lonely and desolate; there was officially none to look after his daughters and his household.[1] In public life, he had lost the erstwhile strong protection of his uncle and his clan; though *Mutīm* was magnanimous enough to provide protection, his position in *Makkah* was now not very safe. The opposition of *Quraysh* had proved irreconcilable and had assumed dangerous proportions. The worse part of the situation was that due to highly intensified persecution, it was not possible for the Muslims to practice *Islām* in *Makkah* without inviting trouble. The Prophet had lost almost all hope of converting anyone from *Quraysh*; spread of *Islām* had nearly come to a halt. It was now almost impossible for the Muslims to coexist in *Makkah* along with *Quraysh*, he thought. The only alternative now left to him seemed to convert some outlying tribe, obtain its protection, and migrate to its location for further preaching of *Islām* to other areas of the peninsula. But due to power and influence of *Quraysh*, even the outlying tribes, especially those having business dealing with them, were highly reluctant to accept the message of *Islām*; the highly disappointing experience of *Tāif* was fresh in his mind. The Prophet, however, had the strongest trust in the mercy and help of God and was sure his mission would succeed. He, therefore, concentrated on the outsiders congregating in *Makkah* and the nearby fairs during pilgrimage and visited the camps of different tribes—*Banū Kindah, Banū Kalb, Banū Hanīfah,* and *Banū Āmir ibn Sasaah*—inviting them to accept him as messenger and profess *Islām*. But none responded favourably, some even resorting to insulting remarks. *Banū Āmir*, though initially showing interest, turned out to be highly ambitious and demanded that in case he gained power in the long run, he should share it with them, a condition to which it was not possible for the Prophet to accede. Ultimately, however, favourable response started coming from the pilgrims of the oasis of *Yathrib* which, according to a *hadīth* of *Bukhari*, the

---

1   *Ever since Khadījah's death, his aunt Khawlah (Wife of Uthmān ibn Mazūn), had been devoting sometime to manage the affairs of his household. But this was not a regular arrangement.*

Prophet had already seen in a dream as the place of his likely emigration. After negotiations during the next two annual seasons of pilgrimage, the development finally led to the *Hijrāh* in September 622.

About the same time (June 620) when the Prophet was receiving green signals from Yathribite pilgrims groping towards solution of the crisis of his community, developments started taking place in his personal life as well which were to resolve problem of his household. After completion of period of mourning of the death of *Khadījah* with whom he had spent twenty-five years in devoted monogamy, he started receiving the idea of remarriage. He had two consecutive dreams in which he saw an angel handing over Abū Bakr's daughter *Āishah* to him wrapped in a silk—a suggestion that the girl was to become his wife. But *Āishah* was then only 6 years old and he was over 50. He, however, thought that if it was the will of God, He would make it possible. Very soon a suggestion came from his aunt, *Khawlah*, that he should marry another wife to look after the needs of his household. She suggested either *Sawdah* or *Āishah* for the purpose, the second name confirming truth of his dream. *Sawdah* was a widow aged about 30 and was the cousin as well as sister-in-law of *Suhayl*, the chief of *Āmir*. She along with her first husband *Sakrān* (brother of *Suhayl*) had emigrated to *Abyssinia* but both were in the first group which returned to *Makkah*. *Sakrān* had died shortly after return.

After due consideration, the Prophet gave acceptance for both the matches. *Sawdah* was only too willing to accept the offer since marriage with the Prophet would greatly enhance her status in the Muslim community, and the wedding took place soon. As for *Āishah*, she was too young to even understand the meaning of marriage. But *Abū Bakr* took it as a great opportunity to cement the closest tie with a person for whom he had the greatest religious reverence. Moreover, about this time, he was again without protection in *Makkah*[1] and the proposed matrimonial alliance would be a source of great strength. He, therefore, persuaded *Mutīm* to forego the promised match which the latter was only too happy to do since he did not want his son to join *Islām*. And so a few months after *Sawdah*'s marriage, *Āishah*'s betrothal to the Prophet took place at a function in which she was not personally present. In later years, she herself recalled that at the time of betrothal she did not even have a clear knowledge of the relationship she had entered into. She had the first inklings of her new status only when after the function she was advised by her mother not to go out for playing with friends and instead call them to her house. *Āishah*'s physical departure to the Prophet's house, however, was to take place after over 3 years in *Madinah* and the marriage would be consummated after she attained puberty.

These two marriages which were first in point of time after the death of *Khadījah* amply show the nature of the Prophet's many marriages which he contracted during the last twelve years of his life. Those who are critical of the Prophet for his multiple marriages and allege that they were the result of his weakness for the fair sex should note that neither of the two marriages was for lust or love; they were measures of social and political arrangement rather than of personal desire. *Āishah* was a small child and definitely had not been chosen for her sexual charm.

---

1   *As per account of the biographers, Abū Bakr had built a small mosque in the compound of his house the wall of which was quite low in height. When he recited the Qurān during prayers in his mosque, being extremely tender-hearted, he wept a lot and the people used to assemble and watch him. The Quraysh were intelligent enough to apprehend that the magical effect of recitation coupled with the highly emotional state of Abū Bakr would lead to large-scale conversions if the practice continued. They, therefore, sent a delegation to Ibn al Dughunnah, his protector, asking him to stop this practice of Abū Bakr as he had promised at the time of giving protection. But Abū Bakr refused to close down his mosque and instead withdrew himself from Dughunnah's protection declaring that God's protection was enough for him.*

As for *Sawdah*, she was middle-aged, had put on weight, and had ceased to be sexually attractive. She was chosen because she was mature and experienced, suitable to take over charge of his household and provide motherly help to his daughters. More importantly, she was from the family of the chief of *Āmir* and through this marriage the Prophet could have had a close link with the tribe; this would have helped him in obtaining support and recognition of an important tribe which he so badly needed at that point of time. Similarly, it was important to establish a stronger tie with *Abū Bakr* who was one of the most important members of the new community. In fact, those days in Arabia it was a practice to contract marriages for forging political alliances. The Prophet was trying to establish a new type of tribe based on religion rather than blood kinship; and in this he decided to use matrimonial ties in a big way.

CHAPTER VII

HIJRAH: THE TURNING POINT

When the Prophet found that *Islām* in *Makkah* was in danger due to the irreconcilably hostile attitude of *Quraysh*, he felt it highly desirable to preach *Islām* to the people coming from outside; this would help him find out a new base for migration of the Muslims and further spread of the faith. Of all the outsiders thus invited by him to the fold of *Islām*, those from *Yathrib* responded quite favourably. Unlike the Makkans, they had no vested interest standing in way of accepting the new religion. Moreover, living in the company of the *Jews*, they were well acquainted with the idea of one God and were psychologically prepared to receive the message of monotheism. From the Jewish rabbis, they had also heard about the likely arrival of a new prophet. Yet, their encouraging response was not solely due to religious appeal of *Islām*; an equally strong motivating factor was their own internal politics—a serious political crisis—for resolving which they badly needed a powerful ideology and a dynamic leader which *Islām* and the Prophet provided.

Located about 250 miles north of *Makkah*,[1] *Yathrib* was an agricultural oasis, a tract of fertile land, which was surrounded by volcanic hills, rocks, and infertile stony grounds. Spread over an area of about twenty square miles, it was not a compact city like *Makkah* but was rather a large settlement of villages inhabited by farmers cultivating dates and cereals. Its economy was predominantly agriculture-based though some trade also used to be carried on. The original inhabitants of the oasis were Jews who are said to have arrived and settled there from the north in the first century AD. They cleared the cultivable land, introduced farming, and lived in compact settlements in which they had erected rather impregnable forts[2] and citadels for safety against nomadic raids. Apart from being farmers, they were skilled in making jewellery, cloth, arms, and wine, their product being quite in demand. We do not know for certain whether these Jews were of *Arab* or Hebrew origin. They may have been refugees from Palestine or original Arab tribes converted to Judaism; but in the seventh century, they were culturally and linguistically indistinguishable from their pagan *Arab* neighbours though they preserved their separate religious identity. At the time of *Hijrah*, there were three main Jewish tribes in *Yathrib—Banū Qurayzah*, *Banū Nadīr*, and the smaller *Banū Qaynuqā*—the last being skilled jewellers residing within the city and running their own market. According to a rough estimate by an author, the total population of the Jews in *Yathrib* at the time of *Hijrah* was over 2,000. But this probably did not include *Qurayzah* and *Nadīr* who used to live outside *Yathrib* proper. *Samhūdī* in his *Wafā ul Wafā* mentions that the Jews of *Yathrib* were divided in more than twenty clans, mostly living as confederates of stronger Arab

---

1   *According to chroniclers, it was at a distance of 11 days caravan journey from Makkah.*

2   *According to one report, there were 59 such fortifications in Yathrib at the time of Hijrah.*

tribes. Subsequent to their settling down, prosperity of *Yathrib* attracted the pagan Arabs and *Banī Qaylah*,[1] who migrated from *Yaman* area in the wake of political instability and breaking of *Mārib* dam following floods, came and settled in *Yathrib* alongside the Jews. In course of time, they got divided into two tribes—*Aws* and *Khazraj*. At the time of the Prophet's arrival, the two pagan tribes had as many as eight clans.[2]

The pagan Arabs acquired the available less fertile land,[3] built their own fortresses on the pattern of the Jews and took to cultivation of dates. Nicknamed 'the fox', the Jews were unscrupulous and scheming; they were moneylenders, exploiting the pagans and concentrating wealth in their hands. Sometimes, pagan borrowers were even forced to mortgage their women and children to the Jews. Due to these reasons the pagans hated them and, according to a story, helped the Christians of the north in their fight against the Jews. On their part, the Jews sought to create friction between *Aws* and *Khazraj* in order to maintain their economic hold and political power. By the seventh century, however, the pagans were more numerous and at a slightly stronger position. But they used to think of the Jews as intellectually superior. The latter used to boast of possessing a superior religion and a scripture. According to an account, a saintly rabbi[4] migrated to *Yathrib* from Syria and informed that the reason for his coming was expected arrival of a great prophet, and the Jews used to threaten the pagans saying that the monotheistic prophet would support them and with his help they would exterminate the pagans as *Ād* and *Imrān* had been slain.

---

1 *They were of Qahtān stock.*
2 *Khazraj had four clans, namely, Mālik, Adiy, Māzin, and Dinār—all collaterals of Banū Najjār.*
   The Aws clans were Banū Abdul Ashhal, Banū Zafār, Banū Hāritha, and Banū Muāwiya.
3 *The Jews had already occupied the most fertile cultivable land known as 'the Heights'. The Arabs could get access to inferior quality of land called 'the Bottom' and this became a source of their irritation and dislike of the Jews.*
4 *His name was Ibn al Hayyabān.*

The real fight in *Yathrib*, however, was not between Jews and pagans but between the two pagan tribes themselves. Due to friction over scarce resources as also tacit instigation by the Jews, *Aws* and *Khazraj* became involved in a long-drawn warfare lasting for more than a century and involving almost all pagan as well as Jewish clans of *Yathrib*. The continual civil war was ruining the land, destroying the crops, and undermining the wealth and power of the oasis. By the time the Prophet started his public preaching in *Makkah*, three bloody battles had already been fought, generating a lot of tension. It had assumed the form of a war of attrition, leaving both sides exhausted and no group likely to get ascendancy. A fourth battle on a larger scale seemed inevitable. It was in view of this impending longer war that the *Aws* sent a delegation to *Makkah* in order to obtain help of *Quraysh*. When the Prophet heard about them, as per his practice, he met them and invited them to *Islām*. One of them, *Iyās bin Muādh*, showed keen interest in the Prophet's talks and told his companions that his message was definitely better than the purpose for which they had gone to *Makkah*, but he was rebuffed by the leader of the delegation. In the meantime, *Quraysh* refused to provide help and the group went back. Shortly afterwards, *Iyās* died, but while dying, he was continually testifying to oneness of God. He is sometimes counted as the first man from *Yathrib* to have entered *Islām*.

The civil war finally culminated in the sanguinary battle of *Buāth* in 618 which involved almost the total population of *Yathrib*. The Jewish tribes of *Nadīr* and *Qurayzah* supported *Aws* while that of *Qaynuqā* sided with *Khazraj*. The battle was fought fiercely, each party determined to exterminate the other. In the first round, *Aws* suffered reverses and fled; in frustration, their general *Abū Usayd* plunged spear in his own leg. The sacrifice of their general inspired them and they returned and fought vigorously, inflicting defeat on *Khazraj*, burning their houses and orchards and proceeding to completely wipe out their enemies, but they were stopped from doing so by implorations of the moderate leaders. The battle was highly destructive and it is said that most of the renowned warriors of the two tribes were killed in its course. In its ultimate result, however, it still remained indecisive; everyone knew that peace was only transitory as claims and counterclaims for blood money would lead to fresh violence. Little did one know at this stage that *Buāth* would turn out to be a blessing in disguise for *Islām*, paving the way for *Hijrah* as later on remarked by *Āishah*. Everyone in the oasis was now totally fed up with violence and there was a strong public opinion in favour of a lasting peace. The people realized that they needed a supreme leader of the type of a king, acceptable to all, to arbitrate disputes and bring about peace and unity. One of the chiefs of *Khazraj, Abd Allāh b. Ubayy,* who had refrained from fighting, probably due to his ambition of becoming such a leader, was seen by many as a possible candidate. We are told by sources that even order had been placed for making a crown for his coronation. He was nonetheless a member of *Khazraj* and his unanimous acceptability was doubtful.

It was in this backdrop that in June 620, during pilgrimage, the Prophet happened to meet six *Khazraj* pilgrims from *Yathrib* at *al Aqabah* in the suburbs of *Makkah*. As per his wont, the Prophet explained to them the tenets of *Islām* and invited them to its fold.[1] As soon as he disclosed his identity, the six Khazrajites became highly excited, making out that he was the same prophet whom the Jews had been talking about. The fact that the new prophet was an Arab and had brought a scripture in Arabic gave them great pleasure. Suddenly, the bright idea that *Islām* with its great message of peace and fraternity would be a powerful instrument in erasing out bitter enmity between *Aws* and *Khazraj*, struck their mind. They also thought that the Prophet with his magnetic personality was sure to be the most suitable leader to arbitrate their disputes and restore peace and unity to the ravaged oasis. Highly impressed by the message of *Islām* and personality of the Prophet, they are believed to have accepted the faith and made up their mind to invite him to *Yathrib* in order to solve their crisis. But since all of them represented the *Khazraj* tribe

---

1 *According to Muhammd Hamidullah, this was his sixteenth attempt at looking out for alliances in order to be able to migrate from Makkah.*

only, they thought it essential to mobilize opinion and support of other leaders of the two tribes in *Yathrib* before formally inviting the Prophet. Therefore, in the language of *Ibn Ishāq*, they told him, '*We have left our people, for no tribe is so divided by hatred and rancour as they. Perhaps God will unite them through you. So let us go to them and invite them to the religion of yours; and if God unites them in it, then no man will be mightier than you.*' They then promised to report back after a year and left.

After going back to *Yathrib*, they carried out a strong propaganda in favour of *Islām* projecting the Prophet as a much more impartial leader compared to *Abd Allāh ibn Ubayy* and a remedy for their predicament; before long, almost every house in *Yathrib* was aware of the Prophet and his message. After roping in a few other leaders, they came back to *Makkah* the next year (621) during *Haj* along with six others, two of whom were from *Aws*. During one of the nights, they confidentially met the Messenger at *Aqabah*, formally embraced *Islām* and took a formal oath of loyalty to *Islām* and of strictly adhering to the basic rules of the faith. The pledge *inter alia* mentioned that they would associate nothing with God, that they would neither steal nor commit fornication nor slay their offspring nor slander others and that they would not disobey the Messenger. They also accepted that if they stuck to these rules of *Islām*, paradise would be their reward and if they committed sins, God might punish or forgive them. This undertaking of the Yathribites with the Prophet is known in history as the First Pledge of *al Aqabah* and is sometimes referred to as the 'pledge of women' also because it did not contain any reference to war for the sake of God.

On the face of it, the pledge was purely religious as it was related to matters of faith only; but from the course of events that followed, it is understood that in the meeting, the Prophet was made welcome to *Yathrib*. Since the group represented different shades of opinion of the oasis, the meeting raised hopes in the Prophet's mind that at long last he was going to find a dependable place of refuge. He might have been realizing that the well-watered land full of greenery lying between two tracks of black stones which he had seen in a dream as his future abode was none other than *Yathrib*; and *Yathrib* had some additional considerations to attract him. Mother of his grandfather, *Salmah* was a Khazrajite and some of his relatives in *Banū Najjār* lived in the oasis. Moreover, in *Yathrib* was located his father's grave and he had spent some of his childhood days there along with his mother. But, it appears, at this stage, he was not really confident of viability of shifting to *Yathrib* unless the number of Muslims adequately increased with new conversions and strong assurance of protection was given. He, therefore, readily accepted the request of the twelve converts to send a religious teacher to *Yathrib* along with them for their instruction in *Islām* and also for inviting others to join the faith. This was all the more necessary as hatred between *Aws* and *Khajraj* was still too strong and so it was not possible for anyone other than a neutral and acceptable outsider to meaningfully preach *Islām*. For the job, the Prophet chose the cousin of his father, *Musāb ibn Umayr*, one of the early Muslims and a recent returnee from *Abyssinia*. He was mature in faith and was quite competent to work as a spiritual guide, handle missionary activities in the difficult situation prevailing in *Yathrib* and at the same time make a realistic assessment of the situation and prepare the way for *Hijrah* which was in Prophet's mind. The deputation of *Musāb* to *Yathrib* is considered the first occasion when the Prophet officially assigned a work of *Islām* independently to an individual. In *Yathrib*, *Musāb* stayed in the house of *Asad ibn Zurārah*, one of the six who had entered *Islām* the previous year.

Although ground was to some extent prepared for spread of *Islām* in *Yathrib*, the attitude of *Aws* was still hostile to it as they suspected that it might be a ploy by *Khazraj* to lull them into submission. Despite their hostile attitude, however, the missionary effort of *Musāb* in the oasis was a grand success. The biographers have recorded events relating to preaching by *Musāb* in detail. What by his eloquence and tactful handling and what by the magic of Quran's recitation, he was able to create a highly favourable ground for conversions. The most dramatic story as described by the biographers was the one of conversion of *Sād ibn Muādh*, the chief of *Abdul Ashhal* clan of *Aws* who initially hated *Islām*. When he saw *Musāb* teaching a group of *Aws* in his garden, he was furious, but since he had relations in *Aws* who had converted to *Islām* and he did not wish to antagonize them, he avoided taking action personally. He, therefore, sent his lieutenant, *Usayd*, chief of *Banū Zafar* clan of *Aws*, to punish *Musāb* and drive him from his land. When *Usayd* reached growling armed with his sword, *Musāb* politely said, '*Won't you sit down and listen. If you like what you hear you can accept it, and if you don't like it you can leave it alone.*' The proposal seemed fair to *Usayd* and he sat down and listened. *Musāb* spoke with great eloquence and recited portions of the *Qurān*, the beauty of which left him highly impressed and he then and there professed *Islām* offering prayers as taught. When he went back to *Sād*, the latter strongly protested and personally rushed, armed with his lance, to teach *Musāb* a lesson. But the same story got repeated, *Musāb* inviting him to listen to his talks first and *Sād* getting mesmerized after listening to recitation and embracing *Islām* instantaneously. After this dramatic event, *Sād* called a meeting of his men and strongly advised them to join *Islām*, which they did; by the end of the day, all men and women of his clan had entered *Islām* en masse. Before long, there were Muslims in almost every Arab family in the oasis except a few pockets of pagan resistance in the clan of *Aws* represented, for example, by the poet and chief, *Abū Qais ibn al Aslāt* and *Abū Āmir*, the father of *Hanzalah*; they thought that *Islām* was corrupting their pure Arabian form of monotheism, that is, *Hanīfiyyah*, and hence opposed it.

Musāb stayed in *Yathrib* and successfully preached *Islām* for eleven months. About a month ahead of the next pilgrimage, he returned to the Prophet to present him his performance report and to brief him about the bright prospects of *Islām* in *Yathrib*. He might have informed the prophet that there was a strong public opinion in *Yathrib* in favour of *Islām* and the people had been looking forward to his emigration to the oasis for restoring peace and unity. He also might have made him aware of the likely arrival of a big delegation of the Yathribites during the coming pilgrimage in order to formally invite him to their city for their religious inspiration and guidance. It appears that satisfied by the assessment of *Musāb* and increased strength of Muslims in *Yathrib*, the Prophet now made up his mind to emigrate. According to a story, he even told his uncle *Abbās* (who though a disbeliever, was his well-wisher and confidant) and his aunt *Umm al Fadl* that he hoped to go and live in *Yathrib* and that the final decision depended on the expected delegation from there. But at the same time he very well knew that abandoning one's tribe and shifting to another place to live under protection of some other tribe amounted to a blasphemy according to the tribal code of conduct and that *Quraysh* would never tolerate this. Moreover, since expansion of the Islamic community at a neighbouring place in alliance with other tribes would be highly dangerous to their interest, they would leave no stone unturned to attack and destroy it. He, therefore, figured out that in the event of emigration, he would definitely be facing armed attacks from *Quraysh*, and so, the strongest possible undertaking from *Khazraj* and *Aws* would have to be taken to protect and support him even to the extent of waging war for the purpose. As for the Jews who constituted a considerable chunk of Yathrib's population, he felt that since *Islām* recognized their prophets and scripture and was in consonance with their general ideology, they would welcome and support him. The Muslims were already facing Jerusalem during prayers; on his advice, *Musāb* had introduced congregational Friday prayers in *Yathrib* on the pattern of the Jews' *Sabbath* a day in advance of the latter. Further, similar to the practice of the Jews, the Muslims started fast of *ashura* in *Yathrib*. The Prophet might have thought that these measures would placate the Jews and they would be siding with the Muslims once he emigrated.

In June 622, during annual pilgrimage, the expected delegation from *Yathrib* did arrive. The group of pilgrims was a larger one which included many disbelievers as well, but as for Muslims, it had seventy-five of them (including two women)—11 from *Aws* and the rest from *Khazraj*. Belonging to leading families of different clans, they represented different shades of opinion of the oasis.¹ Since they were already Muslims, they were keenly desirous of paying respect to the Apostle of God by personal attendance and pledging loyalty to him, but their main intention behind the visit was to persuade him to shift to *Yathrib*. On arrival, they confidentially sent message to the Prophet regarding their intention and requested for a formal meeting. As planned, their rendezvous with him took place secretly in the wee hours of the second night following the pilgrimage, again in the ravine of *al Aqabah*. Classical sources mention that the Prophet's uncle, *Abbās*, accompanied him to the meeting and was the first to start the proceedings.² In his address, *Abbās* pointed out that there was a high degree of threat to the Prophet's life and that ensuring safety and protection to him as offered by the Yathribites would involve the highest degree of responsibility and might result in armed attacks from the enemies of *Islām*. He, therefore, requested the delegation to seriously consider pros and cons of the undertaking which they proposed to enter into. And finally he remarked, *'If you think that you can be faithful to what you have promised him and protect him from his opponents, then assume the*

---

1 *The sources refer to an interesting story that took place during their journey to Yathrib. Included in the group was the enthusiastic Khazrajite chief Barā. During the journey, out of his reverence for the Kābah, he refused to face Jerusalem while praying because in that case he would have been keeping his back towards the Kābah (a situation which a Muslim praying in Makkah could have avoided) and faced the Kābah in violation of the prevailing injunction. When the Prophet came to know about this, he did not approve of this Qiblā though his remark was ambiguous.*

2 *Some western scholars tend to view the important role played by Abbās in this meeting with suspicion. Though a sympathizer and helper of the Prophet, Abbās had not converted to Islām. Classical sources do not mention why the Prophet assigned this important role to him in preference to many highly dependable and competent Muslim Companions including Musāb who was an expert in Yathribite affairs. His role as presented by the biographers is, therefore, sometimes seen as a politically motivated attempt to whitewash his reputation in order to provide legitimacy to the Abbasid Caliphate.*

burden you have undertaken. But if you think that you will betray and abandon him after he has gone out with you, then leave him. For he is safe where he is.' When they wanted to hear the Prophet, he recited from the *Qurān* and said, *'I invite your allegiance on the basis that you protect me as you would your women and children.'* Thereupon the Yathribites, who were now to be nicknamed *Ansār* (Helpers) by the Prophet, firmly and vociferously resolved in one voice to defend the Prophet at all cost and even to fight for his protection. One of them, however, expressed apprehension that in the long run the Prophet might abandon them leaving them to fight the *Quraysh* and their allies alone whom they would be antagonizing by providing protection to him. The Prophet smilingly replied, *'I am of you and you are of me. I will war against them that war against you and be at peace with those at peace with you.'* He also promised that he would never part company with them. Both sides satisfied, the helpers then took oath of fealty as under: *'We pledge to war in complete obedience to the apostle in weal or woe, in ease and hardship and evil circumstances; that we would not wrong anyone; that we would speak the truth at all times; and that in God's service we would fear the censure of none.'*[1] This was what is known as Pledge of the Second *Aqabah*.

Before the meeting dispersed, the Prophet with the help of the group chose twelve of them, who were leading personalities of different clans, as his deputies or representatives (*Naqībs*) to guide them in religious matters and preach *Islām* to unbelievers. Nine of them were from *Khazraj* including *Asād* and *Barā* while three were leaders of *Aws*, one of whom was *Usayd* who was representing *Sād ibn Muādh*. It is sometimes said that this pledge was of the nature of a pact or agreement and had a predominantly political motive on both sides—an alliance of mutual military assistance. In fact, however, an undertaking to wage war in defense of one's religion when its very existence was in danger was nothing but a purely religious matter and it should be seen in that light. The Prophet had so far not been permitted by God to fight or shed blood but had simply been ordered to preach *Islām* patiently and

---

1   *Ibn Ishāq.*

bear with the hostile reaction and excesses of the infidels, leaving the decision about them to God alone. But when persecution of the Muslims exceeded all limits, the very life of the Prophet was seriously threatened and it became almost impossible to practice *Islām*. *Ibn Ishāq* says that it was under these circumstances that slightly before the 'Pledge of War', the Prophet received divine permission to fight for protection of his life and religion against those who wronged them, and this permission came in the form of verse 39 of *Surah* 22 (*Al Haj*): '*To those against whom war is made, permission is given (to fight) because they are wronged; and verily Allāh is most powerful for their aid.*' This was the germ from which the Islamic theory of just war, of *Qitāl* form of *Jihād*, was later to develop. It was after this verse descended that the 'Pledge of War' was undertaken according to the first biographer.

The Prophet was aware that once the *Quraysh* knew about the pact of war with the *Ansār*, they would be furious and would unleash severe violence against the Muslims. He, therefore, advised his followers to immediately undertake *Hijrah* to *Yathrib* where the *Ansār* would take care of their needs. Though the proposition was dangerous since abandonment of mother tribe was likely to invite violent reaction, the Muslims decided to migrate for the sake of God. But it was not made compulsory by the Prophet; those who were not keen and were not in a position to afford the journey or were under strict physical control or watch of the polytheists were allowed to stay back. The exodus of the Muslims immediately started, but it was a heartbreaking exercise since they had to abandon their hearts and homes, sacrifice whatever worldly possessions they had, and say goodbye to their motherland which was so dear to them. Some of them were able to dispose of their properties while most of them had to leave the same to be subsequently captured by the polytheists. Within a month or so, most of the Muslims (about 100 families according to *Ibn Kathīr*) stealthily disappeared from *Makkah*, their houses lying empty and presenting a deserted and desolate look. Sometimes a whole lane would be left empty in the course of a night. The large house of *Abd Allāh ibn Jahsh*, the Prophet's cousin, in the middle of the city lay entirely uninhabited with doors and windows blowing to and fro, and *Utbah* was highly pained to behold the pathetic scene. The city which was earlier so prosperous, so full of life and united, bore a deserted look. Before the departure of the Prophet, most of the Muslims— numbering about 200 as estimated by modern scholars—had deserted *Makkah*; among significant Muslims, only *Abū Bakr* and the Prophet with their families were left out, *Alī* included in the Prophet's family. Some of the other Muslims who stayed back due to genuine reasons were never charged of apostasy or cowardice. The *Qurān* referred to them in verse 14 of *Surah* 4 and declared God's pardon for them.

The *Quraysh* received inklings of conclusion of the pact of *Aqabah* the next morning through a shepherd who had overheard conversation between the Prophet and the *Ansār*. They immediately proceeded to the camp of the Yathribite pilgrims and enquired into the matter, but since the Yathribite Muslims had maintained utmost secrecy and had kept even their polytheist companions in the dark, the shepherd's report could not be confirmed. Subsequently, when they learnt about the development through other sources, they were furious and rushed to the Yathribite camp in order to punish them, but the pilgrims had already left. They could lay their hands only on *Sād bin Ubādah* who was yet to leave; he was captured, mercilessly tortured but was let off due to intervention of some Makkan leaders who knew him. They, however, could not do much to prevent the *Hijrah* as the Muslims secretly performed it in small unobtrusive groups, though as reported by traditions, they were able to detect a few instances of fleeing Muslims and offered resistance. For example, when *Abū Salamah*[1] was leaving with his wife and minor son, he was obstructed by members of his wife's family. A fight broke out in which his son's arm was dislocated. They forcibly detained his wife, *Umm Salamah*, though *Abū Salamah* was able to leave with his son. Having lost both husband and son, Umm Salamah's condition became miserable and after about a year, she was allowed to proceed to *Yathrib* and join them. Another such

---

1 *He is said to be the first to emigrate.*

story relates to *Hishām* who had planned to emigrate along with *Umar*. For mutual protection, the emigrating Muslims used to form small groups of two or three families and travel together. When *Umar* decided to emigrate with family, *Ayyāsh* and *Hishām* tied up their journey with him; the three families were to leave the city separately in order to avoid detection and assemble at an appointed place outside the city. *Umar* and *Ayyāsh* with their respective families reached the meeting point at the appointed time but *Hishām* did not arrive since he was arrested by his people while leaving and put under severe torture which forced him to renounce *Islām*. Umar and *Ayyāsh*, however, proceeded to *Yathrib* with a heavy heart. Though *Ayyāsh* reached *Yathrib*, his brothers followed and deceitfully took him back to *Makkah*, telling him about his mother's miserable condition. There he was made a prisoner and forced to abjure *Islām*. Both he and *Hishām*, however, subsequently re-entered *Islām* and waited for an opportunity to escape. Traditions report another story of *Suhayl*; when he tried to migrate, the polytheists seized his property saying that he had earned his wealth from the Makkans and so he would not be allowed to take it away. He was told that he could leave only after leaving his wealth back. *Suhayl* preferred the second option for the sake of God and left after handing over everything he had. When the Prophet heard about it, he exclaimed, '*Suhayl has made a profit.*'[1]

Now that the *Quraysh* were fully aware of the pact of war and exodus of the Muslims, they grew very angry as well as panicky; angry because abandonment of their tribe by the Muslims was a highly culpable social misconduct deserving severe punishment, and panicky because the development tended to pose serious threat to Makkah's security. They could visualize that a dangerous community of persons who had no regard for ties of kinship, assembling in the safe sanctuary of *Yathrib*, would enjoy freedom to preach and practice *Islām* and would proliferate before long. The apprehension of the Muslims attacking *Makkah* in alliance with the Yathribites to take revenge left them quite alarmed.

---

1   *Ibn Kathīr.*

The fear of the enemies jeopardizing their caravan trade route to *Syria*, which passed through *Yathrib* region, was an additional factor which made them uneasy. About the same time, *Mutīm*, the Prophet's protector died and this further compounded the problem. Now left highly vulnerable without a protector, the Prophet would leave no stone unturned to slip out of *Makkah* and join his followers in *Yathrib*, providing them leadership and making the prospect of an attack on *Makkah* all the more likely, they figured out. The *Quraysh*, therefore, convened a special meeting of the assembly attended by all important leaders to work out a strategy in order to deal with the impending danger. Since some radical course of action against the Prophet was to be decided, *Abū Lahab*, being head of the *Hashīm*, purposefully absented himself. The options of putting *Muhammad* in fetters or exiling him were discussed but rejected; the first because it was likely to lead to an immediate attack by his followers to get him released, and the second since it would enable the Prophet to join his men as the leader and instigate them to lead an attack. At last Abū Jahal's[1] dangerous plan of getting rid of the Prophet without causing a blood feud was accepted. According to this plan, a combined squad of a strong influential and powerful representative of each of the clan specially chosen for the task was to jointly kill the Prophet at one go, each individual striking a mortal blow simultaneously; in that case, responsibility for shedding his blood would be shared by all clans and it would not be possible for *Banū Hashīm* to fight the whole tribe of *Quraysh*, forcing them to accept blood money in lieu of revenge. Thus, a conspiracy was hatched to kill the Prophet and the proposed squad was formed and tasked. The *Qurān* refers to this plot in verse 15/17.

Though most of the Muslims had escaped *Makkah*, the Prophet had not yet planned his *Hijrah* because he had not

---

1   *His real name was Amr but he was surnamed Abū Hakam (father of wisdom) by his people for his sagacity. But owing to his fanaticism and bigotry, the Prophet called him Abū Jahal (father of ignorance) and it was by this name that he came to be known in the annals of Islām.*

received permission for the same from God. We learn from the sources that immediately after the *Quraysh* decided their nasty plot to assassinate him, he received divine information from Gabriel[1] about it who also guided him regarding his next course of action and intimated God's permission for his emigration.[2] The circumstances leading to the Prophet's *Hijrah* and those encountered during its performance have been described by traditions in detail, often embellishing them with miraculous stories and assigning to *Abū Bakr* a laudable role in the episode. After getting posted of the conspiracy, the Prophet at once went to Abū Bakr's place, informed him of the entire development, and asked him to make arrangement for their *Hijrah* at a short notice. *Abū Bakr* had earlier wished to migrate but had been held back by the Prophet. However, anticipating that he would have to emigrate in company of the Prophet, he had arranged two swift camels for the journey and also a guide, *Abdullāh ibn Arqāt*, who though an unbeliever was yet a man of great confidence. Now that it was confirmed that he would be performing *Hijrah* along with the Prophet and that time for the same had come, his eyes were filled with tears in joy and excitement. *Āishah*, who was a small child and was then present, subsequently remembered the occasion and said that for the first time in her life she knew that a person could shed tears with joy also. Therefrom, the Prophet went to his house and informed *Alī* of the entire matter including his decision to emigrate. *Alī* was given an important task; he was to return precious articles of different persons who had deposited the same with the Prophet trusting his honesty. After completion of the task, he was to start his own *Hijrah* and join the Prophet.

---

1 *Ibn Sad reports that the Prophet was informed about the plot by one of his aunts who had overheard conversation when the plan was being decided.*

2 *The great historian Ibn Khaldūn asserts that it was at this time that the Prophet received the first revelation ordering him to make war on his persecutors 'until persecution is no more and religion is for Allāh only' (Q 8:39).*

The same evening the team of young men appointed to kill the Prophet discreetly surrounded his house. But since female voices were coming out of the house and it was against the tribal code of conduct to kill a person in presence of his women relatives, they decided to wait till the intended victim came out. The Prophet who became aware of their presence, decided to hoodwink them; he asked *Ali* to sleep on his bed covering his body with cloth in which he himself used to sleep and masquerade as the Prophet which *Ali* did. The trick worked well, the enemies peeping through the window and remaining satisfied that their target was sleeping. In the meantime, the Prophet stealthily slipped out of the house reciting verse 1–9 of *Surah Yā Sīn*[1]; and though he physically passed through the midst of the enemy, they miraculously failed to see him. In the morning when they saw *Ali* coming out of the bed, to their chagrin they knew that they had been outsmarted. After dodging the enemies, the Prophet rushed to the house of *Abū Bakr.* Now his first priority was to leave the city in order to save his life. It was important to surprise the *Quraysh* by leaving at a time hardly conceivable to them. He, therefore, took *Abū Bakr* along and escaped through a window at the back of the house. Though route to *Yathrib* was to the north, they proceeded southwards in order to give a deception to the enemies. A few kilometers south of *Makkah* the two hid in an unnoticeable cave in mount *Thawr.*[2] As per story recorded by *Ibn Hajār, Abū Bakr* first entered the cave, searched and cleaned it, then closed all the holes in it with pieces of cloth torn off his garment in order to ensure protection from reptiles and then requested the Prophet

---

1 *The last verse reading: 'And we have enshrouded them, so that they see not.'*

2 *According to Ibn Kathir, on way to the cave, Abū Bakr sometimes went ahead of the Prophet and then behind him. When the Prophet asked the reason, he replied: 'O Apostle of God! When I think of those in pursuit, I come behind you, but then I apprehend an ambuscade and I go in front of you.'*

to step in.[1] No one knew about the hiding place except *Abū Bakr's* son *Abd Allāh*, his daughter *Asmā*, and his friend *Āmir ibn Fuhayrah*. Abd Allāh's duty was to collect intelligence from the city regarding plans and activities of *Quraysh* and keep the Prophet posted of developments. *Fuhayrah* grazed Abū Bakr's goats around the hiding place, maintained a general surveillance, covered up the tracks of *Abd Allāh* after he shuttled to and fro, and supplied milk to the Prophet. *Asmā* used to bring food for them to the cave. They stayed in the cave for three days and three nights under constant fear of detection, but the Prophet, while hiding in the cave, underwent the spiritual experience of *Sakīnah*, the great feeling of presence and help of God.

When the *Quraysh* knew that *Muhammad* had managed to escape, they left no stone unturned to trace him out and put him to death. In order to carry out search operations, they immediately deputed their horsemen who started combing all possible escape routes to *Yathrib*. For the sake of providing strong incentive for the job, they even announced a handsome reward of 100 camels to anyone who captured and brought him back. At one point of time, one of the search parties did actually reach entry point of the cave. *Abū Bakr* was highly frightened and whispered to the Prophet that the enemies had almost discovered them. As per a story narrated by *Zurqānī* and confirmed by *Bukhāri*, the Prophet replied: *'Fear not, God is with us.'* *Abū Bakr* went on: *'I fear not for myself but for you. For if I die, I am but an ordinary mortal; but if you die it will mean death to faith and spirit.'*[2] Thereupon the Prophet retorted, *'Even so fear not; we are not two in this cave, there is a third- God.'* The situation was precarious but according to traditions, they were saved by a miracle of God – overnight

---

1   *As per one story, when Abū Bakr's garment proved insufficient, he plucked the last hole with his heel, but was bitten by a snake, when the Prophet was resting his head on his knee and was sleeping. And so despite pain, Abū Bakr did not move his leg, though his teardrops fell on the Prophet's face which waked him up. When the Prophet knew the matter, he put his saliva on the place of bite and Abū Bakr was instantaneously cured.*

2   *The Qurān also refers to the story of the cave in Surah 9— 'Tawbah'.*

growth of an acacia tree covering the entrance to the cave, a just-woven spider's web spread over the entry point and a newly made dove's nest in the hollow of the rock near the entry point with the dove sitting on her eggs. All these camouflaging signs convinced the enemies that the cave was uninhabited and they went back, the Prophet and *Abū Bakr* heaving a sigh of relief. Shortly afterwards, as planned, *Fuhayrah* brought the Bedouin guide along with the camels prepared for the journey. The she-camel meant for the Prophet was named '*Qaswā*'; *Abū Bakr* wanted to gift her to the Prophet but the latter accepted it only on payment for he did not want to get religious significance of his *Hijrah* diluted by accepting the mount as a gift. According to traditions, *Qaswā* was divinely inspired and subsequently remained the favourite mount of the Prophet. *Asmā* brought a bag of provisions for the journey but the bag had no string to hang it on the camel's saddle, so she undid her waistband and used it as a rope for the purpose. For this she earned from the Prophet a title which meant 'she of the girdle'. Simple arrangements for the journey having been made, the small caravan of three camels and four passengers (the Prophet, *Abū Bakr*, *Fuhayrah*, and the guide *Abdullāh bin Arqāt*) left on its great journey of *Hijrah*. The Prophet was highly melancholic at the time of final departure and exclaimed, '*O Makkah! You are to me dearest of all the cities. But your citizens allowed me not to reside here.*'

The journey of the Prophet which now started was extremely dangerous as he was under no one's protection and the horsemen of *Quraysh* were still hunting for him. In order to avoid detection, the efficient guide first headed towards south and then proceeded towards *Yathrib* through circuitous and unfrequented routes, travelling during nights and resting during days. *Ibn Sād* has listed a dozen odd places on way to *Yathrib* where they rested and a few interesting incidents that they encountered. The most famous story is that of *Surāqah bin Malik bin Jushum*, a warrior, who tempted by the reward offered by *Quraysh* had been searching the Prophet alone after receiving clues. He actually sighted the Prophet's caravan but before he could reach it, his horse stumbled thrice resulting in his fall. The portent made him realize that *Muhammad* was a true prophet and was under divine protection. So when he reached the Prophet, he apologized and went back promising not to divulge his whereabouts to anyone on way. It is said that before he left, he requested for and obtained a note signed by *Abū Bakr*; this he wanted to use as a guarantee of peace when the Prophet became great and powerful. As per another story narrated by *Maqrīzī* and *Ibn Kathīr*, the chief of *Aslam* tribe, *Buraidah*, pursued the Prophet's caravan and caught it, but upon the Prophet's exhortations, he and his companions numbering eighty embraced *Islām*. We learn of yet another story of the Prophet having a brief halt at the encampment of *Umm Mabād* who used to supply food and water to the passersby, but on that day, nothing was available. The Prophet then miraculously extracted sufficient milk from the udder of her dry she-goat. During their journey, one morning, they encountered Abū Bakr's cousin, *Talhā*, who was returning from Syria carrying merchandise. From him they received a change of clothes.

After eight days of tiring and hazardous journey involving hardship of sun and thirst, the Prophet reached *Qubā* on the outskirts of *Yathrib* on a Monday noon. There is difference of opinion regarding the exact date of the Prophet's arrival at *Qubā*, but according to modern scholars, he left *Makkah* on 1 *Rabi al Awwal* (13 September 622—Tuesday) and arrived at *Qubā* on 12 *Rabi al Awwal* (24 September 622—Monday). Situated about three miles from *Yathrib*, *Qubā* was the southern extreme of the oasis and now is a great place of orchards and gardens. *Qubā* being gateway to *Yathrib*, all emigrants had passed through it and some of them were still there. Aware of the Prophet's disappearance from *Makkah*, all Muslims in *Yathrib* as well as *Qubā* had been enthusiastically waiting for the arrival of their spiritual leader. Even nonbelievers were considerably eager since the Prophet was shifting to the oasis as the harbinger of peace and unity. Amidst eager waiting, the Prophet reached *Qubā* around noon and was received with great joy. *Qubā* was inhabited by *Banū Amr*, a clan of *Aws*; deciding to stay there for a few days, the Prophet lodged with *Kulthūm*, the chief of the clan. In order to allow sharing of hospitality, *Abū Bakr* was made to stay with a man of *Khazraj* in a neighbouring village called *Sunh*. After a day or two, *Alī* also joined the Prophet having satisfactorily completed the task assigned to him. We learnt from *Ibn al Athīr* that after disappearance of the Prophet, he had been held responsible for his escape and had been subjected to severe maltreatment. While at *Qubā*, a large number of people from *Yathrib* came to greet the Prophet, *Salmān Farsī*[1] one of them, who subsequently entered *Islām* and distinguished himself as a wise and dependable companion. At *Qubā*, the Prophet laid the foundation of the first mosque built in *Islām* and referred to in the *Qurān* (9/108). It was constructed by manual labour of all available Muslims including the Prophet himself and is said to have been completed in fourteen days. The sources do not throw any light why the Prophet decided to stay for a few days at *Qubā* even though he was within a few miles of the destination. Perhaps he was waiting for *Alī* in order to complete *Hijrah* along with him or else wanted to receive confirmation regarding return of the people's deposits which were in his custody before completing the great religious task.

Since there was tremendous restlessness among Muslims of *Yathrib* for the Prophet's arrival and they were sending frantic messages for the purpose, he stayed in *Qubā* for three days only.[2] On Friday morning, accompanied by his companions and escorted by a group of *Banī Amr*, he set out for *Yathrib* mounted on *Qaswā*. On way at noon, they stopped in the valley of *Rānūnā*, the place of *Banī Sālim* clan of *Khazra*j, and offered the Friday congregational prayer which is said to be his first Friday prayer; in it there was a congregation of about 100 persons. Thereafter,

---

1 *He was a Zoroastrian-turned-Christian who used to stay in Syria. He had heard about the newly appeared prophet. Extremely eager to see him, he set out for Arab but on way was sold by unscrupulous merchants and finally became a slave of a Jew of Banū Qurayzah. He had heard about the seal of prophethood and was keen to see that with his own eyes. In his first meeting with the Prophet, he was elated to see and speak to him though he could see the seal of prophethood much later.*

2 *Bukhāri, however, mentions that the duration of the Prophet's stay in Qubā was 14 nights.*

he left for *Yathrib* reaching the destination in the afternoon. The biographers present a picturesque account of his entry into *Yathrib* amidst unprecedented rejoicing, enthusiasm, and fanfare. To his right and left were riding fully decorated armed squads of *Aws* and *Khazraj*; this was a guard of honour and a symbol of protection which they had pledged. Believers and nonbelievers alike came from all directions and joined his procession. Women and children wearing their best clothes lined up the route singing songs describing him as 'the moon of the fourteenth night'. *Anas* later said that he never came across such a happy event in *Yathrib*. People were vying and even fighting with one another to take charge of the Prophet and become his host; some of them even grabbed the halter of the camel requesting him to stay in their house. But the Prophet courteously turned down all offers and remarked, '*Let her (camel) go her way for she is under the command of God. I will stop where the animal sits down.*' After wandering from place to place, *Qaswā*, with halter dropped, ultimately entered the area of *Banī Mālik* branch of *Najjār* and knelt at the entrance of a large walled courtyard which had a few date palm trees and ruins of a building; the place was being used for drying dates. The Prophet dismounted there and said, '*This, if God will, is the dwelling.*'[1] The land was the property of two orphan brothers of *Banū Najjār*, *Suhayl* and *Sahl*, who were under the guardianship of *Asad b Zurārah* (one of the six pledging allegiance in 620). The Prophet desired to purchase the plot but the two brothers insisted on gifting it. He, however, paid the price of ten gold coins as fixed after negotiation and bought it.

Close to the Prophets newly acquired land was the house of *Abū Ayyūb Khālid* of *Banū Najjār* (who had pledged himself at the Second *Aqabah*), and though many other individuals of the locality were insisting to host the Prophet, he decided to stay with *Abū Ayyūb*, perhaps due to kinship with him. The happiness and excitement of *Abū Ayyūb* knew no bounds; he immediately took hold of the Prophet's luggage and guided him to his house. Not willing to show disrespect to his spiritual leader by himself

---

1   *Bukhāri.*

staying above him, he offered the first floor of the house for the Prophet's accommodation, but the latter occupied the ground floor having in mind convenience of a large number of visitors whom he was to encounter every day. *Abū Ayyūb* showed the highest degree of respect and hospitality to his guest; he sent him food both times and whatever was left over, he and his wife used to share taking morsels from where the Prophet's fingers had touched. We learn of a story of accidental breaking of a pitcher full of water in his room; fearing that the water will dip through holes to the Prophet's room causing him disturbance, he used his only quilt to soak water and spoiled the same in the process. Other neighbours also competed with *Abū Ayyūb* in sending food to the Prophet and earning religious merit. Such was the enthusiasm on the Prophet's presence in *Yathrib* that the people in his honour changed the name of the city to *Madinat un Nabi* (city of the Prophet) popularly called *Madinah*; subsequently the city was also called *Madinah al Munawwarah* which meant the illuminated city, a place lighted by the spiritual presence of the Prophet.

The first important decision of the Prophet immediately on arrival at *Madinah* was to construct a mosque for congregational prayers on his newly acquired land. As per his direction, work was started without delay; date trees were cut down and the ground cleared of weeds and shrubs and levelled. Construction was done by personal labour of all Muslims, *Muhājirun*[1] and *Ansar* working shoulder to shoulder. This was the first community project in *Islām* in which all the Muslims participated as a team irrespective of status, the Prophet also joining as a worker carrying bricks like others. While working, they sang songs praising God and requesting for His help. During construction, *Ammār bin Yāsir* was doing exceptionally hard work; overloaded with bricks, he once cried, '*They are killing me.*' The Apostle consoled him and removed dust from his head and face with his own hands. *Ibn Ishāq* calls *Ammār* the first man in *Islām* to build a mosque, but

---

1 *Those Muslims who emigrated from Makkah were given the name of Muhājirun (singular—Muhājir) by the Prophet.*

he does not specify the name of the mosque. According to the Egyptian scholar, *Tāha Hussain*, it was a mosque which he built in *Makkah* before *Hijrah*. Manual work involved in construction was especially hard for the aristocratic Muslims and for this sometimes they used to be the target of taunts. According to a story narrated by *Ibn Ishāq*, while working, *Ammār* used to sing a song composed by *Alī* in which there was a satire for those who did not like the work of dust and dirt. Angered by this, one of the aristocratic Muslims, generally identified as *Uthmān bin Affān*, had an altercation with him on which the Prophet was annoyed and intervened in favour of *Ammār*.[1]

Without any artistic decoration, structure of the mosque was extremely simple in conception and design and was a symbol of Islamic austerity. Covering an area of fifty by fifty yards, it was made of unbaked bricks with pillars of palm trunks supporting roof of palm leaves. Only a part of the mosque area was covered with roof; a greater part was left open within the boundary walls. Since those days direction of prayer (*Qiblā*) was towards Jerusalem, the prayer niche was made towards north, stones, and not bricks being used on either side of it. One gate each was constructed on the remaining three sides, the southern door meant for public entrance and the eastern one, called *Bab an nisa*, reserved for the Prophet's household. The floor of the mosque was left unpaved and used to be muddy during rainy season; it was later covered with pebbles. At the northern end of the mosque was constructed a roofed platform known as *Suffah* (shed), which was meant for those Companions who were like recluses having no family or means of livelihood and who had devoted their entire

---

1 *According to a hadīth, the Prophet once said, 'Ammār is as dear to me as my own face.'*

lives to *Islām*, spending day and night in prayers and recitation.[1]
When construction of the mosque was nearing completion, two
small hut-type dwellings touching the eastern wall were also
constructed to accommodate his two wives. Additional rooms
were constructed in the long run when he had more wives. These
family rooms measuring about nine by fifteen feet each were also
absolutely unostentatious structures with roof as low as could be
touched by hand. Blankets used to be hanged on doors to serve as
shutters. *Zarqāni* rightly pointed out that had these rooms been
kept undisturbed, the world would have seen the simplicity of the
life of the Prophet who was the uncrowned king of the peninsula.
This was the first mosque built in *Madinah* and was, apart from
being a place of worship, to become the centre of all mundane
activities of the community. It subsequently developed into
what now stands as *Masjid al Nabwi*, the second holiest shrine
of the Muslims. Construction of the mosque and residential
accommodation took about seven months during which time the
Prophet lodged with *Abū Ayyūb*.

After completion of construction of the mosque and
residential accommodation, the Prophet took steps to sort out his
household affairs. He sent *Zayd b Harithā* along with *Abū Rāfi* to
bring his family from *Makkah*. When *Zayd* returned with *Sawdah*
and the Prophet's daughters, *Umm Kulthūm* and *Fātimah*, his own
wife *Umm Ayman*[2] and their small son *Usāmah* and also daughters
and son of *Abū Bakr* came along. The Prophet now decided that

---

1   *This group of Companions was known as 'Ashāb as Suffah' (Companions
of the Shed). They used to be always in attendance on the Prophet and
were his spiritual disciples. They used to be sent out as preachers by the
Prophet whenever required. Due to their great poverty, they normally
had nothing to eat. Whenever the Prophet received food in charity, he
used to send it to them; sometimes the well-to-do companions used to
be asked to feed them. Abū Hurairah was one of them. Such was their
poverty that it is said that none of them had two pieces of clothes to cover
lower and upper parts of the body separately. The Prophet had great
regard for them.*

2   *According to Suhaili, Umm Ayman went to Madinah on foot all alone
suffering great hardships.*

his adopted son should, in addition to the elderly *Umm Ayman*, have a younger wife and so he arranged Zayd's second marriage with *Zaynab bint Jahsh*, the beautiful sister of his cousin, *Abd Allāh b Jahsh*. Short-statured and with dark complexion, *Zayd* was not an attractive young man and in the past he had been a slave. *Zaynab*, therefore, considered him of inferior status and was initially not willing to marry him. But when she knew that it was the Prophet's earnest desire, she consented and the marriage took place, though they could not get along well. After a month or so, Āishah's wedding with the Prophet also took place in a very simple way without even wedding feast and she joined the Prophet's household. She was then only 10 or 11 years old and, as per report of *Ibn Sād,* when she was taken for wedding, she was playing on a see-saw with dishevelled hair not aware of the occasion. But though young, she was a precocious child, extremely intelligent and with a remarkably retentive memory; she was able to reproduce conversation between persons even without understanding the meaning. We are told by the sources that even after marriage, she used to play with dolls and friends. The Prophet had great affection and regard for her and never disturbed her games. Despite disparity of age, he always gave her due status as wife; in course of time, she was to become the favourite of his living wives.

Hijrah was not merely a 'flight' or a geographical change of location to save one's life and avoid persecution, as the literal meaning of the term would indicate; nor was it a mere change of one's affiliation from one group to the other, as some writers would have us understand. The term had a great religious significance and meant a religious sacrifice of the highest degree for the sake of God involving abandonment of everything in order to save the faith. In a yet deeper spiritual connotation, it signified liberation of soul from sinful environment and emigration of heart towards spiritual salvation. The *Qurān* in various revelations[1] has amply reflected the positive aspect of *Hijrah*, declaring great religious merit and God's reward in the exercise. Thus says verse 9:20:

---

1   *2:218; 3:195; 4:97; 100; 9:20; 16:41 and 2:53*

'*Those who believe and have left their homes and striven with their wealth and their lives in Allah's way are of much greater worth in Allah's sight. These are they who are triumphant.*' Similarly, verse 2:218 asserts: '*Those who believe and those who suffered exile and fought (and strove and struggled) in the path of Allāh; they have the hope of the mercy of Allāh and Allāh is oft-forgiving, most merciful.*' In modern *Sufi* literature also, *Hijrah* is considered an important stage in the inner spiritual journey of retiring to *Allāh*. Enduring physical hardships of *Hijrah* is treated as a process of self-purification for God's love. It was perhaps due to the religious merit of the glorious act of *Hijrah* that the Prophet extended it by making incumbent on all who converted at other places to emigrate to *Madinah* in order to join the *Ummah*, a point enjoined in the *Qurān* (8:72). In the modern period, *Hijrah* became a paradigm to justify the Muslims' refusal to lose hope in the face of persecution and threat to survival and to seek remedy in mass migration to a more conducive place, as happened in case of partition of India and Pakistan.

From historical point of view also, *Hijrah* was one of the most important events in the life of the Prophet, a turning point in the history of *Islām*, which gave a new direction to the Islamic movement. It opened new gates through which the Prophet took his religious and socio-economic reform movement to final stages of evolution. It led to establishment of the first Islamic community as a social group, a strongly welded brotherhood, based on religion rather than kinship. But the most far-reaching consequence that arose out of circumstances following the *Hijrah* was that *Islām* took on a political form also with establishment of the first Islamic State wedded to a policy to fight back in defense against those who threatened it—an ideology of waging 'just war' (*Qital* form of *Jihad*) in order to save the faith and restore justice and peace. It was this policy which enabled the Prophet to subdue not only *Makkah* but the whole of Arabia in course of time. The first Islamic polity thus established proved the miniature form of the great Islamic Empire which was to develop in later times. *Hijrah* was, therefore, the most formative historical event in the life of the Prophet. It was due to its great religious and historical significance that seventeen years later, *Khalifah Umar* instituted the Islamic calendar on the basis of this event (and not on the basis of birth of the Prophet or date of first revelation, i.e. assignment of prophethood). The commencement of the calendar, however, was not based on the exact time of departure of the Prophet from *Makkah* but on the first day of the first lunar month, viz, *Muharram* falling on 15 July 622.[1]

But though immediate threat of extinction of the Muslim Community was over after completion of the *Hijrah* and there was a strong local wave in favour of *Islām* leading to rapid conversions among *Aws and Khazraj*,[2] its position in *Madinah* was still far from secure. The nascent community found itself beset with multipronged problems that threatened its very survival; the work of reconstruction of the community and establishment of a State to safeguard its interest was to prove extremely difficult. The most serious problem was one of external aggression—a

---

1   *The Islamic Calendar is based on lunar year. A lunar year has only 354 days and 8 hours as compared to 365 days of a solar year. The twelve lunar months of the Islamic calendar are*

　　i.   Muharram (the sacred month)
　　ii.   Safar (the month of departure)
　　iii. Rabi al Awwal (the first month of spring)
　　iv.   Rabi al Thāni (the second month of spring)
　　v.   Jumādi I (the first dry month)
　　vi.   Jumādi II (the second dry month)
　　vii. Rajab (respected month, often called Rajab ul Murajjab)
　　viii. Shabān (the month of budding of trees)
　　ix.   Ramadan (the month of heat and fasting)
　　x.   Shawwāl (the month of function)
　　xi.   Dhū-al-Qadā (the month of truce and rest)
　　xii. Dhū-al-Hijjā (the month of pilgrimage)

2   *According to a rough estimate, immediately after Hijrah the total number of Muslims in Madinah was 200 Muhajirun + 200 Ansār = 400. As referred to by Bukhāri, after a few months a list of Muslims was prepared on the orders of the Prophet and this included the names of 1500 persons. The figures arrived at after the first Islamic census still compared unfavourably with the total population of the oasis which, in the opinion of Muhammad Hamidullah, was around 10,000.*

tremendously growing threat from *Quraysh* who would not leave them in peace even after the *Hijrah*. The success of emigration was a great humiliation for *Quraysh*; the misconduct of the Muslims was blasphemous grossly violating the tribal code of conduct and *Quraysh* would be exposing their own weakness if the culprits went unpunished. More importantly, the rapidly growing strength of *Islām* in *Madinah* challenged political and religious hegemony of *Quraysh* in the peninsula and made them feel unsafe. The Muslims were fast developing potential to lead military attacks on *Makkah* in revenge if not checked at once. Added to the threat of Makkah's security was the fact that the western caravan trade route passed through the Madinan zone of influence; with Islam's power established in the oasis, there was strong apprehension of their trade, on which depended their prosperity and power, being put in jeopardy until Muslim power was neutralized. An anti-Madinah military attack for destruction of the Muslims, therefore, became the cornerstone of their policy and they appear to have started preparations for the same.

They sent a letter to *Abd Allāh ibn Ubayy*, who harboured a strong hatred against the Prophet, threatening him that they would attack and kill all able-bodied men of *Madinah* and enslave their women unless he turned the Prophet out or joined their attack on the oasis and helped them.[1] Making the most of the written threat to the oasis, *Ubbay* tried to foment trouble but withdrew overawed by the growing power of *Isām*. The *Quraysh* also started putting economic pressure on *Madinah* by cutting off trade routes through Madinan region, and this caused shortage of commodities there. Another dangerous measure they took was to instigate the outlying Bedouin tribes against *Islām* and to win them over to join their fight against it. Themselves seething with resentment against *Islām* since it challenged their social order and customs, some of the tribes showed a tendency to align

---

1 *In the opinion of Muhammad Hamidullah, Abū Sufyan had sent another letter to the Ansār in general warning them not to interfere between the Quraysh and Muhammad or give shelter and protection to him. His opinion is based on reference to this effect by Ibn Habīb.*

with *Quraysh*. The *Quraysh* also instigated disgruntled elements within *Madinah*, the Jews, and the hypocrites, against *Islām* using them to obtain intelligence regarding plans and strength of the Muslims. Not less provoking was the news that *Quraysh* meted out worse treatment to the Muslims who had been left behind in *Makkah* and appropriated the belongings and properties left in *Makkah* by the emigrants, which was in utter violation of the tribal code of conduct. Much to the indignation of the Muslims, they also started interfering with their right of pilgrimage; *Sād b Muādh*, who went to the *Kābah* for circumambulation, was badly treated and threatened by *Abū Jahal*. And when the Prophet declared *Madinah* as a sacred city like *Makkah*, animosity of the *Quraysh* further escalated. Various *ahadīth* mentions that, aware of the highly aggressive activities of the *Quraysh,* the Prophet was extremely disturbed and apprehended an open military attack on *Madinah* or assassination attempt on his life any moment. In tension he used to keep awake whole nights, while the Muslims used to guard his house by turn. All Companions used to sleep with weapons and pickets were posted around the city every night to warn the citizens if the enemy made a sudden raid. Thus, ever since emigration, a de facto state of war existed in the oasis.

While the danger of a military attack from *Makkah* was looming large, serious threats were emerging from within the oasis also. The Jews, who constituted a sizeable chunk of the population, had turned alarmingly hostile and were out to destroy *Islām* by their machinations. Initially, they welcomed the Prophet as they thought that he would put civil strife to an end; they also thought that due to Abrahamic connection of *Islām*, he would support the Jews and with his help they would regain political power and get the better of their Christian rivals as well. The Prophet also returned their greetings with similar gestures, visited their chiefs, and tried to befriend their nobles. Adoption of prayers and practices similar to theirs including direction of prayer towards Jerusalem was likely to please them, he thought. But soon disappointment and frustration set in among the Jewish ranks. They were alarmed by the rapidly growing political power of *Islām* and realized that they would have to play a second fiddle to the Prophet. Moreover, the new friendship and unity between *Aws* and *Khazraj* as also the strong solidarity of the Muslim community did not suit them. As they did in the past, they wanted to play one Arab tribe against the other, create discord and strife and themselves dominate the scene. The strong unifying leadership of the Prophet, therefore, left them frustrated and they launched a campaign of 'open seditions and secret treachery'[1] against the Prophet. They started with a war of words which was even more sinister than what *Quraysh* had done. Declaring *Islām* as a false religion and refusing to accept *Muhammad* as a prophet, they attacked his faith on an ideological plain. With malicious intention to arouse doubts in the Prophet's message, the Jewish rabbis and leaders annoyed him with mischievous questions that tended to introduce confusion.[2] In order to stir up old animosity between *Aws* and *Khazraj* and break Islam's unity, a Jewish leader called *Shāh ibn Qays* engaged poets to sing highly provocative war poems of the two tribes which used to be recited during the battle of *Buāth*; this stoked up passions and people of the two tribes were on the verge of physical fight when the Prophet intervened and saved the situation by reminding them of Islamic brotherhood. Out of hatred they mispronounced Quranic words and their poets lampooned Muslim women in violation of the code of conduct. Their hatred of *Islām* was so strong that once when asked in *Makkah*, they openly expressed preference for idolatry as compared to *Islām*.

On one occasion when the Prophet's camels had strayed, they tried to misguide the people by pointing out that he was not a real prophet as he did not even know the whereabouts of his own camels; the camels were, however, traced out when God guided the Prophet and he gave indication accordingly. On another occasion when *Asad* (the first man to pledge fealty) died, as apprehended by the Prophet, they immediately remarked, '*If he*

---

1   *Amīr Ali.*

2   *Names of such Jewish rabbis and leaders who stirred up trouble by asking questions have been listed by Ibn Ishāq.*

were a Prophet his Companion would not have died.' We learn from the biographers that some of them hypocritically joined *Islām* and tried to subvert the faith from within. They used to assemble in the mosque, listen to stories of the Muslims, disseminate doubts by asking questions, and laughed and scoffed at *Islām*. Once when they were plotting against *Islām* in a corner of the mosque, the Prophet overheard them and on his order they were ejected out with some violence. Sometimes, arguments between the Jews and the Muslims used to lead to physical bouts. Once a Jew called *Finhās* used disrespectful language in respect of God saying that not he but God needed his help (he was commenting on verse 2/295 of the *Qurān*). *Abū Bakr* lost temper and hit him on his face, the latter complaining to the Prophet. It was then that verse 3/181 was revealed condemning the remarks of *Finhās*. When a Christian delegation came from *Najrān* and a tripartite religious debate took place between the Christians, the Jews, and the Prophet, the Christians were convinced of the truth of Muhammad's prophethood and, though not joining *Islām*, they resolved not to oppose it. On their request, the Prophet sent *Abū Ubaydah ibn al Jarrah* with judicial authority to sort out their disputes. But the Jews still refused to accept his prophethood. The most dangerous aspect of the Jews' hostility, however, was that they had joined hands with *Quraysh* and the hypocrites, hatching conspiracies against the Prophet and instigating *Quraysh* to attack *Madinah*, and so they were a serious threat to security of the Islamic community. The whole first part of *al Baqarah*, the longest *Surah* of the *Qurān*, relates to the Jewish controversy.

Not less serious than that of the Jews was the threat from a group of enemies who infiltrated the Muslim community pretending as having joined the faith—a group which is known in the *Qurān* as *Munafiqūn* (hypocrites). These 'pseudo-Muslims' were pagan at heart and hated *Islām* because they thought it had robbed them of power; but feeling unsafe to remain unbelievers in the face of growing power of the Muslims, they preferred to climb the bandwagon of *Islām* in order to make hay when the sun shone. That would provide them access to numerous advantages and at the same time make them secure. The conversion of these masqueraders was, therefore, not of conviction, but motivated by worldly reasons. Joining the faith with the concealed intention of subverting and sabotaging it from within, they continuously conspired with the enemies of *Islām*, the *Quraysh* and the Jews. Having free access to all developments within the community, these traitors were thus a more potential danger. The *Surah* of the Cow which was revealed during the early Madinan period gave ample warning of their hidden anti-Islamic agenda. *Ibn Kathīr* points out that in the first part of the *Surah*, there are thirteen long verses on the treacherous designs and activities of the hypocrites whereas only two verses relate to the unbelievers and four concern the believers. Hand in gloves with the Jews, the hypocrites took pleasure in joining them whenever there was an occasion to spread calumny and disaffection against *Islām*. During the occasions of straying of the camels and death of *Kulthūm* and *Asad*, they joined the Jews in mocking at the Prophet. Their uncrowned leader was *Abd Allāh ibn Ubayy* whose ambition to become king of *Madinah* had been frustrated by the arrival of the Prophet. He, therefore, hated the Prophet and abhorred his growing power and popularity. Initially, he vehemently opposed the Prophet, but the strong wave in favour of *Islām* made him realize that he would soon be left isolated and marginalized. He, therefore, accepted *Islām* as a matter of diplomacy and the *Munafiqūn* rallied around him. But his faith was nothing more than a hype, a dissimulation, and the Muslims always doubted his sincerity. We learn from the biographers that behind most of the conspiracies against *Islām*, he used to be the mastermind. The whole *Surah* of the Hypocrites (63) came down about *Ubayy* and his helpers. *Ibn Ishāq* in his *Sirah* has listed out the names of important hypocrites[1] who had been trying to spread sedition against *Islām*, working as fifth column for the *Quraysh*. The Prophet, however, always showed considerable patience and forbearance towards the hypocrites in general and *Ubayy* in particular, hoping in the end to win them over to the faith—a hope in which he was not wrong. He used to

---

1   *Abd Allāh b. Ubbay, Julās, Nabtal, and Mirba were significant of them.*

give *Ubayy* an honoured place in the mosque even allowing him to address congregations of Friday prayers.

Another difficulty within the community related to interpersonal relations among different groups of the faithful themselves. The *Aws* and *Khazraj* had a long history of hostility and bitterness; there was apprehension of old hatred and jealousy getting renewed on sensitive issues. The *Muhajirūn* and *Ansār* had been drawn from totally different backgrounds; differences between them needed to be sorted out and relations regulated. Even within the group of *Muhajirūn* itself, old reflexes of pagan times would sometimes resurface and cause tension between individuals. Added to these irritants was the unique nature of the Islamic community itself. It was for the first time in Arabia that the 'shocking innovation' of having a community based on religion rather than kinship was experimented. This resulted in a member of the community having a dual status; he was at the same time a member of his tribe and also a member of the faith. As a result, his loyalty was torn between tribe and religion. The situation tended to upset social equations and create tension. The difficult task of welding together disparate elements of the community and bringing about complete unity and homogeneity on the basis of the shared faith of *Islām* was to be addressed by the Prophet on priority; every possibility of resurgence of rift and hostility was to be wiped out.

Though the first Islamic community in *Madinah* found itself confronted with serious problems, both from within and without, threatening its very existence, the Prophet showed extraordinary wisdom in handling the situation. After due appreciation and analysis, he initiated a series of innovative measures to ward off the lurking threats and consolidate position of his community. One of the first steps he took was to strongly integrate his community in order to make it a highly motivated and dedicated monolithic group capable of effectively facing the challenges. For this purpose, after holding consultations in a meeting held in the house of *Anas*, he initiated a pact of brotherhood between the Helpers and the Emigrants whereby each *Muhajir* was religiously united with one *Ansār* for mutual welfare and assistance. Thus, *Umar* and *Ibtān b. Mālik, Abū Bakr* and *Kharijah b. Zayd, Abd ar Rahmān b Auf* and *Sād b. al Rabi, Musāb b. Umayr* and

Abū Ayyūb, Bilāl and *Abū Ruwayhah* and *Abū Obaydah b. Jarrāh* and *Sād b. Muādh* stood united in brotherly tie as was the case with all other Emigrants and Helpers. In order to facilitate easy and enduring bond, pairing was done with due consideration to factors like friendship, similarity of temperament, and so on, though rare cases of decision taken by lot are also reported by sources. The biographers have listed all the pairs thus formed by brothering. According to *Maqrīzī*, altogether 186 *Muhajirūn* families were integrated with those of *Ansār*. Perhaps due to his special status, however, the Prophet himself did not choose an *Ansār* but took *Alī* as his brother and similarly united *Hamzah* with *Zayd b Harithā*. Apart from strongly welding relations between members of the community, this innovative measure was to serve a few other collateral purposes, one of which was rehabilitation of the *Muhajirūn* who stood economically uprooted due to *Hijrah* and had now no means of sustenance.[1] Most of them had left behind all their property and had no capital to resume trading, the only profession they knew, but in *Madinah*, there was nothing for them to fall back on except farming for which they had no aptitude. Fraternization with *Ansār* would solve their immediate problem of food and shelter and would also help them acquire expertise in farming while working along with their religious brothers, the Prophet thought. Another motive was to cast off their feeling of loneliness which afflicted them after leaving their families and society behind; this would get them attuned to the changed circumstances.

The system of fraternization introduced by the Prophet was highly successful; the Helpers showed the highest degree of regard for the new bond treating their emigrant brothers better than real ones. The bond of religion was to prove stronger than the bond of blood. Sharing their houses and all belongings, the *Ansār* even requested the Prophet to equally divide their orchards and land between them and their new brothers (*Bukhāri*), but knowing that the *Muhajirūn* did not know anything about cultivation, the Prophet did not agree. The new brotherhood was, however, treated as real kinship, and in consonance with the principle contained in verse 10 of *Surah Anfāl*, the *Muhajirūn* were assigned inheritance

---

1   *Only Uthmān and Abū Bakr had been able to bring along some wealth.*

share in the property of their deceased *Ansār* brothers. However, after the battle of *Badr*, when the *Muhajirūn* did not need such support, this provision was revised by another verse of the same *Surah*. *Bukhāri* refers to a very interesting story showing the great enthusiasm of the *Ansār* for the new brotherhood. According to it, *Sād b. Rabī*, who had been attached with *Abd ar Rahmān b. Auf*, offered to divorce one of his two wives for his new brother, but the offer was declined with thanks. The *Quran* praises the *Ansār* for their magnificent sacrifice and help to *Islām*, declaring rewards for them (59/9 and 8/72).[1] The *Muhajirūn* also displayed considerable self-respect while dealing with their religious brothers; they always tried not to put any extra burden on their hosts. When *Rabī* wanted to share half of his entire wealth with *Abd ar Rahmān*, the latter refused and accepted help only to start his business of selling cheese and ghee in the market. In the course of time, he became a prosperous merchant and married a Madinan girl. *Abū Bakr*, *Uthmān*, *Umar*, and many others likewise started their own business without burdening their *Ansār* brothers. Many, however, had to work as manual labourers in the farms of their attached brothers, while some taught their family members to pay back in kind. According to *Muslim*, after return from *Khaybar*, the *Muhajirūn* returned all properties gifted to them by their *Ansār* brothers.

This unique system of brothering which is unparalleled in history had a great symbolic importance; it drove home the message that it was one's essential Islamic duty to treat all other Muslims as brother.

Out of this, a highly integrated community arose which was called *Ummah*[2]—a novel confederation of people from different

---

1   *In addition, we have a hadīth Qudsi narrated by Muslim which runs as under: 'On the Day of Resurrection God will say—where are those who loved one another for the sake of my grace? Today I shall shade them with My shade; on a day when there is no shade but Mine.'*

2   *It is generally suggested that 'Ummah' is derived from the Arabic word 'Umm' which means mother.*

tribes, clans, and social groups in which faith replaced blood or kinship as the social bond. This religious brotherhood resulted in suppression of all tribal feuds; the age-long enmity between *Aws* and *Khazraj* was forgotten and the people watched their friendship with wonder. The *Ummah* was based on the principle of equality of members irrespective of origin or status; in it members differed from one another not by wealth or genealogical superiority but by degree of piety. The *Ummah* was what has been called a 'super tribe' or 'neo-tribe' (Hodgson) with the Prophet as the *Shaikh*, a social and political head but more powerful than normal tribal chiefs, having absolute religious authority. The Prophet, however, took care to organize the *Ummah* on tribal lines, retaining those tribal customs which did not clash with the principles of *Islām*, '*The Ummah supplemented rather than supplanted the social usage of pre-Islamic Arabia and all its ideas were within the structure of tribalism. It retained pre-Islamic practices in matters of property, marriage and relations between members of the same tribe.*'[1]

Another highly significant political measure taken by the Prophet in order to safeguard position of the Muslim community was to conclude a formal pact or agreement of mutual assistance and cooperation not only with different Muslim tribes but also those of the Jews who were, numerically and in power, a quite important social group in the oasis. The text of the agreement (*Sahīfah*) which has come down to us from the early sources including *Ibn Hishām*, in its nature and contents, was revolutionary for its age and has been hailed as the first written constitution of the world; Muslim historians called it the 'Constitution of *Madinah*' because it showed the outlines of the political arrangement or State which the Prophet established for the first time in *al Hijāz*. Though incorporating various rights and duties of individuals and social groups involved in the agreement, its main objective, however, was maintenance of internal peace and security of the city and its defense in case of attack from external enemies. The Charter was actually meant to officially bind down hostile elements in the oasis, both within

---

1 *Bernard Lewis— 'The Arabs in History'.*

and without the community, who had been conspiring against the *Ummah* and instigating military attack by the *Quraysh*. It was an attempt to weld together conflicting elements of the oasis into an orderly confederation—a modus vivendi with non-Muslims in order to organize a city state. Though veracity of the text of the Constitution[1] was doubted by some Orientalists, its authenticity now stands established. The text is quite lengthy and it can be divided into forty-seven articles though some scholars identify a few more articles in it.[2] The form in which the text is available in the original sources indicates that the Act has two distinct parts; the first (articles 1 to 23) relates to the Muslim tribes/clans, regulating their relations within the *Ummah* and the second (from article 24 to 47) regulates relations with the Jews. Though both the parts have been placed together, it actually appears to be a combination of two separate documents. There is, however, disagreement among scholars regarding chronology of different parts. *Tabarī* and *Ibn Hishām* treat composition of the document as one of the first acts of the Prophet on entering *Madinah*; but historical developments following the *Hijrah* would indicate that some of its parts were probably written down on later dates.

The Constitution of *Madinah* was a great political document; apart from providing glimpses of the first polity established by the Prophet, it contained germs of modern democratic principles of freedom, equality and secularism, far in advance of its age, and stands as a testimony to the remarkable statesmanship of its author. Its explicit provisions, viewed together with implications hidden therein, reveal a number of highly significant features:

- First of all, it made an official announcement of establishment of the Muslim community (*Ummah*) as a distinct social and political group—a federation of the Emigrants and eight *Aws* and *Khazraj* clans. Such a federation remained the nominal form of the Islamic State in the coming times, fresh groups joining the

---

1   *It was for the first time translated in a European language by Wellhausen.*
2   *W. M. Watt identifies as many as fifty articles in the document.*

Ummah on entering *Islām* on equal terms. Each believer was to be brother to all others within the community and everyone was to enjoy equality of status. Peace of the *Ummah* was to be indivisible; no one was to enter into separate peace. The *Ummah* as a whole was to take revenge for blood of a faithful and principles were prescribed for payment of ransom of the prisoners of war and of blood money in order to avoid violence due to vendetta. Blood worth of every Muslim was equalized. The Muslims were to take action against their own men for unlawful acts or excesses in order to suppress crime, and no Muslim was to help a murderer. No Muslim was to kill another Muslim or help an unbeliever. Interpersonal relations of the members within the community thus stood well-regulated.

- The document officially recognized *Muhammad* as a prophet and went to establish his status not only as the political head of the *Ummah* but also as the leading political personality of the oasis. It thus signified assumption by him of secular responsibilities in addition to spiritual role, giving him a privileged position over other tribal heads. Ultimate sovereignty in the Islamic State rested with God and all differences and disputes between parties to the agreement were to be referred to God through the Prophet for adjudication. This in effect made the Prophet head of judicial administration in the oasis in respect of believers and nonbelievers alike. The tribal law of retaliation leading to warfare was thus replaced by a regime of arbitration and peace.

- The Constitution inaugurated a political confederation of Muslim and Jewish communities based on mutual assistance for internal security and defense from external aggression. It marked inception of the idea of one nationality as all social groups that were party to the agreement were to constitute a greater *Ummah* to act collectively for specific purposes. This political arrangement of forming a State based on the modern principle of pluralism with different social groups joining hands for mutual welfare was open to other nonbelieving communities as well and was subsequently extended to the Christians of *Najrān* and other neighbouring areas.

- The Jews[1] were included in the political arrangement of the oasis in a somewhat subordinate position. The main purpose of their inclusion was ensuring their co-operation for defense of *Madinah* in case of attack by *Quraysh*. They were to fight along with the Muslims in such an eventuality and their war expenditure was to be borne by them. While duty-bound to provide assistance in case of attack, they were to be prohibited from undertaking independent military expeditions. The agreement thus provided for compulsory military service by all social groups and everyone was to equally share responsibility for defense of the city. The Jews were not to help or provide protection to the enemy and to make separate peace or agreement.

- Next to defense, the thrust of the agreement was on maintenance of internal peace and security and suppression of crime in the city for which every citizen, whether Muslim or non-Muslim, was, to endeavour. Arrangement of adjudication of all disputes by the Prophet and regulation of payment of blood money were steps in this direction. More important, however, was declaration of the city of *Madinah* (*Jauf* Valley) as a sacred or inviolable (*Harām*) territory on the pattern of *Makkah*; as a consequence, violence or bloodshed in the city was prohibited. This was a significant measure as *Madinah* was now to compete with *Makkah* as a pilgrimage site as well as a trading centre—an indirect attack on religious and economic status of the city of *Quraysh*.

---

1 *The three Jewish tribes of Qaynuqā, Nadīr and Qurayzah did not sign the agreement in the beginning but later on entered into it.*

- Another spectacular feature of the Charter was that it gave to all who joined the Commonwealth as citizens, complete personal security, equal socio-economic rights, and religious freedom. The Jews who entered the agreement were to enjoy security of property and were not to be made to accept *Islām*. In an age of tyranny, violence, and disintegration, the Prophet of *Islām* was thus endeavouring to reconstruct a State and a nation based on universal humanity, liberalism, and tolerance.

As is evident from the 'Constitution of *Madinah*', shortly after arrival in the oasis, the Prophet assumed additional role of a proactive political leader, the ruler of the oasis, implementing ways and means for its safety and security from internal and external enemies. Assumption of a political role has led many Western historians to conclude that after *Hijrah*, the Prophet was concerned more with political rather than religious matters; he became a statesman par excellence, his real motive being empire-building, using religion as a means. '*The seer in him,*' remarks Phillip K. Hitti, '*now recedes into the background and the practical man of politics comes to the fore. The Prophet is gradually overshadowed by the statesman.*' Such a view, however, reflects a superficial interpretation of historical facts and appears to have been inspired by lop-sided coverage by the *Sirah* writers. Compiling their works during the heyday of Islamic imperialism, classical biographers of the Prophet, while dealing with the post-*Hijrah* period, excessively highlighted political aspects of his life tending to ignore religious and spiritual pursuits which were his real objective. They spoke more and more about his wars and diplomacy and remained reticent about evolution of theology and the overall Islamic way of life, development of which was his primary concern. Little did they reflect that the Prophet actually had no intentions of taking up political responsibilities but was compelled to do so by the circumstances. Surrounded by violently hostile elements on all sides, he realized that the only way to ensure survival of his religion was to back it by political power and take recourse to political activism. Perhaps no other way to express and organize religion within the given environment was possible. He used politics as a means to achieve his religious goals and not the other way round. However, this combining of religion and politics,[1] though taxing, did not affect spiritual status of the Prophet who continued to spend most of his time in prayers and activities meant to consolidate his religion.

In the free atmosphere of *Madinah*, the Prophet immediately set himself to the task of not only giving a final shape to his religion but also establishing the Islamic way of life in all aspects as enjoined by revelations. The great mosque was constructed and the five daily prayers (*Salāt*) as well as the one of Fridays were regularly performed in congregation. The egalitarian Islamic code of conduct was enforced; vices of the past like drinking, gambling, usury, and others were cancelled. Soon the official Islamic form of almsgiving, *Zakāt*, was prescribed by several revelations; it was fixed at 2.5 per cent to be spent on welfare of the poor. In the second year of *Hijrah*, fast (*Sawm*) of the month of *Ramadan* was prescribed (Q. 2/183, 185). *Sawm* literally meant abstinence and was an instrument of bringing about purification of soul and self-discipline. Revelations laid down in general what was forbidden (*harām*) and what was allowed (*halāl*) in *Islām*. Within a few months after *Hijrah*, *Adhān* or the practice of loudly summoning the people for *Salāt* at the right time was introduced. Before adoption of the call to prayers, the Muslims used to judge their own time by observing movement of the sun and turn up for prayers at different moments which used to create confusion. Initially, the Prophet thought of appointing men to call the Muslims from their houses for prayers, but that was not found feasible. The idea of appointing a man to blow a horn like what the Jews did or using a wooden clapper (*Nāqūs*) as the Christians those days used to do was examined but rejected by the Prophet. The problem, however, was solved when one night a *Khazraj*, *Abd Allāh ibn Zayd*, saw a dream in which a

---

1 *Intermixing or combination of religion and politics after establishment of the Ummah became a distinctive feature of the Islamic polity in the succeeding ages.*

man in green dress taught him *Adhān* with the same wordings as it stands now. The Prophet said that it was a true vision, and on his direction, *Bilāl* was taught the formula and appointed to pronounce calls for prayers which he started doing from the top of a high-rising building in the neighbourhood of the mosque. This story regarding the introduction of *Adhān* is told by *Ibn Ishāq* and several *ahadīth*. *Abū Dawūd*, however, says that *Umar* suggested pronouncement of the call for prayers which was accepted by the Prophet, and *Bilāl* was deputed for the purpose. *Bukhari* does not mention Abd Allāh ibn Zayd's story but refers to the one relating to *Umar*.

In the post-*Hijrah* period, revelations not only continued but became more frequent and prolific, but their nature and content underwent a change with new political and social developments in the Islamic movement. The emphasis was now on guidance for socio-economic reforms. A series of practical verses laying down new legislation or commenting on current political developments started coming down in a rather prosaic style. In February 624, the *Qiblā* or direction of prayer was finally changed from Jerusalem to the *Kābah* on the basis of a command of God given in a revelation. According to Western historians, this happened when the Prophet lost all hopes of winning over the Jews and decided to focus attention on the Arabs; this would please the Arabs including the *Quraysh* by giving the highest degree of sanctity to the Makkan mosque. The event symbolized widening of Muhammad's mission which was now to cover the whole of Arabia. For 'Arabization of *Islām*', control of *Makkah* was now a religious necessity. But these are mere historical interpretations; what we definitely know is that the change was based on God's command which came down suddenly in the midst of a Friday prayer when verse 2/144 was revealed: '*We have seen thee turning thy face about in the heavens; now we will surely turn thee to a direction which will satisfy thee. Turn thy face towards the Holy Mosque; and wherever you are, turn your faces towards it.*' The move, however, was taken by the Jews as an act of defiance and marked the final break between the Jews and the Prophet.

The most significant change in the outward policy of the Prophet after *Hijrah* was a conscious decision to fight back the enemies who threatened his faith and his community—a resolve to wage wars in defense of *Islām*. This was a great development which was to change the course of history. This attitudinal change, however, did not come about out of his own volition; it was, in fact, the result of compelling circumstances. By disposition, he was peace-loving, had never in his life wielded a weapon, and was extremely tender-hearted, susceptible to human suffering and pain. The religion he was preaching was also one of pure pacifism. God wanted him to warn and preach with patience; offer only passive resistance to insults, persecution, and violence; and leave the fate of the infidels to Him alone. That is why, for more than a decade, he and his followers remained strict pacifists and hated the idea of fighting even in self-defense. When life became unbearable in *Makkah* and their very survival was threatened, they preferred to stealthily migrate rather than fight back. But even before *Hijrah*, the Prophet knew that he was likely to be followed and attacked by the enemies who had sworn to destroy *Islām*, and so a clause about fighting in self-defense had been included in the Second Pledge of *al Aqabah*. The apprehensions of the Prophet came true, and in *Madinah* also, it soon became clear that the polytheists would not leave *Islām* in peace; the Muslims were once again under imminent threat of extermination, now rather heightened due to escalated hatred and animosity of the *Quraysh*. It was under this situation that the Prophet decided to take up arms in order to defend his community against enemy aggression. It was an age of disintegration and violence, and so, it was necessary to use violence in order to put an end to violence. Within the given environment, peace could be achieved only by sword, the Prophet realized. The momentous decision to wage war, however, was not based only on his own assessment; like all other of his important actions, this was also based on the explicit will of God. Soon after *Hijrah*, a few revelations came down which permitted the Muslims not only to fight back in self-defense but also implicitly contained a command for such a course of action:

- *22/39 and 40[1]: 'Sanction is given unto those who fight because they have been wronged; and Allāh is indeed able to give them victory. Those who have been driven from their homes unjustly only because they said—"our Lord is Allāh". For had it not been for Allah's repelling some men by means of others, cloisters and churches and oratories and mosques, wherein the name of Allāh is oft-mentioned, would assuredly have been pulled down. Verily Allāh helpeth one who helpeth Him. Lo! Allāh is strong, Almighty.'*
- *22/216: 'Fighting is prescribed for you and you dislike it. But it is possible that you dislike a thing which is good for you and you love a thing which is bad for you. But Allāh knows and you know not.'*
- *8/39: 'And fight them on until there is no more persecution and religion becomes Allah's in its entirety. But if they cease, verily Allāh doth see all that they do.'*
- *2/190: 'Fight in the way of Allāh against those who fight against you, but begin not hostilities. Lo! Allāh loveth not aggressors.'*

The *Qurān* was thus evolving a theory of just war for suppression of injustice and restoration of peace. Such a war was not to be fought for the sake of material interest or political aggrandizement but was to be a sacred duty exclusively for defending life and religion without recourse to aggression as qualified by verse 2/190. Subsequent revelations were to declare great religious reward for participating and sacrificing life in this duty and curse of God for avoiding it.[2] A well-defined ethics of such warfare was also to develop which enjoined avoidance of killing of noncombatants, destruction of crops and cattle and excesses in any other form. In the post-*Hijrah* situation,

---

1 *Quran 22: 39 is traditionally considered the first verse which gave permission to fight in defence. While some scholars place its revelation immediately before the Second Aqabah, the majority view is that it was revealed during the early months after Hijrah.*

2 *Quran 9/81 and 82; 3/157, 158, 169, and 172.*

Islām represented all that was good and ideal and the Makkan polytheists stood for all the evils of *Jahiliyah*, and therefore, it was the religious duty of the *Ummah* to fight against their aggressors. But even after consolidating its political position during the year following *Hijrah*, the *Ummah* was no match for the powerful *Quraysh*, and so it would have been quite unwise for the Prophet to think of waging a full-scale war against *Makkah*. He, therefore, took recourse to sending small expeditions against their trade caravans on the western trade route. Such an expedition or razzia, called *Ghazwa* in Arabic, was a socially sanctioned Bedouin way of punishing hostile tribes by plundering their goods but, at the same time, taking care to avoid bloodshed lest it should give rise to vendetta. Between June 623 and January 624, the Prophet sent a series of expeditions, all directed against trade caravans of the *Quraysh*. In the history of *Islām*, if an expedition went under the personal command of the Prophet, it was called *Ghazwa* (plural *Ghazawat* or *Maghāzī*); otherwise, it used to be known as *Sariyyah* (plural *Sarayah*).[1] The biographers have listed out eight such expeditions during the period, four of which were *Ghazawat*:

1. The first of these expeditions was sent in the ninth month after *Hijrah* under the command of *Hamzah* with a strength of thirty *Muhajirūn*. Its purpose was to intercept a *Quraysh* caravan which had a strength of 300 riders under the command of *Abū Jahal*. The expedition went to the coastal area in the west near *al Īs* in the territory of *Juhaynah* and confronted the caravan. But the chief of *Juhaynah*, *Majdī*, who was friendly to both, interposed and both withdrew without a fight.

2. This was followed by another expedition of sixty or eighty *Muhajirūn* under the command of *Ubaydah b. al Hārith*. It went to the valley of *Rabigh* in *al Hijāz* and encountered a large *Quraysh* caravan under *Ikrimah b.*

---

1 *Some scholars apply the two terms according to number of men dispatched. If the number of men in an expedition exceeded 100, that was a Ghazwa, while below 100, it was a mere Sariyyah.*

Abū Jahal. There also no fighting that took place except that *Sād b. Abū Waqqās* shot an arrow, the first in *Islām* to have done so. It was on this occasion that two of the Makkans, *al Miqdād* and *Utbah b. Ghazwān*, deserted their group and became Muslims.

3. The next was a very small expedition having only eight *Muhajirūn* (according to some sources—20) under *Sād b. Abū Waqqas* which went as far as *Kharrār* in *Hijāz* but came back without fighting.

4. The first expedition under personal command of the Prophet went to *Waddan* in the South in the territory of *Banū Dumrah*. It went in the twelfth month after *Hijrah* in search of a *Quraysh* caravan but missed the target. The Prophet, however, came back after concluding a treaty of neutrality with *B. Dumrah*. When leaving *Madinah* for this expedition, the Prophet had given charge of the city to *Sād b. Ubādah*. This was for the first time that charge of *Madinah* during the Prophet's absence had been given to someone else and this became a practice for such occasions in future.

5. About a month later, the Prophet led another expedition in the north-west to *Buwāt* along with 200 Muslims.[1] The purpose was to intercept and plunder a *Quraysh* caravan of 1500 camels with 100 riders which were under the charge of *Umayyah b. Khalāf.*[2] But the expedition came back without intercepting the caravan as information about the proposed raid leaked and the caravan changed its route.

6. Another of the Prophet's *Ghazwat* went to the valley of *Dhāt ul Sāq* to intercept a *Quraysh* caravan under *Abū Sufyān*. This was also a big Muslim party with a strength of 200, but the caravan had already passed as

---

1 *Most of the historians believe that like all other expeditions of the period, this one also included only Muhajirūn. Some of the sources, however, suggest that 50 per cent of the Muslims in this expedition were Ansar.*

2 *He was the chief of Jumah and an inveterate enemy of the Prophet.*

the Prophet's information had been received late. The Prophet then proceeded (Oct 623) to al *Ushayrah* in the valley of *Yānbu* which was in south-westerly direction from *Madinah*. Taking advantage of the opportunity, he entered into a treaty of friendship with *B. Mudlij*[1] and also further strengthened his ties with *Banū Dumrah*.

7. About two days after return from *Ushayrah*, a party under an ally of *Quraysh*, *Kurz b. Jābir al Fihrī*, raided the outskirts of *Madinah*, destroyed food-bearing trees, and took away the flock. The Prophet with a party chased him as far as *Safwān* near *Badr*, but *Kurz* managed to escape. This expedition is known as the first raid of *Badr*.

8. So far, none of the early expeditions had been successful. The last one, however, led to bloodshed and created a crisis situation. In Jan 624, the Prophet sent a small party of eight or nine emigrants under *Abd Allāh ibn Jahsh* with direction contained in a sealed cover to be opened only after undertaking journey for two days—a measure taken for the sake of secrecy. Though sources differ regarding the exact purpose of this expedition, *Ibn Ishāq* suggests that it was meant simply for collection of intelligence about *Makkah–Yaman* trade route and also about the general plans and activities of *Quraysh*. When *Abd Allāh* opened the letter after two days of journey, he found the following instruction in it: '*When you have read this letter of mine, proceed until you reach Nakhlah between Makkah and Tāif. Lie in wait there for Quraysh and find out for us what they are doing.*' He followed the instruction and reached *Nakhlah* (though two of his men, *Sād* and *Utbah*, were left behind due to loss of camel) only to encounter a small caravan[2] of only four guards coming from Yaman. It happened to be the last day of *Rajab* when violence was prohibited

---

1 *Mudlij was the tribe of Surāqah who had attempted to capture the Prophet during his Hijrah journey but impressed by him, had become his supporter. His tribe hosted a feast for the Prophet and his companion.*

2 *According to some sources, it was a donkey caravan.*

according to Arab custom. The party found itself confused as the Prophet in his letter had neither forbidden them from fighting nor made mention of the sacred month. Taking its own decision, the party attacked the caravan, killing one (*Amr ibn al Hadramī*) by arrow shot and capturing the merchandise as well as two of the guards (*Uthmān* and *Hakām*) while the fourth one escaped. The group then returned to *Madinah* along with the captured caravan. The incident created serious concern in the *Ummah* as the killing had taken place during the month of truce and retaliation for blood revenge was feared. The Prophet also did not approve the action and refused to accept his one-fifth share of the booty, causing great embarrassment to the members of the justified the killing as well as capture of the caravan[1] even during the sacred month. The Prophet, thereafter, approved the action and expedition. But at this juncture, verse 2/217 was revealed which accepted his share of the spoils. He demanded *Sād* and Utbah's return for release of the two captives to which the *Quraysh* agreed, but one of them (*Al Hakām)* was so impressed by things in *Madinah* that he converted to *Islām* and stayed back. Though the Muslims gained confidence and enthusiasm out of the incident, it created a blood feud and highly infuriated the *Quraysh* who stirred up the whole peninsula against the Prophet, accusing him of desecration of the holy month. It provided a good cause to *Quraysh* to launch an immediate attack on the Muslims.

Based on the impression left by the classical historians, these early expeditions are generally described as military campaigns, a declaration of war against *Quraysh*. They are represented to have been an expression of the pent-up resentment of the Muslims against

---

1 *Q 2/217: 'They will ask you about the sacred month and war in it. Say, war therein is a serious matter, but keeping people from the way of God and disbelieving in Him and in sacred mosque and driving out His people therefrom is more serious with God.'*

the Makkans who had subjected them to ten years of persecution, forced them to abandon their home, usurped their properties, and were now planning to attack and exterminate them. In order to avenge themselves on *Quraysh*, they, therefore, sent these expeditions with the motive of attacking their caravans and taking possession of their goods.[1] On a deeper analysis, however, they may hardly be considered as warlike expeditions, though it is certain that they went out fully prepared to resist attack. Except the last one (*Nakhlah*) in which the party exceeded its authority and indulged in killing and capture of booty without consent of the Prophet, in none of these expeditions fighting or killing or looting of goods took place. If their real purpose was to attack and loot the caravans, it would be difficult to explain the return of the expeditions of *Hamzah* and *Ubaydah* without fight even though they were face to face with *Quraysh*'s caravans. Moreover, the number of fighters in most of these Muslim expeditions was too small to attack large caravans; after the first interception, the *Quraysh* increased the number of caravan escorts, and so, everytime, the Muslims used to be outnumbered. Therefore, calling them military raids intended for fighting does stand to reason. What, then, was the real motive behind these expeditions?

It has been suggested that they were meant not for actual military engagement but for creating a psychological impact to cow down the *Quraysh* and force them to some sort of understanding or negotiation. A show of power and confidence by sending such expeditions would indicate that the *Ummah* was strong enough to take on the mighty *Quraysh* and would restrain them in their designs against the Muslims. It was precisely due to this reason that they threatened to cut-off the highly profitable[2]

---

1   *The Quraysh had appropriated properties of the Muhajirūn left behind in Makkah which was in flagrant violation of the tribal code. Therefore, the Muslims believed themselves to be fully justified in attacking their caravans and taking away the goods in order to recover value of their lost properties.*

2   *According to Sprenger, the annual trade to Makkah through western trade route worked out to a whopping 2,50,000 dinars and 1,60,000 gold pounds.*

Makkan trade route to Syria which was the life-line of their power and prosperity. Frequent attempts to intercept their caravans would make them realize that their trade with Syria would be jeopardized and force them to rapprochement, the Prophet thought. The expeditions were, therefore, not for war but for peace. Another reason behind them was to guard against the impending military attack from *Makkah*. They were basically reconnoitering expeditions intended to collect intelligence regarding designs, movements, war preparations, and alliances of *Quraysh* as also to keep a watch on the general situation in the area. One more collateral purpose of these expeditions was to conclude pacts of friendship and nonaggression with outlying Bedouin tribes specially those located at strategic points along the trade route. It was important to impress the tribes by sending war-like expeditions against a mighty power and thus dissuade them from siding with *Quraysh*. These raids actually resulted in conclusion of military alliances with *Juhaynah* in the north and *Dumrah* as well as *Mudlij* in the south. It has also been pointed out that God's command as well as impending threat of annihilation made it necessary for the Muslims to fight back in self-defense. But thirteen years of pacifism had left them unfit for such a role. The Prophet might have organized these raids for psychological and physical preparation of the *Ummah* and its training in war-like activities. It may, however, be naive to believe that these early expeditions provided the *casus belli* for Makkah's full-scale military attack on the *Ummah* for there were much deeper and fundamental factors behind the clash. Nevertheless, by directly challenging political and economic power as well as honour of the *Quraysh*, they did add fuel to the fire and precipitated the attack which otherwise also seemed inevitable.

CHAPTER VIII

WAR IN THE WAY OF GOD

The early Madinan expeditions, though insignificant in nature, were a prelude to breaking out of active military hostilities between the *Ummah* and the *Quraysh* as well as other elements aligned with the latter or otherwise posing threat to *Islām*; they were followed by a series of 'just wars' that intermittently continued till the death of the Prophet finally resulting in the establishment of political domination of *Islām* on almost the whole of the peninsula. These campaigns were numerous, the classical sources recounting as many as eighty-two of them, but most of them were minor affairs of the nature of traditional nomadic raids involving small number of fighters and should be considered as mere skirmishes rather than wars. Pickthall enumerates sixty-five of them of which twenty-seven were commanded by the Prophet in person, only in nine of which there was hard fighting. The remaining thirty-eight campaigns were sent under other leaders, but the Prophet personally supervised every detail in respect of their organization and tasking. The character of these expeditions, whether they were aggressive or purely defensive, has, however, remained a subject of debate. In later years, when the wars were being terribly fought, a few verses were revealed which gave a general command to fight the infidels not prescribing conditions or restrictions which were there in the previous verses. Three such verses are significant:

- 9/5— *'But when the forbidden months are passed, then fight and slay the pagans wherever you find them and seize them, beleaguer them and lay in wait for them in every stratagem; but if they repent, and establish regular prayers and pay Zakāt, then open the way for them, for Allāh is oft-forgiving, most merciful.'*
- 9/29— *'Fight those who believe not in Allāh, nor the Last Day, nor hold that forbidden which had been forbidden by Allāh and His Messenger, nor acknowledge the religion of truth, from among the people of the book, until they pay Jizya with willing submission, and feel themselves subdued.'*
- 9/73— *'O Prophet! Strive hard against the unbelievers and hypocrites, and be firm against them. Their abode is hell—an evil refuge indeed.'*

On the basis of such revelations, the later generation of Islamic legal scholars and *Qurān* interpreters developed the classical theory of *Jihād*.[1] They regarded the unconditional command to fight in these verses as having abrogated all previous verses concerning fight in defense only. Dividing the world into two spheres, one of believers (*Dar ul Islām*) and the other of unbelievers (*Dar ul Harab*), they asserted that it was the duty of the *Ummah* to bring the whole earth under the sway of *Islām* and to exterminate unbelief. If this was not done, the whole *Ummah* would be sinning, and so, *Islām* was to live in a perpetual state of holy war. They thus advocated fighting against infidels until they converted, that is, an expansionist theory of *Jihād*. Some of the extremist groups like the Kharijites even referred to *Jihād* or fighting against the unbelievers as the sixth pillar of *Islām*. Basing their judgment on such interpretations, many of the Western historians portrayed *Islām* as a 'religion of sword' which advocated violence for spreading the faith. Some of them

---

1 *The word Jihād (mistranslated by Western scholars as holy war), which is commonly but inappropriately used to denote Islamic religious war, is a Quranic term having many shades of meaning. It is derived from the Arabic root j-h-d which means to strive or struggle or exert. As envisaged in the Qurān, it conveys the sense of struggle against evil in the path of God (Jihād fi sabil Allāh) in every possible manner—physical, moral, spiritual, and intellectual—in order to realize God's will. Thus, to lead a virtuous life, preach Islām, spend wealth in the way of God, resist the temptations of the inner self, and fight for religion are all different aspects of Jihād. Fighting or killing (Qitāl) is only one aspect of the all-round struggle to establish Islām, that is, a regime of peace and justice. Qitāl is not an end in itself but a means to a higher and nobler end. Jihād is fought not against visible enemy alone but also against the devil and the self (nafs). According to Ibn Rushd, requirement of Jihād can be fulfilled in four ways—by heart, by tongue, by hands, and by sword. In the Quranic verses commanding fighting in the way of God, the word used is mostly Qitāl and not Jihād.*

The Qurān makes it a duty of all Muslims to carry out Jihād or struggle on all fronts to create a just and decent society as enjoined by Islām. A hadīth makes it clear that Qitāl or fighting, though sometimes vital, amounts to only a minor part of the concept of Jihād. Once on returning from a battle, the Prophet is said to have remarked: 'We return from the little Jihād to the greater Jihād.'

even concluded that the Prophet was a ruthless warrior who waged continuous wars in order to force conversions. These wars were actually aggressive and meant to satisfy his imperialistic ambitions; he used religion for political motives.

Such a view of *Jihād* or *Qitāl* and such an interpretation of the Prophet's life and military campaigns are, however, contrary to the actual historical facts of his life and preaching. In their historical context, the so-called unconditional verses were actually directed against *Quraysh* with whom the *Ummah* was engaged in a do or die fight; and so, they are to be seen in continuation rather than abrogation of the conditional verses. Much before the emergence of Orientalism, the classical doctrine of *Jihād* had been challenged by a new generation of Islamic scholars including *Ibn Taymiyyah* (1263–1328). According to them, *Islām* advocated total peace and coexistence and the theory of unprovoked religious violence was in violation of one of the most important principles of the *Qurān* which forbade use of force for conversion. Verse 2/256 stressed that '*there can be no compulsion in religion.*' Similarly, verse 109/6 mentioned: '*To you your religion, to me mine.*' Moreover, the theory of militant *Islām* is defined by historical facts of the Prophet's life and examples set by him. There is no dearth of historical evidence to prove that he firmly believed in peaceful coexistence of *Islām* with other religions; nor were his military expeditions aggressive or wanton. All of them were fought with strict adherence to restrictions and conditions prescribed by the early verses as also ethics of warfare evolved by the Prophet himself; in none of them was there any excessive violence. Modern scholars have pointed out that in all the fights of the *Ummah* put together, the number of those killed does not exceed 500, both sides included. One would come across a number of instances in which great magnanimity was shown by the *Ummah* and shedding of blood was avoided. Mercy and compassion on the defeated people and humane treatment of the prisoners of wars were hallmarks of the Prophet's policy. In modern times, though the classical view of *Jihād* was made use of by the Islamic terrorist groups and a few fundamentalist regimes like those of Ayotollah Khomeini in Iran and *Talibān* in

Afghanistan, the great mass of the Muslims the world over does not subscribe to the theory of militant *Islām*.

The first but the most crucial battle of the life of the Prophet was that of *Badr*, which was fought against *Quraysh* on 15 March 624 (Friday, seventeenth of *Ramadān*); strangely enough, however, he neither intended nor was ready for this fight at this stage. The *Ummah* was not yet a match for the powerful *Quraysh* and, therefore, confronting them in an open battle was not then included in the Prophet's agenda; what he actually aimed at was to intercept the *Quraysh*'s caravan, capture merchandise, and thereby harass and force them to negotiate so that the Muslims could visit the *Kābah* unobstructed. But it was perhaps the dispensation of God that made the *Ummah* stand face to face with the enemy. The classical biographers have vividly described the circumstances leading to the battle and the course it went through. A whole *Surah* of the *Qurān*— 'al Anfāl' (8–Spoils of War)—is related to the Battle of *Badr* and throws light on its different aspects.

According to the story narrated by the biographers, in the charged atmosphere following *Nakhlah*, the Prophet received information that a large Makkan trade caravan under *Abū Sufyān* (the same which he had missed at *Ushayrah* a couple of months back while it was proceeding to Syria) was returning from Syria. This was the richest caravan of the year having a thousand camels laden with goods worth 50,000 dinars and included weapons also, but escorted only by seventy odd fighters. Almost every significant Makkan had a share in the caravan. In accordance with his policy, the Prophet planned to waylay this caravan and capture booty at *Badr* on the western trade route. Located about eighty miles west of *Madinah* (three days' march from *Madinah*), *Badr* was the site of an annual fair. For this expedition, the Prophet is said to have mobilized a force of 313 Muslims, only 77 of whom were *Muhajirūn*; the remaining of its members were *Ansār* who joined the expedition in large numbers perhaps under the general enthusiasm caused by the incident of *Nakhlah* and also due to prospects of rich booty.[1] The expedition under personal command of the Prophet is said to have departed from *Madinah* on the twelfth day of *Ramadān*. In the meantime, the leader of the caravan, *Abū Sufyān*, got wind of the Prophet's plan and sent words to *Makkah* through *Damdam* of *Ghifār* for reinforcement for the caravan's protection. *Damdam* rushed to *Makkah* and, as instructed by *Abū Sufyān*, made a dramatic appearance in the city.[2] In order to attract immediate attention, he hysterically cut off the ears of his camel, broke its nose, turned its saddle sideways, tore off his own garments and entered the city, standing on its back, loudly appealing to *Quraysh* to save their wealth as well as honour from the Muslims. The Makkans were already seething with anger, determined to take revenge on the Muslims for the killing of *Nakhlah*. When *Damdam* revealed his information, their fury knew no bounds; under the command of *Abū Jahal*, they immediately raised and dispatched a strong force of about 1,000 fighters, all well-trained and effectively equipped and armed. Their army included a cavalry of 100 horses and a train of 700 camels, the infantry wearing armours. All notable leaders of the city joined the force with the exception of *Abū Lahab* who happened to be sick and sent a substitute. The chief of *Jumah, Umayyah b. Khalāf* (the fattest man of *Makkah*), did not intend to join due to old age but was taunted by *Uqbah* as belonging to the group of women, and so in order to save his honour, he also ultimately joined in. Though the *Quraysh* army left without loss of time, it would have been difficult for it to reach *Badr* for protection of the caravan due to distance involved; it

---

1   *The response to the Prophet's call was so overwhelming that those too young also joined the expedition; but they were detected and sent back by the Prophet. On this, Umayr ibn Abū Waqqās cried so much that he was allowed to go along, but as reported by the sources, was killed in the battle.*

2   *According to a story narrated by Ibn Ishāq, three days before the arrival of Damdam, the Prophet's aunt, Atīkah, had a dream which revealed impending disaster for the Quraysh. She told Abbās about that and many in the city knew about it. But Abū Jahal dismissed it as a mere hallucination.*

would, therefore, appear that the real motive of this force was to attack and punish the Muslims rather than protect the caravan.

The Prophet learnt about dispatch of a big *Quraysh*ite army while on the way to *Badr* and was quite frightened. He was aware of the *Ummah*'s weakness; his small raiding party (having only two horses and seventy camels) had not been prepared to face a full scale battle. Apart from being inexperienced in warfare, his men were not properly equipped and armed; some had swords but no shields while some did not have even swords. It was a crisis situation indicating a total change of plan; instead of laying their hands on a rich caravan, they were heading towards a Makkan army more than three times their size. The Prophet knew well that the Makkan army was not likely to retreat without having an engagement with his men. In a move which was to become an important principle of taking Islamic political decisions,[1] he held consultations (*shurā*) with his companions in order to decide whether to retreat or proceed further ready to give a battle to the Makkans. The *Muhajirūn* were strongly in favour of proceeding to *Badr* even if it resulted in confrontation with the Makkan army. Their opinion was voiced by *Abū Bakr* and *Umar* and then by *Miqdād* who said that they would not, like the followers of Moses, tell him to go with his God and fight alone; instead, they would go to any extent fighting with him for his cause. The Prophet, however, was more interested in knowing the reaction of the *Ansar* who constituted about 75 per cent of his army. Their pledge to fight was actually for defending him against attack in *Madinah* only and did not put them under obligation to take part in a military expedition outside their territory. Therefore, when the Prophet repeated his question regarding their opinion on the issue, the *Ansār* realized that their devotion to *Islām* was

1   *It was the principle of the Prophet not to impose his decisions in an autocratic manner and instead to take important decisions after obtaining views and comments from his Companions. He used to give due importance to suggestions and advices of the Companions allowing them to develop their critical faculties. Taking extra-religious decisions by consensus was a hallmark of his policy.*

being doubted and felt rather slighted. On their behalf, *Sād ibn Muādh* expressed unequivocal support to the Prophet under all circumstances including fighting at any place. '*Order us, and by Allāh, we will jump into the sea,*' he said. The Prophet was extremely pleased at the overwhelming and enthusiastic response of his followers in favour of fighting and sacrificing their lives. Since retreating at this stage would have exposed the weakness of the *Ummah*, the Prophet decided to proceed as per his plan; he would still be able to capture the caravan at *Badr* and return to *Madinah* before the *Quraysh* army reached the area, he might have thought.[1] But, aware of the danger that lay ahead, he had special sessions of prayer invoking God's help and gave tidings of a positive response. The precarious situation under which three different parties were heading towards *Badr* at that point of time and the Prophet's desire to avoid confrontation with the Makkan army finds reflection in verse 8/7 of the *Qurān*.[2]

When the Prophet reached *Badr*[3] along with his party, he learnt that the caravan had managed to escape by changing route

---

1   *It is sometimes suggested (M. M. Pickthall and Maulana Shibli Numāni) that attacking the caravan was not the real motive of the Prophet. Even before leaving Madinah, he was aware of the departure of the Makkan army the real aim of which was to attack the Muslims in revenge for the wrong done at Nakhlah. But the Muslims then were a disinclined and ill-equipped lot for a major war and would have despaired if they had known that they were proceeding to face a formidable army. Therefore, the Prophet deliberately concealed the real object of the Ummah's expedition and made a pretext of interception of the caravan. It was the normal practice of the Prophet to hide real motives behind his expeditions, it is argued. It is also said that the Quraysh's army had already advanced more than half-way to Madinah before the Prophet set out for Badr.*

2   *Verse 8/7— 'And when Allāh promised you one of the two bands (of the enemy) that it should be yours, and ye longed that other than the armed one might be yours. And Allāh willed that He should cause the Truth to triumph by His words, and cut the root of the disbelievers.'*

3   *It was during this journey that temporary exemption was granted to the Muslims from the fast of Ramadan while undertaking hard journeys. After announcing this concession, the Prophet was seen prominently drinking water.*

and swift marches. After effecting a safe passage through *Badr* area, *Abū Sufyān* sent a messenger to the Makkan army (which was then a little south of *Badr* at *Juhfah*) informing *Abū Jahal* of the fact and suggesting that reinforcement was no longer required and that the army should go back. After receiving this information, public opinion in the Makkan party was in favour of withdrawal; all the men of the *Zuhra* and the *Adī* clans and many of the *Hāshims* immediately went back. But *Abū Jahal* intransigently opposed withdrawal and persuaded the leaders to continue the march; perhaps he wanted to finally settle scores with the Muslims. Another reason for his insistence was that, in the absence of *Abū Sufyān*, he wanted to cash in on the situation in order to strengthen his political stature in *Makkah*. It was at this stage that *Juhaym* of *Muttalib* saw a dream indicating disaster for *Quraysh* (he even mentioned the names of the Makkan leaders whom he saw being killed), but *Abū Jahal* dismissed him as paranoid and the army proceeded to *Badr*.

After reaching *Badr*, the Prophet was able to ascertain from two water carriers caught by his men that the *Quraysh* army had arrived at *Badr* and was camping beyond the hill of *Aqanqal*. From their statements, he also ascertained their approximate number as well as names of the leaders and remarked, '*This Makkah hath thrown unto you the best morsels of her liver.*' He accepted the tactical suggestion of *Hubāb*, a *Khazraj*, to occupy the wells which were closer to the enemy in order to prevent the latter access to water. Nature also favoured the Muslims at this stage and there was a good shower due to which sandy part of the field which the Muslims occupied became wet and solid while the sloping dry area which was to be occupied by *Quraysh* after crossing the hill became muddy and slippery (Q 2/1, 8/11). The morale of the Muslims was very high and they were bubbling with confidence. They were to win both ways; victory would mean vindication of the faith and involve great religious merit while still greater was to be the reward for getting slain for it would amount to martyrdom (*Shahādat*), that is, direct entry into the paradise. There was, therefore, no fear of death;, and it was this strong religious inspiration—a desire to achieve *Shahādat*—that was to offset the numerical inferiority and other disadvantages of the *Ummah*. But to the Prophet, it was a precarious situation as the very existence of *Islām* was at stake. Moreover, shedding blood of his own men was the last thing he would have desired. He, therefore, made a last attempt to avoid fight and sent *Umar ibn al Khattāb* to the enemy camp for negotiation, but the latter's appeal went unheeded; rather, *Abū Jahal* considered Umar's attempt to negotiate peace as a sign of weakness. In the meantime, *Quraysh* sent *Umayr ibn Wahb* to estimate the number of the Muslims and to confirm if they had any reinforcement in the rear. *Umayr* noticed a grim resolution on faces of the Muslim fighters and, on return, reported the approximate number of the Muslims as well as absence of any further troops in the rear, but also informed: '*I have not seen men but death mounted on camels.*' Apprehending heavy loss of lives of *Quraysh*, he advised them not to fight. '*I do not think,*' he remarked, '*that any man of them will be slain before he shall first have slain a man of you; and if they slay of you a number that is equal to their number, what good will be left in life thereafter.*' Further, in order to avoid war, *Hakīm* of *Asad* (Khadījah's nephew) persuaded *Utbah ibn Rabīah* to pay blood money for the killing of his protectee at *Nakhlah* so that the very reason for fight was eliminated. In his turn, *Utbah* appealed to *Abū Jahal* and others against fighting and shedding blood of men of their own tribe. But *Abū Jahal* was adamant; he knew that the number was in his favour and it was a golden opportunity to get rid of *Muhammad* as well as *Islām*. Accusing *Utbah* of cowardice, he instigated Hadrami's brother, *Āmir*, who tore his clothes and hysterically shouted in favour of fight for revenge. This created a strong psychological impact and set everyone aflame, finally setting scene for a battle between two unequal forces. It was a situation in which it was not possible for either party to withdraw without loss of prestige.

When it became clear that fight could not be averted, the Prophet, showing remarkable qualities of generalship, organized his men in ranks and files and briefed them in strategy and military tactics. They were instructed that after receiving order, they should first bombard the enemies with arrows and stones, drawing sword in the last for close combat only. The fighters were positioned in such a manner that the enemies were to face sun in the eyes. *Musāb b. Umayr* was appointed flag bearer of *Muhajirūn* while *Hubāb* and *Sād b. Muādh* were to hold the standard of *Khazraj* and *Aws*, respectively. Further, on the advice of *Sād b. Muādh*, a hut-type shed or booth of palm branches overlooking the battlefield was constructed from which the Prophet was to watch as well as direct his men. Another purpose behind construction of the booth was that in case the Muslims suffered reverses, the Prophet could retreat to *Madinah* for protection of *Islām* and the remaining Muslims. When the Makkan army crossed the hill and occupied the sloping ground (early in the morning of fifteenth March) facing the Muslim force, *Aswad* of *Makkah* proceeded towards the well in order to forcibly drink water from it, but was killed by *Hamzah*. Thereupon, *Utbah* (who was to take revenge for the blood of his protectee at *Nakhlah*), his brother *Shaybah*, and Utbah's son *Walīd* moved forward and challenged the Muslims for single combats in the traditional Arab style. Initially, three of the helpers (*Awf, Muawwidh*, and *Rawāha*) went ahead in order to face the challenge, but *Utbah* refused to fight with them, saying that he had nothing to do with them and that he would fight only with Qurayshites of equal status. Accepting the demand, the Prophet then loudly ordered *Hamzah, Alī*, and *Ubaydah ibn al Hārith* to proceed and take on the trio. In accordance with their age, *Ubaydah* faced *Utbah, Hamzah* fought with *Shaybah*, and *Alī* encountered *Walīd*. In the single combats that ensued, while *Hamzah* and *Alī* were able to kill their opponents without much effort, *Ubaydah* fell down receiving a fatal injury from *Utbah*; thereupon, *Hamzah* and *Alī* jumped upon *Utbah* who was killed by Hamzah's strike.[1]

The *Quraysh* now advanced shooting a volley of arrows in which two of the Muslims were killed whereupon the Prophet

---

1 *The injured Ubaydah was lifted by Ali and taken to the Prophet. Ubaydah, though badly injured, was anxious to know whether he was dying a martyr; and when the Prophet confirmed it, his soul finally departed.*

loudly announced: '*By God Who holds my soul in his hand, those who fight with courage this day, only advancing and never retreating, and who are slain, will enter paradise directly.*' The announcement did electrify the believers, but the group-fighting which followed went hard against the Muslims in the beginning. In order to save the situation by invoking divine help, the Prophet in his booth prayed to God with earnest devotion: '*O Allāh! Fulfil this day thy promise made unto me.*' Laying his forehead on the ground, he implored: '*O Allāh! If this little band is wiped off this day, none shall ever worship thee till the end of this world.*' And so when the battle had started, the Prophet was praying instead of fighting, and *Abū Bakr* stood near the booth shedding tears, consoling him and requesting him to take control of the battle. Suddenly, while in a trance, the Prophet received indication of arrival of God's help and recited: '*Soon shall the host be routed, and they shall turn their backs.*' (Q 2/45). He informed *Abū Bakr*: '*Be of good cheer, Abū Bakr; the help of God hath come to thee. Here is Gabriel and in his hand is the rein of a horse which he is leading and he is armed for war*' (*Bukhārī*). He then picked up and hurled a handful of pebbles on the enemies and ordered his men to charge. This was a symbolic gesture indicating disaster for the enemy and seemed to have actually turned the tide of the battle in favour of the Muslims.[1]

The will and determination of the Muslim fighters getting redoubled due to personal encouragement by the Prophet, they fought with reckless valour cutting down the enemies. '*The spirit of discipline and contempt of death manifested at this first armed encounter of Islām proved characteristic of it in all its later*

---

1 *In several verses, the Qurān has referred to the help of God to the Prophet in the Battle of Badr:*
    8/9 and 8/50—(Sending of 1000 angels to fight on behalf of the Muslims).
    8/7—(Angels of God slaying the enemy and throwing arrows at them).
    8/26—(Allāh's help when the Muslims were badly outnumbered).
    8/44—(Allāh created an optical illusion under which number of Muslims appeared very large to the Quraysh).

and greater conquests.'[1] Ranged before them were a number of their close relatives, their own sons, fathers, or uncles, yet they never faltered. *Hamzah* and *Alī* were the heroes of *Badr* being responsible for most of the killings. Apart from them, however, some of the lesser known *Ansār* also displayed spectacular bravery while fighting and sacrificed their lives, becoming subject of extollation in the traditions. The two *Ansār* brothers—*Awf* and *Muawwidh*—had taken a vow to kill *Abū Jahal*, the 'Pharoah' of *Quraysh*. After ascertaining his identity, they along with *Muādh* (another brother of *Awf*) attacked and knocked him down with severe injuries. Thereupon, *Ikrimah*, son of *Abū Jahal*, struck *Muādh* and almost cut one of his arms which was left just hanging, but *Muādh* continued to fight with unabated ferocity, and when he felt the hanging limb creating inconvenience, tore it off. According to a source, after the battle was over, *Abū Jahal*, though mortally injured, was still lying with some life in him; at the instance of the Prophet who wanted to know his fate, *Abdullāh ibn Masūd* searched and traced him, cut off his head, and placed it at the Prophet's feet.[2] *Ummayyah b. Khalāf*, who was known for his cruelty against the believers and used to torture *Bilāl* (his former slave), was recognized by some Muslim fighters who wanted to spare his life and instead make him captive, but *Bilāl* noticed him and put him to death. The battle lasted for only a few hours and was over by noon. But it was so ferociously fought by the Muslims that *Quraysh* suffered heavy casualties and fled in panic. As estimated by the historians, about seventy of their men including *Abū Jahal, Ummayyah b. Khalāf, Abul Bakhtarī*, and many other of their notable leaders were killed. In addition, about seventy Makkans were taken prisoner, which included the chief of *Āmir* clan, *Suhayl* (cousin of the Prophet's wife *Sawdah*),

---

1 *Philip K. Hitti— 'History of the Arabs'.*

2 *When the fight was raging, the Prophet advised his men to spare the lives of those who were initially not willing to fight and who had treated him with respect during the Makkan days. One such individual was Abul Bakhtarī. Some of the Muslim fighters tried to make him captive, but he refused to be protected without his friend and courted death.*

and a few close relatives of the Prophet, his son-in-law *Abul Ās*, his uncle *Abbās*, and his cousins, *Aqīl* and *Nawfal*. The Muslims had only fourteen killed which included six *Muhajirūn* and eight *Ansār* (*Awf* and *Muawwidh* among them).[1] After getting routed, the *Quraysh* had fled the battlefield, but since they greatly outnumbered the Muslims, possibility of their regrouping and returning to fight could not be ruled out. The Muslims, therefore, kept a watch till the next morning when they left for Madinah.[2] Under such a situation, individual burial of the slain Makkans not being feasible, the Prophet ordered dead bodies to be thrown into a pit which was done.[3]

The crushing defeat of the prestigious army of *Quraysh*, who used to be considered the strongest military power in *al Hijāz*, at the hands of a hitherto insignificant and numerically much inferior force, was quite unexpected and left the peninsula nonplussed. The historians have attributed reasons like remarkable generalship of the Prophet, better drill and discipline of the Muslims, physical hardiness of the Madinan agriculturists as compared to the Makkan traders, and so on, for this shocking result of the battle. Conversely, it is said that the Makkans failed because they lacked motivation and there was no unity of command in their army as each clan fought independently. But *'the chief reason of the victory was doubtless the greater confidence of the Muslims as a result of their faith,'* says W. M.

---

1 *A complete list of the Makkans killed in the battle and those made captives has been given by Ibn Ishāq in his Sirah. The list of the Muslims who died as martyrs is also given by him.*

2 *Soon after the victory, the Prophet sent Abd Allāh ibn Rawāhah and Zayd to Upper (southern) and Lower Madinah, respectively, to take the good news of their grand success. Great was the happiness among Muslims in Madinah on receiving the tidings. But there was a sad note in the situation as the Prophet's daughter, Ruqāyyah (wife of Uthmān b. Affān), had died due to sickness.*

3 *The dead body of Ummayyah b. Khalāf was not thrown into the pit as it had started disintegrating. We also learn that when the dead body of Utbah was being thrown, his son Hudayfah (who was a Muslim) was full of grief. The Prophet consoled him but he replied that he was sad because his father died without faith.*

Watt. The *Qurān*, however, confirmed that the victory was a part of the divine plan and was made possible by God's help only who sent angels to fight in aid of the Muslims.[1] *'Allāh had helped you at Badr, when you were a contemptible little force,'* later said verse 3/123. And verse 8/17 clearly asserted: *'You killed them not when you did, but it was God who killed them; and you threw not when you did throw your arrows but it was God who threw them.'* There are interesting stories in the traditions which indicate that during the battle several Muslim as well as *Quraysh* fighters felt or visualized the presence of angels. Some had glimpses of angels riding on horses led by Gabriel who was wearing a yellow turban whereas others wore white ones.

In its physical dimensions, the Battle of *Badr* was a minor affair; but it was pregnant with great religious as well as political significance. Religiously, it was taken as a miraculous proof of the truth of *Islām* and tremendously boosted morale of the *Ummah*. The *Qurān* (8/41) described the occasion as the day of *Furqān* which meant a distinguisher between good and evil—a victory of good over evil. The grand victory added to the fame and popularity of *Islām* and in the following months there were large-scale conversions from the Bedouin tribes of *Hijāz*. It was due to its great religious importance that *Badr* became the most celebrated of the battles in the history of *Islām*. In later years, participation at *Badr* became a patent of honour in the *Ummah* because those who joined *Islām* subsequently might have been attracted by success, but the fighters of *Badr* had converted when it was weak and had put their lives at stake during the crisis. Politically, the victory saved the fledgling *Ummah* from extinction and laid the foundation of political power of *Islām*. By inflicting a crushing military defeat on the mightiest power of *Hijāz*, the *Ummah* overnight emerged as a new political power to be reckoned with. With the prestige of the *Ummah* greatly enhanced, the neighbouring tribes were now inclined to align themselves with it. A dark side of the consequences of *Badr*, however, was that it disturbed the balance of power in *Hijāz* and landed the *Ummah* in a situation in which a full-scale war

---

1   *Qurān verse 8/9.*

with the most powerful tribe in Arabia became inevitable. The *Quraysh* would now leave no stone unturned to maintain their control of the region, take revenge on the Muslims, and retrieve their lost prestige. But despite success at *Badr*, there was no reason to believe that the *Ummah* could finally subjugate *Quraysh*. The *Qurān* also warned the Muslims that the victory was only the beginning of their struggle against heavy odds[1] and suggested a long-drawn clash with *Makkah*. The months following *Badr* were, therefore, a time of great tension and anxiety for the Muslims, especially when they heard of *Quraysh*'s large-scale preparations for a bigger attack. Within *Madinah* also, the unexpected victory caused tremendous jealousy; instead of suppressing contumacy, it stimulated the simmering hatred and anger of the Jews and the hypocrites who now plotted against *Islām* more intensely and also started spreading sedition through composition of anti-Islamic poetry. Some even openly criticized the Prophet; exploiting the fear of a larger attack by *Quraysh* in revenge, *Abd Allāh ibn Ubayy* argued that the Prophet had landed *Madinah* in a dangerous situation.

For the *Quraysh* the effect of *Badr* was disastrous in more ways than one. It badly impaired their political status and prestige; their disgraceful military defeat had ruined their reputation. Leaders of different tribes and clans in the region, who were hitherto inclined towards *Makkah*, now started showing tendency to align with the *Ummah*, thus creating two opposing groups in *al Hījāz*. The defeat at *Badr* was also a defeat of the religion of their ancestors; their gods had failed to help them. More important, however, was its consequence on Makkan trade and commerce; the defeat had confirmed the *Ummah*'s domination of the western trade route and exclusion of the *Quraysh* therefrom. Overawed by the astounding military performance of the *Ummah*, *Juhaynah* and other Red Sea tribes now firmly aligned with *Madinah* making it almost impossible for the Qurayshite caravans to pass

---

1 *The Muslims were to be prepared to fight and vanquish the unbelievers in the ratio of 1:10, enjoined verse 8/65. A subsequent verse (8/66), however, lightened the burden to the ratio of 1:2.*

through the route unmolested. It was due to this reason that in the wake of *Badr* the *Quraysh* decided to concentrate on the eastern trade route passing through *Najd* to the Persian Gulf and Iraq. For this purpose they adopted measures to strengthen alliances with *Sulaym* and *Ghatafan* through whose territory the eastern trade route passed. Further, with most of the Makkan chiefs and important individuals killed, the defeat left leadership in the city permanently crippled. *Abū Sufyān* now assumed leadership of the *Quraysh* without any difficulty. In its immediate context, however, the most inflammatory impact of *Badr* on *Quraysh* was the great humiliation involved, a crisis of honour, which their tribal pride could by no means digest. The reaction of one and all was, therefore, one of extreme anger.[1] To avenge the great humiliation now became their one-point programme, and they would put in their entire strength to achieve it. So strong was the urge to punish the Muslims that it was decided to earmark the entire profit (250,000 dirhams according to one source) accrued from Abū Sufyān's trade caravan in order to raise the mightiest possible army, so large and powerful that it would not fail to crush the Muslims. And such was the hatred against the Muslims that *Abū Sufyān* vowed that he would not cohabit with his wife until he had settled scores with them. His fiery wife, *Hind*, on her part, took a vow that she would get *Hamzah* killed and eat his raw liver, for he had slain her father as well as uncle. The *Quraysh* women, on the advice of the Assembly, decided not to mourn their dead lest the Muslims should rejoice at the news; there

---

1 *An example of violent reaction of Quraysh when they heard the news of the disaster at Badr is the story of Abū Lahab as narrated by the biographers. After the defeat, the Makkans were returning to the city in small groups breaking the news. When Abū Lahab received the information from someone, Abbas's wife Umm al Fadl and his slave Abū Rāfi (who had secretly embraced Islām) were nearby. On hearing the news, Abū Rāfi could not conceal his joy and uttered words in praise of Islām. This made Abu Lahab angry who badly assaulted the slave whereupon Umm al Fadl became infuriated and hit Abū Lahab with a wooden post wounding his head. The wound soon developed septic and Abū Lahab died within a week.*

would be no lamentation unless revenge was taken. The men decided not to begin negotiation with the Muslims concerning ransom for their captives in order to get the amount reduced. As a preparatory measure for war, *Quraysh* sent messengers to Bedouin tribes in different directions, appealing to them to join hands in a common fight against the *Ummah* in order to save their religion as well as society from the onslaught of *Islām*.

A secondary consequence of *Badr* was evolution of some Islamic principles for handling of problems arising out of war, and they were based on guidance received from Quranic revelations or decisions of the Prophet. One of such issues was disposal of the prisoners of war.

Despite demand by a majority of Muslims including *Umar* that the seventy captives be put to death, the Prophet agreed with *Abū Bakr* and decided to spare their lives in the hope that their heart would change and they would accept *Islām*. This measure would imply an added humiliation to *Quraysh* and would also earn a handsome profit by way of ransom which was fixed at 4000 dirhams per captive. Only two of the captives, *Nadr* of *Abd ad Dār* (who had mounted a formidable intellectual attack on *Islām*) and *Uqbah* of *Abdū Shams* (who used to physically torment the Prophet), were put to death during the return journey from *Badr*, for they had been the worst enemies of *Islām*; there was no sign of repentance or change of heart in them, and if allowed to return, they would surely have resumed their evil activities. Soon, however, the Prophet and *Abū Bakr* were highly disturbed when a Quranic revelation (verses 8/67, 68, 69)[1] came

---

1   *Verse 8/67*   '*It is not for any Prophet to have captives until he has made slaughter in the land. You desire the lure of this world and Allāh desires (for you) the hereafter, and Allāh is Mighty and Wise.*'

  Verse 8/68   '*Had it not been for an ordinance of Allāh which had gone before, an awful doom had come upon you on account of what you took.*'

  Verse 8/69   '*Now enjoy what you have won as lawful and good and keep your duty to Allāh. Lo! Allāh is Forgiving, Merciful.*'

down which criticized the decision of sparing the lives of the captives out of a consideration of ransom, but finally approved of the Prophet's decision. *Suhayl* (cousin of the Prophet's wife *Sawdah*), who was chief of *Banū Āmir* and important for *Islām*, was one of the first to be released.[1] Another significant prisoner was the Prophet's uncle, *Abbās*, who was dear to him; in fact, the thought of his uncle suffering hardship of imprisonment did not allow the Prophet to sleep the first night and Abbas's ties were loosened on his advice. *Abbās* requested for his release without payment of ransom claiming that he was secretly a Muslim and that he had no money. The Prophet, however, turned down the request and instead asked him to pay the ransom for *Aqīl* and *Nawfal* also, and from his spiritual power, he even told *Abbās* that he had secretly left sufficient money with his wife, *Umm al Fadl*. This spiritual disclosure left *Abbās* flabbergasted and it is said that *Islām* actually entered the heart of *Abbās* at this very point of time. As for *Abū al Ās* (the pagan husband of the Prophet's daughter *Zaynab*), *Zaynab* sent the ransom amount from *Makkah* for his release; her offer included a necklace which she had received from her mother on her wedding day. When the Prophet saw and recognized the necklace, he became highly emotional; on his advice, the necklace as well as the ransom amount was returned and *Abū al Ās* was released. But before he left, the Prophet asked him to send back *Zaynab* to *Madinah* as Islamic law did not permit a Muslim woman to become wife of

---

1   *His clan was quick to send a person to be made hostage in his place which was accepted and he was allowed to return while payment of ransom was received subsequently.*

a pagan man. *Abū al Ās*, who loved his wife dearly, promised to do so with a heavy heart.[1]

Another principle which was adopted by the Prophet following *Badr* and which was to become an important element of the Islamic international law was humane treatment of the prisoners of war.

---

1 *After returning to Makkah, Abu al Ās dispatched Zaynab and her daughter Umāmah to Madinah along with his brother Kinānah. But Quraysh came to know about her departure and their man named Habbār forcibly brought her back. Zaynab, who was pregnant, had a miscarriage due to shock caused by Habbar's attack. Subsequently, when she recovered, she was secretly taken to Madinah by Kinānah.*

Much later, after the battle of Khandaq, a Quraysh caravan in which Abū al Ās was present was captured by Zayd. The seized merchandise as well as captives were brought to Madinah, but Abū al Ās managed to escape. He, however, clandestinely entered Madinah during night, went to the house of Zaynab and requested for help. Zaynab, who was still very fond of her husband, announced her protection for him which was respected by the Prophet. On her intercession, Abū al Ās's merchandise (which he was transporting for others) was refunded and he went back. Impressed by life in Madinah, he soon returned and entered Islām. When asked why he returned the property of the unbelievers, he replied that betraying the trust of others would have been a bad beginning for his Islām.

Subsequently, the policy was endorsed by the *Qurān* (8/70)[1] also which exhorted fair treatment of the prisoners if they showed good conduct or repentance. The great magnanimity shown towards the captives, who were sworn enemies, is a rare example in history and disproves the theory that *Islām* was violent. Each captive was placed jointly in the custody of two or more companions with Instruction to look after their comfort which was scrupulously done. So kind was the treatment offered to the prisoners that one of them is reported to have said, '*Blessings be on men of Madinah; they made us ride while they themselves walked; they gave us wheatened bread to eat, when there was little of it, contenting themselves with dates.*' Despite their poverty, the Muslims did not even refrain from writing off payment of ransom amount in deserving cases. While the more affluent of the prisoners were set free on payment of ransom, there were quite a few who were freed without payment on account of poverty; yet others were asked to teach ten children each which was treated as their ransom. No wonder, some of the prisoners were so impressed by the fair and just treatment meted out to them as also the high

---

1 *Verse 8:70— 'O Prophet! Say unto those captives who are in your hands: If Allāh knoweth any good in your hearts, He will give you better than that which hath been taken from you, and will forgive you. Lo! Allāh is Forgiving, Merciful.'*

moral standard of life in the *Ummah* that they could not resist converting to *Islām*.[1]

One more principle of the Islamic war law which developed in the wake of *Badr* was regarding disposal of booty. All Muslim soldiers had not played equal or similar role in the battle; some

---

1 *A story of one such conversion, as narrated by the historians, was of Walīd, son of the former chief of Makhzūm. His two brothers came to get him released on ransom and made payment after which he set off with them for Makkah. But on the way, he skipped, returned to Madinah, went straight to the Prophet, and professed Islām. In the meantime, his brothers reached following him and angrily asked as to why he spoiled the family's money in ransom when he was to convert. He replied that he did not want to create an impression that he embraced Islām for fear of paying ransom. He, however, went back to Makkah along with his brothers to bring his belongings but was imprisoned there.*

Another such story was of Jubayr bin Mutīm who came to ransom his cousin. He was highly impressed by life in Madinah and listened to recitation of surah Tūr from the mouth of the Prophet. According to Bukhāri, it was then that Islām took root in his heart, but he did not immediately enter Islām because he was to avenge the killing of his brother by Hamzah.

Ibn Sād narrates the interesting story regarding conversion of Umayr (who had estimated the strength of the Muslim army at Badr and had advised the Quraysh not to fight). His son was one of the captives but he had no money to pay ransom. With bitter feelings about the Prophet, he secretly struck a deal with Safwān, who was son of Ummayyah and was likely to become chief of Jumah. According to the deal, he was to go to Madinah and kill the Prophet and Safwān was to take care of his family in the event of anything happening to him. Accordingly, he smeared his sword with poison, went to Madinah, and appeared before the Prophet. Though asked again and again by the Prophet regarding purpose of his visit, he hid the real intention and reiterated that he was there to negotiate ransoming his son. But the Prophet had been made aware of his real intentions by Gabriel and he narrated his entire secret conversation with Safwan in Makkah regarding plot to assassinate him. Shocked by this spiritual revelation, Umayr at once pronounced the Shahādah. His captive son was released and he returned to Makkah where he made many converts though Safwan considered him a traitor. Later on, he returned to Madinah as a muhājir.

had actually fought and killed the enemies receiving injuries, while others had pursued the enemies and physically captured them; there were yet many who had physically collected armours, weapons, and other booty and were not willing to give up what their own hands had taken. Further, there were others who had stayed behind to guard the Prophet; they had performed less actively but demanded equal share of the booty. Thus, immediately after the battle, members of the Muslim army started quarrelling over sharing of the spoils; those who had played a more direct role in the fight demanded a correspondingly larger share. The problem was sorted out by revelation of verse 8/1 which clarified that booty captured was not to be considered a private property: *'They ask thee (Muhammad) of the spoils of war. Say that spoils of war belong to Allāh and the messenger, so keep your duty to Allāh, and adjust the matter of your difference, and obey Allāh and His Messenger, if ye are (true) believer.'* As decided by the Prophet in the light of this and other revelations, one-fifth of the booty was to be reserved for *Allāh*, that is, for welfare of the poor, and the remaining was to be equally distributed; even those who had not participated in the battle or had stayed behind on the instruction of the Prophet were also to get equal share. The direction of the Prophet was strictly obeyed and this became an established rule for distribution of booty in future.

The confidence gained from *Badr* emboldened the Prophet to deal with the contumacious Jews with a strong hand. Despite Islam's acceptance of Judaism as well as its prophets and Muhammad's conciliatory treatment of them, the Jews, right from the beginning, had stubbornly refused to accept *Islām* as an Abrahamic religion, and despite entering into a Covenant with the Prophet, they had been secretly conspiring against the *Ummah* in league with the hypocrites and the Makkan pagans. Their so-called rupture with *Islām* had already taken place before *Badr* and the Quranic revelations were now full of warnings against them.[1] Their reaction to Islam's victory at *Badr* was, therefore, openly hostile; highly jealous and apprehensive of the *Ummah*'s growing power, they decided to clip its wings before it was too late and intensified their conspiratorial activities. Soon after *Badr* when *Abū Sufyān* raided the suburbs of *Madinah*, he was entertained in a secret meeting by the chief of *Nadīr* who passed on secret information to him about the Muslims. Particularly dangerous was the reaction of their reputed poet and leader, *Kāb b. Ashraf* (his father was a *Tai* and mother a Nadirite), who used to identify himself with the Jewish tribe of *Nadīr*. His great wealth had made him a leading Jew. He hated *Islām* and paid monthly allowances to many Jewish scholars who were in agreement with his opinion. The news of routing of the Makkans at *Badr* left him totally shocked; he is said to have then remarked that if the great *Quraysh* nobles had actually been slain, then '*it was better to be inside the earth than outside of it*'. In order to offer his condolences, he immediately sneaked out to *Makkah* where he started composing highly inflammatory verses in the form of elegies or lamentations, stirring up *Quraysh* to redeem their honour and take their revenge. In Arabia, poetry was the most powerful medium of igniting passions and so *Kāb* was playing a highly dangerous role. He was also composing verses of insulting nature against Muslim women.[2] With their increasing treacherous activities and clandestine links with the *Quraysh*, it was now clear that the three major Jewish tribes of *Qaynuqā*, *Nadīr*, and *Qurayzah* were more a security risk to the

---

1 3/118— '*They will do all they can to ruin you, and they love to cause you trouble. Their hatred is clear from what their mouths utter and what their breasts conceal is greater.*'
/120— '*If good befall you, it is evil in their eyes, and if evil befall you they rejoice thereat.*'

2 *After a few months (in August, 624), when Kāb returned to Makkah, there was no let-up in his anti-Islamic activities. According to Ibn Hajār, he was even plotting to treacherously get the Prophet killed. Thereupon, Muhammad ibn Maslama put him to death playing a trick. Whether this was with or without the Prophet's permission or knowledge is disputable.*

Ummah than allies under the Constitution of *Madinah*. They had a sizeable population with a large army and were experienced soldiers. Whereas *Qaynuqā* lived within the city itself, the other two were outside towards south, at a distance of about half-a-day journey from the oasis. Such was the distrust against the Jews that the Prophet apprehended that in the event of an attack on the oasis from *Makkah*, they would join hands with the enemy. It was, therefore, necessary to neutralize them, he figured out. At this stage, a revelation also advised him to take action against those indulging in treachery: *'If thou fearest treachery from any folk, then throw back unto them the covenant. Verily God loveth not the treacherous'* (Q 8/58).

Though all the three major Jewish tribes were conspiring against the *Ummah*, it was the smallest of them, *Banī Qaynuqā*, which was the first to come on the Prophet's radar. Perhaps due to their physical proximity to the *Ummah*, more intelligence was forthcoming regarding their treacherous activities and their hostility had become especially palpable; moreover, as allies of *Ibn Ubayy*, the leader of the hypocrites, they were more to be distrusted. More importantly, however, the Prophet strongly suspected *Qaynuqā* of having leaked out information regarding his plan to waylay Abū Sufyan's caravan. Though smallest of the three Jewish tribes, *Banī Qaynuqā* was the most war-like and quite powerful, both physically and in terms of wealth. With an adult population of over 2,000, it had a fighting force of 700 odd which was more than double of what the Muslims had mustered at *Badr*. Moreover, as reputed metal workers, they had a store of arms and controlled the local market (*Sūq*) including the one of the goldsmiths. In their behavior towards the Prophet, they manifested a spirit of revolt and tended to break the pact with a view to revive old alliance with *Ibn Ubayy*. Not long after *Badr*, the Prophet is said to have addressed their leaders in their market; thinking that the miracle of *Badr* might change their heart, he advised them to refrain from inviting God's wrath by their undesirable activities lest God should punish them as he did the sinners at *Badr*. But their reply was highly defying: *'O Muhammad, you seem to think that we are your people. Do not deceive yourself because you encountered a people with no knowledge of war and got the better of them; for by God, if we fight you, you will find that we are real men.*[1] This was a virtual declaration of war.

After a few months, the simmering tension between *Quaynuqa* and the *Ummah* reached the breaking point when a minor fracas relating to insult of a Muslim (*Ansāri*) woman by a *Qaynuqā* goldsmith led to a crisis situation. The Muslim woman, who had gone to their market wearing a veil, was subjected to eve-teasing by some young Jews who wanted her to unveil. The goldsmith stealthily tied the lady's lower garment with the upper one so that when she rose up, the lower part of her body was partially uncovered. Violation of the Muslim lady's honour could not be tolerated by a Muslim boy who happened to be there; he attacked the guilty Jew and killed him, whereupon the Jews bounced on him and he was also left killed. The family of the deceased *Ansār* demanded vengeance against *Qaynuqā*. Blood had been shed on both sides and the affair could have been easily sorted out by the Prophet's arbitration as per provisions of the Constitution of *Madinah*. But though the Muslims wanted the Prophet to arbitrate the dispute, *Qaynuqā* refused to accept his arbitration and thus violated the pact. Perhaps overconfident of their fighting strength and relying on their former allies of *Khazraj* (*Ibn Ubayy* and *Ubādah ibn Samīt*), they shut themselves into their fortresses, thereby rising in revolt against the *Ummah*. But to their utter dismay, the Muslims besieged them within hours by an army which outnumbered theirs. The expected help from the *Khazraj* did not come. *Ubādah* was a committed Muslim and was not in favour of violating the Covenant, and as for *Ibn Ubayy*, he was too diplomatic to openly come out against the Prophet. The siege lasted for about two weeks after which *Qaynuqā* surrendered unconditionally as was being demanded by the Prophet.

As per the prevailing tribal conventions, *Qaynuqā* deserved the severest punishment, that is, massacre of the whole tribe for treason and violation of the Covenant. There was a Quranic

---

1   *Ibn Ishāq.*

revelation (8/57) also which suggested that the enemy after defeat should be so dealt with as to strike fear in the minds of their supporters. The Prophet, however, always used to treat his enemy with mercy and compassion; and in the instant case, *Ibn Ubbay* was strongly interceding for merciful treatment of his old allies. The Prophet, therefore, took recourse to great leniency and decided that the lives of *Qaynuqā* be spared, their possessions forfeited, and all of them exiled. The *Qaynuqā*, who were expecting a harsher treatment, took a sigh of relief on being spared of their lives and silently left *Madinah* taking refuge with some Jewish tribes in *Wādi al Qura* in the north and eventually settling down at *Adhirāt* on the borders of Syria. The properties left by them were distributed among the Muslims with one-fifth earmarked for the Islamic State. We learn from *Ibn al Jauzī* that the *Ummah* greatly enriched from the weapons (1,500 swords, 300 armour plates, 2,000 spears, and 500 shields) left by *Qaynuqā*. Though the siege of *Qaynuqā* has been called a *Ghazwa*, there was actually no fighting and no shedding of blood. The penalty of expulsion was a highly lenient one and no Jewish clan ever raised any voice against the action. The action was definitely not based on any racial and religious hatred but was purely political. The smaller Jewish clans in *Madinah* who remained committed to the covenant continued to exist side by side with the Muslims in peace. Some sources (*Ibn sād* and *Baihaqī*) mention that even after expulsion, men of *Qaynuqā* could be seen in *Madinah* in small numbers in later times. According to such sources, men of *Qaynuqā* had been permitted to visit the city in the future provided their stay did not exceed three days.

During the year following *Badr*, there were significant developments in the family life of the Prophet also. The first was the marriage of his youngest daughter *Fātimah* with *Ali*. *Fātimah* was now about 20 years old and both *Abū Bakr* and *Umar* wanted her hand. But the Prophet considered *Ali* as the most eligible match for her, though there had been no formal talk from either side in this regard. In fact, *Ali* was hesitant due to his extreme poverty; he had not inherited anything from his father as *Islām* did not permit inheritance from a disbeliever. But now he had acquired a humble dwelling, and so, when the Prophet made the offer, he agreed. Great was the joy of the Prophet and the family members on the occasion of the wedding ceremony which was organized in a very humble manner as per standards of today, but for that time in *Madinah*, the wedding feast was considered one of the finest. *Ibn Sād* describes how the couple was blessed by the Prophet in Ali's own house. Another development that followed was the marriage of *Uthmān* with the Prophet's third daughter, *Umm Kulthūm*, after her sister Ruqayyah's death, and next, the Prophet's own marriage to Umar's widowed daughter *Hafsah*. *Hafsah* was only 18 years old when her husband *Khunays* died after a few months of *Badr*.[1] She was not only beautiful and accomplished but, like her father, was literate which was a rare qualification those days even among men. The sudden death of Uthman's beautiful wife *Ruqayyah* had greatly saddened him. *Umar* offered him *Hafsah* in marriage, but *Uthmān* was not in a mental state to remarry so soon after the death of his beloved wife and so he refused. *Umar* took the refusal as a social slight and offered his daughter's hand to *Abū Bakr*, but *Abū Bakr* also did not respond positively which hurt him even more, and he complained to the Prophet. In order to save the situation, the Prophet himself offered to marry *Hafsah* and also offered the hand of his third daughter *Umm Kulthūm* to *Uthmān*. It was a consummate piece of diplomacy by which the Prophet cemented strong and lasting alliance with two of the most important leaders of the *Ummah*. The marriage of *Umm Kulthūm* and *Uthmān* took place first. Subsequently, after the four-month period of mourning (*Iddah*) had elapsed since the death of *Khunays*, Hafsah's marriage to the Prophet took place in the beginning of 625. The arrival of *Hafsah* was a welcome change for the Prophet's household as a lasting friendship developed between the two young wives, who were daughters of the two leading and friendly figures of the *Ummah*. Traditional stories always present *Āishah* and *Hafsah* as belonging to one group in the household with the elderly *Sawdah* falling

---

1   *It is sometimes suggested that Khunays died due to injuries received in the battle of Badr.*

in line, though the two young ladies used to make fun of her simplicity. According to a story, they once frightened her to the extreme by telling her that *Dajjāl* (a devilish false prophet whose arrival used to be feared by all) had arrived. *Hafsah* is sometimes presented as a charmless wife of the Prophet with a temper like that of her father; sometimes, she used to be plain-speaking to the extent of being impertinent, becoming an embarrassment to her father as well as the household. She, however, had a bright and ever-questioning mind; she had a deep understanding of the contents of the *Qurān* and used to even surprise the Prophet about certain points. She was a major intellectual figure in the early period of *Islām*, a prime source of Prophet's sayings and compiler of the first written copy of the *Qurān*. She was also renowned for the vigor with which she used to fast and devote herself to prayers. She survived the Prophet by thirty-five years.

CHAPTER IX

DEFEAT AND REVIVAL

All sources confirm that immediately following the humiliation of *Badr*, there was a very strong urge on the part of *Quraysh* to take revenge and large-scale preparations for a powerful attack on *Madinah* had started. Strangely enough, however, as compared to the degree of hate and anger, the reaction was rather slow. For about a year following *Badr*, no significant fighting took place. The only offensive taken by *Abū Sufyān* after a few weeks following *Badr* was to lead an expedition of 200 men to the outskirts of *Madinah*. Apart from having a secret meeting with *Sallām b. Mishkan*, chief of *Banī Nadīr*, this group was responsible only for destruction of some palm trees and killing of two of the *Ansār* in the outlying area of *Madinah* called *Urayd*. The party hastily fled when the Prophet proceeded to take it on; while retreating, the Makkans dropped their provisions, mainly flour bags (*Sawīq*) in order to lighten their baggage for getting away quickly. This expedition of *Abū Sufyān* was, perhaps, only of symbolic importance as it was simply meant to fulfill his vow of not practising ablution until he had raided *Madinah*; reconnaissance also might have been one of the aims of this raid.

Apart from this, there was hardly any engagement with the Makkans till the Battle of *Uhud* in March 625. In fact, the western trade route was now almost totally closed to the Makkan trade and *Quraysh* were now sending trade caravans through the eastern trade route passing through *Najd*. For this purpose, they strengthened their alliance with *Sulaym* and *Ghatafān* who lived in the plains of *Najd* to the east of *Makkah* and *Madinah*. These tribes were instigated by *Quraysh* to attack the borders of *Yathrib* and harass the allies of the *Ummah*. Therefore, during the months following *Badr*, the Prophet received warnings of three attempted raids on the eastern borders of the oasis by *Sulaym* and *Ghatafān*. But every time, these projected raids were forestalled by the Prophet who led expeditions against them and they fled back before he reached the point of gathering. In one of these expeditions directed against the *Ghatafān* tribes of *Thalabah* and *Muhārib*, some success was achieved. It was during the Prophet's raid deep inside the *Muhārib* territories that the famous incident of conversion of *Dūthur*, chief of *Muhārib*, took place. On one occasion, when the Prophet was alone and was overcome by sleep under a tree, he was surprised by *Dūthur* with a drawn sword; he threatened to kill the Prophet but was pushed by Gabriel and was overpowered by the Prophet with his sword in the Prophet's hand. The Prophet, however, spared his life and *Dūthur* embraced *Islām*. It was after a long gap following *Badr*, in December 624, that the Prophet received information about one *Quraysh* trade caravan under *Safwān ibn Umayyah* proceeding on the eastern trade route. This caravan was carrying a huge quantity of silver said to be worth about a hundred thousand *dirhams*. An expedition was sent under *Zayd* to waylay this caravan, which he did at *al Qarādah*, a watering place in *Najd*. The Makkans fled in terror, leaving the whole caravan behind, which was captured and taken to *Madinah* with a few captives.

The incident led to acceleration of Makkan preparations for attack on *Madinah*. A large army consisting of 3000 trained, experienced, and well-equipped fighters was urgently raised in which a group of tribes friendly to the Makkans known as *Ahabish* (which included *Thāqif, Kinānah, Abd Manāt*, etc) was also represented, but their presence was rather nominal with *Thāqif* contributing only 100 men and *Kinānah* and *Abd Manāt* one small contingent each. The army included a cavalry of 200 horses and as many camels as the number of men, excluding those meant for transportation of materials. Seven hundred of the fighters were mailed. The army was accompanied by a group of *Quraysh* women, wives of Makkan nobles, led by *Hind*, wife of *Abū Sufyān*. They were meant to beat drums, sing instigating songs, and thereby motivate and encourage the fighters. Also accompanying was an Ethiopian slave of *Jubayr b. Mutīm*; his name was *Wahshī* and he was an expert in throwing javelin, the national sport of Ethiopia. He had been exclusively tasked by his master as well as *Hind* to kill *Hamzah* by spear throw in order to take their promised revenge. In return, *Hind* had promised him freedom as well as handsome monetary rewards. After covering eleven days of journey, the Makkan army under the command of *Abū Sufyān* reached the outskirts of *Madinah* on 21 March 625 and camped at the foot of mount *Uhud* located about five miles to the north-west of the oasis, the place where the famous Battle of *Uhud* was to be fought.

About a week before the arrival of the Makkan army, the Prophet received confidential information regarding its departure through a messenger sent by his uncle *Abbās*, the messenger covering the distance on horseback hurriedly in three days only. The Prophet thus had some time to plan his reaction. It was at this time that he dreamed that he was wearing a strong and impregnable coat of mail and that he was mounted on the back of a ram. His sword was in his hand and he noticed a dent in it, and he also saw some kine which he knew to be his, and they were sacrificed before his eyes. The next morning, he informed the Companions about the same and interpreted it, saying, '*The impregnable coat of mail is Madinah and dent in my sword is a blow that will be struck against myself; the sacrificed kine are some of my Companions who will be slain; and as to the ram, that is the leader of their squadron whom we should slay if God will*' (*Wāqidī*).

In accordance with the interpretation of the dream, the Prophet initially was in favour of remaining within the city of *Madinah* to face the Makkan attack or siege rather than marching out and offering an open battle. In his opinion, he was supported by the elderly Companions as well as *Ibn Ubayy* who said that this was the conventional way *Madinah* always faced its enemy and attacks in the past had always failed. Strategically, this was a wiser proposition as *Madinah* had some impregnable forts for facilitating ambushes of attackers, and because of the topography, siege was likely to be unsuccessful. But convinced of God's help as had come at *Badr*, the younger lots were strongly in favour of an open fight as waiting in the walled city would be interpreted as a sign of cowardice and weakness. Their suggestion was supported by those who had been absent at *Badr* and thought of earning the missed-out religious merit this time. Those whose crops were being trampled and eaten away by Makkan camels and horses also favoured an open fight in order to punish the enemy. The Prophet, therefore, held consultations (*Shūrah*) on the issue. Those arguing for an open battle outside *Madinah* turned out to be in a majority. Though against his wishes, the Prophet agreed to the demand and started preparations for the battle. This decision was taken on 22 March 625 before Friday prayer.[1] The Prophet had already collected intelligence regarding the location and strength of the Makkan army through his informers.

All the Muslim fighters assembled for afternoon prayer after which the Prophet went to his house to dress for the battle while the men waited. On being pointed out by *Sād b. Muādh*, those who had not respected the opinion of the Prophet regarding staying within the walled city and facing the attack, started

---

1 *After Friday prayer Hanzalah appeared before the Prophet and informed that his marriage with Jamilah bint Ubayy was scheduled to be performed that evening. He was the son of Abū Āmir, the Abrahamist and a staunch enemy of Islām, who had deserted to Makkah and was playing a leading role in the attack. Hanzalah wanted to postpone his marriage in view of the impending battle, but the Prophet permitted him to go in for the wedding as scheduled and join him on the battle field the next morning.*

repenting. When the Prophet appeared dressed and armed for the battle wearing a coat of mail, many of them requested him to stay back at *Madinah*. But the Prophet refused and remarked, *'It is not for a Prophet, when he has put on his armour, to take it off until God has judged between him and his enemies'* (*Wāqidī*)[1]. He then mounted his horse *'Sakb'* and marched with his army which had a strength of 1,000 men only, poorly equipped in comparison to the enemy and without any cavalry contingent.

Despite the oath of the Covenant, the Jews had refused to join in on the pretext of *Sabbath*. The troops reached a place called *Shaykhayn*, halfway between *Madinah* and *Uhud*, before sunset and after prayer, halted there for the night. It was at this place that the Prophet detected the presence of eight boys who, despite their tender age, were extremely keen to take part in the battle. They included Zayd's son *Usāmah* and Umar's son *Abd Allāh*, both only 13 years old. Notwithstanding their enthusiasm, they were sent back, but only two of them were retained as they were found to be exceptionally capable, despite their young age. One of the two was *Rāfi*, an *Aws* boy, whom the Companions reported to be a better archer than many of the elders. *Samurah*, an orphan of one of the *Najd* tribes, claimed that he could defeat *Rāfi* in wrestling. The Prophet allowed him to fight and permitted him to join after he actually defeated *Rāfi*. This story as well as a host of traditional accounts indicates that in spite of numerical inferiority of less than one-third and no matching cavalry and equipment, morale of the Muslim troops was very high. Another development that took place at this location was desertion of *Ibn Ubayy* along with 300 hypocrites even without informing the Prophet. This exposed his real character; he plausibly took recourse to this action in order to obtain political mileage out of anticipated defeat of the *Ummah*. This, however, depleted strength of the Muslim army to a mere 700.

Unlike the Makkans, the Prophet had not allowed any woman to accompany the Muslim army at the time it set out.

1   *Q: 3/159.*

260

The enthusiasm of *Nusaybah*, a woman of *Khazraj* who had taken part in the second *Aqabah*, however, led her to take her independent decision. With the intention of tending the wounded and providing water to the thirsty, she rose early the next morning, took her sword and also a bow with arrows, and left for the battlefield joining the Prophet shortly after the battle had started. The mother of *Anas*, *Umm Sulaym*, also followed suit and reached the battlefield with a skin of water soon after *Nusaybah*. During later part of the fight, the two are said to have fought with the enemies like men in defense of the Prophet and earned the latter's praise. After the fight was over, hearing about the believers' death and injuries, a group of about a dozen other women including *Āishāh* and *Umm Ayman* also arrived at *Uhud* for nursing the wounded.

In the early hours of 23 March 625, the Muslim army under command of the Prophet marched from *Shaykhayn* and reached the southern slope of the hill of *Uhud* well before the time for morning prayer. They occupied the higher slope facing the Makkan army which was visible at a distance on the lower ground. To occupy the higher ground was the Prophet's strategic objective which he achieved. The Muslim army was now between the enemy and *Uhud* facing *Madinah* while the Makkans were facing Uhud. After the morning prayer, the Prophet started briefing his men about tactical measures. The highlight of the tactics adopted this time was placement of fifty chosen archers under *Abd Allāh Ibn Jubayr*, a man of *Aws*, on the strategically located hillock of *Ainan* in order to prevent Makkan cavalry from attacking the Muslim infantry from the rear. Their job was to pelt the horses with arrows. '*Horses do not come forward when there are arrows*,' the Prophet said. As quoted by *Wāqidī*, orders of the Prophet on the occasion were as follows: '*Keep their cavalry from us with your arrows. Let them not come upon us from our rear. Be the tide of the battle for us or against us, stay at this post. If you see us plundering the enemy, seek not to have a share in it; and if you see us being slain, come not to our aid.*' The instructions were thus clear enough; they were not to leave their post under any condition except by specific permission of the Prophet. As soon as the Prophet finished briefing, *Hanzalah*[1] reported his arrival. The Prophet next put on another coat of mail and took out, a sword saying, '*Who will take this sword, together with its right?*' Explaining the meaning of 'right', he clarified that the receiver of this sword should keep on striking the foe with it, until its blade was bent. Though *Umar* and *Zubayr* both wanted to take it, the Prophet gave it to *Abū Dujānah*, a man of *Khazraj*, a fearless warrior and a fighter of rare courage. *Abū Dujānah* was putting on a red turban that he never wore except in war, and those who knew him called it a turban of death. The wearing of the red turban meant that he would kill a large number of enemies indiscriminately. After having the honour of receiving the Prophet's sword, he was seen moving around with a flaunting gait which, though not permitted in *Islām*, was allowed by the Prophet on that occasion.

When the sun had risen, the *Quraysh* army was ready in its formation, with 100 horsemen on either wing, commanded in the right by *Khālid ibn al Walīd* and on the left by *Ikrimah ibn Abū Jahal*. At the centre was the infantry under the command of *Abū Sufyān* who was now giving order to advance. Ahead of him was *Talhah* of *Abd ad Dār* holding the banner of *Quraysh*. Two of *Talhah*'s brothers and four of his sons were in close attendance, ready to take the banner in the event of attack on the standard-bearer. *Talhah* had been suitably briefed by *Abū Sufyān* not to get the ignominy of *Badr* repeated. *Musāb* stood in front of the Prophet holding the banner of the Emigrants. Before the engagement started, *Abū Sufyān* stepped ahead and made an attempt to create disunity in the Muslim army. He addressed the men of *Aws* and *Khajraz* and advised them to go away as *Quraysh* had no reason for fight with them. But the *Ansār* responded

---

1 *Hanzalah had consummated his marriage with Jamīlah the previous night. In her sleep, Jamīlah had had a dream which, to her interpretation, indicated martyrdom for her husband. Early in the morning when Hanzalah hurriedly performed ablution and wanted to depart, she clung to him; moved by emotions, he again lay with her. Thereafter, he hastily left for Uhud without even caring for his physical purity, fearing that he might get delayed in reporting for Jihād.*

with angry abuses. Another man who stepped forward with a similar suggestion was *Hanzalah*'s father, *Abū Āmir*. In reply, he was greeted with a volley of stones. Initially with the advance of the Makkan army, the women contingent under *Hind* moved forward in front, beating drums, and singing an old war song:

> *'Advance and we embrace you,*
> *And soft carpets spread.*
> *But turn your backs, we leave you,*
> *Leave you and not love you.'*

Like that of *Badr*, the Battle of *Uhud*, too, was of a short duration, fought from early morning to noon, that is, nearly six to seven hours. Judging from its ups and downs, the battle may be divided into two parts. In the first part, which appears to have been of a shorter duration, the Muslims had the upper hand and had almost won the day, seemingly repeating the performance of *Badr*. But a tactical mistake by their warriors in general and archers in particular turned the tide in favour of the Makkans. During the second phase, the Makkan army was ascendant inflicting heavy casualties on the Muslims, in the end resulting in what may be called their defeat.

The battle began with single combats, the first being fought between *Talhah*, the standard-bearer of *Quraysh*, and *Alī*, who killed his rival in a single blow splitting his skull. Thereafter, the banner successively passed on to two of *Talhah*'s brothers and his four sons who were killed one after the other by *Hamzah*, *Sād of Zuhrah*, *Alī*, *Zubayr*, and *Āsim ibn Thābit*. *Abū Dujānah* fully repaid the trust confided in him by the Prophet and kept the promise of protecting the 'right' of the Prophet's sword. *'He killed every man he encountered as easily as if he had been a reaper and his sword a scythe'* (Martin Lings). *Zubayr*, who was cut up due to the Prophet's perceived favour to *Abū Dujānah*, now realized the wisdom behind his decision. The huge lady, *Hind*, who was urging her warriors on to fight, narrowly escaped being cut down by *Abū Dujānah*, who mistook her for a man, but instantaneously realizing his mistake, withdrew. *Hamzah*, prominent by his huge physique and the ostrich feather which he was wearing on his head, was fighting with great courage, striking down men to his left and right. *Wahshī*, the Ethiopian slave, tasked to kill him, was concerned with his target alone. He had been all through following and watching *Hamzah* from a distance; he got his chance when the latter lifted his sword to attack the last of the standard-bearers and was in a vulnerable position. He immediately positioned his javelin, took a perfect aim from a safe distance, and hurled it at him. It pierced the lower part of his body; he staggered towards *Wahshī* waving his sword but after a few steps collapsed and died. The most prominent hunter of the battle lay there as its principal hunt. Later on, *Wahshī* himself said that he had gone to *Uhud* to kill *Hamzah* only and he did it for the sake of his freedom. *Hanzalah*, romanticized in traditions as '*Ghasāil al Malāika*'—one having been washed in the sky by the angels after martyrdom—was fighting valiantly in the centre when he was suddenly thrust with a spear by one of the fighters felling him down. The attacker killed him outright with a second thrust.[1]

The death of *Hamzah* made little difference to the onslaught of the Muslim warriors and it appeared that the Makkans were going to be routed. The Prophet had taken up his position at a high place at the foot of the mountain along with his close Companions like *Abū Bakr*, *Umar*, and others in order to direct the fight. But gradually, after the battle started, the arena of fight shifted away from the Prophet's side as the Muslims advanced and the Makkans retreated. Now, due to increasing distance, he was not able to see the fight clearly but was having a sense of victory. Ali's white plume, Abū Dujanah's red turban, the yellow turban of *Zubayr*, and the green turban of *Hubāb* were

---

1 *Wāqidī mentions that the Prophet, who was watching and directing the fight from a vantage point up the slope of Uhud, at this point started seeing upwards with amazement and informed those near him that Hanzalah was being washed in the sky by the angels. Afterwards he said to Jamīlah, 'I saw the Angels washing Hanzalah between heaven and earth with water from the clouds in vessels of silver.' She then informed him how Hanzalah had not performed ablution for fear of being late.*

like flags of victory. They were fighting like incarnations of death from whom other Muslim fighters were receiving strength and inspiration. The Makkans continued to retreat until their camp lay open to the Muslims. So far, the strong Makkan cavalry, from which the Prophet had apprehended serious threat, had remained ineffective. One wing of it under *Ikrimah* was behind the Makkan Infantry and was virtually immobilized; the other wing under *Khālid* was repeatedly trying to attack the Muslims from the rear but was effectively being prevented from proceeding by the archers. But at this stage, Muslim warriors instead of pursuing the enemies and completely routing them, under the impression that they had already won the battle, started collecting booty. Watching them doing so, the archers, who had taken position on the hillock in order to check advance of Khalid's cavalry contingent, could not resist their temptation. In violation of the Prophet's running instruction and disobeying the order of their commander, *Abd Allāh ibn Jubayr*, forty of them ran down for booty leaving the rear pass unguarded. This act of indiscipline turned the tide of the battle and ultimately resulted in defeat of the Muslims. The shrewd general *Khālid* took full advantage of the gap created now. His horsemen galloped forward and, slaughtering the remaining ten archers, reached the rear of the Muslim army; he then charged the Muslim infantry from the rear. The horsemen under *Ikrimah* also soon followed his example. The Muslim soldiers turned around to face the cavalry charge but were again attacked by the Makkan infantry from behind as it had now regrouped and come forward. The Muslims were thus caught between 'two fires'. In the ensuing panic, a good number of Muslims were cut down. Many of them ran towards the mountain to take refuge. The Prophet watching this shouted and asked them to return but they paid no heed. The tide of the battle had suddenly changed to the disadvantage of the Muslims. Though a majority of the Muslim warriors kept on fighting, the initial impetus was now lost and weight of numbers became quite palpable. They had to recede step by step, and the scene of the battle moved towards *Uhud* in the direction of the Prophet.

After change of the tide, the battle continued for a few hours and events unfolded in quick succession. The traditional sources present a confusing picture of the sequence of events. However, the sequence given by Martin Lings in his *Muhammad—His Life Based on Earliest Sources* appears most plausible:

- The Prophet was taken into security cover by the Companions available with and around him including the two women. Highly concerned about safety of their spiritual guide, other Companions also started joining him. Among the first to join were two men of *Muzaynah*, *Wahb* and *Hārith*. After sometime, the group of the Prophet's guard had about twenty persons.

- Two times, a small band of Makkan horsemen attempted to approach the Prophet's vantage point to attack him; on both occasions, *Wahb* volunteered to take it on. Single-handedly, he shot arrows on the advancing enemies with such an amazing speed and dexterity that it appeared, as if, not a single man but a group of archers was shooting arrows; the attacking horsemen had to retreat. Then a third group of pedestrian fighters of *Makkah* suddenly emerged in close proximity. The same *Wahb*, responding to the call of the Prophet, drew his sword and single-handedly ran into their midst, fighting with such a contempt of death that whoever saw his fighting never forgot it. Afterwards his dead-body was found with twenty lance injuries apart from several others caused by swords. '*Of all deaths the one I would most fain have died was the Muzaynite's death*,' remarked *Umar* later on.

- After some time, another group of horsemen broke through the rear of the Muslims and rushed towards the Prophet. Five of the *Ansar* volunteered to check it and, drawing their swords, rushed to the enemies. They fought bravely but were killed except one. But the shortfall caused by their death was soon compensated as *Alī*, *Zubayr*, *Talhah*, and *Abū Dujānah*, who were in the midst of the battle, fought their way back and joined the Prophet's side.

- Minutes before their arrival, however, the Prophet's face was hit by a sharp stone thrown by an enemy; it injured his lips and broke one of his teeth with blood oozing from his mouth.[1] Thereupon, *Sād of Zuhrah* and *Hārith* of *Khazraj* along with a few others burst upon the enemies who had to recede away. Then the fatally Injured *Ansar*, who was in the previous group of five, was brought to the Prophet; he died with his head resting on the Prophet's body. It was on this occasion that the Prophet remarked, '*Know that paradise is beneath the shadow of the swords.*' (*Bukhāri*)

- Next, a single horseman named *Ibn Qamiah* of an outskirt clan of *Quraysh*, a ferocious warrior responsible for slaughtering many of the Muslims, suddenly appeared. Before anyone could prevent him, he speedily made his way to close proximity of the Prophet and struck such a powerful blow with his sword on his head which he thought no helmet could resist. *Talhah*, who was standing close by, plunged in between and rather deflected the blow, getting the fingers of one of his hands permanently cut off. Though his spontaneous reaction saved the situation, the sword still hit a side of the helmet driving two of its rings into the Prophet's cheek. Stunned by the shock of the sword-hit, the Prophet fell to the ground whereupon *Ibn Qamiah*, thinking that he was dead, withdrew quickly. But some other enemies closed in to attack further. *Shammās* of *Makhzum*, later described by the Prophet as a 'living shield', stood in his front and fought with unprecedented courage and determination until he was put to death; another man

---

1   *According to one version, the Prophet received stone injury in the beginning of the second part of the battle itself and was taken to a still higher point by the Companions for safety. While being taken, he even fell into a ditch secretly dug and camouflaged by the enemy; he was, however, rescued and taken to the higher slope by the Companions.*

at once took his place supported by *Nusaybah* who was now wielding a sword.

- After galloping back to the battle ground, *Ibn Qamiah* cried at the top of his voice that he had slain *Muhammad* which was heard by all including the Muslim warriors who were still fighting. In a flash, the information reached different corners of the battlefield which started resounding with glorifications of *Al Uzzah* and *Hubal*. Though a rumour, it completely demoralized the Muslims, most of whom stopped fighting and ran helter-skelter. But there were still some who did not lose heart and continued fighting, eager to sacrifice their lives. One such person was *Anas*, son of *Nadr*. While fighting, he bumped into two of his fellows who had stopped fighting thinking that life had no meaning when the Prophet was no more. '*Why sit here?*' he asked the two who replied that the Prophet had been killed. *Anas* said, '*Then what will you do with life after him. Rise and die, even as he died.*' Saying this, he plunged into the midst of the enemies, fought with unbelievable spirit, and achieved martyrdom. *Sād ibn Muādh*, who was also fighting in the centre, saw him fighting and later told the Prophet, '*I could not fight as he fought.*' Afterwards, his dead body was found lying with eighty wounds, so disfigured that no one could recognize him except his sister who did it by seeing his fingers.

- Contrary to what is normally held, rumour regarding killing of the Prophet proved a blessing in disguise. The enemy now felt that since the leader of *Islām*, who was the root cause of strife and the main source of danger to the old order, was no more, there was no reason to continue with the battle. They also felt that they had amply avenged those killed at *Badr*. Therefore, feeling that the battle was now over, most of them relaxed fighting. Those who had surrounded the small group with the Prophet, also now started withdrawing slowly.

They were complacent that they had achieved their main objective.

- As the enemies withdrew, the Prophet, who had regained consciousness, was shifted by the Companions to a glen further up the mountain at a safer point from which they could watch the enemies without being seen. There the Prophet, who was in severe pain, was given first aid. *Abū Ubaydah* drew the metal rings out of his cheek by catching them by his teeth and in the process pulled out two of his own teeth resulting in bleeding from his mouth. The Prophet then remarked, '*Whose blood has touched my blood, him the fire cannot reach*' (*Wāqidī*). But the Prophet's own wound in the cheek was badly bleeding and *Mālik* of *Khazraj* put his mouth to it sucking out the blood.

- When the Prophet along with his group was climbing up the glen, he came across a group of Muslims who had fled and taken shelter on the hill. *Kāb ibn Mālik* in front of them recognized him and shouted with extreme joy that the Apostle of God was alive. The Prophet immediately gestured to him to be silent but the great news spread like fire from mouth to mouth and great was the rejoicing; the defeat had suddenly turned into victory.

- Kāb's loud exclamation was heard by a *Quraysh* horseman named *Ubayy* who was brother of *Ummayyah*. He had sworn to kill the Prophet by hitting him from his horseback. At that moment, after hearing the rumour about the Prophet's slaughter, he was searching his dead body for confirmation at the place which had been vacated by the Prophet's group. When he heard the voice of *Kāb*, he rushed towards it until he reached the Prophet's location. The Companions tried to take him on but were prevented by the Prophet who himself unexpectedly jumped on him with amazing determination; before *Ubayy* could strike his sword on him, he thrust his spear in his neck. Though fatally injured, *Ubayy* managed to gallop back to the Makkan camp and cried that *Muhammad* was alive and had injured him. The Makkans, however, only half-believed his claim as there was every chance of him mistaking another man for the Prophet.

- By the time the Prophet and his party settled down at another safe place, it was noon. They performed *Zuhar* prayer and took some rest.

- The Makkans now after stopping fighting were taking stock of their men killed or wounded; they were also examining the battlefield for assessing losses they had inflicted on the enemy. There was expression of satisfaction on their faces. The battle had left seventy-two Muslims killed which included only three Emigrants (*Hamzah* of *Hāshim*, *Musāb* of *Abd ad Dār*, and *Abd Allāh ibn Jahsh*), the rest being *Ansar*. Only twenty-seven of the Makkans were found dead. While they were searching the dead body of the Prophet, *Wahshī* extracted Hamzah's lever and presented to *Hind* who chewed it in fulfillment of her vow. Thereafter, she went to the dead body of *Hamzah* and cut off his nose, ears, and other parts to vent her pent-up anger and hatred. At her instance, other *Quraysh* ladies, joined by a few men, mutilated almost all the dead bodies of the Muslims, chopping off different parts from them to be worn as 'ornaments of vengeance'. The dead body of *Hanzalah*, however, was not mutilated as his father *Abū Āmir* did not allow it. The uncivilized treatment of the dead bodies by *Quraysh* annoyed their Bedouin allies and lowered their prestige in their mind.

- The *Quraysh* now presumed that the Prophet was alive and was taking shelter somewhere on the hilltop. But there was no point in attacking the mountain and there was also apprehension of the Muslims regrouping and attacking back. They, therefore, after burying their dead, packed up and prepared to depart. But before setting off, *Abū Sufyān* rode to the hill above the gorge and shouted, addressing the Prophet: '*Victory in war goes in turns, our victory today is in exchange for yours at Badr. Now you must vindicate your religion.*' The Prophet asked *Umar* to shout back in reply, which he did: '*Your side and our side are not equal. Our dead are in Paradise; yours are in Hell.*' Then after ascertaining from *Umar* that the Prophet was alive, *Abū Sufyān* loudly announced that he would again fight the Prophet the following year at *Badr*, a challenge heard, accepted, and responded to by the Prophet through a Companion who shouted back to *Abū Sufyān*: '*That is a binding tryst between us*' (*Ibn Ishāq*). *Abū Sufyān* then marched towards the south along with his army.

• The departure of the Makkan army towards south alarmed the Prophet; it might proceed to *Madinah* for an attack, he apprehended. He, therefore, at once sent down *Sād of Zuhra* to find out the things. If they were riding their camels, they were proceeding to *Makkah*, but if they were riding their horses, then they were heading to *Madinah,* he said. If the latter was to be the case, the Muslims were to rush and overtake them to fight and defend their city, the Prophet instructed. Much to his relief, however, *Sād* reported back soon and gave the good news that the Makkan horsemen were riding camels and leading the horses beside them which indicated that they were proceeding to *Makkah*.

After departure of the Makkan army, the Prophet along with his Companions came down to the battlefield in order to find out his dead and injured. He was extremely angry to see the mutilated dead body of *Hamzah* and said that in future, if he gained victory over *Quraysh*, he would also get their dead bodies mutilated even on a larger scale. But then verse 16/126 was revealed which said, '*If you inflict punishment, then inflict only so much as you have suffered; but if you endure patiently, that is better for the patient.*' He, therefore, dropped his vindictive idea. As many as 72 bodies of Muslims, dead or mortally wounded, lying on the ground, presented a highly tragic scene and everyone was full of sorrow. It was then that a group of women from *Madinah* which included *Āishah*, *Umm Ayman*, and *Safiyyah*, after hearing the news of the Makkans departure, arrived to tend the wounded and to get first-hand information about the fate of their dear ones. The dead body of *Hanzalah*, however, presented a unique scene of gratification. There was absolutely no sign of mutilation or tampering with his dead body; his hair was still wet with water even though it was a hot-dry noon. *'None passed him by who did not give thanks, for in his beauty and his peace he was a sign from Heaven, to inform the bereaved of the present state of their martyred kinsmen'* (Martin Lings). The Companions wanted to carry the corpses to *Madinah*, but the Prophet ordered that graves should be dug in the battlefield itself and they be buried where they lay, declaring: *'These men have died fighting in God's cause, and on the day of resurrection God will raise them up.'* Then all the dead were buried, two or three in each grave, after performance of separate prayers for each of them.[1]

After completion of burial, the Prophet left with his men and women, the latter fourteen in all, and reached *Madinah* before the sunset. During the night, he was overcome by an apprehension that the Makkans might return and invade the city. Therefore, immediately after the morning prayer, he asked *Bilāl* to announce that his men should be ready for departure as the enemy were necessarily to be pursued. But he also made it clear that only those should join who had taken part in the Battle of *Uhud* and none

---

1   *When the dead bodies were being searched, the men of Aws were surprised to find one of their men, namely Usayrim, lying in a mortally wounded condition. The reason of surprise was that until the previous day he had not become a Muslim despite their repeated insistence. They asked him how he was in the battlefield without accepting Islām. Though badly injured, he weakly said that after the Prophet's departure from Madinah, he suddenly received God's light, professed Islām, and joined them in the battle early in the morning. After informing this he died, whereupon the Prophet said that he was a man of Paradise. Later on he was known as the Muslim who entered Paradise without ever saying even a single Namāz.*

else. Almost all the men had received major or minor injuries in the battle the previous day and they were getting their wounds attended to. But despite physical incapacitation, they all promptly responded to the Apostle's call and marched with him. They made their first halt about eight miles from *Madinah* whereas the enemies were camping at *Rawhā* not far from that point. It was a critical situation as the Makkan army was still in the area and a second attack, now on the city itself, was not a remote possibility. We know from sources that many of *Quraysh* had had such intentions. In order to save the situation, the Prophet made use of two intelligent tricks. After sunset he ordered that each of his men should lit a fire and spread out. More than 500 beacons thus prepared and lighted, gave the impression of a large army camping there which disturbed *Abū Sufyān*. The Prophet then worked another ruse, and through an informer sent false information to the enemy that the whole city of *Madinah* was in their pursuit including the *Ummah*'s confederates and that the Muslims were hell-bent on revenge. The strategy worked well and left the enemy utterly dismayed leading them to proceed speedily towards *Makkah*. The Prophet and his Companions stayed there for three days, lighting beacons every night, and then went back.

The sudden withdrawal of *Quraysh* from the battlefield in the midst of success amounted to a strategic mistake. For bringing their half-victory to its logical conclusion, they should have followed it up by invading *Madinah* in order to exterminate *Islām* and its followers. Scholars have debated factors responsible for this unwise withdrawal. What motivated them to suddenly order pack-up is found summed up in a statement of *Amr ibn al Ās* as quoted by *Wāqidī*: '*We had heard that Ibn Ubayy had returned to Madinah with a third of the army, and that some men of Aws and Khazraj had stayed in the city. Nor could we be certain that those who had retreated would not return to the attack; and many of us were wounded, and nearly all our horses had been pierced by arrows, so we went on our way.*' However, the real demotivating factor was, perhaps, lack of confidence; or else God blunted their wisdom. Whatever might have been the reason, the decision did prove a blessing in disguise to the Muslims who were in a bad shape and feared that the enemy might turn back to *Madinah*. The Prophet definitely outsmarted them by his strategic ruse.

In its consequences, the Battle of *Uhud* was perhaps neither so decisive nor so significant as it is sometimes made out to have been. It was neither a clear-cut victory of *Quraysh* nor a categorical defeat of the Muslims. At a closer look, *Quraysh* had failed in their main objective; they could neither kill the Prophet nor uproot the Muslims. Of the seventy-two Muslims killed, only three were *Muhajirūn*, the remaining being *Ansar* who had not been their target. Their abrupt withdrawal even when they had an upper hand was an indication of weakness; nor was their military performance altogether impressive. Their reverse in the first phase of the battle had confirmed superiority of the Muslim infantry. The level of performance that they achieved despite marked numerical superiority was not commensurate with their reputation as a military power. Moreover, their success at *Uhud* did not at all help the Makkan economic interest which, to modern Western scholars, was their main objective. The western trade route still remained under domination of the Muslims. *Uhud*, therefore, just provided to *Quraysh* only a momentary psychological satisfaction of having avenged the defeat at *Badr*. It did contain seeds of a subsequent larger attack from *Makkah*.

For the Muslims, though *Uhud* was merely a setback rather than a full-fledged defeat, it did badly shake their confidence. There was a feeling that God's help did not come as it had come at *Badr*. Their disenchantment, however, was soon removed by revelation of verse 3/152 which clarified that their failure was due to their own indiscipline, disobedience, and greed rather than God's disfavour.[1] The battle taught them lessons in managing failures, and as mentioned in revelations, amounted to God's trial of their perseverance and patience. It did also expose the

---

1   *Soon after the defeat, many verses of Surah 3—Āl Imrān—were revealed reflecting on different aspects of the reverse of Uhud. Verses 120 to 188 deal with such matters. They, inter alia, referred to expiation and forgiveness of those who had disobeyed orders on the battlefield as well as hypocrisy of Ibn Ubayy and his men.*

untrustworthiness of Jews and hypocrites, the latter now given the name of *Munafiqūn* in the *Qurān*.

The defeat not only lowered the *Ummah*'s prestige both within and without *Madinah* but also made its position quite weak and vulnerable. Within the city, both hypocrites and Jews were jubilant at the humiliating defeat of the Muslims and now dared to speak out openly against the Prophet. Much to the chagrin of his son, *Abd Allāh*, who was a devout Muslim, *Ibn Ubayy* started loudly criticizing the Prophet for the blunder of going out for an open fight. So many Muslims would not have been killed, had they remained within the city as per his advice, he said. The Jews were equally vehement in their criticism. *Muhammad* was not a prophet but only an ambitious person keen to establish his kingship, because no prophet could have met such a reverse, receiving severe wounds on his own and his Companions' bodies and losing lives of many, they openly talked. In fact, perceiving the Prophet as weakened now, both Jews and hypocrites saw the situation suitable for creating division within the *Ummah* by highlighting each and every sensitive issue; intensification of scheming and plotting for destroying the *Ummah* now became their prime aim. *Umar* came to know about their mischievous remarks and instigations and asked for the Prophet's permission to kill them all. But the Prophet restrained him, calmed him down, and said that such a humiliating situation would not be faced by the Muslims again. The anger of the Muslims, however, found expression when at the next Friday prayer, *Ibn Ubayy* was badly misbehaved by the Muslims who did not allow him to speak and forced him to leave the mosque.

Outside *Madinah* also, seeing the *Ummah*'s position grown fragile, tribes which had been favourably disposed towards *Islām*, now inclined towards *Quraysh*. The pro-*Quraysh* tribes started planning expeditions against the *Ummah* and even dared to ambush and attack small groups of Muslims on move. The situation, thus, had become difficult for the *Ummah*. With the western trade route still under domination of the Muslims and the *Ummah* still powerful enough to continue threatening the old order, there was no let up in the animosity of *Quraysh*. The

Prophet knew that they would not leave him in peace even after the defeat of *Uhud*; the warning of *Abū Sufyān* to face the *Ummah* again after a year at *Badr* let alone, he had strong reasons to apprehend a final and much bigger attack from them which, if not stymied, might destroy *Islām*. On the basis of available trends, he figured out that the final confrontation might not be a straight fight with *Quraysh* alone but a much bigger combination of Arabian tribes under the leadership of *Quraysh*; and this might be extremely difficult for the *Ummah* to take on. After a careful analysis of the situation, the Prophet, therefore, planned a two-fold strategy to deal with the crisis situation. Within the city, it was necessary to deal firmly with hostile elements and get rid of them as and when opportunity came; it was also imperative to ensure cohesion between disparate elements within the *Ummah*, between *Muhajirūn* and *Ansār* on the one hand and *Aws* and *Khazraj* on the other, their relationship being still fragile with *Ibn Ubayy* exploiting every issue to create fissures therein. As regards external policy, the main aim of the Prophet became preventing the Bedouin tribes, especially those located to east and north-east of *Madinah*, from joining the Makkan alliance and obtaining their friendship and support for himself. He knew that for that purpose, a show of force would be necessary; but apart from stick, carrot also would have to be used for winning them over. The two years following *Uhud*, therefore, saw a good number of Muslim expeditions sent against hostile tribes in order to prevent aggressions from them as also to punish them for misdeeds.

The first expedition was sent after more than two months of *Uhud* (June 625) against *Banī Asad* who were close allies of *Quraysh* and, instigated by the latter, were planning a raid on *Madinah*. Another aim behind the move was to demonstrate that the power of *Islām* still remained undiminished. The raiding party consisting of 150 strong and well mounted fighters under command of the Prophet's cousin *Abū Salamah* took the target by surprise. Without much bloodshed, the enemy withdrew and the Muslims captured a large number of camels. About the same time, information was received that the hostile *Hudhayl* tribe from the south was planning to raid the oasis. The Prophet tasked

Abd Allāh ibn Unays of *Khazraj* to eliminate the chief of *Lihyanite* branch of *Hudhayl* because the latter was the most dangerous and hateful enemy of *Islām* and was the root cause of the tribe's anti-Islamic activities. *Abd Allāh* killed the man and escaped. The same month (June 625), however, the *Ummah* received a setback from *Hudhayl*. In retaliation to the death of one of their chiefs, their men ambushed six Muslims at *Ar Rajī*, a watering place in the vicinity of *Makkah*, when they were proceeding to impart religious instruction to some smaller tribes. While four of the Muslims were killed in the encounter,[1] the remaining two, *Khubayb* of *Aws* and *Zayd* of *Khazraj*, were captured and sold to *Quraysh* so that they could avenge killing of their men at *Badr*. *Khubayb* was bought by an ally of *Banī Nawfal* and *Zayd* by *Safwān*. After the sacred month passed, they were taken out for torture and execution. *Wāqidī* narrates a story how the two Muslims courted martyrdom refusing to renounce *Islām* despite brutal torture. Before death, both of them prayed two cycles of *Namāz*. *Khubayb*, in the midst of torture, wished to send peace to the Apostle but had no means. Traditions record that the Prophet at that moment, sitting in Madinah, received his greeting of peace through Gabriel.

It was for the purpose of winning alliance of the powerful tribe of *Āmir* and also as a measure for social rehabilitation of a widow, that the Prophet, soon after *Uhud* (April 625), married *Zaynab bint Khuzaymah*. Daughter of one of the chiefs of *Āmir* tribe, she was the wife of *Ubaydah ibn al Hārith*, a martyr of Badr. She was known for her extremely generous nature winning the epithet *Umm ul Miskīn* (mother of the poor). She, however, died eight months after marriage with the Prophet. Soon after marriage with *Zaynab bint Khuzaymah*, the Prophet invited *Abū*

1　*Those killed included Āsim of Aws who had killed two of the standard-bearers of Quraysh at Uhud. In the battlefield itself, their mother had sworn to drink wine from his skull. The killers, therefore, wanted to sell his head to the lady. But as mentioned in the tradition, Āsim's dead body was miraculously protected by the bees and after sometime swept away by a flood; and the lady could never fulfill her vow.*

Barā, the chief of her tribe to embrace *Islām* along with his men. Giving encouraging response, he requested the Prophet to send a group of Muslims to his tribe for instruction in the new faith. *Banī Āmir* were a branch of *Hawāzin*, their territory located to the south of the hostile *Ghatafān* tribes. The Prophet, therefore, had some reservations, but *Abū Barā* promised protection. He, therefore, selected forty of his knowledgeable Companions and dispatched them for the purpose under command of *Mundhir ibn Amr*, a man of *Khazraj*. Unfortunately, however, when the group of Muslims was camping at *Bir Maunah* en route, a party of *Sulaym*, under instigation by a nephew of *Abū Barā* (he aspired to become chief of *Āmir* in place of *Abū Barā*), raided it, massacring the whole group except two, that is, *Hārith* and *Amr*, who had gone away to pasture the camels.[1] When the duo came back, they were also caught; *Hārith* was done to death after he killed a few of the attackers, but *Amr* was allowed to proceed to *Madinah* in order to inform the Prophet about the fate of the Muslims. Actually, the men of *Sulaym* misinformed *Amr* that the massacre had been instigated by *Banī Āmir*, and through him, they wanted to send wrong information to the Prophet in order to create misunderstanding between the *Ummah* and *Banī Āmir*. *Amr*, while on way back, happened to see two men of *Banī Āmir* sleeping somewhere; in order to take revenge, he killed both of them. This created an embarrassing situation for the Prophet who

---

1   *The group of the Muslims killed included Āmir ibn Fuhayrah, Abū Bakr's slave, who had accompanied the Prophet in his journey of Hijrah. According to a tradition recorded by Wāqidī, when Jabbār, a man of Sulaym, thrust his spear between his shoulders, he cried: 'I have triumphed, by God.' And then, within a flash, his body was lifted into the air by some unseen power until it went out of sight. The men of Sulaym were amazed to see the event and asked Amr, the survivor in the group, as to what was the meaning of the words spoken by Fuhayrah. When it was explained to Jabbār that the word 'triumph' spoken by Fuhayrah meant Paradise, he entered Islām then and there. After the men of Sulaym went back to their tribe, the story was repeated again and again and it led to conversion of many.*

was already highly perturbed by the cold-blooded massacre of his Companions which had damaged the prestige of the *Ummah*.

Not unconnected with the massacre of *Bir Maunah* was the expulsion of the hostile Jewish tribe of *Banī Nadīr* from the oasis. Like other Jewish tribes, the Nadirites abhorred *Islām*. Their animosity heightened due to strong resentment for killing of their poet, *Kāb*, by the Muslims and expulsion of their *Qaynuqah* brothers, they had not participated in the battle of *Uhud* and, after the defeat of the Muslims, had been openly criticizing the Prophet despite being a party to the Covenant. Given reports regarding their collusion with enemies of *Islām* and their scheming activities, they had become an eye-sore to the *Ummah*, a veritable security risk. But still, the Prophet decided to invoke their co-operation in paying the heavy blood money to *Banī Āmir* for the mistaken killing of two of their men. This was because *Banī Āmir* were allies of *Nadīr*. The Prophet, therefore, went to them along with a handful of Companions and requested for their help. The *Nadīr* chief, *Huyay*, responded favourably and invited them to a meal. But clandestinely, he plotted to kill the Prophet by dropping a millstone from the top of a building at the foot of which the Prophet was sitting. The Prophet, however, received warning about the plot divinely through Gabriel whereupon he left abruptly without a word, leaving the Companions there. After returning to *Madinah*, he immediately sent message to the *Nadīr* chief through *Muhammad ibn Maslamah* informing that since they had plotted to kill the Prophet and thereby broken the Covenant, they should permanently leave *Madinah* within ten days, failing which they would be put to death. Contemplating to take advantage of the situation, the leader of hypocrites, *Ibn Ubayy,* instigated the Nadirites to disobey the Prophet's order and promised support. Expecting help also from their sister Jewish tribe of *Banī Qurayzah* as well as *Ghatafan*, who were their allies, *Banī Nadīr* decided to offer resistance. Since this amounted to a virtual declaration of war, the Prophet raised an army and besieged their fortresses. Following exchange of arrows and stones from both sides, there was a continual stream of fresh groups of Muslims joining their army; this swelled up their strength to make it large enough to effectively surround the Nadirites from all sides.

The incident took place in August 625. The siege continued for more than ten days, about fifteen days according to some scholars. The desperately needed help to *Banī Nadīr* did not come from any quarter as neither *Banī Qurayzah* nor *Ibn Ubayy* dared come out openly against the *Ummah*, and *Banī Ghatafān* maintained an enigmatic silence. The situation took a serious turn when ultimately, some of the finest date trees, which were in the sight of the walls, were cut down on orders of the Prophet. Though resorted to with divine permission, this unprecedented step frightened the Nadirites to capitulation. The Prophet ordered them to leave immediately but allowed them to carry only those belongings which their camels could transport, except arms and armours. The act of *Banī Nadīr* amounted to treason of the highest order, and according to conventional tribal norms, they deserved to be put to death; but the Prophet, as usual, adopted leniency and satisfied himself by expulsion only. The unexpected mercy shown by him is one of the many points that disprove the theory of his Western critics that he advocated violence. The Nadirites were not even prevented from receiving back the money which the Muslims had borrowed from them. They, however, went so far as to pull off doors and windows of their houses and left with a caravan of 600 camels with great pomp and show, their women decked up in finest garments and ornaments and slave girls singing songs and playing musical instruments. *'Never had a caravan of such magnificence been seen within living memory. As they made their way through the crowded market of Medina, the camels went into single file, and each one as it passed was an object of wonder, both for the richness of its trappings and wealth of its load.'*[1] Their caravan proceeded to the north; most of them settled at *Khaybar* while some proceeded further towards the border of Syria. In accordance with a Quranic revelation (Q 59/8), the properties left by them (which also included 50 coats of mail, 50 helmets and 340 swords) were distributed among the poor

---

1   *Martin Lings.*

Muhajirūn, thus making them economically independent and relieving the *Ansār* of their burden. The expulsion of *Banī Nadīr* not only removed a source of hazard but overawed the Bedouins, considerably reinforcing prestige of the *Ummah*. On the occasion of expulsion, a whole *Surah* of *al Hashr* (59) was revealed in which the double character of the Jews was exposed.

The image of the *Ummah* further improved by the moral victory achieved at *Badr* in April 626. As per challenge of *Abū Sufyān* at *Uhud* which had been accepted by the Prophet, their armies were to confront each other at *Badr* a year after *Uhud*. As the time of appointment came closer, both of them became conscious of saving their honour by keeping their promise. But it was a year of severe drought and *Abū Sufyān* was not in a position to go in for the expedition as there would be no fodder for the camels and horses. In order to shift the blame to the Prophet, he decided to play a trick. *Nuaym* of *Banī Ashja* (a clan of *Ghatafān*), who was apparently a neutral person, was sent to *Madinah* to discourage the Muslims from proceeding to *Badr*. *Nuaym* went there, spoke to all sections of the oasis, and presented an alarming picture of the forces which *Abū Sufyān* was preparing for the second *Badr*. The Muslims panicked and thought that it would be disastrous to undertake the proposed battle. The Prophet thought that his men might not fully support him. But strongly supported by *Abū Bakr* and *Umar*, he decided to go ahead, declaring, '*I will go forth even if I go alone.*'[1] As originally planned, the Prophet left with 1500 men, many of whom went prepared to trade at the fair of *Badr*. Put in a dilemma, *Abū Sufyān* again tried to hoodwink the Prophet; he set out with 2000 men with the intention of only giving a show of proceeding for battle, but actually returning after a day or two. The ruse, he thought, would deter the Prophet from reaching *Badr*. The Prophet, however, arrived at Badr and spent eight days there, but the Makkans did not turn up. The failure

---

1   *The daring response of the Prophet failed Nuaym's mission and spoilt his chances of getting the promised reward from Abū Sufyān. But he did feel that there was some power in Madinah which was beyond any such influence; impressed by the development, he inclined towards accepting Islām.*

281

of *Abū Sufyān* became a subject of criticism among the Bedouins who were highly impressed by the courage and readiness of the Muslims to face a larger Makkan army a second time.

In June 626, information was received that some clans of *Ghatafān* were again planning to raid the oasis. In order to circumvent the attack, the Prophet immediately marched to the plains of *Najd* with 400 men whereupon the enemy ran away.[1] Not long after this (July 626), the Prophet led a big expedition of 1000 men northward to *Dūmat al Jandal* on Syria border against *Banī Kalb*. They were mostly marauders and used to plunder goods meant for *Madinah*. Moreover, they had an understanding with *Quraysh* and were supposed to attack the oasis from the north at the time of the proposed final onslaught from *Quraysh*. On the *Ummah*'s attack, they ran here and there surrendering their flocks and herds. But the more important result of the expedition was that it frightened the northern tribes and made them aware of the rapidly increasing power of *Islām*.

An indirect though highly significant consequence of *Uhud* was that it led to some Quranic legislation to reform the status of Muslim women. Hitherto, according to Arabian customary law, wife and other female relatives of a deceased male had been excluded from inheritance of property; in case there was no adult son, inheritance went to brothers, nephews, and other agnatic relatives of the deceased. This defect of the customary law came into sharp focus due to the death of a large number of Muslims in the battle of *Uhud*. Almost each of the seventy-two Muslims killed had left behind wives and children who needed social rehabilitation. *Samhudī* narrates that a Muslim woman had lost in the battle not only her husband but also, as a consequence, all her wealth, since she had no son and only daughters. She informed the Prophet of the double misfortune which she was facing due to the discriminatory inheritance law of the time. In order to

---

1 *It was during this expedition that revelation was received regarding shortened prayers (Qasr) during emergencies. Further, it was following this expedition that the Prophet helped Salmān Fārsi get freedom from his Jewish master after payment of the required cost.*

reform the system and facilitate rehabilitation of such affected families, Quranic revelations soon came down which conferred inheritance right on wives and other female relatives. There was, however, still the danger of properties of minor orphans being appropriated by family guardians.

Therefore, apart from conferring property rights on females, the *Qurān* addressed this problem as well. Verses were revealed which prescribed a high degree of religious culpability for such usurpations. Verse 4/2 said, '*Give unto orphans their wealth. Exchange not the good for the bad (in your management thereof) nor absorb their wealth into your own wealth. Lo! That would be great sin.*'

The most important problem, however, was one of effective social rehabilitation of war widows which was most suitably possible by their remarriage. The Prophet, therefore, encouraged Muslims to marry widows who had lost their husbands in *Jihād*. A solution soon arrived by revelation of verse 4/3 which explicitly permitted Muslim males to marry up to four wives: '*And if you fear that you will not deal fairly by the orphans, marry of the women, who seem good to you, two or three or four; and if you fear that you cannot do justice (to so many) then one (only) or that your right hands possess. Thus it is more likely that you will not do injustice.*' The Quranic sanction to polygamy was subjected to vehement criticism by Western historians who saw in it an example of male chauvinism. But viewed in its real historical context, as a measure for rehabilitation of war widows as well as poor, needy, and exploited unmarried women, it was a step for amelioration of the plight of weaker women rather than a license for debauchery. In the seventh century Arabia, there was a shortage of males and surplus of females who used to be treated as mere chattel, and there was no restriction on number of wives and concubines one could have. In such a situation, to restrict the number of wives to only four and condition it by a provision of strict fairness and equal treatment was a measure of radical social reform. Though the degree of empowerment of woman by the Prophet may look discriminatory from modern standard—she could inherit only half of what her brothers could receive and her value as a witness on law was only 50 per cent of that of a male—it was a revolutionary reform far in advance of its age. The Prophet was indeed the harbinger of emancipation of women in history. The reformatory measures adopted by the Prophet in respect of women and orphans went to provide a sense of social security and boosted morale of the Muslims who were to fight for the cause of *Islām* without caring for lives.

In order to give more force to his reformative measure concerning remarriage of widows, the Prophet gave personal examples and married a few of them, though deftly making political use of such matrimonial alliances. Immediately following *Uhud*, he had already married *Zaynab bint Khuzaymah* for cementing alliance with the powerful *Āmir* tribe; she, however, died in January 626. The next month, his cousin *Abū Salamah* died of a wound received in the battle of *Uhud*. His widow, *Umm Salamah*, was only 29 years old and had retained her youth as well as great beauty. She was sister of a powerful leader of *Makhzūm* clan of *Quraysh* and so the Prophet's marriage with her was to prove a useful political connection. Four months after her husband's death (May 626), the Prophet asked for her hand. She was initially hesitant because she had orphan children. She also told the Prophet that she had a jealous nature and since he had more wives than one, there could be rift in the household. But the Prophet persuaded her and she agreed. However, as apprehended by her, her entry to the household did create a cleavage. As reported by *Ibn Sād*, *Āishah* grew jealous of her due to her reputed beauty. The household was to be soon divided into two groups, one more aristocratic represented by *Umm Salamah* and supported by *Fātimah*,[1] and the other which was more plebeian represented by *Āishah* and *Hafsah*.

Not long after Umm Salamah's marriage, the Prophet's marriage with *Zaynab bint Jahsh* took place which sparked off one of the biggest controversies in his history in modern times. The background story of this marriage, as supported by historical

---

1   *Fātimah represented a yet third camp known as Ahl al Bait, the people of the Prophet's family, who subsequently came to be known as the Shiah.*

facts, is that in the early months after *Hijrah*, the Prophet thought that *Zayd*, his adopted son, should have another wife closer to his age. He thought of marrying him to his own cousin, *Zaynab bint Jahsh*, daughter of his real aunt, *Umaymah,* who was the daughter of his grandfather, *Abdul Muttalib*. Since *Zayd* had previously been a slave and consequently had a degraded social status, she was initially not willing. But when she came to know that it was the Prophet's wish and, therefore, God's wish, she agreed and the wedding took place. They, however, could not get along well with each other. For *Zayd*, the marriage was nothing but a cause of embarrassment and humiliation. After sometime, *Zayd* started complaining to the Prophet that she was shrewish with him and he wanted to divorce her. The Prophet knew that *'of all things licit, the most hateful to God was divorce'* (Q 13: 3), and so he persuaded him, again and again, not to divorce her. This fact finds mention in verse 33/37 which was revealed subsequently. But the situation could not be helped and *Zayd* divorced her, bringing the concomitant social disgrace to the lady. The Prophet was always concerned about rehabilitation of widows. In this case, he felt specially bad because he had arranged the marriage with the idea of breaking down the old tribal pride and had shown little regard for Zaynab's feelings. Holding himself responsible for her state, he, therefore, thought of making amends by offering his own hand to her. But there were two problems in effecting the idea. According to Arabian custom of the time, a foster son had the status of a real son and hence such a marriage would be a social taboo. Second, the Prophet was himself not eligible for he already had four wives, the maximum that Islamic law allowed. He, therefore, suppressed his feelings. But then verse 33/37 came down:

> *And when you said to him on whom Allāh has conferred favour and you have conferred favour: Keep your wife to yourself and fear Allāh. And you did hide in your mind that which Allāh was to bring to light, and you did fear mankind whereas Allāh had better right and you should fear Him. So when Zayd had performed the necessary*

> *formality (of divorce) from her, We gave her to*
> *you in marriage, so that (henceforth) there may*
> *be no sins for believers in respect of wives of their*
> *adopted sons, when the latter have performed the*
> *necessary formality for them. The Commandment*
> *of Allāh must be fulfilled.*

The revelation being of the nature of a clear command, question of noncompliance did not arise; the wedding took place for which *Zaynab* was quite willing as, according to tradition, she had always wished to marry the Prophet. Implied in the verse was also the permission to marry more than four wives, but this was for the Prophet alone in view of his special status. The revelation further clarified that relationship with adopted son was only artificial and that there was no restriction in marrying his divorced wife. In future, adopted son was to be named after real father and henceforth *Zayd* came to be known as *Zayd bin Hārithā*. Not less importantly, however, the verse implied that in arranging a marriage, the woman's willingness should be given due importance; unhappy marriage between two unwilling partners was not to be favoured in *Islām*.

The hypocrites and the slanderers, however, made this marriage a point of taunt and criticism. This gave rise to a fabricated story suggesting that the Prophet had fallen in love with *Zaynab* and married her out of lust. This unacceptable and calumnious story was first mentioned by *Wāqidī* who was a known fabricator and coined such fictions due to political motives. Subsequently, *Tabarī* picked it up from *Wāqidī*. Neither *Ibn Ishāq* nor the canonical *hadīth* writers referred to it; *Ibn Hajār* (writer of *Fath al Bārī*) and *Ibn Kathīr* even advised to overlook such false reports due to their apparent wickedness. To some of the Orientalists and fault-finders of the Prophet, however, this was a splendid piece of material; they gave it deep colours and embellishments in order to disparage him. They used it to allege that he had a weakness for the fair sex and he craftly manipulated revelations to further his own actions. According to their lurid version, based on that story, once the Prophet visited Zayd's house for some talks, but he was not present. *Zaynab* was dressing herself or was lightly dressed. She opened the door and the two looked at each other and became conscious of love between them. Though in her late thirties, she had retained her extreme beauty and the Prophet succumbed to her charm. Despite her request, however, he did not enter the house and went back saying, '*Praise be to God Who changes men's hearts*' (*Ibn Sad*). Subsequently, she repeatedly told *Zayd* of the great impression she had made on the Prophet. *Zayd* went to the Prophet and offered to divorce her, if he so liked. Though the Prophet advised him to '*keep his wife and fear God*', his marriage, which had already not been a happy one, was now on the rocks; he divorced her by mutual agreement. The prophet then decided to marry her and, after receiving revelation permitting the same, immediately sent *Salmah*, a maidservant, to *Zaynab* in order to propose. *Zaynab* was extremely happy to get the news, prostrated in thankfulness and gifted her silver bracelets and anklets to *Salmah*.

This colourful story about the Prophet's marriage with *Zaynab* is historically illogical. The history of his life amply shows that he was not a man given to passion and desire and hence such a story is inconsistent with his historical character. When the marriage took place, the Prophet was an old man of 55 years while *Zaynab* was about 40 in a state of declining youth and charm. A meeting between two such persons, who were well-known to each other, rousing such a storm of emotion does not stand to reason. She being his own cousin, he knew her since childhood; if he wanted her for her sexual charms, he could have married her years earlier instead of handing over her hand to *Zayd*. The family relationship between *Zaynab* and the Prophet well negates veracity of any such account. We do discern from the historical analysis of his multiple marriages contracted after Khadījah's death that not only this marriage, but all of them, had been motivated by social and political considerations rather than lust and desire.

After marriage, *Zaynab* joined Umm Salamah's aristocratic group of the Prophet's wives in his household. She was a woman of great piety, fasted much, kept long vigils, and gave generously to the poor. We learn from some sources that at her wedding feast, some of the guests stayed too long and indulged in undesirable talks at the Prophet's house. Following this, some revelations came down which emphasized special status of the Prophet's wives and prescribed their seclusion from public as also wearing of *Hijāb* (veil) by them. They were given the status of *'Mothers of the faithful'* (*Umm ul muminīn*). Further, once married to the Prophet, a woman's remarriage to any other man was prohibited forever. Verse 33/53 said, *'Believers, do not enter house of the Prophet for a meal without waiting for the proper time, unless you are given leave. But if you are invited, enter; and when you have eaten, disperse. Do not engage in familiar talk, for this would annoy the Prophet and he would be ashamed to bid you go; but of the truth, Allah is not ashamed. If you ask his wives for anything, speak to them from behind a curtain (Hijāb). This is more chaste for your hearts and their hearts.'* Verse 33/59 which followed directed about the veil: *'O Prophet! Tell thy wives and thy daughters and the women of the believers to draw their cloaks close around them (when they go abroad). That will be better, so that they may be recognized and not annoyed. Allah is ever Forgiving, Merciful.'* The revelations also stressed the special status of the Prophet and enjoined upon the believers to invoke blessings upon him and give him greeting of peace.

By the end of 626, the Prophet, by a combination of measures, had retrieved the lost prestige and power of the *Ummah*. Yet, there were underlying weaknesses within it. The cementing of relations between different components within it was yet to fully cure; under-surface differences between *Muhajirūn* and *Ansār* on one hand and *Aws* and *Khazraj* on the other still existed. The hypocrites were yet to be reconciled or subdued and still had the potential of creating disturbance on emotional issues. These weaknesses were to get manifested in the expedition of the Prophet against *Banī Mustaliq* in Jan 627.[1] *Banī Mustaliq* of the Red Sea coast were a clan of *Khuzaah* tribe and were allies of *Quraysh*. Under instigation by *Quraysh*, they had designs to raid *Madinah*. The Prophet, however, came to know about their plan and by a quick action made a surprise attack on them at *Murisī* on the Red Sea to the north-west of *Madinah* before they could set out for their proposed raid. Taken by surprise on this lightning attack, ten of *Mustaliq* were killed; their main fighting force under their chief, *Harīth ibn Dirār*, took to flight and the remaining inhabitants of *Murisī* surrendered. It was quite a successful expedition with only one Muslim killed. About 200 families of *Mustaliq* (with a total of about 600 persons including 200 females) were made captives; a rich booty of about 2000 camels and 5000 goats was captured.

The captives included the widowed daughter of the chief, *Juwayriyah*, who was to become the sixth of the living wives of the Prophet. During distribution of the captives, she was allotted to a helper who was demanding a very high price as ransom for her release. She came to the Prophet requesting for intervention. She was a woman of very charming looks and sweet manners. *Ibn Ishāq* says that *Āishah*, who was present with the Prophet at that moment, thought that he would also be equally impressed by her beauty as she had been. As she anticipated, the Prophet actually proposed to pay her ransom and take her as a wife to which she

---

1 *There is a dispute among historians regarding the timing of this expedition. Ibn Ishaq followed by Tabarī suggests that it took place in the sixth year after Hijrah, that is, after the Battle of the Trench. But a majority of historians (Ibn Sād, Ibn Hajār, Baihaqi, Hakim, Musā ibn Uqbah, and others) placed it slightly before the Battle of the Trench and this is generally accepted by modern historians.*

readily agreed.[1] It was perhaps a natural tendency of the classical historians to present every woman who would be married by the Prophet as extremely beautiful and also to give impression as if their hero was a superman, physically capable to love, marry, and satisfy a large number of women. If viewed in correct historical context, however, in this case also as in other cases of his multiple marriages, the motive of the Prophet appears to be political. Captivity of *Juwayriyah* offered a significant political opportunity to win over an important tribe on the western trade route to the cause of *Islām*. It was part of the Prophet's diplomacy to use matrimonial alliances for such purposes and he took advantage of the same. Following the wedding, all *Mustaliq* captives were set free by the Muslims without payment of ransom and a hostile tribe became friendly overnight without effort.

After victory at *Murisī*, the Prophet along with his force stayed there for a few days. During the stay, an incident reflected the still existing tension within the *Ummah*. There was a brawl over ownership of buckets between two local workers, one from *Ghifār* and the other of *Juhaynah*, having tribal alliance with *Quraysh* and *Khazraj*, respectively. The incident caused communal tension between Emigrants and Helpers. Coincidentally, however, a large number of hypocrites had also joined this expedition expecting rich booty. *Ibn Ubayy* along with his mischief mongers took advantage of the situation and stoked it to the limits. He

---

1   *This version is based on the account of Ibn Ishāq. We get slightly different accounts of circumstances leading to the Prophet's marriage with Juwayriah in other sources. According to one, before marriage, her father arrived and offered a number of camels which were short of the proposed offer. Some of the camels he had hidden near a pass. The Prophet, by his spiritual power, informed him about the place where he had hidden them. Highly impressed by this, he along with his two sons then and there entered Islām and Juwayriah followed suit. Another version is given by Hāfiz ibn Hajār. He says that initially the Prophet wanted to keep her as a slave, but her father came with objection. He said that being the daughter of the chief, she had a higher status and, therefore, she could not be made a slave. The Prophet left the decision on Juwayriah herself who was still willing to remain with him; and hence, the Prophet married her after her conversion.*

mischievously blamed the fight on the Emigrants and suggested that they were intruders in *Madinah* needing expulsion. '*By God, when we return to Madinah, the higher and the mightier of us will drive out the lower and the weaker,*' he is said to have remarked. As a result of his instigation, the situation deteriorated; swords were drawn by many on both sides, and a clash might have taken place but for intervention of senior Companions on both sides. The Prophet, who came to know about the mischief of *Ibn Ubayy*, controlled the situation with great difficulty. In order to divert men's minds from the issue, he ordered immediate march despite painful heat of the day. It was during the return journey that Chapter 63 of the *Qurān* (*al Munafiqūn*) was revealed which exposed the double character of the hypocrites and the mischief which *Ibn Ubayy* had played.

Another significant incident connected with *Banī Mustaliq* expedition which took place on the return journey was that which led to *Ifk* or false accusation against Āishah's character. It showed that hostile elements within the *Ummah* were still in a position to indulge in character assassination of family members of the Prophet in order to morally undermine his position. In this expedition, two of his wives, *Umm Salamah* and *Āishah*, had accompanied. At the time of departure from one but the last halt, *Āishah*, who had already occupied her exclusive covered howdah, found that her onyx necklace (presented by her mother at the time of wedding), so dear to her, had fallen down somewhere. She could figure out that she might have dropped it at the place she had been to for attending to call of nature.[1] She, therefore,

---

1 *The clasp of her necklace had become loose. During the early part of the return journey also, at one of the first halts, it fell down and got misplaced. The place had no water and so the Prophet had intended only a brief halt there. But since Āishah could not find her necklace, the Prophet ordered the caravan to halt there for the night. This caused some resentment among the Companions because they thought they would not find water at dawn for ablutions. It was on this occasion that verse 4/43 was revealed which permitted earth-purification in the event of nonavailability of water. The necklace, however, was located at the time of departure from beneath Aisha's camel.*

sneaked out of the howdah and went to search the necklace without being seen by anyone. While she was searching her for necklace, the caravan went off, mistakenly leaving her behind. When she was waiting there alone for help, a young Muslim fighter, *Safwān*, who had been following the caravan due to some reason, reached her location. Recognizing her, he took her along, she seated on the camel and he escorted her on foot. Thus, *Āishah* joined the caravan at the last halt, arriving there alone with the young man, to the astonishment of everyone who watched the scene. The hypocrites exploited the situation and quickly spread a scandal about her character on return to *Madinah*. Gossip spread from mouth to mouth and information reached the ears of the Prophet. Aisha's own cousin *Mistah* and the poet, *Hassān ibn Thābit*, and so on, apart from the hypocrites, were instrumental in spreading the rumour. Though none of the other wives of the Prophet took part in spreading the slander and *Usamah* as well as *Umm Ayman* strongly defended *Āishah*, *Ali* doubted her innocence. When the Prophet asked him about his opinion, he is said to have remarked, '*Women are plentiful and you can always change one for another*.' It was this callous reaction of *Ali* which permanently estranged *Āishah* from him.

For many days, however, *Āishah* had no inklings about the scandal. On return, she fell ill for about twenty days. But she was able to feel a certain reserve or lukewarm attitude on part of the Prophet. When she asked for his permission to go to her parents for getting her sickness attended to, he replied, '*As you will*.' She came to know about the scandal from the mother of *Mistah* only after recovery from sickness. Though the Prophet did not believe the slander, he had been enquiring about the truth from person to person. Taking it as a mischief of the hypocrites, in his speech in the mosque, he even indirectly suggested that *Āishah* was innocent. The scandal, however, created a highly embarrassing situation for him and tended to tear apart the unity of the *Ummah* between believers and nonbelievers of the scandal. Since some of the leaders of *Khazraj* tended to support the accusation, men of *Aws* suggested punitive action against them; the two main components of *Ansār* were on the verge of fight over the issue. It was in this situation that the Prophet went to Abū Bakr's house and sought explanation from *Āishah*. She pleaded her innocence and said that God knew the truth. The problem was, however, solved by revelation of verses 11 to 20 of Chapter 24 (*An Nūr*) of the *Qurān* which confirmed innocence of *Āishah* and condemned the slander as '*a monstrous calumny*'. The revelation also dwelt upon the question of adultery and prescribed penalty for slandering honourable women. Those who had been explicit in spreading the calumny—*Mistah, Hassān, Hamnah,* and others—were scourged accordingly.

The final and the largest attack from *Makkah* came in April 627, over two years after of the battle of *Uhud*. At *Uhud*, victory of *Quraysh* had been only superficial; they had failed in achieving their larger objectives. Soon after defeat, the Prophet was fast recovering the lost reputation of the *Ummah* as a military power and *Islām* was also spreading to remoter areas. It is, however, not known why reaction from them was getting delayed despite their consternation. It appears that they lacked confidence in going alone for the task and, to be doubly sure of success, planned to raise a formidable combined force of many allied nomadic tribes for a combined attack. The delay was occurring since they were not getting the desired active support of an equally powerful tribe. This required support was now provided by the expelled Jewish tribe of *Banī Nadīr* who were desperately determined to avenge their humiliating expulsion from the oasis and recover their land as well as prestige. With extreme hatred of *Islām* comparable to that of *Quraysh*, they were the people who were responsible for activating and goading *Makkah* and organizing the attack. In the beginning of 627, their chief, *Huyay bin Akhtāb* along with other Jewish leaders of *Khaybar* visited *Makkah* and at the *Kabāh*, together with *Quraysh* chiefs, swore a solemn oath to God that they would not fail one another until they had achieved their aim of exterminating *Islām*. Convincing them of help from *Banī Qurayzah* (who they said would renounce their Covenant with the Prophet and join them once their army reached the oasis) and promising to mobilize the Bedouin tribes of *Najd* to provide military support to *Quraysh*, they made them start preparations for the attack. But *Quraysh* still had a latent fear that the Prophet was being helped by some unseen power. In order to remove their misgivings, *Huyay* and the Jewish leaders, posing as having deeper religious knowledge, stressed superiority of paganism over *Islām*. Once *Quraysh* were ready, *Banī Nadīr* took initiatives to mobilize support of a group of nomadic tribes of *Najd* who had grievances against *Madinah*; in case of those having no sufficient desire for revenge, support was obtained by bribery. The *Banī Asad* agreed readily but *Banī Ghatafān* were promised half of the date harvest of *Khaybar* for joining the alliance, and thus a strong force of 2000 was mobilized from the *Ghatafān* clans of *Fazārah*, *Murrah*, and *Ashjā*. A contingent of 700 was also obtained from *Banī Sulaym*.

In this manner, substantial help from seven of the tribes was enlisted by promising a swift victory and easy spoils; and finally, a strong confederate army of over 10,000 was mobilized in which contribution of *Quraysh* alone was 4,000 which included a cavalry of 300. An equal number of horsemen were provided by the confederate tribes, finally making it a strong cavalry of 600 under command of veterans like *Khālid*, *Amr ibn Ās*, and *Ikrimah*. This was said to be the largest army Arabia had ever seen. It was under the formal command of *Abū Sufyān*, but he was no fighter. Perhaps the most renowned fighter in the confederate force was *Amr ibn Abd-Wudd*, who, according to tradition, was considered equal in strength to 1,000 cavaliers. This formidable army marched from different directions and converged in front of *Madinah* near *Uhud* on 31 March 627. This attack being not only from *Quraysh* but launched by a confederacy of a good number of Arabian tribes, the ensuing confrontation is known in history as *Ghazwa al Ahzāb* (Expedition of the Confederates) and is popularly called Battle of the Trench.

The Prophet received information regarding movement of the confederate army about a week before its anticipated arrival. The Muslims panicked to know about its great strength; time was too short for deciding strategy and making preparations for defense. The Prophet knew that with a fighting strength of hardly

3000 without any cavalry, the Muslims were no match for the enemy. The huge confederate cavalry was a specially threatening aspect. The Prophet hurriedly held consultations in which the idea of fighting a pitched battle was ruled out. But even if they remained in the city, how would they deal with the powerful cavalry charge? There seemed to be no answer. A recent Persian convert, *Salmān Fārsi*, however, came out with the suggestion of digging up a deep and wide trench in front of vulnerable portion of the city in order to prevent entry of cavaliers. This practice of defense was prevalent in Persia and *Salmān* well knew its technique. With no alternative stratagem to fall back on, the Prophet approved the idea. The city of *Madinah* was well protected on three directions by clumped plantations, volcanic rocks, and granite hills; it was only from the north that the city was exposed and easy entry was possible. It was, therefore, decided to dig a trench of a length of about 5,000 cubits, with depth ranging from 7 to 10 cubits and width around 10 cubits, in order to block entry from the north. It was extremely difficult to complete such a massive work in a rocky area within less than a week. But under the inspiring leadership of the Prophet, the Muslims, with their morale as high as ever, started the work on a war-footing as per plan prepared by the Prophet himself. Implements were borrowed from *Qurayzah*. Each section of the *Ummah* was made responsible for a specific part of the trench and every Muslim, including the Prophet, performed highly taxing manual labour with unusual spirit singing songs in praise of God:

> *O God, no life is there but life thereafter,*
> *Have mercy on the Helpers and Emigrants.*[1]

Completion of the huge work within six days by unskilled workers despite inclement weather and pangs of hunger is a rare

---

1   *Barā of Aws, one of the teenagers who had been sent back from Uhud due to tender age, later described the great beauty of the Prophet as he saw him working while the trench was being dug. 'More beautiful than him I have never seen,' he said.*

example of a community's cooperative spirit, enthusiasm, and perseverance. Traditions have associated a few stories of miracles performed by the Prophet during the work. It is amusing to learn how rocks too strong to be broken by workers gave way like heaps of sand on impact of the Prophet's saliva and an ordinary strike of shovel. *Ibn Ishāq* tells us an interesting story how *Jābir* of *Khazraj*, moved by leanness of the Prophet during the work, arranged some mutton and barley-bread in his house and invited him for lunch. The Prophet, however, publicly announced the invitation and went to Jābir's house along with a big group of Muslims. *Jābir* and his wife found themselves in a highly embarrassing situation as the food available was sufficient for only a few persons. But the situation could not be helped and the meal was placed in front of the Prophet who blessed it and took the name of God over it. To the utter astonishment of *Jābir*, all ate to satisfaction in groups of tens. There is yet another story referred to by many classical historians, according to which, three strikes by the Prophet by axe to break a large rock gave him vision of Islām's victory of *Syria*, *Persia*, and *Yaman*, a fact which came true only after his death. Digging of the trench was completed well in time after which a contingent of archers and stone-throwers was placed at vantage points on the inner side in order to prevent any cavalier to cross the trench. Excavated rocks and stones were piled up for use as missiles. Care was also taken to gather crops from outlying areas so that the besieging army would find no fodder for camels and horses. The women and children were housed in strong fortresses of the city for safety. With these measures, defense strategy of the Muslims was complete.

The Confederates had planned to launch a simultaneous attack on the city from all sides. But when they reached, the sight of the gaping trench, effectively guarded by the Muslim contingent from behind, left them nonplussed. The moat seemed impassable for the cavalry which was their main strength. They saw this un-Arab innovation for the first time and denounced it as unchivalric. The trench, however, effectively stymied the great military offensive; the attack ended in a siege. The siege is said to have continued for about 25 days during which, instead of usual fight, only intermittent skirmishes took place. The exact chronological sequence of events is not clear, but it appears that for some days in the beginning, the fight was confined to exchange of archery and throwing of stones only.

Unable to cross the trench due to heavy firing of missiles by Muslim defenders or find any other opening, the confederates decided to resort to the method of conspiracy by winning over *Banī Qurayzah*. They would be able to enter the city from south where *Banī Qurayzah* used to live, they thought. *Huyay* contacted the chief of *Qurayzah*, *Kāb ibn Asad*, and tried to convince him of the impending Makkan victory. After some hesitation, *Kāb* agreed to renounce the Covenant and allow them entry. According to some sources, they actually started preparations to launch an attack on the Muslims as part of the Confederates' strategy of diverting the Muslims to this new front in order to enable them to cross the trench. They even attempted to assault the fortress in which the Muslim women had been kept. One of their men who approached the gate of the fortress for reconnaissance is said to have been killed by *Saffiyah*, the Prophet's aunt, who hit his head with a wooden post. The Prophet had information regarding Qurayzah's treachery confirmed with the help of *Sād ibn Muādh* and others. A detachment of 300 Muslims under *Zayd* had to be diverted to the south in order to prevent attack from that side. The treacherous alliance had upset the whole defense strategy of the *Ummah*.

With their morale boosted by the new alliance, the Confederates adopted a new strategy. With a view to keep the Muslim fighters engaged on other fronts and thereby provide opportunity to *Banī Qurayzah* to plan an attack, they launched a powerful attack from three sides, the main being across the ditch. The lead in the northern attack was taken by the old and experienced *Amr ibn Abd Wudd* who was considered the greatest warrior of *Makkah*. Wounded at *Badr*, he had taken a vow not to oil his hair until he had avenged his injury. In a daring action, he along with three other cavaliers (*Dirār, Jubaira,* and *Nawfal*)[1] succeeded in crossing the ditch and challenged

---

1 *According to some sources, Ikrimah was also included in the group.*

the Muslims for a single combat. But so formidable was his reputation as a warrior that no one dared respond to his repeated three challenges. *Alī* wanted to face him at the very first but was restrained by the Prophet. However, when there was no response to his third challenge, the Prophet permitted *Alī*, personally handed over a sword (*Dhul Fiqār* was the name of Ali's sword) to him and wound a turban round his head. The single combat between *Alī*, who was on foot, and *Amr*, who was mounted, has been dramatically described by *Ibn Sād* and other sources. Abd Wudd's sword when struck, pierced through the helmet of *Alī*, and wounded his forehead (this created two permanent scar marks on his forehead for which he was later known as *Dhul Qarnain*—the two horned). However, *Alī* instantaneously recovered and by a single hit of his sword killed *Amr*, whose death broke the backbone of the Makkan offensive. As *Amr* fell, two other horsemen attempted to take on *Alī* but his charge forced them to flee. *Nawfal* while trying to jump back the ditch fell down and was also killed by *Alī*.

The last week of the siege was especially difficult for the Muslims. Food was running short and many were going without food for days together; the weather was highly inclement as it was severely cold. Hungry and tired, harassed by frequent attacks and worried by the menace of *Qurayzah*, they were considering their case as hopeless. The attacks were so numerous and so frightening that even the Prophet failed to perform prayer on some occasions. To add to the problem, the hypocrites were instigating the Helpers to abandon the *Ummah*. Unnerved by such a situation of extreme hardship and constant fear of attack, those who were weak in faith tended to join the hypocrites and retire on one pretext or the other. But the faith of the true believers did not weaken and instead gained strength by the hardship. The *Qurān* echoes the situation well in verses 10 to 13 of Chapter 33 (*Al Ahzāb*):

10. *When they came upon you from above you and from below you, and when eyes grew wild and hearts reached to the throats, and you were imagining vain thoughts concerning Allāh.*

11. *There were the believers sorely tried, and shaken with a mighty shock.*
12. *And when the hypocrites, and those in whose hearts is a disease, were saying: Allāh and His messenger promised us naught but delusion.*
13. *And when a party of them said: O folk of Yathrib! There is no stand (possible) for you, therefore turn back. And certain of them (even) sought permission of the Prophet, saying: Our homes lie open (to the enemy). And they lay not open. They but wished to flee.*

In view of Qurayzah's defection to the enemy camp, it was important for the Prophet to launch his own 'diplomatic offensive' in order to create division in the Confederates also. He knew well that *Ghatafān* and other Bedouin tribes were only reluctant allies of *Quraysh*. They had joined the Confederates for easy plunder rather than out of hostility to *Islām*. But now, they were quite disenchanted and had lost faith in the organizers of the campaign. Deciding to take advantage of mutual recriminations and distrust that had spread among Bedouin allies of the Confederates, the Prophet secretly sent feelers to *Ghatafān* to win them over to his side. He offered a third of Madinah's date harvest to them for the purpose, but they demanded half of the same. In view of gravity of the situation, he even agreed to their demand and was willing to conclude a peace treaty with the clans of *Ghatafān*. A majority of the Companions, however, did not agree to promise any such offer, and finally, the agreement did not materialize. This attempt failing, a successful ruse was resorted to with a view to frustrate the Makkan plan of attack from the south with involvement of *Banī Qurayzah*. This was based on the suggestion of *Nuaym ibn Masūd* of *Ashjā* clan of *Ghatafān*. He was the same person whom *Abū Sufyān* had bribed and engaged in order to create fear in the minds of the Muslims and prevent them from proceeding for the Second *Badr*. Having a feeling that his mission had failed due to some unseen power working in support of the Prophet, he had secretly become a Muslim and had now joined the Confederates with the intention of subverting their campaign. The treacherous alliance between the Confederates and *Qurayzah* made him realize the precariousness of the Prophet's position. With a view to help the *Ummah* out, he secretly planned a deceit in order to break the new alliance and sought the Prophet's permission for playing the trick. Realizing that Nuaym's intentions were sincere, the Prophet gave permission and remarked, '*War involves deceit as well as fighting. Let deceit be your weapon.*' He had influence both on *Quraysh* as well as *Qurayzah* which he deftly used to realize his aim. He secretly went to the *Qurayzah* leaders and created fear in their minds about their fate in case the Confederates failed to exterminate the *Ummah*. In that case, he emphasized, *Quraysh* would go back leaving them on the mercy of the Prophet, and so he suggested that they should not support the Confederates unless *Quraysh* handed over some of their leaders as hostages. The instigations of *Nuaym* worked well and the *Qurayzah* leaders agreed to demand hostages as security. After creating misunderstanding in *Banī Qyrayzah*, he next clandestinely went to *Abū Sufyān* and informed him that *Qurayzah* had no trust in *Quraysh*. Realizing their mistake in opposing the Prophet, they had made a secret alliance with him and they would be demanding hostages whom they would subsequently kill. The misinformation by *Nuaym* infuriated *Quraysh* whose newly created suspicion was confirmed when *Qurayzah* actually demanded hostages in lieu of fighting in their support. Nuaym's deception was a complete success; the *Qurayzah–Quraysh* alliance had broken down due to engineered mistrust.

The prolongation of the siege coupled with inclement weather (it was exceptionally cold and wet) and dwindling provisions had brought about untold hardships on the Confederates. Their horses and camels were dying of hunger as well as arrow wounds. The fourth week of the siege was running without any tangible success and their army was left quite disheartened. And now, *Banī Quaryzah* had also deserted them, which was highly demoralizing. To make the matter worse for them, a strong and bitter wind started blowing from the sea which, after causing distress for three days, finally took the form of a hurricane, so terrible that neither a tent could be kept standing nor a fire remained burning in the Confederates' camp, though that of the Muslims remained rather sheltered from the wind. This turned out to be a God-sent help for the *Ummah* as it made extremely difficult for the Confederates to carry on with the siege[1]. Later on, verse 33/9 confirmed that it was God's special favour to the believers: '*O ye who believe, remember God's favour unto you when hosts come at you and We sent against them a wind and hosts ye saw not.*' The night following the violent storm, *Abū Sufyān* decided not to take the hardship anymore, broke camp, and marched off with his men, and his allies followed suit. His expedition was a complete failure. The so-called Battle of the Trench was not a battle in the real sense of the term; there was no open fight, but only minor skirmishes in which eight of the Confederates and six Muslims lost lives. The *Ummah*, however, suffered a setback when *Sād ibn Muādh*, chief of *Aws*, was fatally wounded. He received an arrow injury in one of his bare hands because the coat of mail he was wearing was too short and left his hands unprotected. After some days, he succumbed to his wound but only after playing a historic role in execution of *Banī Qurayzah*.[2]

The sudden flight of the Confederates, though giving a great relief to the Prophet, did not actually amount to end of the battle for the *Ummah*. This was because though the attacking army had gone back, developments during the siege had demonstrated that an equally dangerous enemy was there within the oasis itself, and that was *Banī Qurayzah*. But for Nuaym's trick, their treason would have led to extermination of the *Ummah*. The Prophet, therefore, decided to get rid of this menace without any further delay. Such an advice had also been divinely given to him through Gabriel (*Ibn Ishāq*). And so, within hours of the retreat of the

---

1   *According to a tradition, this problem from nature had visited the enemy after three days' prayer by the Prophet to God for forcing the enemy to run away.*

2   *The classical historians record a traditional story which said that Sād's dead body, while being carried for burial, was felt by the lifters as extraordinarily light. The Prophet later explained that it was so felt because the angels were carrying it without being seen.*

Confederates, almost in extension of the battle, the Prophet with his 3,000 fighters besieged the fortresses of *Banī Qurayzah* wherein the *Nadīr* chief, *Huyay*, was also taking shelter. *Banī Qurayzah* initially decided to resist, but the siege continued for about twenty-five days. Unable to sustain the siege for such a long period, they requested the Prophet for permission to consult *Abū Lubābah* of *Banī Amr*, who was the chief link between them and *Aws*, with whom they had had a traditional alliance. Permission was granted as it was thought that *Abū Lubābah* would be able to persuade them to surrender. But moved by the wailings of their women and children, he through gesture indicated to them that surrender on their part would amount to their slaughter. For this act of unfaithfulness against *Islām*, *Abū Lubābah* severely repented. For expiation, he is said to have tied himself with one of the pillars of the mosque for about fifteen days (he used to be untied by his daughter for performing prayers only) until, on the basis of a divinely communicated message, the Prophet gave tidings indicating that he had been forgiven by God.

The siege was, however, continuing unabated. The leaders of *Qurayzah* thoroughly discussed their next course of action and weighed pros and cons of different options open to them. The first suggested by *Kāb* was that since *Muhammad* appeared to be a real Prophet, they should enter *Islām* en masse and save their lives and properties. Though some of their men were in favour of this option (three persons from *Banī Hadl*, a branch of *Qurayzah*, and two from *Banī Qurayzah* itself left and entered *Islām*), a majority rejected it. The suggestion of not entering *Islām* but offering to pay a tribute or tax to the *Ummah* was also discussed, but not agreed to. Many thought that they could kill their women and children and attack the Muslim army, catching it unawares, on the day of *Sabbath* when they would not expect such an act. Finally, however, despite *Abū Lubābah*'s warning, they opened the gates of their fortresses and surrendered, hopeful of lenient treatment from the Prophet on intercession of *Aws* who were their allies. The *Aws* did plead for them and requested the Prophet to give them the same lenient treatment as he had given to *Banī Nadīr*. But in view of the dangerous role played by *Banī Nadīr* in organizing an attack against *Islām*, such a course of action would definitely have swelled the ranks of the enemy and would have been an extremely unwise decision. Therefore, not straight away accepting their request, the Prophet with the concurrence of *Aws* appointed one of their own chiefs, the wounded *Sād ibn Muādh*, to pronounce judgment on *Banī Qurayzah*. *Sād* was a highly devoted Muslim known as a man of justice, but at the same time, he was also known for taking tough stands against enemies of *Islām*. The misconduct of *Qurayzah* did not favour leniency and he was well aware of the extremely dangerous nature of their treachery which had brought the *Ummah* on the verge of destruction. Therefore, he decided their fate in accordance with the Jewish law as contained in the *Torah* (Deuteronomy XX— 10–14) for treatment of hostile elements responsible for treason of this nature. According to his decision, all male adults were to be put to death, women and children were to be made slaves and their property treated as booty. The Prophet was known for his leniency in treatment of such defeated hostile elements. In this case, too, as evident from historical accounts, he had not tried to influence Sad's decision as an arbitrator and was perhaps not expecting this type of a severe verdict. But treating his judgment as coming from God, he accepted it and ordered implementation of the sentence. The women and children were segregated and taken away to the city whereas the men, numbering about 600 (more according some accounts but only 400 as per canonical *Hadīth* collections), were executed in small groups, their dead bodies dropped and buried in specially dug trenches.[1] Only one woman, who was responsible for killing a Muslim, was put to death. Those executed included *Huyay* and *Kāb*, the two chiefs.

---

1   *Traditions mention that one Qurayzah man, Zabīt ibn Bātā, who had spared the life of a man of Khazraj during civil wars, was allowed to be spared from execution on the latter's intervention. But in view of the execution of all his tribesmen, he refused the offer and hence was beheaded. However, his wife and children were set free and their property returned.*

This account of mass killing is often used by Western historians to criticize the Prophet for his policy of violence against infidels. The story has been compared with those of Nazi concentration camps. But little do they realize that whereas Nazi atrocities were committed in the twentieth century, the story of execution of *Qurayzah* related to the seventh century when such treatment of hostile elements for treason was an acceptable norm; and this had parallels in the religious history of the Jews.[1] Would it then not be inappropriate to judge this incident by modern standards of natural rights? The classical historians who covered the incident did not express any shock on this massacre. Moreover, the treachery committed by *Banī Qurayzah* was of the most dangerous nature endangering the very existence of the *Ummah*. Sparing their lives would have amounted to allow the ranks of disaffected Jews getting swelled up in *Khaybar* against *Islām*. The situation demanded deterrent punishment as a defensive measure; leniency would have been politically self-destructive. Further, the massacre had not been inspired by any hatred against the Jews and was not of the nature of a pogrom. A good number of Jews still remained in *Madinah*; they never had to complain of the Prophet's hostile attitude towards them, were treated with kindness, and were even given annual grants. The Muslims continued to show great respect for the prophets of the Jews. That the action against *Banī Qurayzah* was purely political is well proved by the fact that the following year, after defeating the Jews of *Khaybar*, the Prophet spared their lives although they had attempted to kill him by poisoning. A modern scholar (*Barakat Ahmad*) has, however, doubted the veracity of the story of execution as some of the contemporary reporters, such as *al Zuhri* and *Qatadah*, make no mention of this event. It is also significant that there is no Jewish version of this massacre. Even Samuel Usque's book *A Consolidation of Tribulations of Israel:*

---

1   *Karen Armstorng has given example of King David of Jerusalem in this connection. He is said to have slain 200 Palestinians after castrating them. Another example is given when Moses had commanded the Israelites to massacre the entire population of Canaan.*

Third Dialogue, which is considered a classic Jewish martyrology, does not make any mention of this incident.

At the time of distribution of seized properties and captivated women and children of *Banī Qurayzah*, a woman named *Rayhānah*, daughter of a Nadirite but married to a man of *Qurayzah*, was accepted by the Prophet as his share. Some Western scholars have described her as a woman of great beauty, but this is a debatable point as sources have not mentioned her that way. They also allege that the Prophet kept her as his concubine as such relation with a slave girl was permitted in *Islām*, but this contention also does not find support in the sources. In the biographical works, there are three versions about *Rayhānah*. According to the first, which is broadly based on the account of *Ibn Ishāq*, she was either chosen by the Prophet or coincidentally fell in his lot. He wanted her to accept *Islām*, but she hated the faith and refused, remaining as his slave. She was lodged with the Prophet's aunt *Salmah* where she subsequently entered *Islām*. The Prophet then offered to set her free and marry her. But she refused the proposal and preferred to live as a slave until she died after about five years. The story given by *Wāqidī* and *Ibn Sād* is, however, different. In their opinion, the Prophet left the final decision to her own choice. In course of time, she embraced *Islām* and the Prophet set her free and married her. There is yet a third story given by *Ibn Minda*, according to which, she was set free, went back to her people, and led a secluded life. Most of the Muslim scholars hold Minda's version as the whole truth. She is, however, generally not accepted as the wife of the Prophet.

The failure of the siege is considered a detrimental defeat of *Quraysh*; it doomed their faith without leaving prospect of recovery in the near future. They had put in their total strength but had miserably failed to uproot the Muslims; their prestige in the eyes of the Bedouins had diminished. Their caravan trade with Syria was now virtually lost to the *Ummah* who had almost taken over the same. No wonder, after their ignominious retreat, the Prophet foretold that this would be the end of Makkan aggression and thenceforth, initiatives would lie with him (*Bukhārī*). Vicariously, the failure of the siege amounted to a significant victory for the *Ummah*. The twin-victory of the Trench and *Qurayzah* immensely enhanced its power and prestige and changed the balance of power in the peninsula in its favour. Within the oasis, it put to an end all opposition and frightened the *Munafiqūn* into submission. After execution of *Banī Qurayzah*, historians do not make mention of any further internal scheming or hostile action. The Prophet now wielded undisputed political power in *Madinah*. Externally too, the *Ummah* gained the status of the strongest regional power, and this found reflection in references made to the Prophet by Byzantine and Persian emperors as '*Powerful king of the Arab*'. Further, the twofold victory sent shockwaves throughout the peninsula making the nomadic tribes feel that *Muhammad* was the man of the future and that antagonizing him would be a dangerous proposition. The tribes, therefore, now inclined towards joining the *Ummah*'s alliance, thus paving the way for building up of a strong *Ummah*'s Confederacy, and those who still clung to the Makkan alliance had to face the wrath of the *Ummah*.

CHAPTER X

TOWARDS PEACE

The Battle of the Trench, although insignificant from the viewpoint of what happened during it, was highly significant for what it led to and what happened following it. It proved a turning point in the Prophet's political history by opening up new avenues. Hitherto, the *Ummah*, surrounded by threats on all sides, had been struggling for its very survival. But now weakening of external as well as internal opponents substantially lowered the threat perception. With his power palpably enhanced, the Prophet now effected a shift in his foreign policy from aggressive *jihad* to that of peace and reconciliation— his religiously cherished goal. *'Now that he was no longer fighting for his life, Muhammad could begin to impose the Pax Islamica upon Arabia.'* (Karen Armstrong). The policy of rapprochement, however, was to go without showing any sign of weakness. The *Ummah* was still faced with dangerously hostile elements. Apart from continuing hostility of *Quraysh*, many recalcitrant nomadic tribes had to be tamed by military power. Moreover, threat from the Jews of *Khaybar*, who had been having alliance with *Quraysh* as well as *Ghatafān*, still loomed large and had the potential of endangering the *Ummah*. Therefore, effective military action of a defensive nature against otherwise irreconcilable enemies could not be dispensed with. It was sometimes necessary to neutralize the potential enemies by diplomatically isolating them. It was also necessary to win over important Bedouin tribes by means of a policy of carrot and stick in order to raise a formidable Muslim Confederacy.[1] Right from the beginning of the Madinan period, the Prophet had believed himself to be the messenger for all Arabs. Spread of *Islām* to the entire peninsula and, by implication, its political unification were now a possibility. But the best way of achieving this aim was through a policy of peace and conciliation.

The first manifestation of the new policy was in respect of *Quraysh* whose enmity with *Islām* was most deep rooted. They had not only repeatedly attempted to kill the Prophet himself but were also hell-bent on altogether exterminating *Islām*. The Prophet was now in a position to settle scores with them; but, on the contrary, he adopted a policy of reconciliation toward *Quraysh* and even started a programme of their appeasement. About this time, there was shortage of food grains in *Makkah* due to famine. *Yamamah* in *Najd* was Arabia's granary, but its chief, who had embraced *Islām*, had prohibited export of foodgrains to *Makkah*. In response to request of some of the Makkans, the Prophet suspended the prohibition. Further, he is said to have sent 500 *dinars* to be distributed among the poor in *Makkah*. He also sent a large quantity of dates to *Abū Sufyān* offering to exchange the same with skins rotting in the latter's warehouses. It is sometimes suggested that he had entered into a secret understanding with *Abū Sufyān* whom he even allowed to take a caravan to Syria unmolested; and that was why the latter was not present in *Makkah* at the time of conclusion of the Treaty of *Hudaybiyah*.

---

1 *During the year intervening between the Trench and Hudaybiyah, several minor expeditions had to be sent by the Prophet in order to discipline pro-Quraysh tribes like Asad, Thalabah and others.*

A more significant step for winning over *Abū Sufyān*, however, was the Prophet's marriage with his daughter, *Umm Habībah* (beginning of 628) who was a Muslim refugee in Abyssinia, now 35 years old. A few months before the treaty of *Hudaybiyah*, the Prophet learnt that the lady's husband, *Ubayd Allāh ibn Jahsh* (the Prophet's cousin and brother-in-law), had expired. *Ubayd Allāh* was a Christian before professing *Islām*, and soon after emigration to Abyssinia, he had reverted to Christianity, to the great distress of his wife. With a view to cement closer tie with *Abū Sufyān*, after completion of the period of waiting, he sent a message to the *Negus* requesting him to arrange his marriage with the widow after obtaining her willingness. *Umm Habībah*, who had just had a dream indicating her marriage with the Prophet, readily agreed, and the marriage took place in absentia. *Khālid ibn Saīd*, chosen by *Umm Habibah*, acted as her guardian and the *Negus* personally solemnized the wedding in the presence of *Jāfar*, celebrating the function and paying 400 gold coins as dower on behalf of the Prophet. After marriage, she joined the Prophet's household sometime in April 628 when he was commanding expedition at *Khaybar*. The Prophet had great respect for the *Negus* and he used to often ask *Umm Habībah* to speak to him about him. The echo of all these measures taken for reconciliation of *Quraysh* may be found in verse 60/7 of the *Qurān*, which said, '*It may be that God ordains love between you and those of them with whom you were at enmity.*' There is reason to believe that, facing suspension of their trade via western route and tired of the war of attrition with *Madinah*, some of the *Quraysh* leaders themselves desired an honourable peace. As had been pointed out by *Khālid ibn al Walīd* at the time of retreat after the Trench, they had now come to realize that *Muhammad* was the man of the future.

What motivated the Prophet to adopt the unexpected policy of reconciliation with *Makkah*? Modern historians have conjectured to find out an answer. The *Quraysh* were the Emigrants' own kith and kin and their city had the *Kābah* which had become an integral part of *Islām*. With great emotional attachment with their birthplace, it was difficult for the Prophet to think of destruction of the city in which violence was traditionally prohibited. Moreover, the city had widespread economic relations, an advanced state of culture, and a group of individuals who had experience in administration as well as high intellectual capability. All these could have been harnessed to build up an Islamic State in the peninsula which the Prophet perhaps had envisaged. Most importantly, however, there was strong political reason for a rapprochement with *Makkah*. In the post-Trench period, the most serious threat to the *Ummah* was from the *Khaybar–Makkah* alliance. *Sarakshī* points out that there was a pact between the two enemies of *Islām*, according to which, if the *Ummah* invaded either of the two, the other was to attack *Madinah*. It was, therefore, highly desirable to neutralize *Makkah* by a peace treaty, isolate *Khaybar*, and put to an end to the threat from the Jews.

In March 628 (month of *Ramadān*), the Prophet took the boldest step in the direction of peace with *Makkah*. Inspired by a dream in which he saw himself performing pilgrimage at the *Kābah* unopposed holding key of the sanctuary in his hand, he decided to go for *Umrah* (the Lesser Pilgrimage) and invited the Muslims, including those from friendly tribes, to accompany. It was made clear that this would be a purely religious affair and not a military expedition. This, however, suited his political programme as he might have been aiming at conclusion of a peace treaty with *Quraysh* during the proposed pilgrimage. Though response from the nomadic tribes turned out to be lukewarm, the *Muhajirūn* were quite excited by the idea of visiting their birthplace. But at the same time, they wondered how they would enter the Sanctuary under the prevailing atmosphere of hostility. Finally, however, a group of 1400 Muslims, mostly *Muhajirūn* and *Ansār*, but also including *Ibn Ubayy* and a few other hypocrites, volunteered to accompany the Prophet. According to some sources, a strong garrison had been left at *Madinah* to guard against apprehended attack from *Khaybar*. The Prophet's wife *Umm Salamah* along with two other women, who had taken part in the Second *Aqabah*, had been permitted to accompany. Attired as pilgrims and taking seventy camels along for customary sacrifice, the party left on the first day of *Dhu al Qadā*, one of the traditional months of truce in which fighting was banned. Since violent reaction from *Quraysh* could not be ruled out, *Umar* and a few others of his ilk suggested carrying of full-scale arms; but the Prophet, who had no intentions to fight and did not want to create misgivings among *Quraysh* whatsoever, did not allow this. Each pilgrim was, however, allowed to carry a sword for safety during journey. *Tabari's* view that after covering some distance, the Prophet ordered stock of arms to be brought and kept sealed, is generally not accepted.

The proposed pilgrimage was a splendid piece of diplomacy. Pilgrimage of the *Kābah* was a traditional right of the Arabs and, hence, adoption of this practice by *Islām* would add to its acceptability. Violence against peaceful pilgrims by *Quraysh* or their prevention from entering the Sanctuary would affect their reputation as its guardian and also alienate the Bedouin tribes. But if allowed to perform pilgrimage, it would amount to a moral victory of the Prophet. The *Quraysh*, thus, found themselves in a dilemma; they were also suspecting the intentions of the Prophet. Nonplussed, their available leaders like *Suhayl*, *Ikrimah*, *Safwān*, and so on[1] decided to stop the Muslims, requisitioned troops of the *Ahābish* (allied tribes living around *Makkah*), and dispatched a cavalry of 200 horses under *Khālid* to prevent their entry to the city. The Prophet received information about this en route from an informer. In order to evade *Khālid*, he changed the route of his caravan and headed to *Hydaybiyah*, about fifteen kilometres south of *Makkah*. At *Hudaybiyah*, his camel *Qaswā* sat down and refused to get up. Considering it a divine indication, the Prophet ordered the Companions to dismount who objected as there was no water at the place. The Prophet is said to have then performed a miracle at this point. An arrow given by him was struck by one of the Companions into a dry waterhole after putting some water rinsed by the Prophet into it. This resulted in gushing out of abundant pure water from the hole.

1 *The sources do not make any mention of Abū Sufyān at this stage which is significant. He was perhaps not in the city and had been to Syria commanding a caravan.*

The Prophet's halt at *Hudaybiyah* dragged on for a number of days as he wanted to proceed further only after convincing *Quraysh* of his peaceful intentions and negotiating peace with them. *Ibn Hishām* reports that immediately on arrival at *Hudaybiyah*, he remarked, '*The Quraysh may ask me anything for charity's shake, I will concede it to them today.*' But *Quraysh* suspected foul play and, in order to ascertain his real intentions, sent three delegations, one after another, to him. The first was under *Budayl ibn Warqah*, one of the chiefs of the *Khuzaah* tribe; the second was led by *Hulays* of *al Hārith* (one of the clans of *Kinānah*), who was commander of the *Ahābish*, while the third was that of *Urwah ibn Masūd* of *Thāqif* from *Tāif.* It, however, appears that none of them had power to negotiate. After talking to the Prophet and inspecting the state of the pilgrims, they were all convinced that the intention of the Muslims was nothing but to peacefully perform religious rites. But despite their recommendation to allow entry to the pilgrims, *Quraysh* intransigently stuck to their stand of preventing their entry. *Hulays*, who had meticulously inspected the sacrificial camels with their marks of consecration and their festive ornaments and was fully convinced of the bona fide of the Prophet, even threatened to withdraw *Ahābish* forces if *Muhammad* was not allowed entry. *Urwah*, who during his meeting with the Prophet had tried to hold the latter's beard in the traditional Arab gesture of familiarity and had, consequently, been snubbed by the Companions, was extremely impressed to notice the great reverence of the Companions for the Prophet and said to *Quraysh*, '*O people, I have been sent as envoy unto kings— unto Caeser and Chosroes and the Negus—and I have not seen a king whose men so honour him as the Companions of Muhammad honour Muhammad. If he comandeth aught, they almost outstrip his word in fulfilling it; when he performeth his ablution, they well-nigh fight for the water thereof; when he speaketh, their voices are hushed in his presence; nor will they look him full in the face; but lower their eyes in reverence for him. He hath offered you a goodly concession; therefore accept it from him*' (*Bukhāri*). However, instead of listening to their pleadings, *Quraysh* tried to create a division in the *Ummah* by inviting *Ibn Ubayy* to perform circumambulations alone, but he refused. In order to force the Muslims to retreat, they even instigated a group of plebeians to assault them. The antisocial elements were captured, but the Prophet set them free.

In order to break the stalemate, the Prophet also sent his envoys to *Makkah*. The first to be sent was *Khirāsh*, a helper, but *Quraysh* did not even hear him, his camel was hamstrung and he himself would have been killed but for the intervention of *Hulays*. As the last resort, *Uthmān ibn Affān* was sent as he belonged to the powerful *Umayyah* clan of *Quraysh* and had many aristocratic connections in the city. The Prophet thought that because of his status he would be able to convince them for peace talks. *Uthmān* was well received in the city, but his message did not have any immediate impact. He was offered to perform circumambulations (*Tawāf*), but he refused to do it without the Prophet. There was, however, delay of a few days in his return to *Hudaybiyah* and rumour spread that he had been done to death by *Quraysh*. This created an explosive situation in *Hudaybiyah* and declaration of war seemed imminent. The Prophet is said to have fallen in a trance, similar to that of receiving revelation, after hearing the rumour. In that state, he summoned the Companions and asked them to swear a special pledge of allegiance to him which they did, one by one, under an acacia tree (the site now commemorated by a beautiful mosque called *Shumaisi*). The special pledge is known as *Bayat al Ridwān* (the Pledge of Good Pleasure—meaning God's final and absolute acceptance of a soul). The incident is referred to in verse 48/18 of the *Qurān* as under: '*Allāh's Good Pleasure was on the believers when they swore fealty to you under the tree. He knew what was in their heart and He sent down Peace of Tranquility (Sakīnah i.e. the Spirit of Peace) to them, and He rewarded them with a speedy victory.*' It is generally believed that this was a pledge by the Muslims to fight *Quraysh* unto death in revenge for *Uthmān's* murder; the Prophet himself called it 'the Pledge of *Uthmān*'. But, hinting at some inner meaning of the fealty, some classical historians suggested that the Companions vowed to follow what was in the Prophet's soul, that is, to obey him wholeheartedly during the crisis. It has also sometimes been suggested that the Prophet had intuition that he was going to enter into a peace agreement with *Quraysh*, the provisions of which were likely to shock the Muslims, and hence the need for the special pledge.

However, even before taking of the Pledge was complete, *Uthmān* appeared at the scene followed by *Suhayl ibn Amr* along with two others (*Mikrāz* and *Huwaytib*) who had arrived to negotiate an agreement. The negotiations were marked by hot arguments, insolence, and arrogance on part of *Suhayl* who obstinately stuck to his stands on different issues, absolutely determined not to allow pilgrimage that year. The Prophet, however, ultimately agreed even to his undue demands showing leniency to the point of weakness. When the agreement was being reduced to writing by *Ali, Suhayl* did not even allow the full formula of '*Bilmillāh*' to be written, saying that he did not know *Ar Rahmān* and *Ar Rahīm* and so, instead of that, only *Bismika Allāhumma* be written thereon. Similarly, he objected to the writing of 'Apostle of God' with the name of *Muhammad* and insisted that '*Muhammad ibn Abd Allāh*' be written. This was too much for *Alī* to tolerate and when the Prophet asked him to rub his epithet off, he refused. Thereupon, the Prophet is said to have himself wiped it out (*Bukhāri* and *Muslim*), a tradition which was made use of by Western historians to claim that the Prophet was not illiterate. It appears, they don't realize that merely reading and writing one's own name does not amount to literacy. However, the terms of agreement, known as the Treaty of *Hudaybiyah*, were finalized and the document was signed by both the parties. The Treaty had four main provisions.

1. The Muslims were not to perform pilgrimage that year but were allowed to do so the following year for three days during which period *Quraysh* would vacate the city in order to facilitate performance of rites of *Umrah* in peace. But they were not to carry arms except swords.

2. There would be a truce for ten years between the two parties including their allies and this truce would grant transit security to individuals of each party in the other party's territory. There was also to be neutrality in the event of war with a third party.

3. Any member of *Quraysh*, in case he became a Muslim and made *Hijrah* without consent of his guardian, would be returned to *Makkah*, but the *Quraysh* would not extradite any Muslim who defected.

4. The Bedouin tribes were to be released from their former obligations and were to choose to enter into alliance with either party, but once entry into alliance was there, terms of the treaty would immediately apply to such clan or tribe.

On the face of it, the terms of the treaty were not only unfavourable but also quite dishonourable to the Muslims, who perceived them as a sort of defeat or surrender. Withdrawal without performing pilgrimage after reaching so close was an utterly humiliating proposition. Further, the truce meant that the Muslims could no longer raid Makkan caravans on which their economy depended. It also amounted to cancellation of the economic blockade of Makkan trade which was their main instrument for putting pressure on *Quraysh*. Moreover, the provision relating to unilateral extradition seemed to accord an inferior status to the Muslims. And, especially infuriating was the actual wording used in the document which rejected the formula of *Bismillāh* and the title of the Prophet. The Companions were, therefore, highly depressed and dissatisfied, though not in a rebellious mood as suggested by some Western scholars.

To make the matter worse, even before the treaty was signed, the episode of *Abū Jandal* took place which left the Muslims seething with anger. *Abū Jandal* was one of the younger sons of *Suhayl* and had embraced *Islām*. His elder brother *Abd Allāh* was already a Muslim and was among the pilgrims. But *Abū Jandal* had been kept under imprisonment by his father at *Makkah*. Coincidentally, exactly at the time of signing of the treaty, he managed to appear before the Prophet after effecting his escape, with fetters still on his body. He begged for protection of the Prophet, but *Suhayl* strongly demanded his custody in accordance with terms of the agreement. The Prophet's repeated appeals to *Suhayl* going in vain, he had to finally give way in order to save the peace. *Abū Jandal*, who was already having black and blue marks of torture on his body, was again beaten up in the presence of 1,400 Muslims and forcibly taken away. The incident was too much for some of the Companions to bear with and *Umar* tended to insolently argue with the Prophet on the issue.[1] He, however, calmed down when the Prophet explained that whatever he had done was in accordance with the will of *Allāh* who would definitely provide a way for relief of *Abū Jandal*. *Umar* still went to *Abū Bakr* and complained to him, but his misgivings were totally removed by the latter's reply, which was the same as that of the Prophet. For his insolent words spoken to the Prophet on the occasion, he was to be sorry throughout his life. It was under this tense situation that the Prophet asked his Companions to perform the rites of *Umrah* at *Hudaybiyah* itself. But, they did not immediately respond to his call which smacked of disobedience (*Bukhāri*). On the wise advice of his wife, *Umm Salamah*, however, the Prophet alone performed the rites, and the Companions soon followed his example, slaughtered animals, and had their heads tonsured. The bunch of their hair was carried towards the *Kābah* by a breeze in a symbolic gesture of God.

Contrary to the initial impression of the Muslims, however, *Surah 'Al Fath'* (48), revealed on the way back to *Madinah*, declared that the Treaty of *Hudaybiyah* was a clear victory of the

---

1 *The actual dialogue between Umar and the Prophet, as quoted by Shibli Numani in his 'Sirat Un Nabi', is as under:*
   'O Messenger of Allāh, are you not the true bearer of God's Message?' asked Umar.
   'Verily, I am,' replied the Prophet.
   'Are we not on the right?' Again asked Umar.
   'Yes, we are,' was the Prophet's reply.
   'Why should we then bear all this insult for our religion?' Umar protested.
   'I am the Messenger of Allāh,' said the Prophet,
   'and can't go against His Will. Allāh will help me.'
   'Had you not said,' Umar asked, 'that we shall perform an ambulation round the Kābah?'
   'But,' answered the Prophet, 'I had not said we shall do it this very year.'

Muslims. Verse 1 and 2 of the *Surah* read: '*Lo! We have given thee a signal victory, that Allah may forgive thee for thy sin that which is past and that which is to come, and may perfect His favour unto thee, and may guide thee on a right path.*' This short *Surah* of 29 verses explained the deeper meaning of the truce. Whereas *Badr* was victory of just over unjust in a war (*Furqān*), *Hudaybiyah* marked the triumph of believers over unbelievers by the Spirit of Peace (*Sakīnah*), signifying Jihad as a struggle for peace. Subsequent developments well proved truthfulness of the Quranic claim; both from the viewpoints of expansion of *Islām* and consolidation of its political power, the Treaty turned out to be a grand victory. '*And there was never a victory greater than this victory,*' aptly said *Ibn Khaldūm*. Indeed, it was an act of great political wisdom of the Prophet. A truce with a powerful enemy opened the door to peace and provided the *Ummah* an opportunity to take on other enemies. If the aim was to neutralize *Makkah* in the event of a military action against *Khaybar*, the same had been achieved; *Khaybar* now stood insulated from its powerful ally and was very soon to be subjugated. Not less importantly, the treaty was an acknowledgement that the *Ummah* now represented a power of equal status rather than a runaway group. Equality of status was also apparent in the clause allowing the nomadic tribes to abandon all alliances and join either of the parties. The tribe of *Khuzaah*, with which the Prophet had matrimonial relation, took advantage of the provision and immediately joined the *Ummah*. Further, Makkah's acceptance of the right of the Muslims to visit the Sanctuary the next year for *Umrah* amounted to recognition of *Islām* as an established religion. Adoption of the traditional Arabic custom of pilgrimage of the Sanctuary by *Islām* was to make it more acceptable to the tribes. The apparent advantage gained by *Quraysh* due to lifting of the economic blockade also suited the Prophet's plans of winning them over and paving the way for their integration into the Islamic system.

The provision regarding unilateral extradition, too, did not have much significance. As explained by the Prophet himself, an apostate from *Islām* was of no use and a new convert to *Islām*, forced to stay in *Makkah*, would gain religious merit from persecution. In due course, this provision went against Makkah's interest itself when a runaway convert, *Abū Basīr*, who was denied entry into the *Ummah* as per terms of the agreement, organized his own force on the Red Sea coast with seventy odd runaway Muslim converts from *Makkah* including *Abū Jandal* and posed a serious threat to the passing Makkan trade caravans. Soon the Makkans approached the Prophet for amendment of the provision in order to allow Makkan converts to make *Hijrah* to *Madinah*, which was done. Thereupon, *Abū Basir*'s band was allowed to join the *Ummah* at *Madinah*, but before that, *Abū Basīr* expired. Last but not the least, the Treaty accounted for unprecedented expansion of *Islām*. The long-drawn war between *Quraysh* and the *Ummah* had, so far, prevented interaction between *Islām* and the nomadic tribes. Now the truce encouraged social interaction as well as free joining of *Ummah*'s alliance by Bedouin tribes; the pagans were in a position to appreciate virtues of *Islām* which led to change of hearts of many. Consequently, within a year or so, the number of Muslims more than doubled; the great *Quraysh* generals *Khālid ibn al Walīd* and *Amr ibn al Ās* also entered the fold of *Islām* not long after *Hudaybiyah*. *Ibn Hishām* points out that the Prophet had gone to *Hudaybiah* with only 1,400 men; just after two years, when he marched to conquer *Makkah*, he had a force of 10,000.

Although the truce of *Hudaybiyah* had saved *Madinah* from attacks from the south, serious threat was still apprehended from the north. This was mainly from the oasis of *Khaybar* (about 184 kilometres north-east of *Madinah*) which was the stronghold of Jewish tribes in Arabia, a veritable hornet's nest of the *Ummah*'s enemies. Reinforced by Jews of *Bani Nadīr* and *Qaynuqah* after their expulsion from *Madinah*, they were implacable enemy of *Islām*, both religiously as well as politically, and were determined to wipe it out. Though their alliance with *Quraysh* had been done away with by *Hudaybiyah*, they still had understanding of mutual assistance with *Ghatafān*. Interpreting the treaty of *Hudaybiyah* as weakness of the *Ummah*, they started actively instigating *Ghatafān* and other smaller tribes of the north to unite against the menace of *Islām* and carry out raids against *Madinah*. In order to get the Prophet eliminated, they are said to have even heavily bribed the expert Jewish sorcerer, *Labīd* of *Madinah*, to kill him by a deadly spell which he did, the Prophet falling sick as a consequence. The spell could be got rid of only with the guidance of Gabriel.[1] The incident strengthened the determination of the Prophet to take action against *Khaybar* from which military aggression was also apprehended. According to his assessment, a combined attack on *Madinah* by *Khaybar*, *Ghatafān*, and some other northern tribes was now imminent, and the probability of a few Arab 'client states' from the extreme north joining hands with them with involvement of even the Roman Empire could not be ruled out. It was at *Khaybar*'s instigation that a group of *Ghatafān* raided the Muslim pasture-land at *Dhi Qarad* (in the vicinity of *Madinah*), killed *Abū Dharr*'s son who kept watch over the herd, and took away twenty camels and his wife. *Tabari* says that this incident took place just a few days before the Battle of *Khaybar*, serving as casus belli.

There was hardly any point in making a pact with the Jewish tribes of *Khaybar* as had been done with *Quraysh*. The three tribes of *Madinah* had earlier entered into a Covenant with the *Ummah* but had broken it at convenient moments. Therefore, the only remedy lay in fighting them and forcing them to subjugation, though their extermination was not the aim. It has sometimes been suggested that by undertaking expedition against *Khaybar*, the Prophet aimed at deflecting frustration of the Muslims which had resulted from the Treaty of *Hudaybiyah*. It might

---

1   *It is said that for casting the spell, Labīd procured a hair of the Prophet through his daughter and tied 11 knots in it after which it was thrown in a deep well. It was possible to undo the spell by untying the knots only. As a result of this spell, the Prophet suffered from weakness and loss of appetite, feeling that something wrong was there. For his rescue, Gabriel came and advised that the remedy lay in recitation of Surahs 113 and 114 over the well. These two Surahs had been revealed during the early Makkan period and Gabriel guided him in respect of their great effect. The two Surahs combined had 11 verses, each verse was to untie one knot. Ali was sent to recite the Surahs over the well which he did and the Prophet soon recovered from his sickness.*

have been an attempt to reward them with rich booty and also to satisfy their urge for action which had been left unfulfilled at *Hudaybiyah*. But such a view is based on conjectures only; the battle of *Khaybar* was a compelling political step in defense. Interpreting that the 'near victory' with rich spoils promised in the recently revealed *Surah Al Fath* was nothing other than conquest of *Khaybar*, the Prophet was convinced of success. Therefore, not long after return from *Hudaybiyah* (April 628), he marched from *Madinah* to invade *Khaybar* with a force of 1,600 men including a cavalry of 200 horses. However, in accordance with a Quranic injunction (Q 6/15), those whose sole motive was booty and who had failed to respond to his summons to participate in the *Umrah* were not allowed this time. The Prophet's wife, *Umm Salamah*, accompanied; a few other ladies, including *Safiyyah*, *Umm Ayman*, *Nusaybah*, and *Umm Sulaym*, are also said to have joined out of their own volition for tending the wounded.

Khaibar was, however, an extremely difficult target. Both in terms of wealth and military strength, it was considered the strongest regional power. Located in well-watered volcanic tract and having highly fertile land, it produced a rich harvest of dates and grains. Highly skilled in metallurgy, its inhabitants were expert in manufacturing arms; their moon-curved swords, sun-catching helmets, and fine bronze armours were considered the best in the desert. They had all the sophisticated war equipment for the age including catapults for hurling stone-missiles and their warriors were well trained as well as experienced. If *Yaqūbi* is to be believed, they had a fighting strength of 20,000. Other sources, however, estimate it as 10,000 whereas their ally, *Ghatafān*, was to provide an additional 4000. The oasis had as many as eight strong fortresses, important of them being *Naīm*, *Nitat*, *Watih*, *Qamūs*, and *Sulalim*. *Qamūs*, built on a steep rock, was the strongest and best fortified; with strong walls built out of rocks, it was considered almost impregnable. It was held by the famous Hebrew warrior, *Marhab*, whose physical strength was proverbial; *Yaqūbi* refers to a tradition claiming it to be equal to a thousand horses. A clan of *Banī Nadīr* headed by *Kinānah* was also settled in this fort. In view of the great strength of *Khaybar*, the decision of the Prophet to invade it with a strength of 1,600 only was considered foolhardy by those hostile to *Islām*, and they were jubilant anticipating a crushing defeat of the *Ummah*. The *Quraysh* are said to have even made bets on the issue.

The morale of the Muslims was, however, quite high as usual. During the march of the army, the poet *Āmir ibn Akwa* was singing inspiring war songs, presenting *Khaybar* as the aggressor. The Khaybarians contacted *Ghatafān* for help and the latter headed with a large army towards *Khaybar* in its support. But the Prophet strategically camped for a few days at *Ar Rajī*, midway between the *Ghatafān* territory and *Khaybar*, so as to create an apprehension that the Muslim army might move to attack *Ghatafān*. Sensing danger, *Ghatafān* are reported to have gone back. According to some sources, they heard a mysterious voice summoning them back to their home while others suggest that they had been bribed by the Muslims. The Muslim army proceeded and reached in front of *Khaybar* before nightfall, but in accordance with the Prophet's principle of not making a night attack, it halted there. The Jews hurriedly held consultations, but theirs was a divided house, and so their clans and tribes decided to fight in separate groups from their own citadels. While they placed their women and children and also their wealth in the forts of *Wati* and *Sulalim*, the provisions were stored in the fort of *Naīm*. There was maximum concentration of the fighting force in the forts of *Qamūs* and *Nitat*. The lack of unity of the Jews, which helped the Muslims and reduced disparity of numbers, has been referred to in the *Qurān*: '*Ill-feeling is rife among them. Thou contest them as a whole, but their hearts are divided.*' (*Surah Al Hashr*—verse 14). Siege of eight separate forts for a long period, however, put steadfastness of the Muslims to a difficult trial.

The siege of *Khaybar* lasted for about a month during which the Muslims showed superior strategic wisdom. For about six days, nothing could be done, but then a spy was caught who gave valuable information about different fortresses. Thereafter, based on intelligence, the fortresses were systematically attacked, one after the other, forcing each to surrender. The exact sequence of events is not clear as the accounts of classical historians differ.

However, it appears that the first fort to be reduced to submission was *Nitat* resulting in killing of the chief, *Salām ibn Mishkam*. It was there that a whole lot of weapons including some 'engines of war' (catapults) fell into the hands of the Muslims which were used in other assaults. Next, attack on the fortress of *Naīm* was brilliantly launched by *Muhammad ibn Maslamah*; the chief *Harīth* was killed and the fort was captured. The stronghold to make the most powerful resistance was *Qamūs* which was the seat of the Jewish champion warrior, *Marhab*, who had never been defeated. Initial attack on this fort was commanded by the Prophet in person. By using palm-trunk battering rams, the Muslims eventually made a small breach in the wall. But for several days, attempt to enter through it was vigorously repelled, even though command was given by the Prophet to *Abū Bakr* and *Umar* by turn. According to *Tabarī*, *Umar* complained of cowardice on part of men whereas the soldiers charged him with lack of courage. At last, the Prophet decided to give command to *Alī*. He is said to have remarked, '*Tomorrow I will give the flag to a man who loves Allāh and his Apostle. Allāh will conquer it by his means. He is no run-away.*' The next morning, he handed over the black standard of *Islām*, called 'The Eagle', to him. *Alī* launched a brilliant attack and killed *Marhab*, splitting his head into two by a single strike of his sword, which was popularly known as *Dhul Fiqār*. After the fall of *Marhab*, the Jews retreated into the citadel and a general assault took place. We get a dramatic presentation of the great physical power and military feat of *Alī* while reducing the fort to submission. During a fierce fight after the assault, *Alī* is said to have lost his shield; in haste, he pulled off a heavy door from its hinges and used it as a shield, holding it in his left hand. *Abū Rāfī*, a Muslim fighter who witnessed the scene, remarked that after the battle was over, he along with seven others could not wield it.[1] *Qamūs* is said to have fallen to the Muslims after a siege of 14 days. As per account of *Ibn Sād*, fight at *Qamūs* left 93 Jews killed against fifteen Muslims. Shortly afterwards, the two remaining forts of *Wati* and *Sulalim* also surrendered.

---

1 *Ibn Ishāq, however, credits Maslamah with the slaughter of Marhab.*

Different fortresses fell to the Muslims at different points of time. As and when they capitulated, booty was captured, surrenderees were made captives, and peace agreement finalized separately in respect of each of them. The general principles of agreement, as enumerated by *Balādhurī* (in his *Futūh*), however, was the same in each case; their lives were spared provided they surrendered their possessions, movable and immovable, without hiding anything and also exiled themselves with their women and children. *Kinānah*, who was caught at *Qamūs*, is reported to have been killed for concealing information regarding the hidden treasure of *Bani Nadīr* in violation of agreement, though the treasure had been discovered. But the veracity of this story was doubted by some sources who said that he was put to death for killing *Maslamah*. However, after occupation of entire *Khaybar* was complete, the Jews requested the Prophet to allow them to retain their houses and land in lieu of an annual payment of 50 per cent of their agricultural produce. The Prophet knew that the Muslims were not skilled in farming and, therefore, in order to save the oasis from becoming a desert, he acceded to the request. But he reserved the right to banish them in the future, if the situation so required. In lieu of payment of the annual tax, the Muslims were to provide protection to *Khaybar*. Thus, the Jews of *Khaybar* henceforth became tenants of the *Ummah* until their expulsion from Arabia during the Caliphate of *Umar. Abd Allāh ibn Rawāha* was appointed collector of the tax and he used to do it every harvest time with exemplary justice and fair play. *Khaybar* represented the first example of the *Ummah*'s occupation of a non-Muslim territory and, therefore, set the general pattern for settlement of non-Muslim areas in the Islamic State in the future. Overawed by the Khaybarian victory of *Islām*, most of the other Jewish settlements of the north like those of *Fadak, Wādi al Qura*, and *Tayma*, in order to forestall Muslim attack, surrendered on similar terms, political power of the Jews in Arabia now coming to an end. *Khaybar* set the example of post-defeat treatment of the conquered people also. There was neither destruction of property nor killing or persecution of the Jews; once the agreement was reached, complete civil liberty as well religious freedom was extended. The copies of *Torah* that were seized by the Muslims during the fight were also returned without any desecration. This conduct was quite in contrast to the manner in which the Romans had treated the Jews when they had conquered Jerusalem in the pre-Islamic period; they had burnt the sacred writings found in the temples and trampled them under their feet. The Prophet was magnanimous enough to even forgive *Zaynab* (daughter of *Harīth* and widowed wife of *Mishkam*) who had attempted to kill him by offering poisoned mutton, though one of the Companions lost his life after consuming the same.[1]

The battle of *Khaybar* produced all the desired consequences for which the Muslims had fought it. The disturbing threat from the Jews of *Khaybar* was left neutralized forever; northern flank of the Muslim State was now as secure as the south had become by the Treaty of *Hudaybiyah*. Further, in addition to payment of annual tax as agreed upon, the booty captured—huge quantities of gold and silver, finest arms and armours and vast herds of horses, camels and cattle, and so on—was so voluminous that financial difficulties of the *Ummah* were over and they suddenly became rich. *Bukhāri* quotes *Umar* as saying, '*We were hungry all the times until the conquest of Khaybar.*' *Āishah* is also said to have remarked, '*It was not until the conquest of Khaybar that I could eat dates to my heart's content.*' It was during the battle of *Khaybar* that *Jāfar ibn Abū Tālib* (the Prophet's first cousin) returned from Abyssinia along with *Umm Habībah* and all other Muslims who had been left behind. It is reported that when he did not find the Prophet at *Madinah*, he reached *Khaybar*, arriving there the day when the last fort surrendered. The Prophet was very fond of him, and on seeing him after fifteen years, there was no limit to his joy.

---

1   *In order to kill the Prophet, the Jewess had prepared poisoned meat of which he tasted only a morsel without swallowing it. He then warned his comrades that it was poisoned. One of his men who had already swallowed a mouthful, died immediately. The woman was brought before the Prophet for judgment. She said that she had done it on account of humiliation of her people whereupon she was forgiven (Bukhāri).*

He is said to have then remarked, '*I do not know what makes me more happy; the conquest of Khaybar or the return of Jāfar?*'

At *Khaybar*, the Prophet happened to choose a young Jewess as his next wife. This was *Safiyyah*, daughter of the deceased *Nadīr* chief *Huyayy b. Akhtab* and now widow of another *Nadīr* chief, *Kinānah*, whom she had married just a couple of months back. According to traditional accounts, she was a lady of great beauty, only 17 years old. She had been made a captive after capture of *Qamūs* and had been earmarked for allotment to a Companion named *Dehyah* of *Kalb*. She was, however, a pious lady who had respect for the Prophet and inclination towards *Islām*. It is said that a few days before attack on *Qamūs*, she had a dream in which she saw a brilliant moon in the sky above *Madinah*; the moon began to move towards *Khaybar* and then fell into her lap. The dream apparently implied that she had a desire to be associated with the Prophet. So, when her husband came to know about her dream, he was angry and gave a blow on her face. When she was brought before the Prophet, mark of the blow was still visible on her face. Hearing of her dream, the Prophet developed some sympathy for her. Moreover, she was a lady of a high family connection, and therefore, her custody as a slave to an ordinary Companion would have been socially anomalous. And more importantly, his own marriage with the Jewess well suited his usual diplomatic policy of entering into matrimonial alliance in order to cement relations with and win over the enemy. He, therefore, set her free leaving the choice on her either to remain a Jewess and join back her people or enter *Islām* and get married to him. She preferred the second alternative and the wedding took place at the first halt during return journey.

Umm Habībah and *Safiyyah* thus entered the Prophet's household roughly about the same time. The former was a well-known lady and all his wives except *Āishah* knew her; as a result, there was no curiosity or alarm among the Prophet's wives about her arrival. But the reputed beauty and young age of *Safiyyah* created misgivings and jealousy among his younger wives, especially *Āishah* and *Hafsah*. She was initially lodged in the house of *Harīthā*, and *Āishah* is said to have gone there concealing her presence in order to personally ascertain her beauty, but the Prophet recognized her. Since *Safiyyah* was a Jewess and daughter of a person who had been a vehement enemy of *Islām*, she used to be made a subject of taunt by *Āishah* and *Hafsah*. But the Prophet always supported her and made her comfortable. Despite initial jealousy of other wives, however, she, being nearer in age to *Āishah* (then 16) and even *Hafsah*, soon joined their group and became pally. By this time, despite Āishah's strong feelings of possessiveness about the Prophet and jealousy of other wives including the deceased *Khadījah* (the Prophet always used to remember her with great respect and fondness to the chagrin of *Āishah*), the Companions knew that she was the wife whom the Prophet loved the most. It was also known that he used to be in the happiest mood when sharing company with her; and so, whenever a person wanted a favour from the Prophet, he used to approach him when he was in Āishah's apartment. She was also conscious of her superior position because she was his only virgin wife. Her special position in the household is well reflected in a *hadīth* quoted by *Bukhāri*: '*Trouble me not with regard to Āishah, for verily the Revelation cometh not unto me when I am beneath the coverlet of a wife except that wife be Āishah.*'

It was during the year 628 that the Prophet dispatched especially chosen envoys along with letters to foreign potentates within and without the peninsula, including the Byzantine and Persian emperors as also kings of Egypt and Ethiopia, inviting them to *Islām*. Information regarding sending of Islamic missions to foreign lands, though based on traditions and referred to by later historians, does not find mention in the *Sirah* of *Ibn Ishāq* and other earliest sources. Due to this reason, some of the Western historians doubt its veracity as, according to their interpretation, the Prophet did not envisage *Islām* as a universal religion; it was simply a religion for the Arabs. We, however, do have some evidence to confirm that dispatch of such embassies represented a historical evolution of the Prophet's religious mission. During the early Madinan phase, a few revelations had emphasized the all-Arab character of the Islamic mission (Q 13/37, 12/2 and 42/7). Subsequently, however, there were revelations that enjoined preaching of the message to entire humanity irrespective of nationality or state. Verse 25/1 said, *'Blessed be He who has revealed the criterion (the Qurān) to His servant that he may warn the nations.'* The last part of the verse has also been translated as *'warner unto all created beings'* and *'all peoples'*, implying a universal or global nature of the mission. Similarly, verse 21/107 read: *'We have not sent thee save as a mercy to all the created beings.'* Moreover, according to traditions, the Prophet had had some spiritual indications regarding spread of *Islām* outside Arabia. While splitting the apparently unbreakable rock during digging of the trench, in the three lightnings resulting from three blows of axe, he had had vision of the castles of the kings of Yaman, Syria, and Iran; this implied spread of *Islām* to these countries. Preaching of the message of *Islām* to countries outside Arabia had, thus, become religiously desirable, if not an integral part of his mission. However, though aware of this aspect of his responsibility, he was totally preoccupied in defense of the *Ummah* from *Quraysh* and had no leisure for sending missions to foreign lands. But neutralization of *Makkah* following the Treaty of *Hudaybiah* provided him opportunity to deliver the message of *Islām* beyond Arabia.

Though exact chronology of sending of these embassies is not known, some of them appear to have been sent before the Battle of *Khaybar* and a few afterwards. In order to authenticate credentials of the envoys, a seal of silver was made with the name of the Prophet inscribed as *'Muhammad, the Messenger of Allāh.'* From different sources, we get names of as many as eight rulers to whom such diplomatic letters were sent:

1. Heraclius, the Roman Emperor of Byzantium.
2. Chosroes II (*Khusro Parwez*), the Sassanian Emperor of Iran.
3. King *Aziz Potiphar* (known as the *Muqawqis*) of Egypt.
4. The *Negus*, king of Ethiopia.
5. *Mundhīr ibn Sāwā*, king of Bahrain.
6. *Al Julanda*, the ruler of Oman.
7. *Haudha ibn Alī*, chief of *Yamāmah*.
8. *Hārith Ghassāni*, the Byzantine governor of Syria.

The content of all the letters was almost the same, that is, an invitation to accept *Islām* or else responsibility to God for keeping the people in error. The letter addressed to the Roman Emperor read: '*In the name of God, Most Compassionate and Merciful. From Muhammad, the bondsman of Allāh and His Messenger, addressed to Hiraclius, the Emperor. Peace to him who follows the guidance. After that I call thee to embrace Islām, which done, thou shalt be safe and be doubly rewarded by God. But if thou heedest not then thou shalt have on thee the sins of thy subjects. O' followers of the Book, come to a doctrine commonly held by you and us, that we worship not any but Allāh, that none of us take others as our Lords; but if you turn back, then bear witness that we believe.*'[1]

The kings who received the letters reacted differently to the Prophet's invitation. The *Negus* of Ethiopia and the ruler of Bharain responded positively and embraced *Islām*. The former is said to have solemnized his conversion at the hands of *Jāfar* who was then present there. *Ibn Ishāq* says that he sent his son along with sixty attendants carrying gifts to pay respect to the Prophet; but the ship carrying the group sank before reaching the shores of Arabia. The Roman Emperor, Heraclius, who was then at Jerusalem following his victory over the Persian Empire, received the Prophet's letter through his Syrian governor. In order to fully appreciate the message contained therein, he wanted to conduct a first-hand enquiry about the Prophet and his religion with the help of some person from Arabia itself. Coincidentally, *Abū Sufyān* was then present in Jerusalem and was produced before the Emperor. Details of dialogue between the Emperor

---

1 *The language of the letter addressed to the Emperor of Iran is reported to be as under:*
   'In the name of God, Most Compassionate and Merciful. From Muhammad, the Messenger of Allāh to Kisra (Chosroes), the Emperor of Iran. Peace to him who followeth the guidance, believeth in Allāh and His Messenger and beareth witness that there is one God and that He hath sent one as His Messenger to all the people of the world that every mortal living be taught to fear Allāh. Embrace Islām, thou shalt be saved, else thou shalt suffer for the sins of the Magis.'

and *Abū Sufyān* have been given by *Bukhāri*.[1] According to account referred to by him, after ascertaining facts, Heraclius was convinced of the truth of *Islām* and was inclined towards it, but could not embrace it due to opposition of his chiefs. The ruler of Syria, *Hārith Ghassāni*, however, was quite enraged to receive the letter and ordered mobilization of his army to attack *Madinah*. This was the beginning of a threat to *Islām* from Syria which subsequently led to the battles of *Mūtah* and *Tabūk*. There was yet a more peculiar reply from the ruler of *Yamāmah*, who wrote back, informing of his intentions to accept *Islām* provided he was given a share in the Prophet's government; this was, however, refused by the Prophet as he had no political ambition of this type.

The great Persian Emperor, after going through the Prophet's letter, found it highly insulting and in anger tore it into pieces. He sent orders to *Bādhān*, his governor of *Yaman*, to produce the Prophet in his court at *Madāin*. *Bādhān* sent two of his representatives to *Madinah* and conveyed the order of the Emperor. The Prophet, however, replied, '*Go and tell him that dominance of Islām shall extend to the capital of Kisra*' (*Tabarī*).

---

1 *After ascertaining facts about character of the Prophet and essence of his message, Heraclius said to Abū Sufyān:*
  '*You say he belongs to a noble family, and Prophets always come from noble families. You said that none from his family ever claimed to be a Prophet. Had it been so, I should have thought his claim to have been the outgrowth of family associations. You admit that none in his family has ever been a king. Had this been the case, I should have supposed him to be ambitious for power. You admit that he has never told lie, and one who does not tell a lie to his fellowmen cannot be expected to weave a lie about God. You said that his followers are weak, and the early followers of every Prophet have been poor people. You say that his religion is gaining ground, a true faith always does so. You admit that he has never deceived anyone, and Prophets never deceive. You say that he teaches prayer, piety and chaste living. If this is true, then his domain will extend to where my feet are placed. I did have a conviction that a Prophet must be born, but was not sure that he would be born in Arabia. I would have washed his feet if I could go there.*'

329

The previous night, he had received information from Gabriel that Chosroes had been killed and replaced as the emperor by his son *Shiravaih*; this spiritually obtained information he gave to Bādhān's messengers who were also asked to advice their ruler to embrace *Islām* and rule Yaman under his suzerainty. The messengers from Yaman went back to their capital at *Sana* and conveyed the Prophet's message as also information regarding murder of the Persian Emperor to *Bādhān*. But even before he could send a man to *Madāin* to find out the fact, a messenger arrived from there and confirmed the news foretold by the Prophet. The development was sufficient to lead *Bādhān* and the two messengers to enter *Islām* then and there and place his kingdom under suzerainty of the Prophet; one of the visions the Prophet had had at the time of digging the Trench came true. The letter of the Prophet addressed to the *Maqawqis*, the ruler of Egypt, was carried by *Hātib ibn Baltaa*. The envoy was well received and though the *Maqawqis* did not embrace *Islām*, he reciprocated invitation of the Prophet by sending a written reply along with gifts through *Hātib* himself. The gift included, apart from cloth, two beautiful slave girls, *Mariyah* and *Sīrīn*, and a white mule (which was named *Duldul* by the Prophet—a name frequently mentioned in traditions). The two girls were Coptic Christians, *Mariyah* being exceptionally beautiful and attractive. According to *Tabarī*, both were real sisters and had embraced *Islām* on way to *Madinah* due to preaching by *Hātib*. Marvelling at Mariyah's beauty, the Prophet married her (sometime in the middle of 628) while her sister was given in marriage to *Hasan b. Thābit*. The claim of some Western writers that she was the Prophet's concubine is firmly refuted by the Muslim historians who, on the basis of strong traditional information, confirm that she entered his household as a duly-wedded wife only and not as a bondmaid. She was lodged in the nearby house of *Harithā* where *Safiyyah* had initially been kept and the Prophet visited her frequently. This caused extreme jealousy among his other wives and was soon to lead to a serious problem in the household. Though the embassies sent to foreign kings met with only partial success, the message of *Islām* was received by all; *Islām* indirectly obtained religious as well as political recognition throughout the Middle East.

For about nine months following the battle of *Khaybar*, the Prophet stayed in *Madinah*. With *Khaybar* subjugated and truce with *Makkah* continuing, this was relatively a period of peace. During the period, about half a dozen minor expeditions were sent against hostile tribes like *Hawazin* in the south and *Ghatafan* in the east. Two of these were directed against *Bani Murrah* in the north who had been harassing the Jewish oasis of *Fadak*, now under protection of the *Ummah*. The first expedition which had a strength of thirty men only resulted in a disaster. Therefore, a second force of 200 strong was immediately sent; the enemy was put to flight with considerable loss of life and capture of captives as well as booty. It was in this expedition that the 17-year-old *Usāmah*, son of *Zayd*, made his debut as a fighter. On being teased for his young age, he chased one of the enemies and killed him even though he was willing to convert. The action of *Usāmah* was not approved of by the Prophet.

It was during this time (probably in the second half of 628) that the Prophet's household developed a crisis situation due to unreasonable demands of his wives. The continuous flow of booty from successful expeditions had considerably improved economic condition of the Muslims. The coming prosperity whetted the desire of his wives also who started demanding a larger share from the Prophet's part of the booty, which he used to spend on the poor. The Prophet had always preached the morally weakening effects of wealth and, therefore, it was not possible for him to meet the demands of his wives. Perhaps, picking up the spirit of independence from the *Madinan* women, they started arguing and squabbling with him on such issues. They were taking advantage of his great regard for women in general and his own wives in particular. When *Umar* learnt about their attitude, he snubbed them including his own daughter, *Hafsah*. Their dissatisfaction, however, was further heightened due to the extra attention which, they thought, the Prophet was now giving to his new wife, *Mariyah*. *Āishah* and *Hafsah* became extremely jealous, and though they knew that their husband was well within his rights, started subjecting *Mariyah* to severe criticism which made her unhappy. In order to avoid unpleasantness, the Prophet shifted *Mariyah* to a house farther away in upper *Madinah*, but this meant his longer absence from other wives and so exacerbated rather than helped the situation. Eventually out of annoyance, the Prophet decided to stop going to *Mariyah* whatsoever. This was, however, not approved of by God and verses 66/1 and 2 (*Surah At Tahrīm*) were revealed which enjoined him to keep on going to *Mariyah*:

1. '*O Prophet! Why in your desire to please your wives, do you impose a ban on what God has made lawful to you. God is Forgiving and Merciful.*'

2. '*God has already ordained you that you be absolved of such oaths. God is your patron. He is All knowing and Wise One.*'

The succeeding verses (66/4 and 5) directly addressed *Āishah* and *Hafsah* and warned them of the probability of divorce:

4. '*If only both of you would turn to God in repentance—and your hearts are already so inclined. But if you uphold each other against him, then surely God is his protector, and Gabriel and the righteous among the believers; and angels too are his helpers.*'

5. '*Were he to divorce you, his Lord might well replace you with better wives—submissive (to God), believing, pious, penitent, devout in worship, given to fasting—previously married and virgins.*'

After receiving the revelations, the Prophet withdrew to a roofed verandah, which was his exclusive space, and stopped going to all his wives. He used to go out to the mosque for prayers only after which again used to withdraw to his porch. This physical seclusion continued for about a month leading to extreme nervousness of his wives. A rumour spread that the Prophet was going to divorce all his wives and the Companions gathered around the house. *Umar* tried to meet him for reconciliation but could get appointment only after repeated requests. Though the

Prophet confirmed to him that he had not yet divorced his wives, he failed to break the ice. The situation could be saved only after revelation of verses 33/28 and 29 (*Surah Al Ahzāb*), popularly known as 'Verses of the Choice'. They ran as under: '*O Prophet! Say to your wives: If you seek the life of this world and all its finery then come, I will make provision for you, and release you honourably. But If you seek God and His Messenger and the abode of the hereafter, then know that God has prepared a great reward for those of you who do good deeds.*' When offered the choice as per command of God, the wives of the Prophet chose 'God and His Messenger' and the crisis was resolved.

In March 629, when one year elapsed after the Treaty of *Hudaybiyah*, the Prophet became eligible to perform *Umrah* as per its terms. It was now time to fulfill his vision of performing pilgrimage unopposed. He, therefore, left for *Makkah* along with about 2,000 unarmed Muslim pilgrims for performance of Lesser Pilgrimage. According to some sources, as a precautionary measure, an armed party of 200 horses was also taken along which was left a few miles behind *Makkah*. As per agreement, *Quraysh* evacuated the city withdrawing to the surrounding hills; the chiefs and important leaders concentrated on mount *Abū Qubays*. From top of the hills they watched in bewilderment the flood of Muslims entering the Sanctuary area uttering '*Labbayk Allahhumma Labbayk*' (Here I am, O God, at Thy Service). Thousands of Muslims, bareheaded and white-robed, making circuits of the *Kābah* and performing other related practices in their own style, made an impressive scene for *Quraysh*. The Muslims stayed in the enclosure of the Sanctuary for three days during which *Bilāl* used to climb on its top and give calls for prayers in his powerful voice; the scene might have been appalling to *Quraysh*. The Prophet during *Umrah* intended to enter the holy mosque but its keys were not handed over to him, the *Quraysh* leaders maintaining that it was not part of the agreement. During the stay of the Muslims, those of *Quraysh* who had secretly embraced *Islām* stealthily came down and happily met their emigrant friends and relatives. It was during *Umrah* that the Prophet's uncle *Abbās* publicly declared his conversion to *Islām* and offered to him his wife's sister, *Maymunah* (who was now a widow), in marriage which was accepted.[1] She was the aunt of the renowned *Quraysh* general, *Khālid ibn al Walīd*; the politically beneficial prospect of winning over the powerful *Makhzūm* clan through this marriage might have motivated the Prophet to accept the offer. The Prophet wanted to stay longer in *Makkah* in order to perform his wedding ceremony in which he intended to invite the *Quraysh* leaders. *Suhayl* and other Makkan chiefs, however, discourteously denied the request for extension of period of stay beyond three days. The Prophet, therefore, ordered the Companions to pack up and march which was done in an orderly manner. Marriage with *Maymunah* was solemnized during return journey at *Sarif*, a few miles from the Sanctuary.

Performance of the Lesser Pilgrimage amounted to a significant moral victory of the Prophet. An orderly performance of the traditional Arabian custom in an Islamic style impressed the Bedouins and became a subject of discussion throughout Arabia. Apart from softening their hearts towards *Islām*, it left *Quraysh* themselves quite impressed (as later confessed by them), who watched simplicity and dignity of the Islamic practice as also behavior of the Muslims with interest. Throughout their stay in *Makkah*, the Muslims had displayed discipline and orderliness which was rare in Arabia; there was neither provocation nor tampering with property left behind by *Quraysh*. No wonder, when the rites of *Umrah* were being performed, *Quraysh* felt that it would have incalculable repercussions and regretted having signed the agreement. The pilgrimage did add to popularity of *Islām*; and it had been made possible by the Treaty of *Hudaybiah*. Following the *Umrah*, more and more Bedouin tribes joined the Islamic confederacy and number of the Muslims started further swelling up. It was soon after return from *Makkah* that two of the illustrious warriors of *Quraysh*, *Khālid ibn al Walīd* and *Amr ibn al Ās* visited *Madinah* and entered *Islām*. Having been responsible for killing of a large number of Muslims, they feared vendetta.

---

1 *Maymunah was the twelfth and last wife of the Prophet. At this point of time, however, she became the tenth living wife of the Prophet.*

But the Prophet promised that entry to *Islām* wiped out all debts and represented an entirely new beginning. Conversion of these two great generals subsequently proved a source of tremendous strength to *Islām*. It was during the pilgrimage that *Alī* suggested that Hamzah's daughter *Umārah* should not be left amongst the idolaters. She was, therefore, taken along to *Madinah* in *Fatimah's* hawdah. But after reaching *Madinah*, *Ali*, *Zayd*, and *Jāfar* hotly argued for taking over her custody. Eventually, the Prophet intervened and her guardianship was given to *Jāfar*. However, soon after return, the Prophet's daughter *Zaynab* died, which was an occasion of great grief in the household. But then, the tragedy was somewhat compensated by the happy tiding that the Prophet's wife, *Mariyah*, was expecting a child. The Prophet had not had a child from any of his wives after *Khadījah*, and so it was a great experience of joy for the entire *Ummah*.

The next important event in the Prophet's history was the Battle of *Mūtah* (Sept 629) which was fought against the combined force of the Syrian governor of Byzantine Empire, different other north Arabian tribes settled along the Syrian borders and also Byzantine imperial army. Under Roman cultural influence, these frontier tribes had embraced Christianity and acted as vassals of the Byzantine Empire. They had adopted a stance of extreme hostility to *Islām* and had been violently reacting even to peaceful missionary and diplomatic activities of the Prophet. Earlier, on receiving the Prophet's letter of invitation to *Islām*, the Ghassanide governor of Syria had threatened to invade *Madinah* and even unsuccessfully tried to mobilize the Byzantine army for the purpose. About three months after *Umrah*, the Prophet sent a group of fifteen Muslims to preach *Islām* to one of the tribes on the Syrian border at *Dhat al Talh*, but all except one were killed. A lone messenger sent next to the governor of *Basrah* was also intercepted by a Ghassanide chief of *Balqā* region named *Surabhil* and was put to death in violation of the then prevailing international law. These provocations were serious enough to invite a reaction from the *Ummah*. More importantly, however, after neutralization of both *Makkah* and *Khaybar*, it was now from the extreme north that the Prophet had now been apprehending a serious threat. According to some sources, he had been receiving intelligence about designs of the frontier tribes to invade *Madīnah* with the help of the Byzantine army. It was, therefore, necessary to send some powerful expedition against them in order to keep them in check.

Though not confirmed by the sources, on the basis of historical analysis, some modern historians have suggested that *Mūtah* was part of a much bigger northern policy of the Prophet, which had religious as well as political motives. With prospects of Islamisation of the whole of Arabia getting crystallized, it was now a part of the Prophet's mission to preach *Islām* outside it. The territories of the frontier tribes standing like a gateway to the outer world, their association with the *Ummah*, with or without conversion, might have been a high-priority political target of the Prophet. Further, since Arabia was fast converting to *Islām*, it was necessary to explore new areas for conducting raids which was the main economic activity of the Bedouins. In order to satisfy their strong urge for fight, finding out new outlets for directing their energy outside Arabia was also a political necessity.

In order to act before it was too late, the Prophet, therefore, organized a big army of 3,000 men and dispatched it to the Syrian border under his personal supervision and briefing. Unexpectedly, however, this time command was given to his adopted son, *Zayd b. Harithah*. *Zayd* was an ex-slave and so working under his command was not liked by many high-born Companions, but the Prophet's decision was final. It, however, appears that he had some intuition regarding the highly hazardous nature of this expedition. Therefore, he made it clear that in case *Zayd* happened to be killed, *Jāfar* would take over command, and in case of the latter also getting martyred, *Abd Allāh ibn Rawāhah* was to assume command. The well-known general *Khālid* also accompanied the army. When the Muslims reached the Syrian border, they came to know that almost all frontier tribes had combined together against them and had also managed to rope in a large Byzantine imperial force which was lavishly equipped. The Emperor was himself present along with a big army in *Balqā* area. As the sources would have us believe, combined strength of the enemy force was about one lakh, alarmingly outnumbering the Muslim army. Realizing the gravity of the situation, *Zayd* held consultations and was in favour of informing the Prophet and waiting for further instructions. But *Abd Allāh ibn Rawāhah*, who was a passionate poet as well as an indomitable warrior, enthusiastically insisted on fighting, emphasizing that attaining martyrdom rather than victory was their ultimate aim.[1] Moved by his words, the Muslims decided to fight, but as the slope of the land was against them, they shifted southwards to a place called *Mūtah* (in modern Jordan) and obtained favourable ground for launching attack. *Zayd* with his comparably tiny force charged the enemy giving surprise, but was killed. *Jāfar* then took over command, fought recklessly, but also met with a heroic death. The next commander as appointed by the Prophet, *Abd Allāh ibn Rawāhah*, too, fell fighting. Though no further arrangement regarding command had been instructed by the Prophet, the experienced *Khālid* was next given command by the senior Companions. A military genius of rare ability and a master strategist, he immediately rearranged the Muslim army and put up a fierce fight breaking eight swords in his hand. The charge was so powerful that not only the enemy advance was checked, but as a knee-jerk reaction, they withdrew back enough to enable the Muslims to effect an orderly retreat. But while doing that, *Khālid* adopted a stratagem of deception by so arranging his men as to make the enemy believe that reinforcements had arrived; and thus, he managed a safe retreat which was in itself an achievement.

In the battle only about a dozen Muslims lost their lives. All the three martyred commanders fought like heroes, but courage and valour displayed by *Jāfar* while fighting was made a subject of extollation in the traditions. When his right hand was severed, he held the standard in the left, and when that was also cut off, he

---

1   *It is said that Rawahah had an intuition that he was going to achieve martyrdom. On way to the north, he was found reciting some self-composed verses expressing desire to be left behind in Syria, that is, achieve martyrdom (Wāqidī).*

is said to have caught hold of the flag with his teeth (*Ibn Kathīr*). He achieved martyrdom only after receiving ninety cut injuries, all frontal and none on the back (*Bukhārī*). It was in context of his reckless fight that, later on, the Prophet had a vision of Paradise in which he saw him flying with wings like those of angels, and thenceforth, he came to be known as *Jāfar Tayyar*. We learn from the traditions that when the Battle of *Mūtah* was being fought, space between *Mūtah* and *Madinah* had been miraculously folded for the Prophet, who was able to spiritually watch the entire sequence of events including death of the three commanders. The sources confirm that, much before *Khālid* returned, he had told the story about death of his three favourite Companions to his men in *Madinah*. He even visited the houses of *Zayd* and *Jāfar*, consoled their family members and wept and sobbed before the Muslim army arrived back. Though highly grieved by the result of the battle, he praised Khalid's performance and called him *Saifullāh* (sword of *Islām*). However, when the Muslim army under *Khālid* actually reached *Madinah*, the people called them runaways from the path of God and threw dust on them. But the Prophet said that they were not deserters and they would fight again (*Wāqidī*).

The spirit of *Islām* as shown in reckless fighting by the Muslims at *Mūtah* did impress the enemy. Nevertheless, it was a serious setback and prestige of the *Ummah* in the north had received a beating. Encouraged by their success at *Mūtah*, in the following months, the northern tribes of *Balī* and *Qudaah* reportedly started organizing a force on the Syrian border with intent to invade *Madinah*. The Prophet, therefore, sent *Amr ibn al Ās* (whose mother was a woman of *Balī* tribe) along with 300 men in order to check them. *Amr* was instructed to fight where necessary and win over allies where possible. After reaching the Syrian border, however, *Amr* came to know that the enemies were in greater numbers and requested for reinforcements. The Prophet immediately dispatched another group of 200 fighters under *Abū Ubaydah*. He was a senior Companion and a competent general, but in view of seriousness of the situation, he willingly worked under the command of the newly converted *Amr* which pleased the Prophet. However, as the Muslim army advanced, the enemy dispersed; there was no significant fighting except a brief exchange of arrows at a place. *Amr* was also able to establish alliances with a few friendly tribes. The expedition against *Balī* tribe (Oct 629) refurbished the image of the *Ummah* to some extent.

———————

CHAPTER XI

THE MISSION FULFILLED

The setback at *Mūtah* was perceived by *Quraysh* as weakness of the *Ummah*; thinking that it was no more invincible they tended to adopt a defiant attitude and did not even bother to abrogate terms of the Treaty of *Hudaybiyah*. This was to provide a good opportunity to the Prophet to take steps for Makkah's subjugation; and he made a brilliant use of it. Following the Treaty of *Hudaybiyah*, *Khuzaah* tribe had made an alliance with the *Ummah* while their old rival, *Banī Bakr*, had joined *Quraysh*. Towards the end of 629, a clan of *Banī Bakr* (*Banū al Dil*), aided and abetted by *Quraysh*, made a surprise raid against *Banū Kāb*, a clan of *Khuzaah*. *Tabarī* reports that *Quraysh* had provided weapons to the aggressors and some of their leaders including *Suhayl*, *Safwān,* and *Ikrimah* had even participated in the attack under cover of darkness. The men of *Khuzaah*, after loss of a few lives, took refuge in the sacred area of the Sanctuary in which violence was prohibited. But the attackers perpetrated violence even in that area, causing death of twenty odd people.

The incident amounted to a breach of the Treaty and the *Khuzaah* immediately sent a deputation (under *Amr ibn Sālim*) to the Prophet remonstrating and requesting for help. The Prophet was angry to listen to the story and promised action.

Apart from the fact that the incident provided him an excellent pretext for proceeding against *Quraysh*, breach of agreement was a serious offence necessitating punitive action. The Prophet hated bloodshed, but he hated even more aggression and treachery. Moreover, bloodshed in the sacred area was a crime which involved sanctity of the *Kābah*. He, therefore, sent a messenger to *Quraysh* and asked them either to pay blood money for those killed or break alliance with *Banī Bakr* or, as a third alternative, to abrogate the treaty of *Hudaybiyah* itself. We are told by *Zurqānī* that *Quraysh* conveyed acceptance of the third alternative which amounted to declaration of a state of hostility. However, the saner *Quraysh* leaders soon realized gravity of the consequences that might ensue out of this decision. As expected by the Prophet, they immediately dispatched their most diplomatic leader, *Abū Sufyān* to *Madinah* in order to persuade him to renew the treaty for ten years, but he was snubbed by the Prophet. So, in order to influence him, he went to his daughter, *Umm Habībah*, but she treated him badly and did not allow him to even sit on the Prophet's mat, saying that he was an unclean polytheist. He is said to have next approached *Abū Bakr, Umar, Fātimah*, and *Alī* requesting for intercession, but in vain. Failing to get the treaty renewed, *Abū Sufyān* went back to *Makkah* disappointed, but his peace initiative at this time, with realization that the *Ummah*'s conquest of Makkah was inevitable, did help him get better treatment from the Prophet in the long run. W. M. Watt suggests that during his visit to *Madinah*, he was persuaded by *Alī* and others for a peaceful surrender of *Makkah*, though classical sources do not mention this in clear terms due to their obvious bias against the *Ummayyads*.

After departure of *Abū Sufyān*, the Prophet did not lose time to ask his followers to get ready for an expedition. The allied tribes were also informed to prepare and join in. But he kept the destination a secret, leaving everyone guessing. Obviously, he wanted to take *Quraysh* by surprise, giving them no time to prepare for fight. It was his aim to avoid violence inside the Holy City which was a religious requirement. Moreover, by temperament and also due to Islamic obligations, he loathed bloodshed especially of those who were his own kith and kin. One of the Companions, *Hātib b. Abū Baltaah*, who happened to get some wind regarding the Prophet's plan to invade *Makkah*, secretly dispatched a letter to *Quraysh* through a woman warning them. But the Prophet came to know of it through Gabriel and the letter was intercepted. Though *Umar* wanted to behead him, the Prophet pardoned him as he had participated in the battle of *Badr* and his action was due to a genuine personal reason with no malafide.[1] The Muslim army left *Madinah* on tenth of *Ramadān* (January 630). Since *Sulaym*, *Muzaynah*, *Ghatafān*, and other tribes had also joined in, strength of the army was such that *Madinah* had never seen before. As the force moved towards south without knowing the destination, more and more nomadic tribes joined in, finally making the strength to about 10,000. Midway between *Madinah* and *Makkah*, the Prophet's uncle *Abbās*, who had left *Makkah* for good and was shifting with his family to join the *Ummah*, happened to meet the army. He reported to the Prophet and making out that the target was *Makkah*, pleaded for lenient treatment of *Quraysh*. Intending to use *Abbās* for conveying message regarding great power and strength of the Muslim army to *Quraysh* and persuading them to surrender without fight, he sent him back to *Makkah*. The Muslim army proceeded further and encamped at a junction called *al Zahrān* not very far from *Makkah*. The destination was still not known and there was confusion as roads branched off to *Tāif* in the south and *Najd* in the east as well from this point. This uncertainty about destination was to create another problem. The southern tribe of *Hawāzin* which had remained hostile to *Islām*

---

1 *Actually, unlike other emigrants, his family was in Makkah. He apprehended a general massacre of the Makkans by the Muslim army. Therefore, in order to save lives of his family members, he had intended to pass on information to Quraysh.*

apprehended that the Prophet was advancing against them. They, therefore, started assembling their own army at *Tāif*, the city of goddess *al Lāt*.

With a massive Muslim army camping close by, *Quraysh* became nervous and, after hurried consultations, sent *Abū Sufyān* along with *Hakīm* (Khadījah's nephew) and *Budayl* of *Khuzaah* to find out actual plan and intentions of the Prophet. While proceeding, they came across *Abbās* (he was riding *Duldul*, the Prophet's mule, for safety as well as unobstructed movement), who immediately took them to the Prophet for a dialogue. As a psychological stratagem, the Prophet had ordered each man in the camp to light a fire after dusk so as to give impression of an extraordinarily huge army camping. The sight extremely frightened *Abū Sufyān* who appeared before the Prophet along with *Abbās*; during talks, he could gather that the Prophet intended to attack *Makkah*. On invitation of the Prophet to *Islām*, *Hakīm* and *Budayl* at once read the *Kalimah*, but as reported by *Tabarī*, *Abū Sufyān* hesitated in reading the second part of it, that is, accepting *Muhammad* as a prophet. In the morning, however, when he watched the prayer, the ambiance left him highly impressed and he entered *Islām*. His profession of *Islām* at this stage might have been of convenience rather than conviction and opinions differ about it. However, in order to use his influence over *Quraysh* for ensuring occupation of *Makkah* without bloodshed, the Prophet announced that the Muslims will not inflict physical harm on a Makkan provided he took refuge in Abū Sufyan's house or in the Sanctuary or simply remained closed in his own house. This gave a sigh of relief to *Abū Sufyān* who was then advised to proceed to *Makkah* and announce the concession promised. It is suggested by some historians that these developments in which *Abū Sufyān* played a significant role were prearranged. He knew that the Prophet's conquest of *Makkah* was inevitable and, therefore, was working for a rapprochement for quite some time in order to safeguard his own position of leadership in *Makkah*.

The Muslim army marched forward to *Makkah* on Feb. 1, 630. *Ibn Hishām* confirms that before departure, care was taken to instruct the soldiers not to engage in fighting unless attacked and also not to lay hands on properties of *Quraysh*. In order to create further psychological impact on *Abū Sufyān*, the Prophet made it a point to ask *Abbās* to take him to a dominating place so that he watched the size and power of the Muslim army. The sight of an enormous flood of fighters, lavishly equipped with arms and armours, marching impressively in squadrons of different tribes, left *Abū Sufyān* utterly awestruck as he had never seen such a scene before. The last squadron was of the Prophet himself consisting of Emigrants and Helpers; the armours put on by them gave it a greenish-black colour. The standard was being carried by *Sād ibn Ubādah* who was shouting provocative slogans suggesting large-scale violence. This highly frightened *Abū Sufyān*, but the Prophet promptly declared that the day was one of mercy and forgiveness and not of fighting and bloodshed. In order to silence *Sād*, the flag was handed over to his son *Qays* on the Prophet's order. *Abū Sufyān* then rushed to *Makkah* and, at the top of his voice, warned the quickly gathered crowd of *Quraysh* of the great strength and determination of the Muslim army. He also advised that it would not be possible for them to resist the Prophet's army and suggested surrender without fight. The Prophet's offer of sparing their lives if they went indoors or to the Sanctuary or his own house was also explained. His wife, *Hind*, who was standing near him, became infuriated, caught him by moustaches, abused him, and asked the people to kill this 'miserable protector of a people'. But *Abū Sufyan* again and again repeated his warning whereupon, out of scare, the people went either to their houses or the Sanctuary.

Before entering the city, the Prophet segmented his army into four divisions—the right command under *Khālid*, the left under *Zubayr*, and the central segment further subdivided into two divisions, one under *Sād ibn Ubādah* and the other led by *Abū Ubaydah*. As directed, they entered the city from four directions and closed in at the centre. While making entry, the Prophet himself was on the back of *Qaswā* with *Usāma b. Zayd* seated with him. Noticing that there was no preparation by *Quraysh* for resistance, and his heart's desire to conquer *Makkah* without bloodshed was going to be fulfilled, he lowered his head, as if prostrating, in thanksgiving and recited *Surah al Fath*. The Makkans offered no resistance and the streets were empty with people remaining indoors. It was only to Khalid's regiment that some resistance was offered by *Ikrimah*, *Safwān*, and *Suhayl* who had gathered a force with the help of some allied tribes on *Abū Qubays*. They attacked the Muslims killing two of them whereupon *Khālid* charged them, putting them to flight and leaving a dozen or more Makkans dead. *Ikrimah* and *Safwān* escaped while *Suhayl* ran to his house and locked the door. The Prophet was quite angry to learn about this incident, but when the defensive nature of the reaction was explained, he treated it as having been ordained by God. *Makkah* had been conquered virtually without bloodshed.

Since it was the Prophet's decision not to enter any house, his red tent was pitched not far from the Mosque. *Umm Salamah*, *Maymūnah*, and *Fātimah* who had accompanied were waiting for him in the tent. His first act after reaching the tent was performance of ablution followed by prayer of eight cycles of *Namāz* in thanksgiving. Then after a brief rest, he mounted his camel, headed to the *Kābah*, and made seven rounds of it (touching the black stone in each round) along with the Companions uttering *Allāh-u-Akbar*, the whole city resounding with the magnification which symbolized victory of *Islām*. Thereafter, he along with the Companions pulled down and burnt all the 360 idols kept around the Shrine reciting verse 17/81: 'Say: *Truth has come and falsehood has disappeared. Falsehood is always bound to wither away*.' Next, after some prayer at the Station of Abraham, he went to the *Zamzam*, drank water from *Abbās*, and confirmed forever the traditional right of *Hashīm* to water the pilgrims. After that, taking keys of the Holy House from its keeper, *Uthmān b. Talhah*, he entered it along with a few others. The inner walls of the *Kābah* had paintings of pagan deities and different prophets and angels including Abraham, Jesus and Mary. He ordered all the pictures to be obliterated which was done. According to *Maqrīzī*, all paintings were rubbed off except that of Abraham while *Azraqī* narrates that the pictures of Jesus and Mary were left out, but these views are debatable. The Islamic purification of the *Kābah* was, thus, completed.

While the Prophet was removing the remnants of idolatry from the *Kābah*, crowd of the Makkans, which included those who had taken shelter in the Sanctuary and also many who had assembled there, was watching the scene. The Prophet made it a point to address them. After praising and thanking *Allāh*, he said, '*O people! Listen to me. All the arrogance, the distinctions, the pride and all the claims of blood of the times of ignorance are under my feet today. O Quraysh! Allāh has destroyed the arrogance of the times of ignorance and he has destroyed the pride of race. All men are children of Adam and Adam was a handful of dust.*' After advising them to shun hate, family-pride, blood-revenge, and other vices, he recited verse 49/13 of the *Qurān*, which condemned racism: '*Mankind! We have created you from a male and a female; and made you into peoples and tribes, so that you might come to know each other. The noblest of you in God's sight is the one who fears God most. God is all-knowing and all-aware.*' This verse is considered the magna carta of Islamic equality and brotherhood.

Remembering the past damages of the most heinous nature for which they had been responsible, *Quraysh* expected vengeance and were extremely scared. But they were left extremely amazed as well as relieved when, showing the highest degree of magnanimity, the Prophet announced a general amnesty for all Makkans in a highly dramatic manner. As recorded by *Ibn Qayyīm* (in his *Zad al Maād*), he asked them, '*What do you think of the treatment that I am about to accord to you?*' They replied, '*O noble brother and son of a noble brother! We expect nothing but goodness from you.*' Then reciting verse 12/92 in which *Yūsuf* had forgiven the misconduct of his brothers,[1] the Prophet remarked, '*Go your way for you are freed ones.*' But he remembered to order proclamation throughout the city that everyone who had an idol in his house should immediately destroy it. After finishing his speech, the Prophet withdrew to the hill of *Safā* (where he had first preached his family) to accept allegiance of those who were willing. Hundreds of men and women lined up and entered

---

1   '*No blame (shall fall) on you this day; may God forgive you! And He is the Most Merciful of those who show mercy.*'

Islām taking oath of fealty on the Prophet's hand. According to some sources, allegiance from females was taken by *Umar* on the Prophet's advice. It is reported that many hesitated to accept *Islām* and paid political homage only. Nobody was, however, forced to convert. But, impressed by the virtues of *Islām* and character of the Prophet and also as a result of missionary preaching by *Muādh b. Jabal*, who had been appointed for the purpose, the whole of *Makkah* was soon to enter *Islām* en masse. It is said that the crowd on *Safā* which entered *Islām* included *Hind, Umm Hakīm* (wife of *Ikrimah*), and the two surviving sons of *Abū Lahab*, in whose conversion the Prophet was interested.

It is, however, mentioned in the sources that the general pardon announced by the Prophet was not absolute and excluded ten of the Makkans who were inveterate enemies of *Islām*; they had been responsible for highly abominable crimes or dangerous propaganda against *Islām*. But the exact number of such proscribed individuals is debatable as the sources give differing versions; nor is there unanimity regarding identity of the condemned individuals who were ordered to be executed. But it is commonly understood that *Abd Allāh b. Khatāl* and his two slave girls, *Fartāna* and *Quraibah*, figured in the list. *Abd Allāh* had initially converted to *Islām*, but subsequently killed his clients, apostatized, and ordered his two singing slave girls to castigate the Prophet in songs. Another repulsive character included in the list was *Abd Allāh b. Saīd*, the foster brother of *Uthmān ibn Affān*. This character has become famous due to mention in Salman Rushdie's *The Satanic Verses*. He had entered *Islām* before *Hijrah* and used to note down revelations for the Prophet; but subsequently, suspecting genuiness of the Prophet, he reverted to polytheism, returned to *Quraysh*, and started spreading stories about falsification of revelations by him.[1] Others

---

1 *According to this unreliable story, once the Prophet recited part of a revelation as 'Alīmun Samīun' (Allāh is knowing and hearing). But in order to test the memory of Prophet, he slightly changed the text to 'Alīmun Hakīmun' (Allāh is knowing and wise). Since the Prophet failed to notice the alteration, Abd Allāh apostatized and started propaganda against him.*

of the blacklisted individuals, as claimed in different sources, were *Habbār* (who had attacked the Prophet's daughter, *Zaynab*, resulting in her abortion), *Wahshī* (who had killed *Hamzah*), *Miqyās b. Subāba*, and even *Ikrimah b. Abū Jahal*. Most of these proscribed persons either hid or ran away from *Makkah* in order to avoid punitive action. But, hearing the news of the Prophet's attitude of mercy and forgiveness, they returned and, through intercession of their relatives, were forgiven and allowed entry into the fold of *Islām*. Even *Wahshī*, who had fled, was later on pardoned, but the Prophet asked him not to show his face to him in the future. According to *Bukhāri*, of the ten or more such persons, only one, that is, *Abd Allāh b. Khatāl*, was executed whereas Shibli Numāni has doubted all the stories of execution.

In a number of ways, the conquest of *Makkah* was a great event and it is difficult to find a similar example in history. A revolution had been brought about virtually without bloodshed. The defeated Makkans were the worst enemies of the Prophet and *Islām*; for twenty years, they had subjected the *Ummah* to the highest degree of atrocities, ranging from wicked persecution to exile and even to repeated military attacks for extermination. Victory over the same people, in the same city, evoked painful reminiscences of crimes committed by them. They now lay totally at the mercy of the Prophet and expected the worst type of vengeance. But it was a perfect example of conquest by a Prophet rather than a king. Bearing no grudges, remembering no wrongs done and evincing no desire for revenge or wealth or power, he meted out a rare treatment of courtesy and kindness to his bitterest foes. '*The day of his greatest triumph over his enemies was also the day of his greatest victory over himself*' (Stanely Lane-Poole). No Makkan was physically harmed, no woman was molested, and no attempt was made to deprive anyone of his property. Even the houses of the Emigrants which were now under occupation of others were not taken back. There was neither curtailment of civil rights nor any coercion to convert. Reconciliation rather than retaliation was made the general policy. Even the keys of the *Kābah* were restored to the former keeper, *Uthmān ibn Talhah* (who had just the previous year, at the time of *Umrah*, refused to hand over the same to the Prophet), and he was made their custodian forever. The Prophet while doing this act of rare magnanimity only recited verse 4/58: *'Allāh commands you to restore trusts to their owners and if you decide between people, decide fairly.'*

The conquest of *Makkah* was a vindication of the Prophet's Islamic mission and amounted to fulfillment of the most important part of It; it was also a vindication of his policy of peace. His objective behind the expedition was not to punish *Quraysh* but to abolish idolatry, take control of the House of God, and purge it of all traces of polytheism; and the purpose had been achieved. The aim was also to bring about Islamisation of *Makkah* which was the strongest centre of paganism and tribal values. The process of assimilation of this bastion of the old order commenced immediately on conquest; soon the city was to enter *Islām* en masse and was to become a stronghold of the Islamic movement. The fall of *Makkah* also cleared the way for absorption of other nomadic tribes to *Islām*. The Prophet stayed in *Makkah* after its conquest for fifteen days during which he consolidated Islamic administration of the city and instructed people in *Islām*. Delegations were sent to preach the faith. *Khālid* was sent to *Nakhlah* to destroy the idol as well as temple of *al Uzzah* which he successfully did, sending shockwaves to *Thāqif* regarding fate of their goddess *al Lāt* at *Tāif*.[1] It is recorded in some of the sources that *Khālid* next proceeded to collect taxes from *Banī Jadhimah*, who had entered *Islām* but were not paying *Zakāt*. However, under some confusion or having no faith in *Khālid*, the men of *Jadhimah* took up arms at his approach and surrendered only after heated arguments. But *Khālid* killed some of them. The Prophet

---

1 *According to a story recorded by Wāqidī, when Khālid reported back to the Prophet after destroying the temple as well as idol of al Uzzah, the Prophet asked whether he had also destroyed embodiment of her evil spirit. Khalid replied that he had not seen anything of that nature there. The Prophet then ordered him to return and destroy her. Khālid went back to Nakhlah and there, out of the ruins of the temple, a highly scaring naked black woman came out with long and wildly flowing hair. Drawing his sword, he cut her down and, thus, completed his mission.*

was highly annoyed with him when he came to know about killing of the Muslims. He is said to have immediately gone to the *Kābah* and denounced *Khālid*'s act three times, calling God to be witness that he bore no responsibility for it. He, however, sent *Alī* with adequate money to pay compensation for those killed which he did. Before leaving territories of *Banī Jadhimah*, *Alī* distributed the balance amount left with him also among them which was appreciated by the Prophet.

In its immediate consequence, however, the Islamic conquest of *Makkah* produced a dangerous reaction from the nomadic tribes of south and south-east who were hostile to *Islām*. They were generally known as *Hawāzin* and included other sister-tribes like *Nasr, Jusham, Sād b. Bakr, Thāqif,* and others. These tribes were quite war-like and had a history of hostility towards *Quraysh* as well. When the Muslim army was camping at the junction of *al Zahrān*, under the apprehension that it would head towards them, they had started mobilizing troops at *Tāif*. But even though the Prophet invaded *Makkah* and had no intentions of attacking them, they did not stop mobilization of their forces and jointly (but excluding *Kāb* and *Kilāb*) assembled their army in the valley of *Awtās*, to the north of *Tāif,* under command of their reputed warrior, *Mālik ibn Awf,* who was the ruler of the main *Hawāzin* line. Perhaps for their encouragement during fight, they had even brought their women, children, and all properties to the place of concentration, their total strength estimated at 20,000 as per some sources. Shocked by destruction of the temple of *al Uzzah*, they were anticipating a Muslim attack on the shrine of their main goddess *al Lāt* at *Tāif* and were determined to protect it at any cost, and that might have motivated them to bring in their entire lot along with cattle. Another reason which might have goaded them was their concern about fate of their religion and culture at the hands of *Islām* after collapse of *Makkah*. Anticipating that there might be confusion in *Makkah* in the wake of Muslim attack and occupation, they thought that it was a highly favourable time to launch an attack and overcome both their enemies. This would lead to their emergence as champions of paganism and nomadism in Arabia which *Islām* threatened to engulf. According to sources, their attack on *Makkah* was imminent and the Prophet received information about their plan.

Since the Prophet did not want the Holy City to become a battleground, he decided to take on *Hawāzin* in their area itself. Therefore, appointing *Attāb b. Usayd* as administrator of the city, he marched towards *Awtās* along with his entire force brought from *Madīnah*, now reinforced by 2,000 Makkans which included *Abū Sufyān* and his son, *Muāwiyah*, and a group of yet-to-convert Makkans (*Safwān* and *Suhayl* included). The huge army of 12,000 was now better equipped as the Prophet had spent 30,000 dinars borrowed from *Abd Allāh b. Rabīah* for the purpose; hundred coats of mail had also been borrowed from *Safwān*. As the army marched, *Abū Bakr* was expressing overconfidence in its power and strength. '*We shall not this day be worsted by the smallness of our numbers,*' he is said to have remarked, but this type of tall-talks was not appreciated by the Prophet. In the meantime, the *Hawāzin* army had advanced to the valley of *Hunayn* located between *Makkah* and *Tāif*. Acting on the strategic suggestion of their blind but highly experienced military advisor, *Durayd b. al Simmah* (head of *Jusham* tribe), they deployed some of their contingents in the ravines on either side of the valley in such a manner that they were not visible. The rest of the fighters were deployed opposite the gorge so that they would face the approaching enemy from a prominent and visible position. This was a deadly deployment as *Durayd* had planned to first surprise the enemy by an ambush and then charge them. When the Muslim army entered the valley in the morning twilight, with *Khālid* leading the cavalry ahead (consisting mostly of *Sulaym* tribes) followed by the Makkans, it was subjected to a powerful ambuscade by shooting volleys of arrows from both sides accompanied by a strong charge from the front. *Khālid* failed to contain the charge, a general rout ensued and the Muslim soldiers ran back in confusion, suffering heavy casualties. However, the confidence-inspiring presence of the Prophet (who was on back of *Duldul*) saved the situation. He, along with some veteran Companions, held the ground firmly at some distance behind and called back the fleeing men. On his order, *Abbās*, in his powerful and resounding voice, reminded them of the pledge they had taken at *Hudaybiyah*; thereupon, the soldiers came back shouting '*labbayk*! *Labbayk*! (Here we are! Here we are!)'. Thus reorganized quickly under personal supervision of the Prophet, the Muslim army launched a powerful counterattack. This time as done at *Badr*, the Prophet threw a handful of pebbles towards the enemy invoking help of God, and this symbolic act is said to have turned the tide of the battle.

The *Hawāzin* warriors fought bravely but could not stand the charge for long, suffered heavy casualties and took to flight, leaving behind the lines their women and children. Their commander, *Mālik*, retreated with the men of *Thāqif* to the fortified city of *Tāif*. The main branch of *Hawāzin*, while fleeing, was pushed as far as *Nakhlah* inflicting much slaughter after which they ran to the hills to save their lives. Some of the sources report that *Khālid*, who was notorious for his savagery, killed a few children and women at *Hunayn* whereupon the Prophet reiterated his command not to harm such innocent persons. The turning of tide of the battle from defeat to victory was indeed miraculous and was seen by the believers as a manifestation of God's help. The *Qurān* was soon to confirm that the victory was a gift of God. Verses 9/25 to 27 said:

> *Indeed, God has helped you on many occasions. On the day of Hunayn, when you took pride in your great numbers, they proved of no avail to you—for the earth, despite all its vastness, became (too) narrow for you and you turned back, in retreat. God caused His tranquility to descend upon His Messenger and the faithful and sent down forces which you did not see. He punished those who denied the truth—for such is the recompense of all who deny the truth. Then after that, God will turn in His mercy to whom He wills; God is forgiving and merciful.*

About 6,000 women and children left behind by the enemy were made captives. The booty captured is said to have been the largest ever, and according to sources, included 24,000 camels, 40,000 sheep and goats, and also 4,000 ounces of silver. But since *Mālik* along with a large chunk of enemy had run away to *Tāif*, which was the last significant stronghold of resistance in the area, the Prophet decided to attack it without delay. Therefore, dispatching the captives as well as booty to *Jirānah* (about ten miles from *Makkah*) under the charge of *Budayl*, he led his army to *Tāif* and besieged the fort. While proceeding to *Tāif*, the fort of *Mālik* at *Liyyah* was destroyed. Overcoming *Tāif* was, however, not an easy task. The fortification there was one of the strongest and *Thāqif* were expert in defeating siege. Moreover, they had provisions enough to last for about a year. Due to heavy shooting of arrows, it was not possible for the Muslims to approach the fort. Even catapults and battering rams which had been borrowed from *Banū Daws* were rendered ineffective due to firing of red-hot iron missiles by the enemy putting tanks to flames. In order to psychologically weaken the enemy, the Prophet attempted to win over the slaves of *Tāif* by promising them freedom if they joined *Islām*, but only twenty out of eighty of them could be attracted and the step failed to create much impact. The Muslims then threatened to destroy vineyards of *Tāif* which made the enemy nervous, but the Prophet abandoned the idea on humanitarian grounds on their request. Convinced of futility of continuing the siege any longer and due to the approaching sacred month, the Prophet ultimately withdrew and went to *Jirānah*. The siege lasted for about twenty days and accounted for eighteen deaths of Muslims.

After reaching *Jirānah*,[1] the Prophet addressed himself to the task of distribution of booty and captives. He expected arrival of a delegation from *Hawāzin* for swearing fealty and so it was delayed for a few days, but when no delegation came, distribution was done. Taking cue from a revelation (verse 9/60), which permitted preferential treatment of those whose hearts were to be reconciled, the Prophet gave a greater share from the spoils to some of the *Quraysh* leaders (like *Abū Sufyān*, his sons, *Hākim b. Hizām*, and others) and a few tribal chiefs, though they were wealthy people. Even *Suhayl* and *Safwān*, who had not yet embraced *Islām*, were given larger shares. On an average, the selected *Quraysh* leaders and tribal chiefs received 100 camels or its equivalent each whereas *Muhajirūn* and *Ansār*, who were poor but had higher status as believers, could get only four camels each. This action of the Prophet, though criticized by some of the Orientalists as a 'bribe' in order to win loyalty of the recent converts, was actually from his one-fifth share of booty and had the sanction of the *Qurān*. Nevertheless, the discrimination led to some feelings among the Helpers that the Prophet was favouring his own kinsmen in disregard of their contribution to *Islām*. They feared that the Prophet would now prefer to stay in *Makkah* along with his kinsmen. When the Prophet learnt about their feelings from *Sād ibn Ubādah*, he assembled all the 4,000 Helpers and delivered a highly emotional speech, clarifying his position. He fully acknowledged the services rendered by *Ansār*, explained the insignificance of wealth, made them aware of weak faith of the new converts and the Quranic permission to use gifts as a means of strengthening it. He categorically announced that *Ansār* were

---

1   *At Jirānah, the Prophet had the pleasant surprise of meeting his foster sister, Shaymā. She was daughter of Halīmah and Hārith, foster parents of the Prophet, with whom he had spent his early childhood. Shaymā being slightly elder to him, used to take care of as well as play with him. She was one of the captives of Hunayn and had been arguing with the guards, claiming that she was the Prophet's sister. When produced before the Prophet, he recognized her and was full of joy, but his eyes filled with tears to learn that his foster parents were no more. Shaymā chose to enter Islām but returned to her clan; she was sent back with rich presents.*

preferable to him compared to others and that he would never desert them and always remain in *Madinah*. The full text of his speech has been quoted by *Ibn Ishāq*. However, as a result of his powerful speech, grievances of the Helpers stood fully redressed, tears flowed from their eyes, they apologized and were fully reconciled. The incident illustrated that due to its conglomerate character, some tension still existed within the *Ummah*, but the personality of the Prophet was a highly unifying factor which kept them integrated.

No sooner had the Prophet completed distribution of booty and captives than the expected delegation from *Hawāzin* arrived which included brother of the Prophet's foster father, *Hārithah*. Some of them were already Muslims; the remaining now entered *Islām* and demanded return of their relatives who had already been distributed as slaves. Although there was some hesitation, especially among tribes, to return property already received, on persuasion they agreed and the captives were returned to their people. It was about this time that, responding to a secret invitation by the Prophet, the *Hawāzin* commander *Mālik b. Awf,* stealthily escaped from *Tāif,* reported to the Prophet and entered *Islām*. His family members and possessions were returned and the Prophet made him commander of the Muslim community of *Hawāzin*; he was also tasked to fight against *Thāqif* of *Tāif*. Subsequently, he made hell of the *Thāqif*'s life and gave them no peace until they surrendered and entered *Islām* after about a year. The victory of *Hunayn* had been seen by the people, both believers and unbelievers, as sort of a miracle. Moreover, the nomads of the area had come in contact with the magnetic personality of the Prophet and were greatly influenced by it. As a result, more and more nomadic groups started professing *Islām,* swelling ranks of the Muslims. It was at *Jirānah* that a good number of pagan Makkans including *Safwān* and *Suhayl* also entered *Islām*.

From *Jirānah*, the Prophet retired to *Makkah*, performed *Umrah*, and then returned to *Madinah*. Even before reaching *Madinah*, *Uruwah* of *Thāqif* appeared before him and embraced *Islām*. He was the same person who had visited the Prophet at *Hudaybiyah* for talks on behalf of *Quraysh* and had been highly impressed to notice great reverence of the Muslims for their leader. During the battle of *Hunayn*, he had been out to Yaman, but when he heard stories regarding the miraculous victory and great magnanimity of the Prophet, his heart changed. After accepting *Islām*, he obtained permission, after repeated requests, to proselytize the new faith among *Thāqif*, but, as warned by the Prophet, was put to death by them. A great event of the post-*Hunayn* period was the keenly awaited birth of the Prophet's son, *Ibrahīm* (so named by the Prophet himself) to *Mariyah*. The Prophet was tremendously happy on the occasion and there was great rejoicing in *Madinah*. After return from *Makkah*, he stayed in *Madinah* for about six months. This was a period of comparative peace, only a few expeditions being sent during it. The first was Ali's expedition to destroy the shrine of *Manāt* at *Qudayd* on the Red Sea. Subsequently, *Alī* led an expedition against the Christian tribe of *Tayy* (north-east of *Madinah*), but the real object was destroying the pagan temple of *Fuls*. The previous chief of this tribe, *Hātim*, who was renowned for his generosity and noble qualities, was now dead, succeeded by his son *Adī*. The expedition was successful; although *Adī* escaped, *Hatim's* daughter was captured and brought to *Madinah*. But she was sent back respectfully by the Prophet in view of good reputation of her father. After sometime, *Adī* along with others of *Tayy* embraced *Islām*. It was about this time that the *Negus*, king of Ethiopia (who, according to traditions, had converted to *Islām*), expired. The Prophet is said to have performed funeral prayer for him in absentia at *Madinah*. It was later heard that a light was constantly seen shining over the King's grave in Abyssinia.

The next important but the boldest step of the Prophet was to lead an expedition to *Tabūk* in the north. By this time, the Islamic State had emerged as the strongest military power of Arabia. The nomadic tribes, throughout the peninsula, were now contemplating to forge alliance with it, with or without conversion. There was no significant challenge from any part of Arabia. But a serious threat still existed from the north, that is, Syria, which was part of the Byzantine Empire. The Christianized Arab tribes of the Syrian frontiers were also quite hostile to the growing power of *Islām*. The Prophet might have been having his larger northern policy of finding out an outlet to Syria in order to direct the pent-up energies of the Bedouins; he might have had an ambition to take the message of *Islām* to farther territories; he might also have been realizing that a clash with the Byzantines was inevitable and it was necessary to lead expeditions to the north for training of his men, and there might have been a strong urge to avenge the defeat of *Mūtah*. We are, however, not sure about these conjectural factors accounting for the Prophet's decision to lead a campaign against the Byzantine Empire. What we definitely know from the sources is that he received information from the visiting Nabataean traders that the Byzantine Emperor, Heraclius, after his grand victory over the Persians, had now planned to attack *Madinah* shortly. It was also reported that the Emperor had advanced one-year full salary to his soldiers for arranging provisions for long operations in Arabian deserts and had even drafted the frontier Arab tribes of *Lakkm*, *Judhām*, *Amla*, and *Ghassān* for launching attack on *Madinah*. There were also rumours afloat that the imperial army had already marched to *Balqah*. Thinking that offence was the best defense, the Prophet decided to take on the advancing enemy en route and ordered mobilization for a large expedition. It was the month of October; weather was excessively oppressive and date-harvest was ready for picking. Moreover, the Byzantines had a formidable reputation as a military power; a direct confrontation with them was felt to be an extremely hazardous proposition. Since stakes involved were very high, the Prophet this time did not maintain any secrecy and openly announced the target. The allied tribes as well as *Makkah* were directed to send all available armed and mounted men for the campaign. However, due to unfavourable timing and difficulties as well as hazards involved, response from less devout Muslims and the nomadic tribes was lukewarm. The hypocrites seized on the opportunity to create disaffection, suggesting that it was an unwise decision of the Prophet and might result in disaster. The leader of the hypocrites, *Abd Allāh b. Ubayy*, though willing to accompany, was exempted by the Prophet due to sickness. It is reported that even four of the hardcore *Ansār* (*Abū Khaythamah, Kāb b. Mālik, Murarah b. Rabī*, and *Hilāl b. Umayyah*) failed to join mainly to avoid discomforts involved. The unfavourable situation and the hurried manner in which the expedition was organized coupled with hazards involved in launching a direct offensive against the then mightiest power of the world, strongly indicated that the Prophet was acting under compelling circumstances.

However, it was not such an unpopular expedition as it is sometimes made out to have been. Most of the Muslims joined it with usual enthusiasm and the wealthy Companions competed with one another in contributing funds for equipping the troops. Traditions tell us that *Uthmān* alone financed mounting and equipment for 10,000 men, that is, one third of the total strength. *Umar* did not lag behind and gave half of his wealth, but *Abū Bakr* presented a rare example by contributing his entire property to the cause. But despite these contributions, it was still not possible to mount all the volunteers. Verse 9/92 of the *Qurān*[1] has immortalized the memory of 'the seven weepers' of *Banī Ghifār* who could not be mounted and were sent back to their extreme grief. It was because of this incident that thenceforth *Banī Ghifār* came to be known as *Banū al Bakka* which meant the tribe of weepers.' *Alī* had been left behind by the Prophet to look after his family, but he was subjected to taunts by hypocrites who alleged that he had become a 'burden' and the Prophet wanted to get rid of him. The Muslim army had already left and covered a considerable distance. But *Alī* could not bear with the taunts, speedily proceeded and overtook the Prophet. When the Prophet asked, he explained the reason for his arrival. The Prophet told *Alī* that he was to him what Aaron was to Moses except that he was the last prophet; and satisfied by the Prophet's remark, he went back as instructed. This remark of the Prophet is often used by the *Shiāh* scholars to claim that he intended to

---

1   'Nor (does any blame) attach to those who came to you to be provided
    with mounts, and when you said, "I can find no mounts for you," they
    went back, and tears welled up in their eyes with sadness, since they could
    not find any way to contribute.'

declare *Alī* as his successor. After departure of the army, one of the four good believers who had stayed back, *Abū Khaythamah*, was full of repentance, set out alone and joined the Prophet at *Tabūk*. According to some traditions, during onward journey, the Prophet miraculously made water gush out of a dried-up spring, but another version says that the Prophet prayed and clouds suddenly came giving abundant ┅

The army that was raised to confront the Byzantines had a strength of 30,000 strong with a cavalry of 10,000 horses, the largest ever assembled in Arabia. It left *Madinah* in October 630 and, after a difficult march, reached *Tabūk* on the Syrian border, halfway between *Madinah* and Damascus (about 700 km from *Madinah*). The army camped there for about twenty days, but the information regarding mobilization of the enemy turned out to be a hoax as no trace of it was found; nor was there any attempt by Heraclius to confront the Muslim army. According to a story, the Emperor had had a dream in which he saw Syria being conquered by a 'circumcised man'. That was why he did not react even to the presence of a large Muslim army camping at the doorsteps, and even sent a gift of gold coins to the Prophet. The dream had had such an intense impact on his mind that he even proposed to conclude a treaty with the Prophet which, however, could not materialize due to stiff opposition of his generals. No frontier tribe also was ready for war; rather, dismayed by military preparation of the *Ummah*, they were inclined to conclude treaty with it. Taking advantage of the situation, the Prophet concluded alliances with the Christian king, *Yuhunna*, of *Aylah* in modern Israel, two Jewish settlements of *Jarba* and *Adhruh* in modern Jordan and *Maqna* on the Red Sea coast. According to terms of treaties, they were to pay an annual tribute by way of poll tax (*Jizyah*) for protection by the *Ummah* and were not to be forced to convert. Further, *Khālid* was dispatched with a strong force to invade the fortresses of *Dumāt* al *Jandal* on the route between *Madinah* and Iraq. Hunted by *Khālid*, its Christian ruler (*Ukaydir*) ran to *Madinah* and entered into a similar protective agreement with the Prophet.

During return journey from *Tabūk*, disgruntled elements continued grumbling and criticizing the expedition. If some sources are to be believed, there was even a plot to kill the Prophet by pushing him over a cliff. It was, therefore, necessary to quell dissension even though it was not significant enough. The Prophet had been invited by some doubtful characters to consecrate a new mosque at *Qubā*. Actually, however, this mosque had become a centre of disaffection and the same was confirmed by a revelation (Q 9/107 & 108).[1] Therefore, before reaching *Madinah*, the Prophet sent his men who set the mosque on fire. After arrival in *Madinah*, he looked into conduct of the people who had not joined the expedition. While some offered acceptable excuses, the three good believers who had failed to accompany were socially boycotted; they were not allowed to even interact with their wives and other family members. But being good Muslims, they repented and lived in *Madinah* as outcasts for about fifty days when they were forgiven in accordance with God's decision[2] conveyed through verse 9/118. The Prophet's firm handling of the dissenters after return from *Tabūk* eliminated disobedience and opposition forever. The return from *Tabūk* was an occasion of great sorrow since the Prophet's daughter *Umm Kulthūm* (wife of *Uthmān*) had died.[3] Soon, the leader of

---

1 *'Then there are those who built a mosque to cause harm, to spread apostasy and disunity among the believers—as an outpost for those who from the outset warred on God and His Messenger. They swear, "Our intentions were nothing but good," but God bears witness that they are lying. Do not set foot in it. Only a house of worship, founded from the very first day upon piety, is worthy of your setting foot therein. In it are men who love to be purified and God loves those who purify themselves'* (Verse 9/107 and 108).

2 *'He has turned with mercy to the three whose case was deferred, when the earth, for all its spaciousness, closed in upon them, and their own souls seemed straitened to them and they realized that there was no refuge from God except in Him. He turned to them so that they might turn to Him. God is the Ever Forgiving, the Most Merciful'* (Verse 9/118).

3 *She was the Prophet's third daughter to die during his lifetime. He was survived by his youngest daughter Fātimah only.*

the hypocrites, *Ibn Ubayy*, died of sickness. The Prophet himself led his funeral prayer and prayed for him after his burial even though *Umar* protested against it. Verse 9/84 had forbidden such a treatment of a hypocrite,[1] but according to traditions, God's command contained in this verse was not applicable to *Ibn Ubayy* for, due to approaching death, he had undergone change of heart and had become a true Muslim, and this was known to the Prophet. Traditional accounts, however, differ as to the state of faith in which he had died.

Although, there was no actual fighting at *Tabūk*, the expedition turned out to be a significant achievement and its general impact proved quite beneficial to the *Ummah*. Mobilization of such a large army and boldness to challenge the mightiest power of the time spread an awe of the growing strength of the Muslims. The hostile Arab tribes of the frontiers, who had been a potent source of threat were frightened into submission; the threat was now permanently removed. Moreover, by entering into pacts with them, the Prophet was able to secure the Byzantine frontier and create a buffer zone between it and the Islamic State. In its final analysis, *Tabūk* left prestige of the *Ummah* as a military power significantly enhanced; and though without conversion, the message of *Islām* had reached the northern frontiers and beyond. No wonder, the year following *Tabūk* was to witness a flood of delegations from different parts of the peninsula for concluding protective alliances.

In the post-*Hijrah* period, in order to protect his nascent community, the Prophet had adopted a calculated policy of contracting alliances of mutual assistance or, at least, of benevolent neutrality with the nomadic tribes; his aim was to build up an Islamic confederacy to counter attacks from *Quraysh* and their confederates. But response from them was not encouraging as *Quraysh* were the leading military power of the region and they were frightened to alienate them. Moreover, there was an

---

1 *'And never (O Muhammad) pray for one of them who dies, nor stand by his grave. For they denied God and His Messenger, and died rebellious'* (Verse 9/84).

intrinsic hostility to *Islām* as it was perceived to challenge their ancestral religion and culture. After the fall of *Makkah*, however, the *Ummah* emerged as the most powerful military power of the peninsula. The nomadic tribes now stood seriously threatened by the *Ummah* and, as a natural reaction, tended to approach the Prophet for entering into protective alliances. The defeat of the Persian Empire by the Byzantines in 628 and its consequent weakening further changed the balance of power. As a result, tribes located in southern and eastern parts of the peninsula, which had hitherto remained under protection of the Persian Empire, were now inclined to seek protection of the Muslim State. And now after the *Ummah*'s unopposed expedition to *Tabūk*, the northern tribes also looked up to the Prophet for protection. Therefore, in the year 631, the process of Arabian tribes forging protective alliances with the Prophet gained great momentum. A series of delegations of nomadic tribes from different corners of the peninsula flocked to *Madinah* for the purpose, assuming the form of what may be called a pro-Islamic movement. The year (ninth year of *Hijrah*) is, therefore, known in history as the 'Year of Deputations' (*al Wufūd*).

Generally, these delegations were politically motivated, but they often resulted in the tribe's conversion to *Islām* en masse or in substantial part. In dealing with such tribes, the Prophet showed remarkable wisdom; since Islamic values totally challenged their way of life, he was satisfied with political submission only and did not insist on conversion. But he did not fail to utilize such occasions for preaching *Islām*; this often paid dividends leading to large-scale conversions, though many of them might have been of convenience rather than conviction. As per pattern evolved, the tribes seeking alliance had two options open to them. Those who accepted *Islām* were to give up idol worship, adopt Islamic practices, provide troops when required, and pay a religious tax (*Zakāt*); in lieu, they were to get protection. But in case a tribe wanted to keep its ancestral religion and declare political allegiance only, the pact envisaged payment of a poll tax (*Jizyah*) in exchange for protection and religious freedom.

The first to approach for peace pact after *Tabūk* were *Banī Thaqīf* of *Tāif* who had been put under tremendous military pressure by *Mālik*, the converted *Hawāzin* leader. Since most of their neighbouring tribes had already entered *Islām*, they stood surrounded by Muslim communities and were left totally isolated, their position becoming precarious. They, therefore, sent a delegation to the Prophet seeking peace and protection. But their request was conditional; they wanted to retain the temple of *al Lāt* for three years. Their request was rejected, whereupon they repeated the same, successively reducing the period to two years, one year, and finally one month only. The other special terms they wanted included exemption from five daily prayers, permission to drink wine, and also freedom to indulge in extramarital sex while travelling on business trips. All their requests were, however, categorically rejected by the Prophet as they were un-Islamic. Nevertheless, they not only signed the agreement but also entered *Islām*. The only concession given to them was that the Prophet agreed to allow them not to destroy the idol of *al Lāt* with their own hands. He deputed *Mughīrah* (nephew of *Uruwah*) and *Abū Sufyān* for the purpose, the former destroying the idol with his own hands. It is said that *Abū Āmir*, father of *Hanzalah*, and *Wahshī*, the negro who had killed *Hamzah*, had taken shelter in *Tāif*. When *Tāif* submitted, *Abū Āmir* fled to Syria and died a fugitive, but *Wahshī*, acting on advice of some people, went to *Madinah*, surrendered to the Prophet, and entered *Islām*. However, the Prophet, though accepting his conversion, ordered that he should not show his face to him.

The subsequent part of the year witnessed a flood of delegations from all directions including the distant regions of south and east. *Ibn Ishāq* gives a detailed description of embassies received from tribes like *Tamīm, Āmir, Sād b. Bakr, Abdul Qays, Hanīfah, Rayyi, Kindah, Zubayd, Hārith*, and others. The kingdom of *Yaman* and also the four kings of *Himyar* sent delegates, the latter sending letters informing about their acceptance of *Islām*. In his *Tabaqāt*, *Ibn Sād* has devoted fifty pages to details of a few dozen delegations received by the Prophet during the year including those from far-off lands of *Hadramawt* and *Omān*.

The delegations used to be courteously received, treated well, and accommodated in the Mosque; in many cases, religious discourses took place leading to conversion. Conclusion of treaties, however, was not always a smooth process and in a few cases, difficulties were encountered. For example, two successive delegations from *Banī Āmir*, led by *Āmir b. al Tufayl* and *Arbad b. Qays*, refused to submit to the Prophet. In return for accepting *Islām*, the first asked the Prophet to name him as his successor, and on refusal, he returned without entering into agreement. But he died of cancer on his way back home. The second leader also refused to convert but subsequently died due to lightning. Their intransigence, however, could not stop the people of *Banī Āmir* to soon enter *Islām*. Similarly, in the delegation from *Banī Hanīfah* was included a person named *Musaylimah* who, though converted in the beginning, later on claimed himself to be a prophet. As learnt from traditions, the delegation from *Banī Tamīm* included their poets and orators who challenged the Muslims for a competition in poetry and oratory which was done; but they were defeated, leading to their acceptance of *Islām*. A delegation was received from the Christian community of *Najrān* also which had sixty people, mostly chiefs and religious leaders including *Abū Hārithā*. They raised a number of questions about *Islām* and critically examined Quranic description of Jesus and his religion. Their questions to the Prophet were answered in a number of verses of *Surah* 3 (*Āl Imrān*) revealed on the occasion. One of the verses revealed was 3/61, which said, '*And if anyone should argue with you about this (truth) after the knowledge you have received, say to them "Come! Let us gather our sons and your sons, our women and your women, and ourselves and yourselves; and then let us pray earnestly and invoke the curse of God upon the liars."*' As per command contained in this verse, the Prophet proposed imprecation, but due to fear, the Christians declined to accept the challenge. They, however, entered into a treaty, according to which, in return for payment of taxes, they were to receive religious freedom as well as protection of the Islamic State.

By the end of the Year of Deputations, mission of the Prophet in terms of Islamisation of Arabia was almost complete. Though allegiance of a few of the tribes was still political only, conversions to *Islām* had been on an amazingly large scale; *Islām* had now spread to every corner of the peninsula and had become what may be called its state religion. Almost all pagan tribes had embraced it, and those who still remained Christians or Jews were under the *Ummah*'s protection. Acceptance of *Islām*, however, implied simultaneous adoption of its social, political, economic, and moral code and the whole life of a Muslim required to be regulated by what the *Qurān* and the Prophet had said. As the newly converted communities of distant lands themselves requested, teachers were sent in all directions for imparting religious instructions, *Muādh ibn Jabal* and *Abū Musā* to the extreme south with special briefing. The religious instructors were often invested with judicial authority for settling disputes and restoring peace in far-off lands. Apart from missionary perspectives of the delegations, however, they had great political import. In fact they represented a pro-*Ummah* movement of a political nature as well. By his exceptional political genius, the Prophet, for the first time in the history of Arabia, had brought about political unification of the peninsula. The foundations of the first ever State had been brilliantly laid on which edifice of the great Islamic Empire was to be built in later times. The process of knitting together the whole of Arabia under the *pax Islamica* had been completed, all tribes and communities living together in peace.

Another significant development of this year was performance of formal pilgrimage (as distinct from Lesser Pilgrimage or *Umrah*) by the Muslims under the leadership of *Abū Bakr*. When the time of pilgrimage came, the Prophet was fully occupied in receiving delegations, and so, he deputed *Abū Bakr* for the job, who left with 300 Muslim pilgrims. But soon after his departure, a revelation came which the Prophet thought it extremely important to proclaim to the polytheists assembled for pilgrimage in *Makkah*. But because of the highly significant nature of the revelation and, more importantly, due to the fact that a revelation was being transmitted for the only time by a person other than himself, he decided that it would be done by a man of his house only. He, therefore, chose *Alī* and sent him to *Makkah* along with a copy of the revelation, with direction to personally read out to the pilgrims in the valley of *Mina*. *Alī* speedily travelled and joined *Abū Bakr* before he reached *Makkah*. The newly revealed verses were the first twelve ones of *Surah* 9 (*At Taubah or Al Barāat*), the only *Surah* which does not begin with the formula of '*Bismillāh*'. The absence of God's names of mercy in this *Surah* was, perhaps, because of stern commandments against the pagans which these verses contained. Until this time, no official Islamic order had been issued for regulating performance of pilgrimage of the House of *Allāh*. These verses put strict restrictions on entry of the idolaters to the Sanctuary and, therefore, are known as the Proclamation of Immunity (from obligation toward idolaters). On the day of the Feast, when all the pilgrims were assembled in the valley of *Minā* to sacrifice their animals, *Alī* read out the verses. After finishing recitation of the twelve verses, *Alī* explained the gist of the message contained therein in the following words: '*I am ordered to declare unto you that no unbeliever shall enter Paradise. No unbeliever shall, after this year, perform the pilgrimage; nor shall any one be allowed to make the circuit of the Holy House unclothed. Whosoever has a treaty with the Apostle, it shall be respected until its time expires. Four months are given to the tribes that they may return to their houses in security. After that the obligations of the Messenger shall cease*' (*Ibn Qayyīm*). The proclamation meant that from the next year, no idolater was to be allowed to perform pilgrimage and desecrate the Sanctuary with performance of heathen rites; and those polytheists who permanently lived in the sacred area were to either convert or leave. It also amounted to official derecognition of idolatry in Arabia. The Islamic theological doctrines had already evolved by this time; with proclamation of these prohibitive injunctions, the Islamic regulatory arrangement about the *Kābah* was almost complete. The only important aspect left now was prescription of the Islamic rites and rituals for performance of *Haj*, and these were to be established the following year when the Prophet himself was to perform *Haj*.

During the whole tenth H. year, the Prophet remained in *Madinah* preoccupied in receiving delegations from different tribes and making arrangements for their assimilation into the Islamic State. But in one of the early months of the year, his happiness came to an end by the serious illness of his infant son, *Ibrāhīm*, who had been born to *Mariyah* some fifteen months back. He had begun to walk and even talk, being a source of great happiness to the Prophet. The Prophet continually visited him during illness, but as ill luck would have it, the child expired in his own arms. This was an occasion of his great sorrow, forcing tears to continually flow from his eyes. When pointed out that lamentation was forbidden in *Islām*, he replied that it was a prompting of tenderness and mercy and was not unpleasant to God. The thought of the child entering Paradise and getting reunited in the other world, however, comforted him and *Mariyah*. The Prophet himself led the funeral prayer. The rest of the year passed off under heavy engagements. But he did have an intuition that his mission having been completed, the end of his life was not far, and this feeling was reflected in his activities when the month of *Ramadān* came. It was his normal practice to make a retreat in the Mosque for special prayers during the middle ten days of the month. But this time, he retreated for another ten days until the end of the month. Further, as informed by *Bukhāri*, he confided to *Fātimah*: '*Gabriel reciteth the Koran unto me and I unto him once every year; but this year he hath recited it with me twice. I cannot but think that my time hath come.*' By this time, the Quranic commandment (Q 2/196, 197, and 3/97) making pilgrimage of the *Kābah* or *Haj* compulsory for every Muslim once in the lifetime provided he had means to do it, had been revealed. '*Pilgrimage to the House is a duty to God for anyone who is able to undertake it,*' commanded verse 3/97. But after it became a mandatory part of *Islām*, the Prophet had himself not performed the pilgrimage and hence the correct Islamic rites and rituals for its performance had not yet been officially established. In the eleventh month of the year (*Dhū al Qadā*), the Prophet, therefore, announced that he himself would lead pilgrimage in the following month (*Dhū al Hijjā*)—the month during which pilgrimage used to be traditionally performed. Great was the response to his call and a large number of Muslims including those from desert tribes, numbering more than one lakh according to some sources, flocked to *Madinah* for the purpose. Leading them, the Prophet left *Madinah* for pilgrimage accompanied by all his wives and also *Fātīmah*. *Abū Bakr* was accompanied by his wife, *Asmā*; at one of the initial halts, she gave birth to a son. *Alī* was, however, not accompanying as in the month of *Ramadan* he had been sent by the Prophet to *Yaman* to preach *Islām* to some contumacious tribe in the area.[1] He reported back to the Prophet directly in *Makkah* and participated in the *Haj*.

The Prophet set out from *Madinah* five days before the end of *Dhū al Qadā* and reached *Makkah* on the eleventh day, that is, sixth of *Dhū al Hijjā*. Apart from personal performance of *Haj* which was a religious obligation, his main collateral objective was to establish forever the rites and rituals of the annual pilgrimage for the Muslims. He, therefore, made it a point to thoroughly teach the Companions about all actions and rituals involved by personal practical demonstration. At the very first halt (*Dhū al Hulayfah*), he entered into the sacral state of *Ihrām* by donning a special garb consisting merely of two white pieces of cloth covering the upper and lower parts of the body. The rules of *Ihrām* were explained to all Muslims who followed suit. The *Ihrām* symbolized equality and humility of all believers before God and was understood as a metaphor for how the people would appear from the grave on the Day of Judgment to confront the Creator. He then proceeded further, the entire crowd intermittently chanting after him the slogan of *Haj* (*Talbiyyah*)[2] throughout the journey, and this was to be frequently repeated during the pilgrimage, the entire area resounding with the magnification. The ceremonies of pilgrimage appear to have started on the seventh of the month,

---

1   *Alī had proceeded to Yaman with a small cavalry of 300 horses. But the group he was to call to Islām attacked his party. Though at first defeated, they again regrouped and fought. Alī, however, broke their resistance and finally they submitted and converted to Islām. Their delegation to Madinah was the last one to report to the Prophet before his death.*

2   *'At your service, O God! At your Service! You have no partner!'*

the first part of which was *Tawāf* or making seven rounds of the *Kābah*, which the Prophet did after kissing the black stone as he entered the Sanctuary. He then went to the Station of Abraham and performed two cycles of prayer. Thereafter along with others, he went to the hill of *Safā* and jogged back and forth seven times between it and the hill of *Marwah* (the action known as *Sa'y*), uttering special prayers. The *Sa'y* recalled *Hājar*'s frantic search for water after Abraham was forced to abandon her and *Ismāīl* in the desert. This was followed by his visit to the *Zamzam* where he drank its water. Next, returning to the Mosque, he entered the *Kābah* along with *Bilāl, Usāmah*, and the keeper of the keys. But realizing that it would not be possible for every pilgrim to enter the House, he later indicated that it was not to be followed by others. After reaching this stage, the Prophet made it clear that the rites performed so far were parts of *Umrah*, and next rituals constituting the main *Haj* would be performed only by those who had brought sacrificial animals. All pilgrims who had not brought sacrificial animals were, therefore, directed to desacralize themselves by removing the pilgrims' garb. Some of the pilgrims, however, hesitated to change into normal dress and halt their pilgrimage, which annoyed the Prophet. '*Whoever angers the Prophet of God will taste of the fire*,' he disclosed in anger and repeated his command; thereupon thousands of pilgrims including the Prophet's wives and *Fātimah* terminated their pilgrimage. At this stage, *Alī* also reported back from *Yaman* and was informed of the Prophet's command. But finding him keen to perform full pilgrimage, the Prophet gave some of his sacrificial animals to him, and so he continued with the rituals of *Haj*.

On the eigth day of the month, the Prophet rode to the valley of *Minā* followed by the rest of the pilgrims. After prayers and spending the night there, the next morning (ninth day), riding on his camel, he, followed by other pilgrims, reached the valley of *Arafah* (Mount of Mercy), about thirteen miles east of *Makkah*. At noon, he rode on to the valley of *Uranah* in the same locality. It was at this place that while sitting on his camel, he delivered his famous sermon in a loud voice addressing a great multitude of pilgrims. Special care was taken by him to ensure that his words were fully listened to and understood by the audience. *Rabīah ibn Umayyah* worked as the crier, repeating his speech sentence by sentence. As narrated by *Ibn Ishāq*, main points of the speech delivered were:

> *O men, listen to my words. I do not know whether I shall ever meet you in this place again after this year. Your blood and your property are sacrosanct until you meet your Lord, as this day and this month are holy. You will surely meet your Lord and He will ask you of your works. I have told you. He who has a pledge let him return it to him who entrusted him with it. All usury is abolished, but you have your capital. Wrong not and you shall not be wronged. God has decreed that there is no usury and the usury of Abbās b. Abdul Muttalib is abolished, all of it. All bloodshed in the pagan period is to be left unavenged. Satan despairs of ever being worshipped in your land, so beware of him in your religion. Postponement of a sacred month is only an excess of disbelief whereby those who disbelieve are misled.*

> *You have rights over your wives and they have rights over you. Lay injunctions on women kindly, for they are prisoners with you having no control of their persons. You have taken them only as a trust from God and you have the enjoyment of their persons.*

> *I have left with you something which if you will hold fast to it you will never fall into error—the book of God and the practice of His prophet, so give good heed to what I say.*

> *Know that every Muslim is a Muslim's brother,*
> *and that the Muslims are brethren. It is only*
> *lawful to take from a brother what he gives you*
> *willingly, so wrong not yourselves. O God, have*
> *I not told you?*

This beautiful address contained the summary of his life's teachings and had remarkable eloquence as well as clarity; it was neither poetical nor mystical but was a practical presentation of the faith—the crux of *Islām*. Immediately following the speech, there was a revelation which the Prophet publicly recited for the knowledge of all: '*Those who deny the truth have this day despaired of ever harming your religion. So do not fear them. Fear Me. Today I have completed your religion for you and completed my blessing upon you. I have chosen for you Islām as your religion*' (Q 5/3). This is considered the last revelation which completed the *Qurān*, but it was very significant as it indicated that the Prophet's mission was complete. *Abū Bakr* heard the revelation and, to his great grief, immediately realized that the Prophet's life was soon to come to a close. It is said that not much before this revelation, another revelation came down, which was Chapter 110 (*Surah An Nasr*, meaning succour) of the *Qurān*: '*When God's help and victory come, and you see people entering God's religion in multitudes, then glorify your Lord with His praise and seek His forgiveness. He is always ready to accept repentance.*' This *Surah* is considered the first Quranic indication of the Prophet's approaching death. *Bukhāri* mentions a *hadīth* according to which, when it was revealed, *Umar* asked *Abdullāh b. Abbās* to explain its meaning. The latter said that command to pray for forgiveness in it meant that time for the Messenger of God to part company was approaching.

After the Prophet's speech, the ritual prayers were prayed and the rest of the time at *Arafah* was spent on meditation. But after sunset, the Prophet along with other pilgrims proceeded through the narrow mountain pass to *Muzdalifah* near *Makkah* (which is within the sacred precinct). There, everyone spent the night in the open, engaged in prayers and meditation. With no tent pitched for accommodation, this was one of the most

371

ascetic phases of *Haj*. At this location, the pilgrims on his advice collected small pebbles for stoning Satan, symbolically represented by three pillars (*Jamarah*) at *Aqabah* in the valley of *Minā*. The next morning (tenth day of *Dhu al Hijjā*), he led the pilgrims to the adjacent valley of *Minā* where two rituals were performed poignantly replicating the crisis situation faced by Abraham in fulfilling God's command to sacrifice his son *Ismāīl*. The first was hurling seven pebbles by each pilgrim on the *Jamarah* which was meant to reenact Abraham's rejection of the Satan's temptation to disobey the divine order. The second was sacrifice of animals (*Qurbāni*) commemorating the sheep that God ultimately accepted from Abraham in place of his son.[1] The Prophet himself sacrificed sixty-three camels, one for each year of his life. This was followed by shaving of heads of the pilgrims. When the Prophet's head was shaved, the Companions competed with one another for obtaining locks of his hair, but the Prophet allowed *Khālid* to take it, who was highly pleased and kept it reverently. The Prophet next, followed by the pilgrims, visited the *Kābah* and spent the next three nights in *Minā* during which the pilgrims were allowed to repeatedly move from there to the *Kābah* and perform more *Tawāf*, *Sa'y*, and stoning. Thus was completed the first Islamic *Haj* by the Prophet, fixing the rites and rituals of it for the future. This was a brilliant assimilation of the pre-Islamic Abrahamic tradition of pilgrimage of *Bait Allāh*,

---

1 *Muslims all over the world indirectly participate in this ritual of Haj by simultaneously offering sacrifice of animals at their homes—the occasion being celebrated as Īd al Adhā, the festival of sacrifice.*

a seven-day affair[1] involving a symbolic and emotional series of rituals reenacting the faith-testing events in the lives of Abraham, *Hājar*, and their son *Ismāīl*. Integration of the age-old practice of pilgrimage with Islamic reorientation as an integral part of the new faith provided a splendid platform for get-together of the *Ummah* and its spiritual renewal every year. Performance of this first Islamic *Haj* by the Prophet is known in history as the 'Farewell Pilgrimage' because it was for the last time in his life that he had visited *Makkah* and the *Kābah*.

During the return journey of the Prophet to *Madinah*, an interesting development concerning *Alī* took place. In his eagerness to meet the Prophet and perform pilgrimage with him, *Alī* had hurriedly reached *Makkah* leaving his troops behind in the south. Included in the booty captured after his expedition was a huge quantity of linen which was enough to clothe his whole army. But he had decided to hand over the same to the Prophet untouched. However, during his absence, his deputy commander allowed the men to change clothes out of the new linen. This, he thought, would satisfy his men as they had been out on expedition for about three months and change of clothes was required for

---

1   *The main functions of seven days of Haj have been described by Muslim Scholars as under:*

Day One *(seventh day of Dhū al Hijjā)—Day of Az Zeenah, that is, adoring of sacrificial animals.*

Day Two *(eigth day of Dhū al Hijjā)—Day of Tarwiyyah, that is, providing drinking water to animals and storing water for the following days.*

Day Three *(ninth day of Dhū al Hijjā)—Day of Arafah which is of special prayer.*

Day Four *(tenth day of Dhū al Hijjā)—Day of An Nahr, that is, sacrificing animals in Minā.*

Day Five *(eleventh day of Dhū al Hijjā)—Day of Al Qarr that is settling down in Minā.*

Day Six *(twelfth day of Dhū al Hijjā)—Day of the first departure when it is permissible to return to Makkah.*

Day Seven *(thirteenth day of Dhū al Hijjā)—Day of the second departure when all pilgrims will depart from Minā.*

their proper appearance in *Makkah* during the festival. When the troop was approaching *Makkah*, *Alī* rode out to meet his men. Noticing them in new garments, he was annoyed and ordered them to return their new clothes. This caused great resentment among the soldiers; and when the Prophet knew about it, he tried to remove their grievance saying that *Alī* was only scrupulously performing his duty towards God and should not be blamed. His words, however, could not satisfy the soldiers who again complained to the Prophet against *Alī* on way back to *Madinah*. In response, the Prophet inter alia remarked, '*Whose nearest I am, his nearest Alī is.*' Later, when he halted at *Ghadir al Khumm* (well of *Khumm*), he gathered all the men and, taking *Alī* by the hand, repeated his earlier statement and added a prayer: '*O God, be the friend of him who is his friend, and the foe of him who is his foe*'; and thereupon, resentment against *Alī* was over (*Ibn Kathīr*). The *Shiāh* scholars have used this incident to suggest that in this way, the Prophet had declared *Alī* as his successor. Some even claim that the incident amounted to 'coronation' of *Alī* as the *Caliph* as this was immediately followed by revelation of verse 5/67 in which the prophet was commanded to proclaim the message which had been sent to him by God. They also claim that verse 5/3 which referred to completion of the religion of *Islām* and which was the last revelation, was revealed immediately after this incident. It is further said that after the incident, the Prophet placed a turban on the head of *Alī* and the Companions congratulated him.

After pilgrimage, the Prophet returned to *Madinah* in the last week of *Dhū al Hijjah* (March 632), and since then until his death (about two and a half months later), he stayed there only. His mission was complete; *Islām* had fully evolved and was firmly established in the whole of Arabia. There was nothing much to do and most of the time used to be spent on prayers. One important development of this period was emergence of a few pretenders who themselves claimed prophethood, thereby challenging *Islām* and the Prophet. One of them was *Musaylimah* of *Banī Hanīfah* (a Christian tribe of *Yamāmah*). He had the audacity to even send a letter to the Prophet in which he wrote: '*From Musaylimah* the Messenger of God to Muhammad the Messenger of God, peace be on thee! It hath been given me, to share with thee the authority. Half the earth is ours, and half belongeth unto Quraysh, although they are a people who transgress.' Two other such imposters were *Tulayhah*, a chief of *Banī Asad*, and *Aswad b. Kāb* of Yaman. There was also a woman of *Tamīm* named *Sājah* who claimed to be a prophetess. Though their claim to prophethood amounted to a revolt, *Islām* was by this time too powerful and well-entrenched to be seriously threatened by such minor imposters. The Prophet, therefore, did not take any immediate action against them. *Aswad* had gained some military power, but due to his misconduct, his very followers rose against him and he was assassinated. Subsequently, *Tulayhah* was defeated by *Khālid* and he became a true Muslim, and *Musaylimah* was killed by *Wahshī*. Another significant development that took place hardly fifteen days before the Prophet's death was his order to mobilize a large army (of the strength of about 3,000 as per some sources) for sending an expedition to Syria under command of Zayd's son *Usāmah* who was hardly 20 years old. He also ordered a large number of elder Companions of noble birth including *Abū Bakr* and *Umar* to join the expedition under him. The elderly Companions, however, at first resented their placement under an inexperienced youngster of an inferior social status (*Usāmah* was son of a client, that is, *mawali* dependent on *Hāshim*), and there was some criticism, but the Prophet firmly stuck to his decision. *Usāmah* was ordered to lead his army to *Balqā* and *Dārūm* (in Palestine) which were in vicinity of *Mūtah* where his father had been killed. He was also suitably briefed by the Prophet in strategic matters with direction to organize the force and set out without delay. He was to take the enemy by surprise in the early hours and return quickly. By appointing *Usāmah* as the commander, the Prophet perhaps wanted to give him an opportunity to derive satisfaction by avenging his father's death and also earning a reward in lieu of martyrdom of his father. Moreover, having full confidence in his martial capabilities, he thought, this would establish the principle that efficiency and not age was to decide status in *Islām* without distinction of social status. But what motivated the

Prophet to order sending of such a hurriedly decided and high-stake expedition against territories of the Roman Empire at this stage of his life? Though we know that the Prophet was quite concerned about the anti-Islamic elements still existing in the extreme north, the sources do not allude to any serious threat from them at this point of time; nor was there any intelligence input suggesting any plan from Syria to direct an attack on the *Ummah*. The sources, however, do mention that the Prophet wanted to avenge the defeat of *Mūtah*, and this might have been the aim of the Prophet behind Usamah's expedition. However, taking cue from the fact that *Alī* had not been asked to join it, some *Shia* writers would suggest that his real aim was to ensure unobstructed assumption of *Khilāfat* by *Alī* during the absence of most of the potential claimants; this was because the Prophet well knew that he was going to die before the return of the expedition. But there is no historical basis for such a contention.

It is said that the very next night after he ordered preparation for the Syrian expedition, the Prophet, accompanied by his freedman, *Abū Muwayhibah*, visited the cemetery of *Madinah* called *Baqī*. There he prayed for the people lying in the graves and revealed to *Abū Muwayhibah*: '*I have been offered the keys of the treasuries of this world and immortality therein followed by paradise, and I have been given the choice between that and meeting my Lord and Paradise.*' When he was requested by his Companion to choose the first one, he informed that he had already chosen the second option. The next morning, he was afflicted by illness with severe headache followed by fever. This sickness of the Prophet continued for about twelve days (from first to twelfth *Rabi al Awwal*), took a serious turn after a few days, and proved fatal. Since he had throughout led a highly regulated life, he had never had any serious sickness previously. Some sources indicate that this sickness was the delayed after-effect of the poisoned mutton offered by a Jewess at *Khaybar* which he had chewed. During his illness, however, he was in great pain, but he bore the sufferings with remarkable calmness and serenity. The traditional sources have left a detailed account of events that took place during his illness, though their sequence is difficult to determine. These developments have, however, been interpreted differently by *Sunni* and *Shia* writers in order to suit their conviction.

On the first day of the headache, he went to *Āishah* to inform her of his suffering but *Āishah* herself was having headache and moaned, '*O my head!*' The Prophet replied that this time it was his headache that was the main concern. But he also joked with *Āishah*: '*Would it distress you if you were to die before me so that I might wrap you in your shroud and pray over you and bury you?*' And *Āishah* retorted back that in that case he would straight away go to one of his other wives for spending the night. During the first few days, despite headache and fever, the Prophet was leading prayers in the mosque and performing his daily activities. His condition, however, deteriorated on the fifth day and he shifted to Āishah's apartment for being attended to, with concurrence of the other wives. When only three days were left in his death, his condition is said to have worsened; with splitting headache and debilitating fever, it was difficult for him to go to the mosque for leading prayer. But he had some important matter about which he was keen to instruct his Companions. He, therefore, asked his wives to pour seven skins of water from different wells on his body so that the fever subsided and he could go to the mosque. This having been done, he, supported by *Alī* and *Fadl b. Abbas*, could reach the mosque and sit in the pulpit. His head was tightly bound with a piece of cloth to relieve pain. The first thing he uttered was a prayer for forgiveness of those killed at *Uhud*. Then he said, '*God has given one of his servants the choice between this world and that which is with God, and he has chosen the latter*' (*Ibn Ishāq*). *Abū Bakr* could make out that this was an indication of his imminent death and burst into tears, saying, '*Nay, let us ransom for you ourselves, our wives and children.*' The Prophet feared that Abū Bakr's emotion might move others to weep in which case he might not be able to impart to the people his remaining message. So he made a gesture to him to be silent and in order to calm him down said, '*See to these doors that open on to the mosque and shut them except one from Abū Bakr's house, for I know no one who is a better friend to me than he.*' He further added: '*If I were to choose a friend among men (meaning that his real friend was Allāh) I would choose Abū Bakr in companionship, faith and brotherhood until Allāh brings us together in his realm.*' Thereafter, he switched over to the subject of Usamah's expedition to Syria. He had received words that some of the Companions were critical of the leadership of *Usamah*, saying '*he has put a young man in command of the best of the Emigrants and Helpers*'. He had also felt that the people had been tardy in joining the expedition. In order to drive home his message, he remarked, '*O men, dispatch Usamah's force, for though you criticize his leadership as you criticized the leadership of his father before him, he is just as worthy of the command as his father was*' (*Ibn Ishāq*).[1] The next part of his address related to *Ansār*. He advised: '*Emigrants, be good to the Supporters, for they were close to me—the refuge I sought. So extol the good in them and overlook their faults.*' This address of the Prophet was on the occasion of *Zuhar* prayer and this is said to have been the last prayer personally led by him.

After this address, when the Prophet went back to Āishah's apartment, his pain became more severe and he found himself physically incapacitated to lead prayers in the mosque. So when the time for the next prayer came, he asked the people to inform *Abū Bakr* to preside over prayers in the mosque.[2] But *Āishah* tried to persuade the Prophet to change his decision saying that his father was a delicate man with a weak voice and wept much

---

1 *Due to the Prophet's reiterated instruction, the Companions hurried on with their preparations and Usāmah along with his army went out to Jurf, not far from Madīnah, and encamped there. But Usamah was receiving frequent reports about condition of the Prophet from his mother. When he came to know that the Prophet's condition had been critical, he decided to stay on there and proceed further only after his condition improved.*

2 *This point is strongly used by some scholars to claim that the Prophet wanted Abū Bakr to succeed him as Khalīfah. They argue that though the Prophet did not directly nominate him as Khalīfah after him because the Qurān decreed that the affairs of the Muslims were to be settled by consultations amongst themselves, he suggested it to the people in different ways—by letting him lead prayers, by letting him head pilgrimage of the Kābah and by praising him as the best companion he ever had.*

when he read the *Qurān*. However, despite her frequent requests, the Prophet repeated his order and curtly remarked, '*You are like Joseph's Companions; tell him to preside at prayers.*' Later on, she explained, '*My only reason for saying what I did was that I wanted Abū Bakr to be spared this task, because I knew that people would never like a man who occupied the apostle's place, and would blame him for every misfortune that occurred, and I wanted Abū Bakr to be spared this.*' It is said that on one of the occasions when *Abū Bakr* was absent and *Umar* tried to lead the prayer, the Prophet heard his voice and did not allow it, saying, '*Where is Abū Bakr? Nay, Allāh and Muslims will resent this.*' Some of the traditions mention that on one of the last days of his illness, when he was in great pain and many of the Companions had gathered around him, the Prophet said, '*Give me pen and ink and I shall write for you what would make you never go astray.*' Some of the Companions hurried to do so, but a few including *Umar* opposed that saying that the *Qurān* already included everything. They probably thought that the Prophet's condition was too serious to permit of this type of strain. When the Prophet saw them arguing, he was annoyed and said, '*Leave me now, it is not right that people dispute in the presence of their Prophet.*' This story, though mentioned by *Bukhāri*, however, does not find mention in Ibn Ishaq's *Sirah*.[1]

It is clear from the sources that for quite some time the Prophet had a premonition about his approaching death and he had also been giving clear indications that the illness he was suffering from would prove fatal. During his illness, *Fātimah* used to frequently visit him; on such occasions, *Āishah* used to slightly withdraw giving the father and the daughter privacy to talk. One of his last days, when she came, *Āishah* noticed the Prophet whispering something to her whereupon she started weeping. Then suddenly he whispered something else which made her smile. When she was leaving, *Āishah* asked her about the secret of her sudden

---

1 *Some Shiāh writers suggest that on this occasion, the Prophet wanted to leave his will or written direction nominating Ali as his successor. But Umar perceived this and so he opposed getting written down any such instruction by the Prophet.*

change of behavior, but she refused to divulge it. However, later on, she revealed to her: '*The Prophet told me he would die in that suffering whereof he died, and therefore I wept. Then he told me that I would be the first person of the people of his house to follow him, and therefore, I laughed*'[1] (*Bukhāri*). According to another story, the Prophet did not wish to die with any personal property with him. One of his last days, he remembered that he had seven dinars which he had kept with *Āishah*. He took them from her and said, '*What would Muhammad do if he met his Lord and this was with him?*' and then he gave them away (*Ibn Sād*). A day prior to his death, his wives brought some medicine and with the help of *Abbās*, forcibly made him swallow it. The Prophet was annoyed and forced everyone there to take the same medicine except his uncle *Abbās*. That day, the condition of the Prophet was critical and he was rather in a delirium. But it appears, the medicine gave him some relief, and the next morning (Monday, the last day of his life), fever abated and he felt better; despite extreme weakness, he decided to attend the dawn prayer. Supported by *Alī* and *Fadl*, he went to the mosque. The prayer had already begun, led by *Abū Bakr*, and the Prophet's face was full of joy to see his followers praying. When the people saw him in a better condition, their hearts leapt with joy and they started making way for him even during prayer, but he made a sign to them to attend to it. *Abū Bakr* sensed that the Prophet had arrived and he was about to leave his place to allow him to lead the prayer, but he put his hand on his arm and asked him to continue, himself quietly sitting beside him to pray. His face was radiant, reflecting gladness and satisfaction. '*I never saw the Prophet's face more beautiful than it was at that hour,*' said *Anas*. This was the last prayer of the Prophet. It is said that after prayer, he turned to the people and spoke in a loud voice: '*The fire is stirred high and temptations come like dark patches of the night. I have not allowed you except what the Qurān allows, and I have not forbidden you except what the Qurān forbids. After me you will differ much. Whatever agrees with the Qurān is from me; whatever differs from the Qurān is not from me.*'

---

1 *Fātimah actually died ten weeks after the Prophet's death.*

Great was the happiness of the Muslims at this perceived recovery of the Prophet. *Usāmah*, who used to frequently visit the Prophet, arrived and, seeing him in a better state, took permission for departure of his army; he rode back to *Jurf* and ordered the soldiers to get ready for the march. *Abū Bakr* also took permission and left for Upper *Madinah* to see his wife. The Prophet went to Aisha's apartment with the help of *Alī*, *Fadl*, and *Thawbān*, and *Abbās* followed them. At this point, *Abbās* took *Alī* apart and, telling him that he was recognizing death in the face of the Prophet, proposed to talk to him regarding vesting of authority after him. But *Alī* said, '*By God I will not, for if the authority be withheld from us by him, none after him will ever give it to us*' (*Ibn Ishāq*). During illness, the Prophet most of the times used to lie on Āishah's couch with head resting on her lap or breast, and now also he was in the same position. It is reported that when he was so lying, the brother of *Āishah* entered the room with a tooth stick in his hand which the Prophet saw and gave expression as if he wanted it. *Āishah* took it, softened it by chewing, and gave it to the Prophet who brushed his teeth energetically despite weakness. But soon after that, his condition deteriorated; fever went up, causing restlessness, and he wiped his face several times after dipping his hand in a bowl of cool water. Then he lost consciousness, but after about an hour, he opened his eyes and weakly said to *Āishah*, '*No Prophet is taken by death until he hath been shown his place in Paradise and then offered the choice, to live or to die.*' And *Āishah* could make out that he had chosen the other world. She heard him utter verse 4/69 and the last words murmured by him were, '*O God, with the supreme communion*' (*Ibn Sād*). After that, his head became heavier on her breast. The soul of the Prophet had departed, but *Āishah* could not understand; when his other wives began crying, she laid his head on a pillow and joined in lamentation. It was the noon of Monday, 12 *Rabi al Awwal* of the eleventh year of *Hijrah* (corresponding to 8 June 632) and a few days were left in his age to complete 63 years; interestingly, it was the same lunar day he had been born.

The news about the Prophet's death spread like a wildfire. Though, in the light of his repeated indications followed by serious sickness, his death was expected, it nevertheless created a crisis-like situation. The Prophet was a leader of his men who was not only their greatest inspiration and the strongest pillar of support but also the readily available guide in both religious as well as temporal matters. They were so much devoted to and dependent on him that it was extremely difficult for them to reconcile to the idea of life without him. How will they lead their lives without the Prophet? Who will provide the succour, protection, and guidance? These were the questions in everyone's mind, and there was a sense of insecurity. The extraordinary situation caused by his death was further compounded by the fact that the Prophet had not nominated his successor. How is the vacuum going to be filled up? Under such a situation, the reaction of the people was either one of shock mixed with panic or of disbelief.

When it was felt that the Prophet was going to die, *Umm Ayman* had sent information to *Usāmah* at *Jurf* where *Umar* and other senior Companions were also camping. After receiving information, *Usāmah* ordered postponement of the march and rushed along with others to see the Prophet. On way they were told that death of the Prophet had already taken place. *Umar*, however, refused to believe it; due to misunderstanding of a verse of the *Qurān*, he was under the impression that the Prophet would outlive a few generations. Even though he went to the Prophet's house immediately and saw him dead, he still did not accept that he had actually died. He started telling the people in the mosque that the soul of the Prophet had only temporarily gone, and it will return to give life to him after forty days, as had happened to Moses. In the meantime, *Abū Bakr* hurriedly arrived as the news had reached him. He went straight to Aisha's apartment where the Prophet was lying, uncovered his face, and kissed him, saying, '*You are dearer than my father and mother, you have tasted the death which God had decreed; a second death will never overtake you.*' Then he went out to the mosque where *Umar* was continuing his address, trying to convince the people that the Apostle was absent in spirit only and would soon return. He was even threatening to attack those who disagreed. *Abū Bakr* tried to make him quiet, but he did not pay any heed. The people, however, recognized his voice and turned to him in order to listen to his address. After praising God, *Abū Bakr* said, '*O men, if anyone worships Muhammad, Muhammad is dead; if anyone worships God, God is alive, immortal.*' Then he recited verse 3/158: *Muhammad is nothing but an apostle. Apostles have passed away before him. Can it be that if he were to die or be killed you would turn back on your heels? He who turns back does no harm to God and God will reward the grateful.*' Abū Bakr's speech had a salutary effect and removed confusion from the minds of the people. Listening to recitation of the verse, which came as if they heard it for the first time, they all accepted the truth. Abū Bakr's handling of the situation was indeed splendid. Even *Umar* was now reconciled to the fact. He later on said, '*By God, when I heard Abū Bakr recite these words, I was dumbfounded so that my legs would not bear me and I fell to the ground knowing that the Apostle was indeed dead.*'

It appears, after everyone mentally accepted the situation, it was decided that burial of the Prophet would be done the next day. *Ibn Ishāq* says that *Alī* along with *Zubayr* and *Talhah* withdrew to his own house, while most of the Emigrants gathered around *Abū Bakr* in the mosque. It was then that a person came and informed that many of the *Ansār* had assembled in the hall of *Banī Sāidah* (a clan of *Khazraj*) of whom *Sād b. Ubadah* (who was sick but had been taken to the hall lying on bed) was the chief. He also revealed that they were discussing transfer of authority after the Prophet, were not in favour of being ruled by anyone except a man of *Yathrib*, and were about to pledge their allegiance to *Sād*. The information was quite disturbing and so, urged by *Umar*, *Abū Bakr* went along with him to the meeting place, also joined by *Abū Ubaydah*. When they reached, some other *Muhajirūn* also joined them. Seeing them, one of the helpers delivered a speech in which he glorified *Ansar*'s role in helping *Islām* and reiterated their decision not to surrender authority to *Muhajirūn*. *Umar* wanted to speak in reaction but was restrained by *Abū Bakr* who himself spoke. He pointed out that the *Ummah* was now spread throughout Arabia and tried to convince them that the Arabs as a whole would not accept as ruler anyone other than a man of *Quraysh*, who because of the tribe's pre-eminent position, would be acceptable to all. Then he suggested that either *Umar* or *Abū Ubaydah* should be recognized as leader of the *Ummah*. Thereupon one of the helpers suggested that there should be two authorities, and this led to heated arguments and the meeting was on the verge of ending in a fiasco. But then *Umar* intervened and pleaded the case of *Abū Bakr*. Pointing out that the Prophet's command to *Abū Bakr* to lead the Muslims in prayers amounted to his will that he should be his successor. He further mentioned that by selecting *Abū Bakr* as the *Khalifah*, they would be giving authority to the next best man of the *Ummah*, the Companion who was best trusted and loved by the Apostle. Umar's words moved the *Ansār* who felt that he was expressing only the wish of the Prophet. Taking advantage of the softening of attitude, *Umar* seized the hand of *Abū Bakr* and pledged allegiance to him followed by *Abū Ubaydah* and other *Muhajirun* and then by all the helpers present excepting *Sād*, who is said to have never acknowledged him as *Khalifah*.

The next morning, when *Abū Bakr* was to lead the prayer in the mosque, *Umar* addressed the congregation. He described *Abū Bakr* as the best of the Companions, the only person who accompanied the Prophet when he hid in the cave during the *Hijrah* journey (a fact recalled in the recently revealed verse 9/40) and declared him as the head of the *Ummah*; thereupon the whole congregation rose and pledged loyalty to *Abū Bakr*, except *Alī* who did so later. Then *Abū Bakr* delivered his inaugural speech in which, after praising God, he said, *'I have been given authority over you but I am not the best of you. If I do well, help me, and if I do ill, then put me right. Truth consists in loyalty and falsehood in treachery. The weak among you shall be strong in my eyes until I secure his right if God will; and the strong among you shall be weak in my eyes until I wrest the right from him. If a people refrain from fighting in the way of God, God will smite them with disgrace. Wickedness is never widespread in a people but God brings calamity upon them all. Obey me as long as I obey God and His apostle, and if I disobey them you owe me no obedience. Arise to prayer. God have mercy on you'* (*Ibn Ishāq*). Some of the Companions hurriedly holding meeting in order to decide the issue of transfer of authority and indulging in heated arguments even though the Prophet was still lying unburied do appear to have been unbecoming of them. In fact, despite strong religious unity, the *Ummah* still had group loyalties within it based on political aspirations. The action of a group of *Ansar* to hold a separate assembly for unilateral selection of ruler immediately following death of the Prophet amounted to a dangerous separatist move and tended to disrupt the *Ummah* at the very beginning. It was, therefore, a compelling necessity for leaders like *Abū Bakr* and *Umar* to intervene and sort out the issue in order to save unity of the community, and the situation appears to have been efficiently handled by *Abū Bakr*.

After the prayer, the Prophet's family members decided to prepare his body for burial. Despite suggestion by some that he be buried in *Makkah* or Jerusalem, it was decided to bury him in *Madinah* itself. When the time for giving bath to the Apostle came, everyone involved was spiritually guided to wash him with his garment on. Washing was performed by *Alī*, *Abbās* and his two sons (*Fadl* and *Qitham*), and *Usāmah*. It is said that on request *Aws b. Khawli*, a *Khazrajite*, was also allowed entry to represent the helpers. *Abbās* and his sons helped *Alī* to turn the body while *Usāmah* poured water over it,[1] and *Alī* washed the body touching only the garment. The traditions tell that as the act of washing was performed, the holy body emitted highly pleasant smells, and *Alī* repeatedly said, *'Dearer than my father and my mother, how excellent are you in life and in death.'* It is said that even a day after death, the Apostle seemed to be merely sleeping, with the only difference that there was no breathing. After washing, the Prophet's body was wrapped in three shrouds. A disagreement, however, arose as to which place the holy grave should be dug. Some suggested it to be in the mosque where he used to address the people. But this was not favoured as during illness *Āishah* had heard the Prophet curse such people who had adopted the grave

---

1   *It is said that Shuqran, the Prophet's freedman, also joined and helped Usāmah in pouring water.*

of their prophet as a place of worship. Others suggested the main cemetery of *Madinah*, *Baqī al Gharqad*, but *Abū Bakr* solved the problem by informing that the Prophet himself had remarked, '*No Prophet dieth but is buried where died.*' And so, the spot just below the couch he was lying in Āishah's room was chosen for the purpose. *Abū Talhah Zayd*, the undertaker of *Madinah*, is said to have dug the grave. During the whole day, the people of *Madinah* paid visit to the Apostle and prayed over him in small groups, first the men, and then women and children. Late in the night, the beloved of the people was laid in his grave by *Alī* and others who had prepared him for the burial. Unprecedented was the sorrow in the city. The Companions were asking each other not to mourn but were weeping themselves.

APPENDIX I

A CHRONOLOGICAL LIST
OF THE PROPHET'S WIVES
(BASIC FACTS ABOUT THEM)

Sl. no.	Name and family	When married	Age at the time of marriage	Year of death	Motive behind marriage	Remarks/ distinguishing features
1.	Khadījah bint Khuwyalid of Asad	595 AD	About 40 years (but some sources mention it to be 28)	619 AD	- Liking for each other - In order to lead a happy conjugal life	Aristocratic, twice widowed and wealthy trader of Makkah - An exemplar of Islamic womanhood - Bore six children to the Prophet.

| 2. | Sawdah bint Zamān (cousin of Suhayl, Chief of Āmir tribe) | June, 620 AD | About 30 years | 654 AD | - Rehabilitation of an Abyssinia-returned devoted Muslim widow.
- Utilising her maturity and experience for taking care of his daughters and looking after the household affairs.
- To cement political tie with Āmir tribe | - A middle-aged hefty and simple lady without much sexual charm. |
| 3. | Āishah bint Abū Bakr of Tāym | Betrothal in 620 and marriage in 624 AD | 6/7 at the time betrothal and about 10 at the time of marriage | 678 AD | - In pursuance of a dream which he thought was decision of God.
- A social and political move to create closer tie with a powerful Muslim leader.
- Not guided by consideration of charm or beauty as she was merely a child, not knowing meaning of marriage and still playing with dolls. | - Subsequently grown into a beautiful and intelligent lady with remarkable memory.
- Favorite wife of the Prophet.
- The only virgin wife of the Prophet |

4.	Hafsah bint Umar ibn al Khattāb of Adi clan—a widow whose husband died due to injuries received in the Battle of Badr.	Beginning of 625 AD	18 years	665 AD	- To sort out rift among leaders of the Ummah as Abū Bakr and Uthmān had refused her hand. - To rehabilitate a war widow which was the Prophet's policy. - To establish closer tie with one of the most powerful leaders of the Ummah	- Good looking, accomplished, and literate, she was an authority on the Qurān. - Outspoken, she used to assert her independence and indulge in trickery along with Āishah to the annoyance of the Prophet.
5.	Zaynab bint Khuzaymah of Āmir—a war widow whose husband had become a martyr at Badr	April, 625 AD	-	8 months after marriage	- Rehabilitation of a war widow who was a devoted Muslim	- Extremely generous, she used to take great care of the poor. - Known as 'Mother of the Poor'.
6.	Umm Salamah w/o Abū Salamah who died of wounds received at Uhud (sister of a powerful leader of Makhzūm clan.)	May, 626 AD	29 years	676 AD	- Rehabilitation of a war widow. - For cementing a useful political connection.	- Good looking, intelligent and wise lady. - Used to give valuable advices to the Prophet on important matters.

7.	Zaynab bint Jahsh, (the Prophet's cousin) divorced by the Prophet's adopted son, Zayd.	626 AD (shortly after marriage with Umm Salamah)	Approaching 40 (according to some sources, about 30)	642 AD	- In order to make amends for forcing on her marriage with Zayd which could not last—Zayd divorced her and the Prophet felt himself responsible for bringing social disgrace to the lady. - In order to fulfill God's Quranic command.	- Extremely beautiful, known in her circle as 'the beautiful'. - A woman of great piety known for her fasts and night prayers. - The marriage became a subject of historical controversy due to criticism by Western scholars.
8.	Juwayriyah d/o Chief of Banī Mustaliq defeated by the Prophet in January, 627 AD Umm	January, 627 AD	20 years	655 AD	- Motivated by political consideration of winning over an important hostile tribe.	- Having charming looks and sweet manners.

| 9. | Habībah d/o Abū Sufyān of Umayyah clan. | Beginning of 628 AD | 35 years | – | - Rehabilitation of a devoted Muslim widow who had entered Islam in the very beginning.
 - Establishing alliance with the powerful. Umayyah clan and the most influential leader of Quraysh.
 - A political marriage. | - She had emigrated to the Abyssinia along with her husband, Ubād Allāh (a cousin of the Prophet) who was previously a Christian. In Abyssinia, he reverted to Christianity and became excessively addicted to alcohol, getting alienated from his wife. After his death, her marriage with the Prophet was performed in Abyssinia (Aksum) in absentia under the care of the Negus on the Prophet's request. She went to Madinah to join the Prophet in April 628 AD. |

10.	Safiyyah d/o the deceased Nadīr Chief Huyayy and widow of another Nadir Chief, Kinānah. A young Jewess captured during the Battle of Khaybar.	April, 628 AD	17 years	–	- In order to cement relations with and win over the Jewish enemies.	- Of reputed beauty—known as 'the small lovely-looking girl'. - Only Jewish wife of the Prophet.
11.	Mariyah, a Coptic Christian slave girl gifted to the Prophet by Muqawqis (King of Egypt)	Middle of 628 AD	–	637 AD	- In order to show that he was friendly with and honoured Christianity - To win political friendship of the Christian powers.	- The only wife of the Prophet having Christian background. - The Western writers treat her as the Prophet's concubine. But, based on reliable sources, the Muslim scholars hold that she entered the life of the Prophet as a converted and duly-wedded wife.

						- Extremely beautiful and attractive-curly haired. - Buried in Baqī with other wives indicating that she had the status of a wife. - Mother of the Prophet's son Ibrahīm, the only issue the Prophet had from any wife other than Khadījah.
12	Maymūnah (widowed sister of wife of the Prophet's youngest uncle Abbās and aunt of Khalid ibn al Walīd of Makhzūm.	March, 629 AD	30 years	681 AD	- To cement ties with and win over the powerful Makhzūm clan.	- Twelfth and the last wife of the Prophet and also the last to die.

- Following execution of the Jewish tribe of *Banī Qurayzah* (May 627 AD), a young widowed Jewish woman named *Rayhānah* was captured and became the share of the Prophet. According to some sources, in order to show that he had no ill will against the Jews and could honour a Jewess, the Prophet wanted to marry her after her conversion to *Islām*, but she refused and stayed as his slave. The Western scholars treat her as his concubine while some sources mention that she entered Islam and married the Prophet. Yet other sources mention that, though subsequently accepting *Islām*, she did not marry the Prophet and remained honourably in seclusion until her death in 630 AD. She is, however, generally not included in the list of the Prophet's wives.

• Some sources refer to one more marriage of the Prophet (in 631 AD) with *Asmā bint Numān*, a kindite woman of *Najd*. Following an alliance, her father had drawn a marriage contract and sent her to *Madinah* to live as his wife. But, as mentioned by *Ibn Sād*, she was extremely beautiful, and therefore, *Āishah* and *Hafsah* grew jealous of her. On arrival, they welcomed her and applied henna on her hands and feet; thereafter, pretending to give her love advice, they taught her to repeat words on meeting the Prophet which were actually a formula for divorce. The Prophet took her words as a powerful repudiation of the marriage and immediately sent her back despite her protest that she had been tricked. *Ibn Hishām*, however, refers to yet another marriage of the Prophet with *Āmrah* of *Kilāb*. As per some sources, the story of the trick related to her, and not to *Asmā*. Though mentioned by *Tabarī* and *Ibn Sād*, the story about these two marriages is not given credence by the historians and they are not listed as the Prophet's wife.

• The chronology of the Prophet's multiple marriages is the strongest testimony of the fact that they were not entered into for the sake of deriving normal marital pleasure but were motivated by strong social and political considerations. For twenty-five long years after marriage with *Khadījah*, he remained a strict monogamist, and this was the period of his youth with abundant resources to afford other wives of his liking. Almost all his subsequent marriages were entered into during the brief period from 624 to 630 AD, when he was too old to be guided by considerations of love and pleasure, and this was also the period of his heaviest political preoccupation. It would not be difficult to discern that while some of them were contracted for forging political alliances, others were to set examples as a measure of social reform for rehabilitation of war widows as well as orphans. It appears that those levelling the allegation that these multiple marriages were entered into due to his weakness for the fair sex have wittingly or unwittingly failed to take note of and explain these aspects of his serial marriages.

APPENDIX II

**DESCENDENCY CHART OF THE
PROPHET'S LINE OF QURAYSH TRIBE**
(QUARAYSH OF THE HOLLOW)

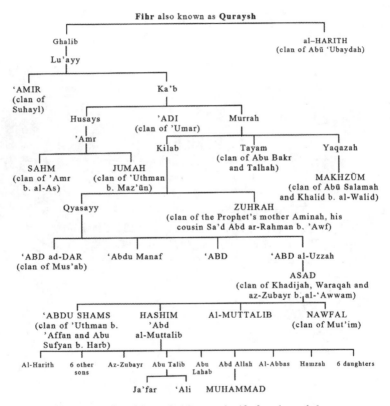

Names mentioned in capital letters signify founders of clans.

APPENDIX III

FAMILY TREE OF THE PROPHET

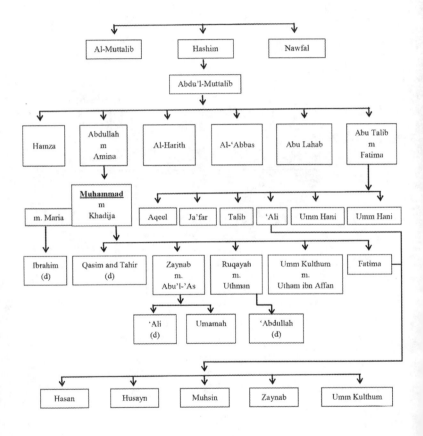

Index of Names, Places, and Terms

Printed in the United States
By Bookmasters